ISBN 978-0-265-09708-3
PIBN 10944789

SELECT CASES

REPORTED IN

THE SEVERAL COURTS

OF THE

UNITED STATES AND GREAT BRITAIN,

IN THE YEARS

1847, 1848 AND 1849.

SOME ENTIRE, BUT MOSTLY IN A CONDENSED FORM.

BY

ASA KINNE.

VOLUME IX.

NEW YORK:
CORNISH, LAMPORT & CO., PUBLISHERS,
No. 8 PARK PLACE.
1852.

CONTENTS.

CONTENTS.

CONTENTS.

KINNE'S LAW COMPENDIUM,

FOR 1849

ABATEMENT.

The law is well settled, that if a woman is sued while *sole* and marries during the pendency of the suit, she cannot plead the supervenment coverture in abatement.—*Hailman* v. *Buckmaster*, 3 *Gilman's R.*, p. 498. *Ills.* (1847.)

(TREAT, J., *cited Gould's Pl.*, 263, *sec.* 87; 1 *Chitty's Pl.*, 484; *King* v. *Jones*, 2 *Lord Raymond*, 1525.)

It is no answer to a plea in abatement, alleging that the defendant was dead at the commencement of the suit, that in the progress of the suit he appeared by attorney, as a dead man cannot appear by attorney. —*Massey* v. *Steele's Adm'r* 11 *Alabama R.*, p. 340. (1847.)

ACCIDENT—RAILROAD.

Where, in consequence of the neglect of the agents of a railway company to chain or put blocks under the wheels of cars left standing on a track, constructed on a pier used as a public highway, one, who was crossing the track at a point over which it was necessary for him to pass in order to reach his vessel, moored to the pier, is, during a dark night, and without any fault on his part, run over and seriously injured by the cars, which had been put in motion by a strong wind, he will be entitled to recover damages to the extent of the injury sustained. *Brown* v. *Pontchartrain Railroad Company*, 8 *Robinson's La. R.*, p. 45. (1847.)

(*Schmidt & Roselius cited Civil Code, arts.* 2294, 2295, 1928, *sec.* 3; 11 *Touiller, No.* 121, *p.* 153; *Merlin's R., vol.* 26, *verbo Quasi-Delit; Domat, vol.*, 1 *b.* 2, *tit.* 8, *sec.* 4; *Ibid. tit.* 9, *Des Engagemens, &c., pardes cas fortuits;* 2 *La.*, 73; 7 *La.*, 575; *Graham on New Trials,* 417; *Sayer's Law of Damages,* 214 *et seq.;* 2 *Wilson,* 205; 2 *Wend.*, 432; 17 *Mass.*, 503; 9 *Serg. & Rawle,* 94; 2 *Aiken,* 255; 2 *Hill,* (*S. C.*) 573; 4 *Hammond,* 500, 514; *Wright,* 603; 4 *Wash. C. C.*, 106; 4 *Serg. & Rawle,* 15; 7 *Mass.*, 187; 7 *Cowen,* 485; 6 *Petersd. Abridg.*, 634.)

ACCOMMODATION ENDORSER.

Where a maker of a note executes a mortgage on his property to indemnify his accommodation endorsers on the note, the holder of the note will be entitled to the benefit of the mortgage, and may in Equity subject the mortgaged property to the satisfaction of his debt, nor can the endorser by a release of the mortgage deprive the creditor of that right.—*Dick et al.* v. *Mawry,* 9 *Smedes & Marshall's R.*, *p.* 448. *Miss.* (1848.)

(THACHER, J., *cited* 1 *Story Eq.*, 481, *sec.* 502; 6 *Smedes & Marshall,* 139.)

ADMINISTRATOR.

The principle of the rule, that where a person becomes a surety in a note to be used for a particular object, the principal cannot divert it from that object without the surety's assent; applied as between the principal's administrator and the surety, in favor of the latter, to the proceeds of such a note remaining in the principal's hand at his death.

The administrator's claim to retain the proceeds is no better than that of the intestate would have been if he had been living.—*Lee* v. *The Highland Bank,* 2 *Sandford's Ch. R.*, *p.* 311. *N. Y.* (1847.)

THE bill was filed by Leonard Lee on the 12th day of April, 1844, against the Highland Bank, and John W. Brown, Esq., as administrator of Gilbert Ogden Fowler, late of the village of Newburgh, deceased; praying to have a note delivered up and cancelled. The note was for $1500, dated December, 27th, 1843, and payable the first of May ensuing; was made by the complainant, payable to Mr. Fowler, endorsed by him, and was discounted by the Highland Bank, on the day of its date. The bank received from Lee the discount on the note, and delivered to him their draft on a New York Bank for the $1500. It being found in Mr. Fowler's room after his death the same evening, endorsed by Lee, it was returned to the cashier of the bank by Mr. Fowler's son and was never used.

The opinion of the Court states all the other facts that were deemed material.

Stevens, for complainant.
Reeve & Reynolds, for the defendants.

The Assistant Vice-Chancellor.—The Highland Bank having received the draft issued upon discounting the note in question, the same day that they parted with it, have very properly left the controversy to be settled between the complainant and the administrator of Fowler. The case has been argued on the footing that the draft, which was in Fowler's possession at his death, had come to the hands of the administrator.

On this basis, I think there will be no difficulty in arriving at a result which will be equitable in regard to the remarkable circumstances of the case, as well as conformable to established principles.

The facts are involved in much obscurity by the sudden death of Mr. Fowler. The transaction was not a mere exchange of notes, which of itself implies mutual benefit and accommodation. This is shown by Lee's paying the discount on the note to the bank, and delivering to Fowler a draft for the whole $1500, and by the admission in the answer that Lee made his note and procured the draft solely for the accommodation and benefit of Fowler; while there is no pretence that Lee was to be benefited in any manner by the operation.

I take these facts to be established. Mr. Fowler, being confined to his room by sickness, sent for the complainant and procured him to give a note for $1500, payable to Fowler's order, to take it to the Highland Bank at Newburgh, of which Fowler was president, have it discounted, pay the discount, take the $1500 in a sight draft of that bank drawn on a New-York Bank, and deliver the same to Mr. Fowler. This was all done for Fowler's sole benefit and accommodation.

The object which Fowler had in view, and for the promotion of which the complainant thus lent his credit, is stated in the bill; and I think it is substantially proved by the circumstances and the testimony of Isaac V. Fowler. The latter says his father was to pay to one of the heirs of his deceased brother-in-law $1500 on the occasion stated in the bill, or one not materially variant; and that on the 24th of December, his father told the witness that he would send to the witness in New-York, by the middle of that week, a draft for $1500 to pay to that heir.

This draft procured for Fowler by the complainant, was obtained on Wednesday of that week. It was drawn on New-York on a letter sheet, so as to be sent by mail. The coincidence of circumstances, in the absence of proof of any other occasion or object which Fowler had for such a draft, leads to the conclusion, that it was obtained for the specific purpose of being remitted to his son, and paid to his brother-in-law.

It is not probable that Fowler made his request of the complainant, without informing him at least in general terms for what he wanted the accommodation, and I am bound to infer that he stated the object truly.

His death the same evening, while the draft still laid upon his table, in his sick room, prevented its ever being applied to the intended object.

The complainant therefore by the note in question, became the surety for Fowler, to raise money and obtain a draft for a specific object and purpose. The money was raised and the draft procured, but owing to the sudden death of the principal, it never was applied to that object. For the determination of the point, it is deemed to be remaining in the hands of the administrator of the principal.

And the question is, which has the better right to the draft, in equity; the complainant, in order to withdraw the note he lent, or the administrator, to distribute it among the creditors of Fowler?

There can be but one answer to this question in the forum of conscience; and the law concurs in that response. The administrator's claim is no better than Mr. Fowler's would have been, if he had lived, and instead of using the draft for the purpose intended, had repudiated that intention, and taken it to the bank and sought to apply it on some of his current liabilities there.

When a person becomes the surety for another in a note, to be used for a particular object or purpose, the principal cannot divert it from that object, without the surety's assent. And if he do so divert it, neither he, nor any one with notice of the diversion, can maintain any action upon it, or set up any right by virtue of the transaction.

This principle will be found in *Denniston* v. *Bacon*, 10 *Johns.*, 198; *Wardell* v. *Hughes*, 3 *Wend.*, 418; *Brown* v. *Taber*, 5 *Wend.*, 566; *Woodhull* v. *Holmes*, 10 *Johns.*, 231; *Skilding* v. *Warren*, 15 *Johns.*, 270; *Beers* v. *Culver*, 1 *Hill*, 589; *Grandin* v. *LeRoy*, 2 *Paige*, 509.

In *Bonser* v. *Cox*, 4 *Beavan*, 379, 384; *S. C.*, 5 *Lond. Jurist*, 164, a, John Cox made a joint and several promissory note with Richard Cox, to Messrs. Monells, for which the Monells were to advance the amount to Richard by two drafts at three months each. Instead of advancing the drafts, they made the advance in cash immediately. *Lord* LANGDALE, Master of the Rolls, held that John Cox, the surety, was thereby discharged. He also held that it made no difference, if it were shown that the money was applied for the purposes intended by the surety.

On these grounds, I am satisfied that the administrator of Fowler is not entitled to retain the draft as against the complainant; and the bank having received it, they must deliver up the note in question to the complainant. They must also refund to him the sum paid by him for the discount of the note.

The decree must be without costs. Mr. Brown was acting as administrator, and could not with safety relinquish the claim without the sanction of a Court; while the other defendants stood in the situation of stakeholders, ready to yield to either party with the assent of the other, and incapable of deciding the nice question at issue between them.

ADMINISTRATOR DE BONIS NON.

An administrator *de bonis non* of a solvent estate, can only recover from his predecessor, whether he has been removed, or has resigned, the assets which remain in his hands, in specie, unconverted. A settlement of his administration can only be made between him and the distributees, or legatees of the estate.—*Nolly* v. *Wilkins*, 11 *Alabama R.*, *p.* 872. (1847.)

ADMINISTRATOR—SECURITY.

Where an appeal has been entered by the intestate in his life time, and the security, good at the time, becomes insolvent pending the appeal, the administrator of the deceased is not bound to give additional security. —*Latimer et als* v. *Adm'rs of Ware*, 2 *Kelly's R.*, *p.* 272. *Ga.* (1847.)

Motion to compel the defendants to give additional security on the appeal entered in this case by their intestate in his lifetime. Heard before Judge Wright, in Floyd Superior Court, October Term, 1846.

Motion overruled in the Court below, assigned for error.
For the facts, see the opinion of the Supreme Court.

Hansell, for the plaintiffs in error.

Hooper & Mitchell, and *Akin*, for the defendants.

By the Court—Lumpkin, J., delivering the opinion.

The plaintiffs in error recovered a judgment against Robert Ware, who entered an appeal, in terms of the law, giving security which was deemed amply sufficient at the time. Ware died pending the appeal, and a motion was made, at the last October term of Floyd Superior Court, to compel his administrators to give additional security, on the ground, that the original security had become insolvent, or failing to do so, to have the appeal dismissed. Judge Wright refused the application, and this is now assigned as error.

An appeal being a proceeding unknown to the common law, we must look to our own Statutes for guidance in this question. It provides that either party, plaintiff or defendant, being dissatisfied with the verdict of the jury, may enter an appeal, "*provided* the person or persons so appealing shall, previous to obtaining such an appeal, pay all costs which shall have arisen on the former trial, and give security for the eventual condemnation money, *except executors and administrators, who shall not be liable to give such security, &c.*"—*Prince*, 426.

Is it not manifestly absurd, to exempt the representative of an estate from giving any security whatever when the appeal is entered by him, and to hold him bound to do so, because the security becomes insolvent which was given by the testator or intestate in his lifetime? It is true, that the rules of Court declare, that "if the security, good at first, becomes insolvent pending the appeal, the party appealing shall give other good security in the discretion of the Court, or the appeal shall be dismissed." *Hotchkiss*, 943. But this rule must be construed in reference to the existing laws of the State; and the Judges who framed it will not be presumed to have intended it to apply to administrators and executors. Even if interpreted literally, as it is insisted it shall be, it does not embrace the present case; it exacts additional security from the "*party appealing*" only; whereas this call is made, not on the original defendant who entered the appeal, but upon his representatives. Did it become necessary to do so, we should unhesitatingly uphold the judiciary act exempting executors and administrators from giving security, and set aside the rule as bench law. We are of the opinion, however, that there is no repugnance between them.

Why should these administrators be required to give security? The creditors of the estate are entitled to nothing beyond the assets. That these will be safely kept and legally and faithfully distributed, they have ample security upon the administration bond. Surely it cannot be expected that the administrators will involve themselves or their friends in personal liability apart from the correct administration of the estate. Trustees are never required to go further than to give security for the proper management and appropriation of the trust fund.

There is good reason in requiring the party himself, if in life, to strengthen the appeal bond, before he should be allowed the privilege of litigating his rights longer; he might waste his property and leave his creditor virtually remediless even with a judgment in his favor. But this the administrators cannot do; they have already given security well and truly to administer the goods, chattels and credits of their intestates, and to deliver and pay over the same to such persons as are entitled to the same according to law.—*Prince*, 228.

Were more than this demanded, all prudent persons would either decline undertaking the office of administrator, already too onerous, or else they would forbear or refuse to prosecute beyond the first trial, the just claims of their intestate, rather than incur the risk which it would involve. Justice to the rights of widows and orphans, as well as creditors, forbids such a decision.

It is contended, and with a good degree of earnestness, that by adopting the foregoing views, the plaintiff is placed in a worse situation by the death of the defendant than he would have been had he lived; that had the debtor survived, he could have been forced to give additional security, whereas his substitutes are relieved, notwithstanding they may continue the controversy which he left pending at his death.

Perhaps, after all, there is some confusion in respect to the legal maxims. *Actus Dei nemini facit injuriam*—that no one shall be injured through the act of God. Now it is true, and it would be unreasonable if it were otherwise, that those things which are inevitable as storms, tempests and lightning. Which no industry car avoid, no policy prevent, something in opposition to the act of man, shall not operate to the prejudice of those to whom no laches can be imputed. Thus if a sea-bank, or wall, which the owners of particular lands are bound to repair, be destroyed by tempests, without any default in such owners, the commissioners of sewers may order a new wall to be erected, at the expense of the whole level.—*Rex* v. *Somerset, Commissioners of Sewers*, 8 *T. R.*, 312.

So, also, where land is surrounded suddenly by the rage or violence of the sea, without any default of the tenant, or if the surface of the meadow be destroyed by the eruption of a moss, this would be no waste, but the act of God; that *vis major* for which the tenant is not responsible. —*Simmons* v. *Norton*, 7 *Bing.*, 647.

Again, if the condition of a bond was possible at the time of making it, and becomes impossible by the act of God, the obligor shall be excused; as if a lessee covenants to leave a wood in as good plight as the wood was at the time of making the lease, and afterwards the trees were blown down by a tempest, he is discharged by his covenant.—1 *Reports*, 98.

So much for the illustration of the rule. On the other hand, it cannot be disputed that death is one of those dispensations of Providence which occasions frequently, not loss merely, but absolute ruin, to innocent sufferers. Take the case of landlord and tenant: where the premises are destroyed by fire, the latter is liable to the payment of rent until the tenancy is determined, although the landlord is not bound to rebuild, notwithstanding he has recovered the value from an Insurance office.—*Paradine* v. *Jane, Aleyn*, 27.

By the common law, the death of a *sole* party to a suit pending the proceeding, was always productive of delay and expense by the abatement of the action. In *personal* actions the right itself is forever gone. Where credit is extended not upon the property, but the probity of the debtor, his death, which is the act of God, takes from the creditor all hope of reimbursement; so that were it true as urged by the plaintiff in error, that under this construction, by the death of Ware he is placed in a worse condition than he was before, still that would interpose no legal objection to the doctrines. And, whatever else may or may not inflict an injury, it is our province to see to it, that the law works no wrong in our hands. That *actus curiæ meminem gravabit*.

The judgment of the Court below must be affirmed.

AGENT.

An agent who admits money in his hands belonging to his principal, is liable for interest thereon from the time he received it.

He who has fraudulently received, *or* wrongfully detains the money of another, is chargeable with interest thereon from the time he received it.—*Anderson et al.* v. *The State of Georgia.*, 2 *Kelly's R.*, *p.* 370. *Ga.* (1847.)

(NISBET, J., cited *Dodge* v. *Perkins*, 9 *Pick.*, 368; *Weeks* v. *Hasty*, 13 *Mass.*, 218; *Wood* v. *Robins*, 11 *Mass.*, 504; *The Commonwealth* v. *Crevar*, 3 *Binn.*, 121; *Gillet* v. *Maynard*, 5 *Johns.*, 88; *The People* v. *Gasherrie.*, 9 *Johns.*, 71; *Greenly* v. *Hopkins*, 10 *Wend.*, 96; *Crawford* v. *Willing*, 4 *Dall.*, 289; *Slingerland* v. *Swart*, 13 *Johns.*, 296; *Brown* v. *Campbell*, 1 *S. & R.*, 179.)

When a party, dealing with an agent, takes his promissory note, with a knowledge of his agency, and of the liability of the principal for the debt for which the note is given, he thereby discharges the principal; and the contract cannot be afterwards rescinded, and a new one made, by which the principal will be bound, without his knowledge and assent. *Paige* v. *Stone et al.*, 10 *Metcalf's R.*, *p.* 160. *Mass.* (1847.)

(HUBBARD, J., cited *Paterson* v. *Gandasequi*, 15 *East*, 62; *Wilkins* v. *Reed*, 6 *Greenl.*, 220; *French* v. *Price*, 24 *Pick.*, 13; *Green* v. *Tanner*, 8 *Metcalf*, 411.)

An agent by whom a contract has been executed, and who has been released by the plaintiff from any liability to him, may be examined as a witness in an action on the contract, to prove the extent of his powers. —*Miller* v. *The New Orleans Canal and Banking Co.*, 8 *Robinson's La. R.*, *p.* 236. (1847.)

(GARLAND, J., cited 13 *La.*, 216; 9 *La.*, 52; 2 *Starkie*, 767-9.)

Where funds are placed in the hands of an agent to make purchases, and a balance remains in his hands, after the purchases are completed, he is not liable to pay interest on such balance before the commencement of the suit, unless a special demand was made.—*Williams* v. *Baxter*, 3 *M'Lean's U. S. R.*, *p.* 471. (1847.)

The plaintiff delivered a note to an agent for collection, and the agent delivered it to an attorney with whom plaintiff had no communication. It was *held* that the agent was not absolved by showing that an attorney intervened. It was his duty to superintend the collection and receive the money, and in the absence of any proof on his part, showing exertions to collect the money from the attorney who received it, he will be held accountable.—*Harrold et al.* v. *Gillespie et als.*, 7 *Humphreys' R.*, *p.* 57. *Tenn.* (1847.)

Where an agent buys land with the money of his principal, and takes a deed conveying the title to himself, or upon the sale of the land thus situated, takes notes for the purchase money in his own name; it is competent for the principal to prove the fact by parol testimony, and assert his title to the land in the one case, and to the money in the other.—*Andrews et al.* v. *Jones*, 10 *Alabama R.*, *p.* 460. (1847.)

Where an agent paid out the money of his principal in discharge of a debt due by another; it was *held*, that the principal had no cause of action against him for whose benefit his money had been paid. No one can be made a debtor without his consent.—*Young* v. *Dibrell*, 7 *Humphreys' R.*, *p.* 270. *Tenn.* (1847.)

In order to charge one with a contract alleged to have been made with his agent, the authority of the agent, and that it has been strictly pursued, must be clearly proved.—*The Bank of Hamburgh* v. *Johnson*, 3 *Richardson's R.*, *p.* 42. *S. C.* (1847.)

Where the alleged authority of an agent is by parol and for a specified purpose, the principal may prove the nature and extent of the agency by the agent, unless otherwise disqualified.

When the question is, whether the agent did or did not exceed the authority given to him as agent, he is equally liable to the losing party, if he exceeds his powers, for the damage done thereby; and is a competent witness without a release.—*Crooker* v. *Appleton*, 25 *Maine R.*, *p.* 131. (1847.)

An agent who receives notes to be deposited with an attorney for collection, but collects the money himself, is not entitled to insist on a demand before suit against him.—*Brazier* v. *Fortune*, 10 *Alabama R.*, *p.* 516. (1847.)

AGREEMENT.

An agreement made by a railroad company, with a person owning land adjacent to the railroad, to establish and maintain a permanent turnout track, and stopping-place, at a particular point, in the neighborhood of his property, and to stop there with the freight trains and passenger cars of the company, is, in substance, the grant of an easement, or servitude, which is to be binding upon the property of the railroad company, as the servient tenement, for the benefit of the owner of such adjacent property, and of all those who shall succeed him, in his estate, as owners thereof. And such an agreement to be valid must be in writing.

The negative easement, which the owner of the dominant tenement is to acquire by such an agreement, is an incorporeal hereditament; the right or title to which can only pass by grant, or deed under seal, or be acquired by prescription.

The provision of the Revised Statutes, declaring that no estate or interest in lands, or any trust or power over them, shall be created or granted, except by operation of law, or by a deed or conveyance in writing, &c., is sufficiently broad to prevent the acquiring of an easement in land by a verbal agreement merely.

A parol executory agreement, between an individual and a railroad company, that the latter shall continue to stop with their cars at a particular place, adjacent to his property, as a permanent arrangement, is void by the statute of frauds; because from the nature and terms of the agreement it is not to be performed in one year from the making thereof. —*Pitkin* v. *The Long Island Railroad Company*, 2 *Barbour's Ch. R.*, *p.* 221. *N. Y.* (1848.)

(The Chancellor cited 1 *Pardessus Traite des Servitudes*, *ch.* 1; *Fentiman* v. *Smith*, 4 *East*, 107; *Hewlins* v. *Shippam*, 7 *Dow.* & *Ryl.*, 783; 5 *Barn.* & *Cres.*, 221; *S. C.*, 2 *R. S.*, 145, *sec.* 6.)

By an agreement between D. and W., D. was to furnish goods for a store and pay all the expenses, and W. was to transact the business of the store, and receive half the profits, as a compensation for his services. *Held*, in an action against W. and D. for goods sold and delivered to D., that they were not partners, and that D. only was liable for the goods. *Bradley et al.* v. *White et al.*, 10 *Metcalf's R.*, *p.* 303. *Mass.* (1847.)

(Hubbard, J., cited *Denny* v. *Cabot*, 6 *Metcalf*, 82; *Blanchard* v. *Coolidge*, 22 *Pick.*, 151; *Vanderburgh* v. *Hull*, 20 *Wend.*, 70; *Ambler* v. *Bradley*, 6 *Vermont*, 119; *Loomis* v. *Marshall*, 12 *Conn.*, 69; *Story on Part.*, *secs.* 36, 38.)

The endorser of a bill or note may, before the paper matures, make a valid agreement to waive a presentment and notice of non-payment. Such an agreement does not require a consideration to support it.—*Coddington* v. *Davis et als.*, 3 *Denio's R.*, *p.* 16. *N. Y.* (1848.)

(Jewett, J., cited 2 *Inst.*, 183; 10 *Rep.*, 101; 1 *Selw. N. P.*, 10*th Ed.*, 358; *Story on Prom. Notes*, *sec.* 271; *Leffingwell* v. *White*, 1 *Johns. Cas.*, 99; *Story on Bills*, *secs.* 371, 373.)

AMENDMENT.

A sheriff cannot amend his return so as to avoid a motion pending against him, neither can his deputy, so as to discharge his principal.—*Howard et als.* v. *Union Bank*, 7 *Humphreys' R.*, *p.* 26. *Tenn.* (1847.)

(Green, J., cited *Mullins* v. *Johnson* & *Rayburn*, 3 *Humph.*, 396.)

AMENDMENT OF RECORD.

Where a judgment was recorded upon a bond and warrant of attorney, and at the time the judgment record was left at the clerk's office, to be docketed, the attorney omitted to leave the warrant of attorney, but left it the next day in the office; from which place it was taken away by another person, through mistake, and lost, and the clerk docketed the judgment without having previously signed the record; *Held*, that these were errors which the Court had power to remedy, by permitting an amendment of the record.—*Williams* v. *Wheeler*, 1 *Barbour's R.*, *p.* 48. *N. Y.* (1848.)

(EDMONDS, J., cited *Lee* v. *Curtis*, 17 *Johns.*, 86; *Seaman* v. *Drake*, 1 *Caine*, 9; *Close* v. *Gillespie*, 3 *Johns.*, 526; *March* v. *Berry*, 7 *Cowen*, 344; *Hanmer* v. *McConnell*, 2 *Ham.* 32; *State* v. *Cherry*, 2 *Dev.*, 550; *O'Driscol* v. *McBurney*, 2 *Nev. & Man.*, 59; *Lowry* v. *Catlin*, 2 *Vt.*, 365; *Chamberlain* v. *Crane*, 4 *N. H.*, 115; *Bank of Newburgh* v. *Seymour*, 14 *Johns.*, 219; *Mechanics' Bank* v. *Minthorne*, 19 *Johns.*, 244; *Patton* v. *Massey*, 2 *Hill*, 475; *Commonwealth* v. *Winstons*, 5 *Rand.*, 546; *Cheetham* v. *Tillotson*, 4 *Johns.*, 499; *Hubert* v. *Hardenburgh*, 5 *Halst.*, 222; *Bank of Kentucky* v. *Ashley*, 2 *Pet.*, 329; *Prevost* v. *Nichols*, 4 *Yeates*, 479.)

ANCIENT LIGHTS.

One who erects a house in a city or town, on the margin of his lot, with a window opening upon the lot of the adjoining proprietor, does not thereby acquire such a right to the use of his window as to deprive the adjoining proprietor of the right to build on his lot, in any manner his judgment or fancy may dictate.—*Ray* v. *Lines*, 10 *Alabama R.*, *p.* 63. (1847.)

(ORMOND, J., cited *Gwin* v. *Melmoth*, 1 *Freeman's Ch.*, 505.)

ANNUITY.

Where a person is entitled, under a will, to an annuity for life, payable semi-annually, out of the income of real and personal estate in the hands of trustees, his interest in such annuity, beyond what is necessary for the support of himself and his family, may, under the provisions of the Revised Statutes, be reached by a creditor's bill, and applied to the payment of his debts.—*Sellick* v. *Mason*, 2 *Barbour's Ch. R.*, *p.* 79. *N. Y.* (1848.)

ANTE-NUPTIAL AGREEMENT.

Where a husband and wife, in order to carry out an ante-nuptial agreement, conveyed personal property to a trustee, with directions to hold a part of it for the sole and separate use of the wife, with a power to the wife to alien or devise it, such part goes, if she dies intestate, to her next of kin, free of all claim on the part of the husband.—*Marshall* v. *Beall*, 6 *Howard's U. S. R.*, *p.* 70. (1848.)

(*Jones* cited *Clancey*, 43, 51; 2 *Roper, Husband and Wife*, 157; 2 *Story Eq.*, *secs.* 1378—1383; 7 *Johns. Ch.*, 229; 6 *Gill & Johnson*, 349.

Catron, J., cited *Ward* v. *Thompson*, 6 *Gill & Johns.*, 349; *Watt* v. *Watt*, 3 *Ves.*, 241; *Garrick* v. *Camden*, 14 *Ves.*, 372; *Bailey* v. *Wright* 18 *Ves.*, 49.)

APPRAISERS.

Where appraisers are chosen by parties to determine the amount of a claim arising under an agreement between them, with power to such appraisers to appoint an umpire to decide between them in case of their disagreement, they may appoint such umpire immediately, without waiting until a disagreement has arisen between them.

It is not a valid objection to an award made upon such a submission, that one of the appraisers signed the same, with the umpire. The authority originally given to the appraisers ceases upon the appointment of an umpire by them; and if either of them subsequently signs the award, his signature is a mere nullity. The award is the act of the umpire.—*The Mayor &c. of New York* v. *Butler*, 1 *Barbour's R.*, *p.* 325. *N. Y.* (1848.)

ARBITRATION.

Where accounts between the parties were submitted to arbitrators, a portion of which were in suit and secured by attachment, and an award was made of a certain sum to be paid to the plaintiff, otherwise the action should proceed, which payment was refused. *Held*, that the submission and award was no bar to the maintainance of the suit.

Where an auditor was appointed in such case, who merely re-affirmed the award of the arbitrators, which included in it matters not in suit, the report was set aside.—*Elliot* v. *Quimby*, 13 *New Hampshire R.*, *p.* 181. (1847.)

Assumpsit, on account annexed to the writ, and for use and occupation.

After suit brought, and before the same was entered, the parties submitted the accounts between them to arbitrators, who awarded $12 41 to the plaintiff, and costs. An attachment of property had been made upon the writ, and the award provided that the action should not be estopped until the $12 41 was paid, and that the award should remain in the hands of one of the arbitrators until this condition was complied with.

The sum awarded was not paid, and at the term of Court at which the writ was returnable, the action was entered. The defendant pleaded the general issue with notice of set-off, and also the award, in bar of the farther maintenance of the action.

An auditor was appointed by the Court to state the accounts between the parties. On the hearing before the auditor, evidence was offered of the submission of the accounts of the parties to arbitrators, and their award, and the auditor reported, affirming the award as conclusive in the suit.

In the accounts presented to the arbitrators, various items were considered and allowed, which were not embraced in the present suit.

The plaintiff moved for judgment on the report of the auditor, but the defendant objected. 1. Because the award was binding on the parties, and was a bar to the farther maintenance of the suit. 2. That the auditor's report was void, because various matters were considered in it which were not included in the present suit.

On these exceptions the case was transferred to this Court for such order thereon as the Court should direct.

Bellows, for the defendant.—A general submission of a cause to arbitrators, is a dismissal of the suit. *Ex parte Wright*, 6 *Cowen*, 399. This is the case, although the arbitrators have done nothing. The Court will not look beyond the submission. *Larkin* v. *Robbins*, 2 *Wend.*, 505. If, before plea pleaded, all actions be submitted to arbitration, the defendant may plead the fact in bar of the further maintenance of the suit.—*Towns* v. *Wilcox*, 12 *Wend.*, 503.

It is also held, that where there is a submission of all demands which either party had against the other, the award is a conclusive bar to an action for any demand subsisting at the time of the submission and award.—*Wheeler* v. *Vanhouten*, 12 *Johns.*, 311.

Ainsworth, for the plaintiff.

UPHAM, J. It is undoubtedly correct that an agreement for the submission of a cause is ordinarily a discontinuance of the suit; and that, as a general rule, where there has been a submission of all demands, an award is conclusive against a suit, on any demand subsisting at the time of the submission. Where, however, parties have submitted all demands to arbitrators, and they have made their report, it may still be shown, in an action afterwards brought on a particular demand, that it was not in dispute, and not laid before the referees, and the action may be maintained.—2 *N. H. Rep.*, 26, *Whittemore* v. *Whittemore*; 5 *Mass.*, 334, *Webster* v. *Lee*; 9 *Mass.*, 320, *Hodges* v. *Hodges*; 2 *Verm.*, 417, *Buck* v. *Buck*; 5 *Greenl.*, 192, *Bailey* v. *Whitney*; 4 *Vermont*, 210, *Hayes* v. *Blanchard*.

Courts in such cases go behind the submission to see what construction the parties gave to it, and what was in fact included under it; and where an award is pleaded they will not hold themselves concluded by the mere fact of an award, but inquire what was actually decided by the arbitrators.

Where a submission has been made, but the arbitrators have refused to sit, the submission is not necessarily a discharge of the action, unless such expressly appears to have been the intention of the parties. The submission is often made on an express understanding, or an implied presumption, that the referees will act, or the suit shall proceed; and if they attempt to do so under such circumstances, the whole attempt at submission fails. Where a submission of a suit has been made, and the arbitrators award conditionally the payment of a certain sum, or that the suit shall proceed, we hold it to be so far subject to their direction that the award will be binding in this respect. In this case the arbitrators agreed on an amount due the plaintiff, but held the award in their own hands, subject to the condition that if the amount was not paid, the action was to proceed.

The agreement of submission was by parol, and for aught that appears the arbitrators acted fully within the terms of the submission, as understood by the parties. There is, therefore, no good reason to hold the action is discharged, or that the parties intended this should be the case, unless the award was paid so as to discharge the suit. This has not been done, and the whole proceeding falls to the ground.

The appointment of an auditor by the Court was, under the circumstances, perfectly proper. The case would of course proceed precisely as though there had been no attempt at submission or award in the suit. The auditor has, however, transcended his authority, in passing on matters submitted to the arbitrators, but not embraced in the suit. His report must, therefore, be set aside or recommitted, that it may be corrected in this respect.

Report recommitted.

ASSAULT AND BATTERY.

In an action of trespass for an assault and battery, the Court permitted the plaintiff to prove, that he was a poor man with a large family, and that the defendant was a wealthy man, with no children, and but a small family. The Court also instructed the jury, "that if they found the defendant guilty, in assessing the plaintiff's damages, they had a right to take into consideration the circumstances of the parties:" *Held*, that the Circuit Court decided correctly in admitting the evidence and in giving the instruction.

In actions of trespass for assault and battery, the condition in life and circumstances of the parties are peculiarly the proper subjects for the consideration of the jury in estimating the damages. They may take into consideration the pecuniary resources of the defendant, and may give exemplary damages, not only to compensate the plaintiff, but to punish the defendant, according to the circumstances of the case.

The amount of damages to be recovered in actions for personal injuries, rests so much in the discretion of juries, that Courts will not disturb their verdicts on the ground that the damages are excessive, unless it is manifest that they have been governed by passion, partiality, or corruption. To draw such a conclusion, it is not enough that the damages, in the opinion of the Court, are too high, or that a less amount would have been a sufficient satisfaction for the injury. It must be apparent, at first blush, that the damages are glaringly excessive.—*McNamara* v. *King*, 2 *Gilman's R.*, *p.* 432. *Ills.* (1847.)

TRESPASS for an assault and battery in the Kane Circuit Court, brought by the appellee against the appellant. The cause was heard before the *Hon. John D.* CATON and a jury, at the September term, 1845, when a verdict and judgment was rendered for the plaintiff below for $650 damages.

The evidence in the case is sufficiently stated in the opinion of the Court.

The cause was submitted to the Court on the plaintiff's abstract, and the defendant's brief.

Thomas & Lincoln, for the appellant.
Wilson, for the appellee.

In actions for personal injuries Courts will not set aside verdicts for excessive damages, unless the damages are so excessive as to make it manifest that the jury acted from passion, partiality, or corruption; and to enable the Court to draw the conclusion, it is not enough that, in their opinion, the damages are too high, or that much less damages would have been a sufficient satisfaction for the plaintiff.—*Coffin* v. *Coffin*, 4 *Mass.*, 40; 8 *Burr.*, 609; 3 *Com. Dig.*, 3, 57; *Johnson* v. *Moulton*, 1 *Scam.*, 532.

In Coffin v. *Coffin*, before cited, *Chief Justice* PARSONS says: "Judges should be very cautious how they overthrow verdicts given by twelve men on their oaths on the ground of excessive damages." "And it must be a glaring case, indeed, of outrageous damages in a tort, and which all mankind at first blush must think so, to induce the Court to grant a new trial, for excessive damages." There is a manifest difference between cases, where the damages may be estimated, as in promises and trespasses for goods, and where the damages are matters of speculation, and are ideal.

2. A Court will not grant a new trial where substantial justice has been done between the parties, although the law arising on the evidence would have justified a different result.—*Smith* v. *Schultz*, 1 *Scam.*, 491; *Wheeler* v. *Shields*, 2 *Scam.*, 350; *Cox* v. *Stitchen*, 1 *Bos. & Pul.*, 339; 2 *T. R.*, 4; *Hunt* v. *Burrell*, 5 *Johns.*, 139.

3. The jury have a right in assessing the plaintiff's damages in an action of trespass for an assault and battery, to take into consideration the wealth and condition of the defendant. His wealth affords a criterion by which the jury may judge as to the amount they ought to impose upon him, as "smart money," in the nature of a penalty for his con-

duct. A thousand dollars would be no greater penalty to a man worth ten thousand dollars, than would be a hundred to a man worth one-tenth as much.

4. There was no error in allowing proof to go to the jury that the plaintiff was a poor man with a large family. The business and circumstances of a plaintiff in actions of this character are proper subjects for the consideration of the jury in assessing the damages which he may have sustained. It is the policy of the law to protect the persons and property of the poor. The consequences of an assault upon a poor man, who has a family dependent upon his labor for support, by which he is maimed for life, are surely more serious than they would be to a man in affluence. 1 *Mass.*, 12. In the case of *Reed* v. *Davis*, 4 *Pick.*, 216, which was an action of trespass for an assault and battery, the Supreme Court of Massachusetts says: "Now that circumstance [the poverty of the plaintiff] was to be taken into consideration by the jury. There is nothing more abhorrent to the feelings of the citizens of a free government than oppressing the poor and distressed under the forms and color of, but in reality in violation of, the laws. An intelligent and impartial jury may and ought to be influenced by the proof of such an act committed by the defendants." And again: "The plaintiff was poor. He had seen better days, but had been reduced in his circumstances. He was not thought able to do any thing in vindication of his rights at law. But in this the defendants miscalculated." "They (the jury) have proceeded upon higher grounds of damages than those which arise merely from bodily wounds and bruises. These considerations are sound and should be cherished," &c.

The case of *Lincoln* v. *the Saratoga Railroad Co.*, 23 *Wend.*, 425, was an action on the case for negligence, by "which the plaintiff had his leg broken." The Court in that case say: "And for that purpose (assessing the plaintiff's damages) the nature of the plaintiff's business, its extent, and the importance of his personal oversight and superintendence in conducting it, may be shown." "The amount of business, the ability and attention of the plaintiff, the business season, the comparative inexperience of the partners, the money pressure in the market, and the like,—all this may be very proper for the consideration of the jury, and entitled to such weight in connexion with all the circumstances of the case, in their estimate of the loss and damages, as they may think it deserves."

The opinion of the Court was delivered by

TREAT, J.—This was an action of trespass, assault and battery, commenced in the Kane Circuit Court, by George A. King, against Charles McNamara. The defendant pleaded "not guilty," and several special pleas, on which issues were formed. The cause was tried by a jury. On the trial, the Court allowed the plaintiff to prove that he was a poor man with a large family; and that the defendant was a wealthy man, with no children, and but a small family. The defendant objected to the introduction of this evidence. At the instance of the plaintiff, the

Court instructed the jury, that if they found the defendant guilty, in assessing the plaintiff's damages, they had a right to take into consideration the circumstances of the parties. The defendant excepted to the instructions. The jury returned a verdict in favor of the plaintiff for $650. The Court overruled a motion for a new trial, and judgment was entered on the verdict. The defendant excepted, and incorporated the whole of the testimony in a bill of exceptions. He has appealed to this Court, and now assigns for error the several decisions of the Circuit Court, in admitting the evidence objected to, in giving the instruction, and in refusing to grant a new trial.

The evidence is voluminous, and will not be here particularly stated. It has been carefully examined and considered. In the opinion of the Court, it shows an aggravated case of assault and battery without any attending circumstances to justify or excuse it. The defendant assailed the plaintiff with a deadly weapon, and severely wounded him; the result of which was a dangerous illness for several weeks. We cannot say that the damages were excessive. The amount of recovery in actions for personal injuries rests so much in the discretion of juries, that Courts will not disturb their verdicts on the ground that the damages are excessive, unless it is manifest that they have been governed by passion, partiality, or corruption; and to draw such a conclusion, it is not enough that the damages, in the opinion of the Court, are too high, or that a less amount would have been a sufficient satisfaction for the injury. It must be apparent at first blush that the damages are glaringly excessive. —*Coffin* v. *Coffin*, 4 *Mass.*, 1; *Coleman* v. *Southwick*, 9 *Johns.*, 45; *Com. Dig.*, "Damages," E. 7.

We are also of the opinion, that the Circuit Court decided correctly in admitting the evidence, and in giving the instruction. In actions of this kind, the condition in life and circumstances of the parties are peculiarly the proper subjects for the consideration of the jury in estimating the damages. Their pecuniary circumstances may be inquired into. It may be readily supposed that the consequences of a severe personal injury would be more disastrous to a person destitute of pecuniary resources, and dependent wholly on his manual exertions for the support of himself and family, than to an individual differently situated in life. The effect of the injury might be to deprive him and his family of the comforts and necessaries of life. It is proper that the jury should be influenced by the pecuniary resources of the defendant. The more affluent, the more able he is to remunerate the party he has wantonly injured. In this class of cases, the jury may give exemplary damages, not only to compensate the plaintiff, but to punish the defendant. The standard of damages is not a fixed one, applicable to all cases, but is to be regulated by the circumstances of each particular case.—*Grable* v. *Margrave*, 3 *Scam.*, 372; *Reed* v. *Davis*, 4 *Pick.*, 216; *Lincoln* v. *S. & S. Railroad*, 23 *Wend.*, 425.

The judgment of the Circuit Court is affirmed with costs.

Judgment affirmed.

ASSIGNMENT.

A general assignment executed by an insolvent debtor, to his brother, who at the time was unfit to attend to business by reason of a lingering disease, which the assignor believed was incurable, and of which he died, was held for that cause to be fraudulent and void as against creditors.

The selection of such an assignee furnishes a strong presumption of an intent on the part of the assignor to keep the control and disposal of the property.

The assigned property was almost wholly fees earned in the office of sheriff. The assignor's deputy continued to receive and collect the same after the assignment, and to dispose of them as he had done previously, except that he paid over to the assignor only on the assignee's direction. This was held to be evidence of fraud in the assignment.

So of an understanding that the assignee should allow to the assignor a weekly sum for his services, the same being nominal.

An assignment by a sheriff of fees due and to become due, having for one of its objects an indemnity of his sureties against future misappropriation of moneys which should be collected on executions, is void.—*Currie et als.* v. *Hart et als.*, 2 *Sandford's Ch. R.*, *p.* 353. *N. Y.* (1847.)

The bill was filed on the 23d day of August, 1842, against Monmouth B. Hart, on the return of an execution unsatisfied, to reach his equitable interests and things in action.

In his answer the defendant set up the execution by him of a general assignment to James H. Hart, for the benefit of his creditors, dated May 10, 1842, and delivered June 10, 1842.

The complainants, on the 24th of February, 1843, filed a supplemental bill making James H. Hart a party defendant, and charging that the assignment was fraudulent and void against them as creditors of M. B. Hart. J. H. Hart put in an answer on the 3d of June, previous to which he had at his own request been removed from the trust as assignee, and Cornelius Bergen appointed in his stead by an order of this Court dated May 31, 1843.

On the 24th of October, 1843, a second supplemental bill was filed, making Bergen a party. The suit was brought to a hearing on the pleadings and proofs.

It appeared that M. B. Hart was the sheriff of the City and County of New York, for three years, commencing on the 1st day of January, 1841, and C. Bergen was one of the sureties in his official bond.

The assignment to James H. Hart embraced all M. B. Hart's property and effects, including the debts due to him as sheriff, with all the future receipts of the office of sheriff. Its trusts were, *first*, to pay demands against him as sheriff thereafter to be incurred, and such as should accrue against him and his sureties in his official bond. *Second*, to pay all the demands for which James H. Hart was liable for him as endorser or otherwise. *Third*, to pay $4,200 of borrowed money to Benjamin F. Hart. And *Fourth*, to pay all the other creditors of M. B. Hart rateably.

The other material facts will be found stated in the opinion of the Court.

Buckham & Gerard, for the complainants.

Hart, for the defendant, M. B. Hart.

Rockwell & Tallmadge, for C. Bergen.

The Assistant Vice-Chancellor.—I doubt very much whether any interest passed to James H. Hart, the assignee, in the future credits and receipts which were expected to accrue in the sheriff's office, after the date of the assignment. The effect of such instruments, when they operate by way of agreement or estoppel, *Wright* v. *Wright*, 1 *Ves.*, 409, would probably be limited and restricted so as to cease whenever they came in conflict with the equitable lien or priority of a creditor's bill against the assignor. This point, and the grave questions of public policy which are presented by an assignment of a sheriff's whole official fees which are thereafter to accrue, are of so much importance as well as difficulty, that I prefer to leave them to the decision of judges who will do them better justice than I can, if there are other grounds upon which the case can be better determined.

In respect to the sheriff's fees which had accrued when the assignment was made, they are like debts due to any other individual.

I will examine the objections to the assignment, as applicable to those fees.

First. The general terms used in declaring the second trust, render its validity questionable. They provide for discharging all legal demands and liabilities which might thereafter be incurred, in and about the management and discharge of the duties of the assignor as sheriff, and all legal claims upon the office or against him as sheriff, which might thereafter arise, &c., &c.

It appears by the testimony, that claims of this character frequently arose, both before and after the assignment, in consequence of the assignor's omission to pay over moneys collected by him on executions. This class of claims was of course founded upon a plain violation of his official duty, and an assignment made in contemplation of such official misconduct, and intended to secure the sheriff's sureties from its consequences, would, in my opinion, be void. The trust in this instrument is sufficiently broad to include such claims, and was sustained at the hearing as properly and justly applicable to them. It would, perhaps, be too harsh to avoid it because it may include a void preference, when there is no expression of a design to provide for such a preference.

But, after reading the testimony of the under-sheriff and the coroner, it is difficult to resist the conclusion that this species of claim was a prominent consideration and motive for making the assignment. And if it were, I think, the object being unlawful, the trusts could not be upheld.

I will waive this point, and proceed to the other objections made by the complainants.

Second. The selection of the assignee, is one of the alleged evidences of a fraudulent intent in making the assignment.

The assignment was executed on the 10th day of June, 1842. It bears date a month earlier, but I find no evidence that it was drawn up prior to that day.

It is proved by a letter of M. B. Hart, dated 21st June, 1842, (which is proper testimony, as he was then in possession of the assigned effects,) that Doctor Hart, the assignee, had been confined to his bed and room for fifteen days, with a disorder which the physicians declared to be a decline or consumption. The letter shows that M. B. Hart did not believe that his brother would ever recover, and that his only hope was in his brother's going to Rio Janeiro to spend the ensuing winter. He says in the letter, that he has determined to make an assignment to the doctor of all his fees, &c., as if the assignment had not then been executed; but as the case stands, the date of its delivery was the 10th of June.

It also appears that Doctor Hart never recovered from the attack mentioned in the letter, which was consumption; and that he was never afterwards able to attend to business to any extent deserving of mention.

This is the case therefore of an insolvent debtor making an assignment in trust for creditors of all his property, and even of his future expectations, to a brother, who as he knows is prostrate with a disease which he believes is incurable, and knowing also that if curable, it will, for a year to come, entirely prevent him from giving any personal attention to the discharge of the duties of assignee.

In *Reed* v. *Emery*, 8 *Paige*, 417, the CHANCELLOR decided that an assignment by a debtor in failing circumstances to an assignee who is known to be insolvent, is *primâ facie* evidence of an intent to defraud the creditors of the assignor, and sufficient to overcome the general denial of fraud in the answer.

In *Cram* v. *Mitchell*, 1 *Sandford's Ch.*, 251, I decided the same point upon an assignment made to three near relatives, all of whom were preferred creditors; one of the assignees being stone blind, another too illiterate to write and scarcely able to read, and the third residing at so great a distance from the property and residence of the assignor, that he could not devote his attention to it, and instead of that, appointed an agent on the spot to look after his interests as a creditor.

The selection of such assignees, furnishes strong presumption of an intent, on the part of the assignor, to keep the control of his property in his own hands and under his own disposal. This is the natural and inevitable result, when the assignor is physically or mentally incompetent to act efficiently, as well as where his distance from the scene of action precludes his personal care and supervision.

On this ground, I am persuaded that the assignment in question is fraudulent as against the creditors of M. B. Hart.

Third. The management of the assigned property is the next point made against the assignment.

The property consisted almost exclusively of the fees earned, and to be earned, in the sheriff's office.

It appears by the testimony that for nearly eleven months after the transfer of the property, there was no change whatever in the custody and control of those things in action, or in the receipt of such as were paid. During all this period, the under-sheriff, who attended in the office and had the charge there during Mr. Hart's whole term, received all the moneys paid in for fees and services. He received them as such under-sheriff, and not as agent or in behalf of the assignee; and he paid them out and disposed of them precisely as he had done before the assignment was made, except that he says what he paid over to the sheriff himself was so paid by J. H. Hart's direction. This merely aggravates the apparent fraud, for it shows that the assignee's only active interference was to place money in the assignor's hands in contravention of his duty as trustee. The reason assigned for the assignee's omission to take possession, is its intrinsic difficulty, and his continued ill health. The difficulty is all imaginary, provided the assignment were made in good faith. A clerk placed in the office, a notice to the deputies and the under-sheriff, and to the indebted attorneys, renewed from time to time in respect of the accruing fees, would have answered the purpose.

The ill health of the assignee, if it had been wholly unforeseen, would have obviated the inference arising from his personal inattention; but would not excuse the total omission to act through others. And this omission, coupled with the assignor's knowledge of the situation of his brother when he made the transfer, furnishes presumptive evidence that he made it with the intent to hinder and delay his creditors.

In reference to the household furniture, &c., assigned, it then was, and has ever since been, in the possession of M. B. Hart. An execution would probably have been upheld against all the claims interposed to protect it; but the requisite parties are wanting to warrant me in deciding that question.

I do not think that the voluntary assignee could have held these chattels, against the mortgage and the executions which were charges upon them. His omission to interfere, therefore, does not furnish any evidence of a fraudulent intent.

Fourth. There is one other circumstance which deserves notice. Mr. Hart's son testifies that Mr. Hart received from the assignee, ten dollars a week for his services, up to the time his term of office expired.

If the assignment were valid to pass the earnings of the office after its date, these payments were made to the assignor wholly out of the fund he had set apart for his creditors. His services, so far as it is proved, consisted of his official title and dignity as sheriff, and of nothing more.

Watkins, who in May, 1843, enacted the part of receiver under J. H. Hart, also paid out money on M. B. Hart's orders drawn upon the under-sheriff.

And in his examination before the master, under the order for a receiver in this suit, M. B. Hart testified, that J. H. Hart allowed him to draw from the fees of the office sufficient for the support of his family, in compensation for his services, and that his salary was fixed at $2,000 a year; but he had not drawn out at any thing like that rate. This examination was in March, 1843, while M. B. Hart continued in possession of the things in action assigned, and it must be received as competent testimony against the assignee.

The result of the evidence on this head clearly shows, that although not expressed in the instrument, it was understood and agreed, when the assignment was made, that the assignor should receive his support out of the effects assigned.

This, of itself, is sufficient to establish an intent fraudulent towards creditors.

I have not adverted to the course of things after the first of May, 1843. The receivership of Watkins, during that month of May, was really absurd. He received some moneys from the under-sheriff, and paid them out, principally as directed by him, without apparently knowing why he received or paid them. It is plain that he did not succeed in learning much about the assigned property, or in getting any control over it.

After Mr. Bergen became the trustee, matters undoubtedly assumed a different aspect. But the change came too late to efface the indelible badge of fraud which had been stamped upon the assignment, by the circumstances which I have considered and detailed.

It is impossible for me, upon the evidence, to resist the conclusion, that this assignment was intended to hinder, delay, or defraud creditors; and it must be declared to be void against the complainants accordingly.

They are entitled to a decree for the payment of their debt, interest and costs, out of the fund upon which they obtained a lien by their bill.

ASSIGNMENT—MORTGAGE.

Until proceedings are had for the purpose of enforcing a mortgage, the interest of the mortgagee may be assigned without deed, by a parol transfer of the debt and mortgage.

And the assignee may maintain an action upon the mortgage in his own name, notwithstanding the evidence of the debt is not in form negotiable, or is not assigned in such manner that he can maintain a personal action in his own name upon that.

No action can be maintained upon a mortgage, in the name of the mortgagee, after the mortgage has been assigned so that the assignee can maintain an action in his own right.—*Rigney* v. *Lovejoy*, 13 *New Hampshire R.*, *p.* 247. (1847.)

(*Ainsworth* cited 4 *Kent's Com.*, 159–60, *and cases there cited;* 4 *Conn.*, 235; 7 *Mass.*, 138; 4 *Johns.*, 41; 2 *Greenl.* 132; 3 *Pick.*, 484; 5 *N. H.*, 430; 7 *N. H.*, 94; 11 *Johns.*, 534; 1 *Johns.*, 580; *Doug.*, 610; *Roberts on Frauds*, 275.)

ATTACHMENT.

A non-resident cannot sue out an attachment against the property of a deceased non-resident debtor.—*Hemingway* v. *Moore et al.*, 11 *Alabama R.*, *p.* 645. (1847.)

(Ormond, J., cited *Loomis* v. *Allen*, 7 *Ala.*, 708.)

ATTORNEY.

A plea by an attorney of a party indicted for an assault committed with intent to rob, is a nullity; the defendant must plead in person.—*McQuillon* v. *The State of Mississippi*, 8 *Smedes and Marshall's R.*, *p.* 587. *Miss.* (1847.)

(*Guion & Walker* cited *Chitty's Crim. Law*, 416, 436, 472; *Stephen's Crim. Law*, 290; *Barbour's Crim. Treatise*, 300, 304; *Arch. Crim. Prac.*, 93.)

If one place a note in the hands of an attorney for collection, instructing him to pay the proceeds in satisfaction of a debt due by him to another, that other being also a client of the same attorney, this is an actual appropriation of the fund, which places it beyond the future control of the party so instructing, and which he cannot revoke by an after assignment.—*Alexander* v. *Adams*, 1 *Strobhart's R.*, *p.* 47. *S. C.* (1847.)

An attorney or solicitor cannot withdraw his name after it has been entered upon the record, without the leave of the Court, and the service of a citation upon him, in case of appeal, is as valid as if served on the party himself.—*United States* v. *Curry et al.*, 6. *Howard's U. S. R.*, *p.* 106. (1848.)

The provision of the statute making it a criminal offence for an attorney, counsellor or solicitor to buy any bond, bill or other *chose in action* for the purpose of bringing suit thereon, applies to the purchase of a *chose in action* for the purpose of instituting a suit thereon in Equity, as well as to a purchase in order to bring a suit thereon at law.—*Baldwin* v. *Latson*, 2 *Barbour's Ch. R.*, *p.* 306. *N. Y.* (1848.)

(The Chancellor cited *Hall* v. *Gird*, 7 *Hill*, 586.)

One attorney confides a note to another for collection, and takes his receipt, but without giving instructions with respect to the ownership. After the money is collected, it is remitted to the payee of the note, whose name however was endorsed on the note. This remittance, the payee not being the owner, will not discharge the collecting attorney from liability to his immediate principal, nor will the action of the latter, for the money, be defeated by proof that he was himself the agent of the endorsee, unless that person has asserted his right to the money as against his agent.—*Lewis et al.* v. *Peck et al.*, 10 *Alabama R.*, *p.* 142. (1847.)

The plaintiff's attorney is not liable for the defendant's costs, where the plaintiff removed from the state pending the suit, but only where he was a non-resident when it was commenced.—*Alexander* v. *Carpenter* 3 *Denio's R.*, *p.* 266. *N. Y.* (1848.)

Where an attorney charges himself with an amount collected for his principal, and charges the principal with his fee, the jury may infer a promise from the attorney to pay the balance.—*Cameron, Ex'r,* v. *Clarke, Smith & Co.*, 11 *Alabama R.*, *p.* 259. (1847.)

An attorney has no right to purchase real estate under his client's execution, for such client, unless specially authorized.—*Washington* v. *Johnson*, 7 *Humphrey's R.*, *p.* 468. *Tenn.* (1847.)

The attorney in a case has not power, as such, to employ assistant counsel in the suit at the expense of his client; and an employment by him will not bind his client, unless it can be fairly inferred, from the facts in the case, that such authority was given to him by the client.—*Paddock* v. *Colby et al.*, 18 *Vermont R.*, *p.* 485. (1847.)

An attorney at law, in the absence of instructions to that effect, has no authority to give day of payment, upon receiving security from the debtor.—*Lockhart* v. *Wyatt*, 10 *Alabama R.*, *p.* 231. (1847.)

ATTORNEY AND CLIENT.

The admission by the attorney of record of a fact for the purpose of trial, binds his client, and is conclusive of the fact admitted.—*Stark et al.* v. *Keenan, Ex'x*, 11 *Alabama R.*, *p.* 818. (1847.)

An attorney, to whom a promissory note is committed for the purpose of collection, by the payee, derives no authority, from the mere fact of the employment, to endorse and transfer the note, in behalf of his client, to a third person, so as to enable him to maintain an action for the benefit of the payee.—*White* v. *Hildreth*, 13 *New-Hampshire R.*, *p.* 104. (1847.)

Counsel, who with the consent of the client, withdraws from a case, after having rendered beneficial services, does not thereby lose his right to compensation for the services rendered, unless at the time of his withdrawal, he waives or abandons his claim to compensation.

An attorney at law cannot recover more than he agreed to receive, by proof that his services were worth more.—*Coopwood* v. *Wallace*, 12 *Alabama R.*, *p.* 790. (1848.)

ATTORNEY IN FACT.

One who has been constituted attorney in fact, to receive the money of an absent debtor, but refuses to do so, and under his power appoints another to receive it, may in his return to a writ of attachment, properly deny that he has any moneys, goods, &c., of the absent debtor.

One appointed under a power of attorney, is the attorney of the principal, and not of the attorney who appointed him.—*Burrell* v. *Letson*, 1 *Strobhart's R.*, *p.* 239. *S. C.* (1847.)

AUCTION.

All fraudulent acts and all combinations, having for their object to stifle fair competition at the biddings at auction sales, are unlawful.

Where the parties agreed, that if the defendant would not bid upon a note against the plaintiff, at an auction sale which was to be had thereof as part of the effects of a bankrupt, that the plaintiff would discharge a demand in his favor against the defendant, *it was held*, that such agreement was unlawful and void.—*Gardiner* v. *Morse*, 25 *Maine R.*, *p.* 140. (1847.)

(*Randall* cited *Howard* v. *Castle*, 6 *T. R.*, 642; *Bexwell* v. *Christie*, *Cowp.*, 395; *Jones* v. *Caswell*, 3 *Johns. Cas.*, 29; *Thompson* v. *Davis*, 13 *Johns.*, 112; *Doolin* v. *Ward*, 6 *Johns.*, 194; *Wilber* v. *How*, 8 *Johns.*, 444; *Fuller* v. *Abraham*, 6 *Moore*, 318; *Gulic* v. *Ward*, 5 *Halst.*, 87; *Piat* v. *Oliver*, 1 *McLean*, 295.)

AUCTIONEER.

Sales made by auctioneers, stand upon the same footing as those made by private individuals, and require that some note or memorandum should be made and signed by the party to be charged, to render them valid and obligatory upon the purchaser.

An auctioneer sold at public vendue a certain house and blacksmith's shop, with a leasehold interest in the lot on which the buildings were located. The premises were struck off, and the following memorandum made by the auctioneer, on the back of the lease, with a pencil: "$200........$3,50.......Richard Burke." No other memorandum of the sale was made. *Held*, not to be binding on the bidder to whom the property was struck off, there being nothing in the case, as shown by the evidence, to connect the memorandum with any particular house or lot, or with any terms or conditions of the sale, which would tend to prove the contract between the parties.—*Burke* v. *Haley*, 2 *Gillman's R.*, *p.* 614. *Ills.* (1847.)

THIS suit was originally commenced before a justice of the peace in Jo Davies County, by the defendant in error, for the sum of $81 91, being the difference in the sale of property sold at auction. Judgment was rendered before the justice for the amount claimed, against the plaintiff in error, from which judgment he appealed to the Circuit Court of Jo Davies County. At the June term, 1845, of said Court, a verdict was rendered against him for the above sum of $81 91.

Campbell & Pratt, for the plaintiff in error.

Sales at auction of real estate are within the Statute of Frauds.—*Gale's Stat.*, 315, *Simonds* v. *Catlin*, 3 *Caine*, 84; 2 *Johns.*, 260.

There was no sufficient memorandum made by the auctioneer to take the case out of the statute.—3 *Johns.*, 419.

On the subject of auction sales generally, see 1 *Esp. N. P.*, 101; 2 *Esp. N. P.*, 659; *Walker* v. *Constable*, 1 *Bos. & Pul.*, 306; 7 *Vesey*, 341; 13 *Vesey*, 456; *Sugden on Vend.*, *ch.* 1, *p.* 25.

Churchman, for the appellee.

Our statute applies to executory contracts; the English did not.—*Roberts on Frauds*, 112, 125, 129; *Simon* v. *Motivos*, 3 *Burr.*, 1920.

The principal conditions were sufficient to bind the purchaser.—2 *Esp.*, 231.

Campbell, in reply.

The doctrine laid down in *Simon* v. *Motivos*, 3 *Burr.*, 1920, is not the law, and has not been for years.

The opinion of the Court was delivered by

PURPLE, J.—The defendant in error sued the plaintiff in error before a justice of the peace of Jo Davies County. The suit was removed into the Circuit Court by appeal, and then tried at the June term, 1845. The bill of exceptions exhibits the following state of facts: There was a house and blacksmith's shop situated upon a lot in Galena, in which the representatives of Farnan held a leasehold interest. William Montgomery, a witness, called by plaintiff below, testified that he was a public auctioneer in Galena, that said plaintiff employed him to sell said interest in the house, shop, and lot, at public auction; that he advertised the property for sale in a newspaper, and offered it at public auction on the day designated in the advertisement; that defendant below bid for the property aforesaid the sum of ——, and also the sum of —— for a sign-post; that he immediately wrote in pencil mark on the lease describing the premlses, the words and figures following: "$200 . . . $3 50 . . . Richard Burke;" that defendant below signed no instrument whatever relative to said sale, nor did he pay any thing on the same; that witness afterwards wrote a notice to Burke, which is not set out in the bill of exceptions; that he afterwards again exposed said property to sale, and that it was purchased by one Patrick Barnes; that the demand here sought to be recovered is the difference between the two sales; that he never made any tender of a conveyance of the property in question to the defendant below, except as by the notice before mentioned, previous to the commencement of this suit.

Philip A Hoyne testified, that he served the notice before mentioned on the defendant below. This was all the evidence.

The counsel for the defendant below requested the Court to instruct the jury: "That the Statute of Frauds applies in auction sales of lands as well as private sales, and that to take such sales out of the statute, a memorandum in writing is necessary, signed by the party to be charged, and that if the property, or any part of it in this case was an interest in lands, unless the contract was reduced to writing, it is void; and the plaintiff cannot recover for such interest." This instruction was refused, and the Court charged the jury: "That auction sales of lands were not within the Statute of Frauds, and that the memorandum made by the auctioneer in pencil mark on the lease was sufficient to charge the defendant."

The defendant below excepted to the opinion of the Court in refusing the instruction asked, and in giving the one before recited. Other exceptions were taken upon the trial, and other errors have been assigned, but we deem them unimportant. We shall, therefore, only notice these two questions:

First, Whether sales of lands or interests therein made at public auction are within the Statute of Frauds; and,

Second, Whether the memorandum here made is sufficient to exempt the case from the operation of the statute.

Upon the first point, there seems to have been some conflict of opinion among the Judges of the English Courts. In the case of *Simon* v. *Motivos*, 3 *Burr.*, 1921, it was held that sales made at public auction were not within the statute. But *Lord* ELLENBOROUGH, in the case of *Hinde* v. *Whitehouse*, 7 *T. R.*, although he does not expressly decide the question, it not being necessary in that case, distinctly states that he is of a contrary opinion. All the recent decisions seem to admit the principle, and we think with sufficient reason in their favor, that sales made by auctioneers stand upon the same footing as those made by private individuals, and require that some note or memorandum should be made and signed by the party to be charged, to render them valid and obligatory upon the purchaser.

There is no difficulty in determining the other question presented in this case. The statute of this State, *Rev. Stat.*, 258, provides that "no action shall be brought whereby to charge any person upon any contract for the sale of lands, tenements, or hereditaments, or any interest in or concerning them, for a longer period than one year, unless the promise or agreement upon which such action shall be brought, or some memorandum or note thereof shall be made in writing and signed by the party to be charged therewith, or some other person, thereto by him lawfully authorized."

The only written memorandum made in this case by which the purchaser at the sale is sought to be charged, is the one made on the back of the lease of the premises sold, as follows: "$200 . . . $3 50 . . . Richard Burke." This was made by the auctioneer at the time of sale. Neither the notice containing the terms and conditions of the sale, nor the lease, nor the memorandum upon the back of the same, were produced upon the trial. There is nothing in the case, as shown by the evidence, to connect the memorandum with any particular lot or house, or with any terms or conditions of the sale, which would tend to prove the contract between the parties. The auctioneer, it is true, by law is the agent of both the vendor and purchaser, and a memorandum signed by him would be binding on the latter, provided it was sufficient, either in itself, or when connected with other written or printed evidence, to show what was the contract of the parties. From the entire absence of all such testimony, the Court should have given the instructions asked for by the counsel for the defendant below, and withheld the instruction given.

It has been insisted upon in the argument by the counsel for defendant in error, that the Statute of Frauds was not pleaded in this case, and that said defendant had no notice that the defendant below designed to avail himself of its benefits until the conclusion of the testimony in the cause. The Court has heretofore held that a party who intends to take advantage of this statute, must plead the same, or in some other form rely upon it. This case being an appeal from a justice of the peace, no written pleadings are necessary in the Circuit Court. But the proceedings in this case clearly show that the defendant below relied solely on the statute for his defence.

The judgment of the Circuit Court is reversed with costs, and the cause remanded with directions to that Court to award *a venire facias de novo*.

Judgment reversed.

AWARD.

When an award is about being made, between a principal and one of two sureties, touching certain moneys, alleged to have been placed in his hands for the payment of the debt, the other surety will be bound by it when made, either by assenting to it when made, or by being present, with full knowledge that it is about being made, and not dissenting.—*McGehee* v. *McGehee*, 12 *Alabama R.*, *p.* 83. (1848.)

(ORMOND, J., cited *Evans* v. *McKinney, Litt. Sel. Cases*, 262; *Watson on Awards*, 175; *Kingston* v. *Phelps, Peake*, 227.)

An award in replevin, finding property in defendant, the goods having been delivered to the plaintiff by the sheriff, is sufficient.

An award was filed on the 26th of February, in a leap-year—the 17th of March falling on a Sunday—the plaintiff is entitled to enter his appeal on the 18th.—*Harker* v. *Addis*, 4 *Barr's R.*, *p.* 515. *Pa.* (1847.)

(Burnside, J., cited *In re John Goswiler*, 3 *Pa.*, 201; *Sims* v. *Hampton*, 1 *Serg. & Rawl.*, 411; *Roberts' Dig.*, 207, 208.)

At common law it was not necessary that a submission to arbitrators should be in writing, except where the controversy related to land, or to some matter in respect to which it was incompetent for parties to make a valid and binding agreement by parol. And where a submission is verbal, without any provision therein that the award shall be in writing, a verbal award is valid at common law.—*Valentine* v. *Valentine*, 2 *Barbour's Ch. R.*, *p.* 430. *N. Y.* (1848.)

(The Chancellor cited *Billings' Law of Awards*, 9; *Kyd on Awards*, 7; *Walters* v. *Morgan*, 2 *Cox's Ch. Cas.*, 369; *Cable* v. *Rogers*, 3 *Buls. R.*, 311.)

BAGGAGE—LOSS OF.

A stage contractor is a common carrier, and liable as such for all loss of baggage, &c.; and the practice of requiring freight for baggage, if over a certain weight, illustrates well, that baggage under that weight is virtually and fully paid for by the personal passage money of the traveller.

The fact, that stage contractors do not enter the baggage upon the way-bill, which is not a contract, but *ex parte* altogether, and for their own use, does not alter their liability as common carriers for the loss of such baggage.

Evidence of the contents of a trunk, lost from a stage-coach, though only *prima facie*, and light, is legal and competent for what it is worth. —*Peixotti* v. *McLaughlin*, 1 *Strobhart's R.*, *p.* 468. *S. C.* (1847.)

Tried before *Mr. Justice Wardlow*, at Columbia, Spring Term, 1847.

The defendant was a mail contractor, and owner of a line of stage coaches, in which, with the mail, passengers and their travelling baggage were carried between Columbia and Cheraw. The plaintiff was a passenger from Columbia to Camden, and on the way, without apparent negligence on the part of the contractor or any of his agents, the plaintiff's trunk was cut from behind the coach, and rifled of its contents. By this *sum. pro.*, the plaintiff sought reparation for the loss he had sustained.

The presiding Judge held, the defendant was liable as a common carrier.

*In the list which accompanied the coach from one end of the line to the other, called the *way-bill*, the plaintiff's name was entered, but no mention made of his baggage. The evidence showed, that the baggage of a passenger was never noticed in the way-bill, unless it exceeded a certain weight, and then an extra charge was made. He considered that the passage money paid by the plaintiff was a compensation for the transportation of ordinary baggage as well as of himself.

He held evidence of the contents of the trunk when it left Charleston, a few days before, as pertinent to the inquiry concerning what the trunk contained when it left Camden, although it appeared that the plaintiff had opened it in Columbia.

Decree for the plaintiff. The defendant appealed, and moved the court to reverse the decree on the following grounds:

1. Because his Honor erred in deciding that a stage contractor was liable as a common carrier.

2. Because his Honor erred in deciding that, when the way-bill named the passenger alone, and there was no mention made of baggage on the way-bill, the stage contractor was liable for baggage lost, as a common carrier.

3. And for a new trial; because his Honor erred in admitting evidence to prove the contents of the lost trunk when it left Charleston, and when said trunk was not placed on the stage coach of the defendant, until it was brought to Columbia.

Black, for the motion.—There is no case, in our State Reports, applicable to stage-coach contractors, as common carriers. Baggage is not named in the way-bill, as a part of the goods contracted for; and the way-bill is the evidence of the contract. If the Court intends to say they are common carriers, let it not be under oppressive restrictions. Let them have some protection. Let the way-bill contain an entry of what baggage they are to carry. In *Middletown* v. *Fowler, et al.*, 1 *Salk.*, 282, it was held, that they were exempt as common carriers, *nisi*, &c.

(*Porcher*, contra, cited *Wolf* v. *Somers*, 2 *Camp.*, 351; *Clark* v. *Gray*, 3 *East*, 564; *Allen* v. *Seawall*, 2 *Wend.*, 327; *Pardy* v. *Drew*, 25 *Wend.*, 459; *Butler* v. *Baring*, 2 *Car. & Payne*, 12 *Eng. Com. Law*, 287.)

Richardson, J., delivered the opinion of the Court.

The strict liability of common carriers by the common law has been fully recognized in this State, in many cases, and the general doctrine is established. The liability of ferrymen as common carriers, so often adjudged, is very analogous to the present case. The ferryman takes over a man—say for ten cents; but the man carries a pack. There can be no doubt the ferryman would be liable for the loss of the pack, although he takes no toll separately for the pack. So if the contents of a wagon, or of the load upon a horse, be lost; because all must be, necessarily, placed in the custody of the ferryman. The stage contractor, the ferryman, the boatmen, railroad companies and wagoners, are alike carriers over the public highway, and stand all in the same parity of reasoning, i. e., they come within the same necessary and strict legal policy of guarding against robberies or cheats by those who, having the custody, are enabled to do wrong secretly. Inn-keepers, for the same reason, come under similar law, although not separately paid for the traveller's baggage. In regard to stage contractors, the practice of requiring freight for baggage, if over a certain weight, illustrates well that baggage under that weight is virtually and fully paid for, by the personal passage money of the traveller. And it would be inconsistent to distinguish the contractor's liability or exemption, by the weight of the baggage. And I would say, that in the United States, with our very moving and no less migratory people, the laws against common carriers are of great practical and every-day importance; and apply readily to stage coaches, railroads, and all travelling vehicles. Accordingly, in the neighboring States, and especially in New-York, where there is great experience, the judicial decisions on such liability of stage contractors are many. There can be little doubt, therefore, that they are liable as common carriers. The case does not require the consideration of extreme cases, or extraordinary instances of rich merchandise conveyed under the name of travelling baggage. Upon the second ground of appeal, the Court cannot perceive how the way-bill, which is merely an entry or record kept of the passengers by the stage contractor, for his own use, can make any difference. It is not like a bill of lading or a contract, but *ex parte* altogether. Lastly, the evidence of the contents of the lost trunk may have been only *prima facie*, and light. But it was plainly legal and competent for what it was worth, and sufficiently supports the Circuit decision on the fact.

The motion is therefore dismissed.

BANK.

When a note is made payable to a bank, and signed by a surety, presented to the bank for discount and refused, and afterwards discounted by a third person, without the knowledge of the surety, an action will not lie at the suit of the bank, for the use of the person discounting the note, against the surety.

Such an action will lie against the principal in the note, if sued separately.—*Clinton Bank of Columbus* v. *Ayres et al.*, 16 *Ohio R.*, p. 282. (1848.)

(*Dennison, Jr.*, cited 2 *Ohio*, 24; 6 *Ohio*, 150; 3 *A. K. Marsh.*, 430; 6 *J. J. Marsh.*, 131; 1 *Chit. Pl.*, 2, 3; 3 *Bing. N. C.*, 829; 12 *Johns.*, 190; 3 *T. R.*, 148, 6 *N. H.*, 535; 20 *Johns.*, 288; 4 *T. R.*,

470; 16 *Pick.*, 579; 6 *Ohio*, 246; 8 *Ohio*, 529, 11 *Ohio*, 65; 5 *N. H.*, 267; *Ang. & Ames on Corp.*, 104. 66, 230; 12 *Wheat.*, 68; 2 *Cranch*, 127; 3 *Pick.*, 335; 1 *Pick.*, 297; 9 *Wheat.*, 702–3; 2 *Burr.*, 1226; 1 *Black. Com.*, 75, *note* 8; 2 *Kent's Com.*, 53; 10 *Eng. C. L.*, 156; 1 *Selwyn N. P.*, 122; 1 *Chit. Pl.*, 511–12; 556–7; *Gould's Pl.*, 331, 345; 2 *Hall*, 195; 5 *Cow.*, 466; 8 *Cranch*, 30; 13 *Wend.*, 78; 2 *Phil. Ev.*, 130; 2 *Stark Ev.* 77–9; 11 *Ohio*, 489; 12 Ohio, 112.

Finch & Ranney, contra, cited *Utica Bank* v. *Ganson*, 10 *Wend.*, 315; *Bank of Rutland* v. *Buck*, 5 *Wend.*, 66; *Chenango Bank* v. *Hyde*, 4 *Cow.*, 567; *Farnsworth* v. *Sweet*, 5 *N. H.*, 267; *Pillons et al.* v. *Van Mierop et al.*, 3 *Burr.*, 1663; *Powell* v. *Waters*, 17 *Johns.*, 176; *Conway et al.* v. *Bank of U. S.*, 6 *J. J. Marsh.*, 129; *Denniston* v. *Bacon et al.*, 10 *Johns.*, 198.)

A bank is answerable for the acts of its agent. And it is immaterial how notes get into circulation, if they come into the hands of the holder *bona fide*.—*White* v. *How et al.*, 3 *McLean's U. S. R.*, *p.* 291. (1847.)

Where a bank loans the notes of other banks, which circulate in payment of debts, but are in fact from twenty to twenty-five per cent. below specie par, the contract is usurious, and the bank is only entitled to recover the specie value of the notes at the time they were lent, without interest.—*Bondurant* v. *The Commercial Bank of Natchez*, 8 *Smedes & Marshall's R.*, *p.* 533. *Miss.* (1847.)

(*Bullock* cited 3 *S. & M.*, 285; 7 *Yerg.*, 547; *Cox* v. *Rowley, lately decided in La.*, 1 *Yerg.*, 243, 444; 12 *Pick.*, 565; 5 *Mon.*, 477; 7 *Mon.*, 263; 1 *J. J. Marshall*, 47; *Planters' Bank* v. *Sharp*, 4 *Smedes & Mar.*, 75.

Clayton, J., cited *Bank* v. *Hays et al.*, 1 *Yerg.*, 243; *Harrison* v. *Bank of Kentucky* 2 *J. J. Marshall*, 140; *Bank of the State* v. *Ford*, 5 *Iredell*, 698.)

Money fraudulently obtained from a bank may be sued for before the note given to the bank for the same becomes due.

A forged note to the bank is no payment, and the bank may sue for the money advanced by it.—*Gibson* v. *Stevens*, 3 *McLean's U. S. R.*, *p.* 551. (1847.)

A bank cannot legally be taxed for railroad stock pledged to it as collateral security for a debt.—*Waltham Bank* v. *Inhabitants of Waltham*, 10 *Metcalf's R.*, *p.* 334. *Mass.* (1847.)

BANK CHARTER.

It is now the settled law, that an inquiry into the violation of its charter by a bank or other corporation, can only be had in a direct proceeding, instituted for the purpose, by the government; and not in a collateral way, by individuals.—*The Grand Gulf Bank* v. *Archer et al.*, 8 *Smedes & Marshall's R.*, *p.* 151. *Miss.* (1847.)

(CLAYTON, J., cited *Flecker* v. *Bank of U. S.*, 8 *Wheat.*, 388; *Vidal* v. *Girard's Ex'rs*, 2 *How.* (*S. C.*) 127; 16 *Mass.*, 102; 3 *Ran.*, 143; 4 *Shepley*, 224; *Bank* v. *Hammond*, 1 *Rich. Law R.*, 228; *Com. Bank of Manchester* v. *Nolan*, 7 *How.*, 508; *Wade* v. *Amer. Col. Society*, 7 *S. & M.*, 663; *Bank of Port Gibson* v. *Nevitt*, 6 *S.*, *M.*, 513.)

BANK—PROTEST.

When a note is deposited with a bank for collection, when due, it is a sufficient demand if the teller of the bank, presenting the note, inquires of the book-keeper whether a deposit has been made to pay the note, and is informed there are no funds to pay it.

The demand is good, though the teller acted as clerk of the notary public who protested the note.

The teller represented the bank, and it was responsible for the money if paid.

The notice was made out by the clerk, but signed by the notary, and the Court will not presume a fact, not proved against the face of the paper.—*Browning* v. *Andrews*, 3 *McLean's U. S.R.*, *p.* 576. (1847.)

Joy & Porter, for plaintiff,
Hand, for defendant.

OPINION OF THE COURT.—This is a motion for a new trial. The plaintiff brought this action against the defendant as endorser of a promissory note, payable at the Bank of Michigan. At the trial the defendant objected to the evidence of the presentment of the note to the bank, and demand of payment when it became due; and also as to the sufficiency of the notice. The objections were overruled and the evidence was permitted to go to the jury, with a reservation of the questions of law.

1. The note was presented to the bank and a demand of payment made, by the clerk of the notary, who, it is alleged, had no authority to make the demand.

This point was raised in *Sacrider* v. *Brown*, 3 *McLean*, 481, but it was not decided, as the decision turned upon the illegality of the protest.

In that case the Court referred to *Loftly* v. *Mills*, 4 *Term*, 475, to the views of *Mr. Chitty* and his correspondence with the associations of notaries of Liverpool and London on the subject, and to the 3*d and* 4*th of*

Hill's Reports, and the Court say, "If it were admitted that a notary's clerk may make a demand of payment, yet it is very clear that the clerk cannot make the protest."

From the evidence in this case it appears the note was deposited in the bank for collection; that Alexander H. Sibley, the teller of the bank, was the clerk of the notary, and when the note became due he inquired of the book-keeper whether any funds had been deposited to meet the note, who replied, after examining the books, that no such deposit had been made. The teller at the time held the note in his hands, presenting it to the book-keeper. We think this was a sufficient demand. The bank had possession of the note for collection and was responsible for it. The note was payable at the bank, and it was the duty of the maker to deposit funds for that purpose. No deposit was made, and this fact being ascertained by the book-keeper, who enters all deposits, at the request of the holder of the note, nothing more was necessary. Had the funds been placed in the bank, the possession of the note by the bank would have authorized the teller to deposit them to the credit of the plaintiff.

In the *Bank of Utica* v. *Smith*, 19 *Johns.*, 231, the Court decided, "That a demand of payment of a note by a notary, or a person having a parol authority for that purpose, or the lawful possession of the note, is sufficient." The note, on payment, would have been surrendered, and wherever this may be lawfully done by the holder, he may make the demand.

2. It is insisted that the notice was insufficient.

In support of this objection a late decision of the Supreme Court of Michigan is referred to, as governing the question of notice.

The notice was directed to the defendant, informing him, that the note of John H. Galts for $428 87, endorsed by the defendant and payable at the Bank of Michigan, was protested for non-payment on the 9th of July, 1838, and that the holders look to him for payment. The form of this notice seems to have been taken from the one sanctioned by the Supreme Court in the case of *Mills* v. *The Bank of U. S.*, 11 *Wheat.*, 431. "The law has prescribed no particular form of such notice. The object of it is merely to inform the endorser of the non-payment by the maker, and that he is held liable for the payment thereof."—*Bank of Alexandria* v. *Swann*, 9 *Peters*, 33. "The notice is sufficient if it state the non-payment: and it is not necessary to state expressly, for it is justly implied, that the holders look to the endorser."—3 *Kent's Com.*, 2*d ed.*, 108; *Lenox* v. *Leverett*, 10 *Mass.*, 1; *Wallace* v. *Agry*, 4 *Mason*, 336; *Kenworthy* v. *Hopkins*, 1 *Johns. Cases*, 107.

The late decision in Michigan, not yet reported, is understood to overrule the above cases and what has, heretofore, been considered the settled law upon the subject in this country and in England. Whether this be the case or not can be of but little importance to this Court. The question is not local and does not arise under any statutory provision. Notice is required by the statute, but the form of the notice is not given. Indeed, had a form been adopted by statute, essentially changing the form which has been observed here and in England for more than half a century, and which has been sanctioned by Courts that recognize the law merchant, we should hesitate to give the statute a retrospective effect. It would seem vitally to bear upon prior contracts, in changing the nature of their obligation.

The Courts of the United States follow the settled construction of the statutes of a State, by its Supreme Court. But the above is a question of general commercial law, and does not depend upon the construction of a statute. The reason which influences the Supreme Court to follow the States in the construction of their statutes, it would seem, should influence the State Courts to follow the rule of decision of the Supreme Court of the Union on questions of general law.

The notice purports to have been signed by Henry R. Sanger, notary public, and the body of it is in the handwriting of Sibley, the teller of the bank. It seems to have been the practice of the notary to leave blank notices signed by him with Sibley, who filled them up and gave them the proper directions, but the witness is not able to state whether, in this case, the name of the notary was signed to the notice before or after it was filled up. As the signature of the notary is proved to be genuine, the Court will not presume a fact, nor should a jury be authorized to do so, against the face of the paper.

The motion for a new trial is overruled, and judgment.

BANKRUPT.

In an action upon a promissory note, where the bankruptcy of the maker is alleged in his defence, and the certificate of discharge is attempted to be impeached on the ground of a prior fraudulent sale of goods to a third person, which he did not include in his schedule of effects, the purchaser is a competent witness.—*Loud* v. *Pierce, Maine R., p.* 233. (1847.)

Where a certificate in bankruptcy is interposed as a defence to a pre-existing debt, it may be invalidated by proving fraud in its procurement. —*Suydam & Co.* v. *Walker et als.*, 16 *Ohio R., p.* 122. (1848.)

(Hitchcock, J., cited 2 *Howard*, 202, 209; 1 *Denio*, 75, 332, 519.)

BANKRUPTCY.

If the maker of a negotiable promissory note obtain a discharge in bankruptcy, and subsequently, upon an adequate consideration, promise to pay the debt, an action may be brought against him upon the original contract, and the creditor may avail himself of the new promise in answer to a plea of bankruptcy. But this new promise does not revive the original *negotiable* character of the instrument. It is a promise to the party alone, to whom it is made, and is not negotiable, or assignable, so as to permit a recovery thereon in the name of a third person.

In an action by the endorsee against the payee of a negotiable promissory note, if the defendant plead a discharge in bankruptcy, a replication of a new promise to the payee, prior to the endorsement, will be a departure from the declaration.—*Walbridge* v. *Harroon*, 18 *Vermont R.*, *p.* 448. (1847.)

Assumpsit upon a promissory note, executed by the defendant, and made payable to Joseph A. Wing, or order, and by Wing endorsed to the plaintiff. The defendant pleaded his discharge in bankruptcy, under the act of Congress of August 19, 1841, in bar of the action; to which the plaintiff replied, that the defendant, subsequent to his being decreed a bankrupt, and previous to his obtaining his certificate of discharge as a bankrupt, and previous to the time when the note was endorsed by Wing to the plaintiff, and while Wing was the owner and holder of the note, promised to pay the note to Wing, according to its tenor. To this replication the defendant demurred.

The County Court—Redfield, J., presiding—adjudged the replication insufficient, and rendered judgment for the defendant. Exceptions by plaintiff.

Wing, for plaintiff.

Bankruptcy is a personal privilege, and no one can take advantage of it, except the bankrupt himself. He must, if a joint contractor, be sued with the other contractors.—*Roberts* v. *McLean*, 16 *Vt.*, 608; 1 *Chit. Pl.*, 48, 52; *Lawes' Pl.*, 703; *Allen* v. *Butler, et al.*, 9 *Vt.*, 122. The suit must be upon the original contract, and not on the new promise. —2 *Stark. Ev.*, 210; *Williams* v. *Dyde et al.*, *Peake*, 68; *Trueman* v. *Fenton*, *Cowp.*, 544; *Gailer* v. *Grinnel*, 2 *Aik.*, 349; 1 *Chit: Pl.*, 61; *Birch* v. *Sharland*, 1 *T. R.*, 715. And it makes no difference, whether the promise is before or after the discharge, if it is after the decree in bankruptcy.—1 *Chit. Pl.*, 61; *Cowp.*, 527, 544; 2 *Stark. Ev.*, 211; *Roberts* v. *Morgan*, 2 *Esp.*, 736.

The certificate of bankruptcy does not remove the debt, but, when waived by a new promise, the old debt is restored, the same as if the defendant had never availed himself of his discharge. When waived, it is the same as though it had never existed. It is the same as the statute of limitations, or the plea of infancy, with this exception,—the statute of limitations is waived by an unqualified admission that the debt is due; while to remove the bar, created by a discharge in bankruptcy, or by infancy, there must be an express promise, to pay; but, when the bar is removed, the action must, according to all the authorities referred to, be brought on the original contract, and not on the new promise.

No case can be found, where it has been held, that a note lost its negotiability by reason of any decree in bankruptcy, or that the assignee or endorsee of a note signed by a bankrupt or an infant, which had been revived after decree in bankruptcy, or after the defendant had arrived at full age, or after the statute of limitations had been removed by an admission of the debt, could not maintain an action in his own name on the note thus revived, the same as if there had never been any defence to the note. The case of *Trueman* v. *Fenton*, *Cowp.*, 544, was in the name of the endorsee, but no question was made in reference to the negotiability of the note.

Peck, for defendants.

The decree of bankruptcy and discharge rendered the note *functus officio*. The discharge of the defendant discharged the debt for which the note was given. The plaintiff, then, took nothing by the assignment, but an equitable interest in the debt; in other words, he cannot sustain an action in his own name as endorsee, as the note has no legal existence.—*Baker* v. *Wheaton*, 5 *Mass.*, 509. The debt, though discharged, is a sufficient consideration to support an express promise to pay it. A bare acknowledgment of the debt, as in the case of a debt barred by the statute of limitations, will not avoid the discharge. In this all the authorities agree.—*Lynbury* v. *Wrightman*, 5 *Esp.*, 198.

If the action had been brought in the name of the payee, he might have recovered, on proving an express promise to pay the note. So, if the promise had been made to the plaintiff after the note was assigned, he might recover on a declaration properly framed. The difficulty in this case is, that he seeks to recover upon a promise made to the payee before the transfer. This is not within the issue and is a departure.—*Dupuy* v. *Smart*, 3 *Wend.*, 135; *Moore* v. *Viele*, 4 *Wend.*, 420; *Dean* v. *Crane*, 1 *Salk.*, 28; *Sarrele* v. *Wine*, 3 *East*, 409; 2 *Saund.*, 37, *f*, *note*.

The opinion of the Court was delivered by WILLIAMS, C. J. This action is brought by the endorsee against the maker of a promissory note. The defendant pleads a certificate of discharge in bankruptcy. The plaintiff has replied a new promise to Wing, the payee, made after the decree in bankruptcy and before the note was endorsed to the plaintiff. To this replication there is a demurrer, and joinder in demurrer. The question is, whether this note is still to be considered as negotiable; and, as such, capable of being transferred to the plaintiff, together with the benefit of the promise made to Wing.

It seems to be settled by authorities, that, when a debt is discharged by a certificate of bankruptcy, if the debtor, for an adequate consideration, promise to pay the same, an action may be brought on the original contract, and the creditor may avail himself of such new promise in answer to a plea of bankruptcy. In this particular it is assimilated to a promise to pay a debt barred by the statute of limitations. The cases, however, are widely different. In bankruptcy a debt is discharged by the operation of the certificate. A recovery can only be had on the new promise, founded on sufficient consideration. A debt, on which the statute of limitations has run is not discharged; the remedy, only, is taken away, and the remedy may be restored by a promise, or acknowledgment, made without any consideration therefor. The debt and the remedy remain in the latter case, as they were originally. In bankruptcy the debt is discharged, and the new promise alone gives the action. This new promise does not revive the original negotiable character of the instrument; it is a promise to the party alone, to whom it is made, and is not negotiable, or assignable, so as to permit a recovery thereon in the name of a third person. The replication, therefore, of a promise to Wing could not aid the plaintiff in this case, and was a departure from the declaration.

The cases of *Baker* v. *Wheaton*, 5 *Mass.*, 509, *Depuy* v. *Smart*, 3 *Wend.*, 135, and *Moore* v. *Viele*, 4 *Wend.*, 420, are very clear on this point,—that a note, discharged by a certificate of discharge in bankruptcy, or insolvency, is *functus officio*, ceases to be negotiable, and that no action can be sustained thereon by any other person, than the one to whom the promise was made. The principle of those cases we recognize and are disposed to adopt, inasmuch as no case is produced, which recognizes a different principle.

The judgment of the County Court is therefore affirmed.

BETTING.

Money knowingly lent to be staked on the event of a horse-race, cannot be recovered back.—*Ruckman* v. *Bryan*, 3 *Denio's R.*, *p.* 340. *N. Y.* (1848.)

(BEARDSLEY, J., cited *Gibbons* v. *Gouverneur*, 1 *Denio*, 170; 9 *Anne*, *c.* 14, *sec.* 1; *Chit. on Cont.*, 712; *Barjeau* v. *Walmsley*, 2 *Stra.*, 1249; *Robinson* v. *Bland*, 2 *Burr.*, 1077; *Alcinbrook* v. *Hall*, 2 *Wils.*, 309; *Wettenhall* v. *Wood*, 1 *Esp.*, 18; *McKinnell* v. *Robinson*, 3 *M. & W.*, 434; *Canaan* v. *Bryce*, 3 *Barn. & Ald.*, 179; *Langton* v. *Hughes*, 1 *M. & S.*, 593; *The Gas Light & Coke Co.* v. *Turner*, 5 *Bing. N. C.*, 666; *De Begnis* v. *Armistead*, 10 *Bing.*, 107; *Chit. on Cont.*, 696, 714.)

Where two resident citizens of Vermont went into Canada for the purpose of making a wager in reference to the result of a Presidential election then pending in the United States, and, while there, made the wager, and each deposited the amount of money wagered by him in the hands of a stakeholder, who was a citizen of Canada, with written directions to pay the whole amount to the one or the other of the parties, according to the event, it was *held*, that the contract must be treated as illegal, by the Courts of this State, to the same extent that it would have been, if made within the State.

And the loser, having, after the event was determined, but before the stakeholder had delivered the stake to the winner, notified the stakeholder of his revocation of the contract, and demanded the money which he deposited, was allowed to recover back the amount of his deposit, in an action of *indebitatus assumpsit* against the stakeholder.

As between the *parties* to an illegal wager, where money, or other property has been advanced by one to the other upon the making of the contract, the wager is revocable at any time before the event happens.

But, as against a *stakeholder*, a revocation before the event happens is not necessary; but the loser may demand of him a return of his deposit, until, with the loser's express or implied assent, it has been paid over to the winner.—*Tarleton* v. *Baker*, 18 *Vermont R.*, p. 9. (1847.)

INDEBITATUS ASSUMPSIT for money had and received, money paid, laid out and expended, and money lent. Plea, the general issue, and trial by jury.

On trial the plaintiff gave evidence tending to prove, that about the 1st of August, 1840, the plaintiff and one George M. Kidder agreed, at St. Albans, in this State, to meet each other at Dunham, in Lower Canada, on the 5th day of the same August, and there deposit with the defendant, as a stakeholder, the sum of three hundred dollars,—the plaintiff to deposit two hundred dollars and the defendant one hundred; that on the 5th day of August the plaintiff and Kidder did meet at Dunham, and requested the defendant to receive the said money as stakeholder; that the defendant received the money, and agreed to pay it over according to certain written directions, signed by the plaintiff and Kidder, which were then delivered to the defendant, and which were in these words: "Dunham, L. C., August 5th, 1840. Enclosed three hundred dollars, to be paid George M. Kidder in case William Henry Harrison is elected President of the United States the next Presidential election in the United States; and in case Martin Van Buren is elected President of the United States, to be paid to Mr. A. G. Tarleton; it is farther understood and agreed, that, in case of the death of either of the said candidates before the next Presidential election, then one hundred dollars of the within is to be paid to Geo. M. Kidder, and two hundred to Mr. A. G. Tarleton.

The plaintiff also gave evidence, tending to prove, that, on the 28th day of November, 1840, one Levi Stevens, having a power of attorney from the plaintiff to receive the money deposited by the plaintiff, called upon the defendant, at Dunham, and demanded the money, and that the defendant then refused to deliver it to him; and also evidence tending to prove that Kidder was notified, by the plaintiff's direction, on the 31st day of October, 1840, that the plaintiff revoked the wager.

The defendant introduced the depositions of James Smith and William Walker, who testified, in substance, that they were counsellors at law in Canada, and that by the laws of Canada, a stakeholder may be called upon to pay over the money, deposited with him by the parties laying a wager, to the winning party, after the occurrence of the event which is to decide the wager, the stakeholder being bound by the agreement at the time of receiving the deposit, unless the wager is illegal; and that, by the same laws, a wager as to the result of a foreign election is not an illegal wager; and that, in case of the refusal of the stakeholder to pay the money to the winner, the winner may maintain an action against him therefor.

The defendant also gave evidence tending to prove, that, at the time the wager in question was made, Kidder refused to make any wager in the United States.

The Court instructed the jury, that the wager in question, being made by citizens of this State, was illegal by the laws of this State, notwithstanding it was made in Canada; that it is incident to every wager, that either party may rescind the wager, so long as the event is undecided; that, if the plaintiff rescinded the wager in question on the 31st of October, 1840, either party had the right, at any time thereafter, to take his money from the defendant; and that, if the defendant was forbidden by the plaintiff, or his agent, on the 28th of November, 1840, to pay over the money to Kidder, he had no right afterwards to make payment of the same to Kidder.

The jury returned a verdict for the plaintiff. Exceptions by defendant.

Stevens & Seymour, for defendant.

1. The contract being made in Canada, and to be performed there, the *lex loci contractus* must govern.—*Sherrill* v. *Hopkins*, 1 *Cow.*, 103; *Van Schaick* v. *Edwards*, 2 *Johns. Cas.*, 255; *Ruggles* v. *Keeler*, 3 *Johns*, 263; *Andrews* v. *Herriott*, 4 *Cow.*, 508.

2. The laws of foreign countries must be proved like other facts, before they can be received in Courts of Justice.—*Lincoln* v. *Batelle*, 6. *Wend.*, 475; *Francis* v. *Ocean Ins. Co.*, 6 *Cow.*, 429; *Case* v. *Riker*, 10 *Vt.*, 484. In this case the plaintiff offered no evidence, to show that the contract was illegal by the laws of Canada, or that, by those laws, he had a right to rescind. On the other hand, the defendant has proved that, by the laws of Canada the wager was legal. The plaintiff is presumed to know the laws of the country, where he enters into a contract; but there can be no legal presumption, that the defendant knew the laws of this State, not being within its jurisdiction.

3. If the contract is illegal, a Court of Justice will not interfere between the parties,—the principle of public policy being, *ex dolo malo non oritur actio.*—*Yates* v. *Foot*, 12 *Johns.*, 1; *McKeown* v. *Laverty*, 3 *Wend.*, 494; *Lyon* v. *Strong*, 6 *Vt.*, 222.

4. The common law of England recognizes the validity of wagers, as legal contracts.—*Jones* v. *Randall*, *Cowp.*, 37; *De Costa* v. *Jones*, *Cowp.*, 729; *Pope* v. *St. Leger*, *Salk.*, 344; *Lynell* v. *Longbotham*, 2 *Wils.*, 36; *McKeown* v. *Laverty*, 3 *Wend.*, 494.

Hoyt & Nutting, for plaintiffs.

1. The liability of the depositor, or stakeholder, depends upon the contract between the depositors.—9 *Conn.*, 169; 8 *B. & C.*, 221.

2. The contract in this case amounted simply to a wager, by two citizens of Vermont, as to the result of a Presidential election. This Court very early decided all wagers to be illegal, as opposed to sound

policy and good morals, *Collamer* v. *Day*, 2 *Vt.*, 144, and the Legislature of this State have made it highly penal for any man to "win or lose any money, or other valuable thing, by betting on the election of any person to any office."—*Rev. Stat.*, c. 51, *sec.* 14; *Rust* v. *Gott*, 9 *Cow.*, 169, *and note.*

3. The plaintiff insists that, if the wager be rescinded, and the stakeholder notified thereof any time before he actually pay over the money to the winner, either party may recover the amount deposited by himself. —*Allan* v. *Hearn*, 1 *T. R.*, 56; *Cotton* v. *Thurland*, 5 *T. R.*, 405: 15 *Eng. Com. Law*, 204; 16 *S. & R.*, 147.

4. It does not appear by the case, that the wager was made in Canada. The parties met at St. Albans, and agreed upon the terms and conditions of the wager. And the plaintiff submits, whether the subsequent meeting at Dunham, and depositing the money with the defendant, was any thing more than a part performance of that agreement.

5. The depositions introduced by the defendant do not prove what the law of Canada is, in a case like the present.

6. The Courts of this State should give no operation whatever to any foreign law, which legalizes in any way, or tends to encourage, wagering in reference to our elections.—1. Because such contracts are against sound policy;—2. Because they are opposed to good morals; and, 3. They are in open and direct violation of a public law of this State.—2 *Kent*, 458; *Story's Confl. of Laws*, 203; 13 *Mass.*, 26.

The opinion of the Court was delivered by

ROYCE, J.—In this State, a wager, like the one in question, would be altogether illegal; not only at common law, as tending to promote corruption and a spirit of gaming, and therefore opposed to public policy,—but as being, moreover, expressly prohibited by statute. And so far as the law of Canada was shown upon the trial, it would seem to correspond with the English common law. It is doubtless true that in Canada, as in England, wagers upon indifferent subjects are valid, and that an action will lie to enforce them. The evidence from Canada speaks of wagers that are not illegal, in contradistinction to those that are so, without giving instances of the latter class. But we are bound to suppose, that the exceptions to the validity of wagers in their law are not essentially more restricted than those in English common law. Hence we infer, that it is a requisite in the law of Canada, that a wager shall not tend directly to promote immorality, nor to contravene public policy. The evidence clearly implies that a wager between their citizens, upon the result of an election there, is regarded as illegal. And we cannot doubt, that if two of their citizens, with a view to evade the laws of their own country, should come into the United States and make such a wager, it would be pronounced illegal by the Courts of Canada. Indeed, this would be but an instance of applying a conservative and self-protecting principle, which is believed to pervade the jurisprudence of all civilized nations. As between the parties to the present wager, we accordingly consider that it should be treated by the Courts of this State as none the less illegal for having been made in Canada. The parties were resident citizens here, and their resort to Canada, as the place of concluding the contract, was obviously designed as an evasion of our laws. And we are at liberty to presume that the defendant was aware of all this, and must have known, that, within the jurisdiction of Vermont, he might, under proper circumstances, be made subject to liability.

The case will therefore depend upon the views to be taken of an illegal wager. It is urged, that no remedy should be afforded in such a case, whether as between the parties to the wager, or in favor of either against a stakeholder. The want of such a rule, not only as applicable to illegal wagers, but to all contracts arising *ex turpi causâ*, has, indeed, been regretted by several of the English Judges, and the rule itself receives direct countenance from some of the New-York cases. But the common law does not at present, as we believe, sanction the denial of its remedies in such extensive and unqualified terms. We deem it well settled, that an illegal wager is revocable at any time before the event happens; and that such a revocation, like the rescission of other contracts, places the parties *in statu quo*, and of course entitles them to a return of their deposits. Such I understand to be the rule as between the parties themselves, when money or other property has been advanced on a stake by one to the other, upon the making of such a wager. It is said to be founded in the justice and policy of allowing to each party a *locus penitentiæ*, while the contract remains exetutory. I think it might also be referred to acknowledged principles, resulting from the illegality of the contract. But according to the case of *Cotton* v. *Thurland*, 5 *T. R.*, 405, followed by *Lacaussade* v. *White*, 7 *T. R.*, 535, and expressly confirmed by *Smith* v. *Bickmore*, 4 *Taunt.*, 474, a revocation before the event happens is not necessary, as against a stakeholder, but the loser may demand of him a return of his deposit, until, with the loser's express or implied consent, it has been paid over to the winner. This is at present the received doctrine in the case of an illegal wager.—*Chit. on Cont.*, 687, *and cases there cited*. The event of an *illegal* wager cannot, of itself, confer a right of property upon the winner. It is only when he gets possession as owner, and that with the loser's unrevoked assent, that the stake becomes his in the nature of an executed gift. In the meantime, the stakeholder, being a mere depositary, without any interest in the stake, is legally bound to restore to each party his own contribution, if thereto required. And according to these views, there can be no doubt, upon the facts appearing in the present case, but that the plaintiff established a right to recover back his deposit of the defendant.

Judgment of County Court affirmed.

BILL AND ANSWER.

To entitle a complainant to an order authorizing him to be examined as a witness, to prove the facts stated in his bill, against an absent defendant who has not appeared in the cause, it should be stated in the bill, and sworn to, that the complainant has not the means of proving the matters which he wishes to establish, except by his own oath, without an answer and discovery from the absent defendant.—*Anonymous*, 1 *Barbour's Ch. R.*, *p.* 408. *N. Y.* (1847.)

This was an application for a reference to a master to take proof of the facts stated in the bill, as against an absent defendant who had not appeared in the suit.

Forsyth, asked for a provision to be inserted in the order, authorizing the complainant to be examined, to prove, by his own oath, the facts stated in the bill.

The Chancellor said it was not a matter of course to permit the complainant to be examined to prove the allegations in the bill, as against an absentee. He said the complainant should state in his bill, and verify it by his oath, that he cannot prove the matters charged in the bill, except by an answer and discovery from the absent defendant, unless he is permitted to prove them by his own oath. That upon such a bill, inasmuch as a discovery could not be obtained from an absentee who did not appear, the complainant might be permitted to prove the facts as to which a discovery from the defendant would be necessary, if he appeared in the cause, and did not suffer the bill to be taken as confessed against him after such appearance.

BILL OF DISCOVERY.

To maintain a bill of discovery in a defence at law, the plaintiff must state a case which, if established, would constitute a good defence at law, and he must then state some fact, material to such defence, which he wishes to establish by the confession of the defendant.—*Nieury* v. *O'Hara*, 1 *Barbour's R.*, *p.* 484. *N. Y.* (1848.)

(Harris, J., cited *Story Eq. Pl.*, *secs.* 319, 325; *Newkirk* v. *Willet*, 2 *Caine's Cas. in Er.*, 296; *Williams* v. *Harden*, 1 *Barb. Ch.*, 298.)

BILL OF EXCHANGE.

A negotiable bill of exchange or promissory note must be for a fixed sum, and must be payable in money, and the time of payment must be such that it will certainly arrive; though the day of payment may depend upon a contingency.—*Henschel* v. *Mahler*, 3 *Denio's R.*, *p.* 428. *N. Y.* (1848.)

(The Chancellor cited *Colehan* v. *Cooke*, *Willes*, 393; *Strange*, 1217, *S. C.*)

A bill of exchange, payable twelve months after date, when the nominal day of payment falls on *Sunday*, is, notwithstanding, allowed three days of grace, and is properly protestable on the *Wednesday* following. —*Wooley* v. *Clements*, 11 *Alabama R.*, *p.* 220. (1847.)

(GOLDTHWAITE, J., cited *Chitty on Bills*, 410, *a*, *and note* 1; *Story on Bills*, *secs.* 337, 338.)

An acceptor of a bill of exchange is not liable to the payee or endorsee for damages caused by non-payment, but only for the amount of the bill, with interest and costs of protest.—*Bowen et als.* v. *Stoddard*, 10 *Metcalf's R.*, *p.* 375. *Mass.* (1847.)

(HUBBARD, J., cited *Bain* v. *Ackworth*, 1 *Rep. Con. Ct.*, (*S. C.*,) 107 *Riggs* v. *Lindsay*, 7 *Cranch*, 500.)

BLANK NOTE—ENDORSER.

Where a note is endorsed in blank, and it does not appear that the holder had notice of any restrictions or limitations upon the extent of liability to be incurred, the endorser thereon will be liable to such holder, even though the note be filled up with a greater sum than the endorser expected or intended.—*Fanning* v. *The Farmers' and Merchants' Bank of Memphis*, 8 *Smedes & Marshall's R.*, *p.* 139. *Miss.* (1847.)

BOND.

Upon a bond conditioned to save harmless and indemnify the obligee against his *liability* as the maker of a promissory note then held by a third person, *and to pay the same*, or cause it to be paid, the obligee may, without having paid any thing, recover the amount of the note against the obligor, upon his failure to pay the holder.

But he cannot recover the costs of a judgment obtained against him on the note, where he has not paid them.

Where the note is past due at the time of the execution of such a bond, the obligee is bound to make payment to the holder immediately; and if he fail to do so, a suit may be maintained on the bond without delay.

The defendant cannot, in an action on such a bond, set up usury in the note.

An agreement to indemnify one against a demand, is of the same legal import as an agreement to indemnify him against his *liability* for the demand.—*Churchill* v. *Hunt*, 3 *Denio's R.*, *p.* 321. *N. Y.* (1848.)

(*Hill, Jr.*, cited *Thomas* v. *Allen*, 1 *Hill*, 147; *The People* v. *Corbett*, 8 *Cowen*, 520; *Webb* v. *Lansing*, 19 *Wend.*, 423; *Bearce* v. *Barstow*,

9 Mass., 45, 48; *De Wolf* v. *Johnson*, 10 *Wheat.*, 367; *Pratt* v. *Adams*, 7 *Paige*, 615, 639, 641.

Pierson, contra, cited, *In Re Negus*, 7 *Wend.*, 499; *Douglas* v. *Clark*, 14 *Johns.*, 177; *Aberdeen* v. *Blackmar*, 6 *Hill*, 324; *Hammond* v. *Hopping*, 13 *Wend.*, 505; *Reed* v. *Smith*, 9 *Cow.*, 647; *Chitty on Cont.*, 706, 709; *Ord on Usury*, 105.

Beardsley, J., cited *Hurlst. on Bonds*, 40; *Bothy's Case*, 6 *Rep.*, 31; *Shep. Touch.*, 369; *Farquahar* v. *Morris*, 7 *D. & E.*, 124; *Port* v. *Jackson*, 17 *Johns.*, 239, *and authorities there referred to*; *In Re Negus*, 7 *Wend.*, 499.)

It is the essence of a bond to have an obligee as well as an obligor; it must show upon its face to whom it is payable.

The defect cannot be supplied by showing a delivery to a particular person.—*Phelps* v. *Call*, 7 *Iredell's R.*, *p.* 262. *N. C.* (1847.)

A surety to an attachment bond, who is a necessary witness for the party, may be made competent by the execution of a new bond, with sufficient surety, and it is the duty of the Court to permit such substitution to be made.—*Drinkwater* v. *Holliday*, 11 *Alabama R.*, *p.* 134. (1847.)

Falsely putting a witness' name to a bond, which is not required to have a subscribing witness, does not vitiate the bond, and is not forgery. —*State* v. *Gherkin*, 7 *Iredell's R.*, *p.* 206. *N. C.* (1847.)

BOND—HUSBAND AND WIFE.

Where a bond was executed to husband and wife, in consideration of property delivered by the husband to the obligor, conditioned for the delivery of certain specific articles of property to the obligees, during their natural lives, for their support, it was *held*, that the wife had an equitable interest in the bond, and might legally cancel it, after the decease of her husband.

And where the wife, in such case, after the decease of her husband, cancelled the bond executed to her husband and herself, and received, in lieu thereof, a bond to herself, conditioned for general maintenance through life, it was *held*, in the absence of all proof of fraud, that the obligor was not chargeable as her trustee, by reason of such second bond.

An obligation to maintain a person through life is a mere personal matter, and, where the consideration did not move from the person to be supported, cannot be attached by trustee process.—*Briggs* v. *Beach*, 18 *Vermont R.*, *p.* 115. (1847.)

BOND AND MORTGAGE.

If a person take a bond and mortgage to himself, with a condition to support him and his wife during their lives, an action upon the mortgage, to enforce the performance of the condition, for the benefit of the wife, after his decease, must be brought in the name of his administrator.

The widow cannot lawfully enter for condition broken.

If she marry again, and reside with the second husband, without any claim for support, it must be considered as voluntarily waived for the time being; and in order to constitute a breach of the condition, subsequently, there must be a demand of the support required, and a refusal.

It is not necessary to make the demand upon the land mortgaged, unless that be the place where the support is to be furnished.

The widow may make a valid demand, notwithstanding she has married again; and it may be made upon the administrator of the mortgagor, in case of his decease.

But she cannot make the duty more onerous by contracting another marriage; a second husband would have no right to participate in the support; and she must be ready, when she makes the demand, to receive it at a convenient place, if none be designated, and in such manner as the terms of the obligation require.—*Holmes* v. *Fisher*, 13 *New Hampshire R.*, *p.* 9. (1847.)

Writ of Entry, to recover possession of a tract of land in Richmond. The action was founded upon a mortgage made by John Day to Othniel Day, the plaintiff's intestate. Plea, the general issue.

Upon the trial it appeared in evidence that Othniel Day was formerly the owner of the land, and on the 16th of May, 1818, conveyed it to his son, John Day, taking back a mortgage to himself, to secure the performance of the condition of a bond executed, at the same time, by John Day, the mortgagor.

The condition of the bond was, that "if the said John Day, his heirs, executors and administrators, do and shall, well and truly support and maintain Othniel Day, and Rebecca Day, his present wife, in sickness and health, befitting persons of their age and degree in life, with clothing, lodging, washing, mending, and every other necessary of life, and also pay all debts and taxes that the above-named Othniel Day now oweth, and also pay to the above named Othniel Day two dollars per year, to be paid in the month of October annually, without fraud or deceit, and at the death of the above-named Othniel Day and Rebecca Day give their bodies a Christian-like burial, then the said bond is to be null and void, but otherwise to remain in full force and virtue."

Othniel Day died in June, 1819. His widow, Rebecca Day, lived with her son, John Day, until July, 1829, at which time she married one Bancroft, and went to reside with him.

John Day died in October, 1832, leaving a widow and six children.

The defendant subsequently married his widow, and was appointed guardian of three of the children, the eldest of whom is fourteen years of age. They reside upon the premises with the defendant and his wife. There was evidence that the defendant is poor and intemperate.

Subsequent to the decease of John Day, said Rebecca requested John Parkhurst, who was administrator of his estate, to provide her with suitable support. He took time for inquiry, but afterwards refused to do any thing on the subject. She then entered upon the demanded premises, about four years prior to the commencement of this suit, (the land being at that time left vacant and unoccupied by the defendant,) leased them, and received the rents until April, 1840, when the defendant entered claiming the same.

Said Rebecca, since her second marriage, has lived with her husband, Bancroft, and has been supported by means independent of any aid from the bond, or the mortgaged premises.

No claim for support has at any time been made upon the premises.

A verdict was taken by the plaintiff, by consent, subject to the opinion of this Court upon the foregoing case.

Chamberlain, for the defendant, contended that the plaintiff, as administrator of Othniel Day could not rightfully maintain this suit; and that no suit could be maintained without a demand for support upon the premises.

Edwards, for the plaintiff.—The bond makes provision for the support of the wife, as well as that of the husband. To avail herself of this provision for her support, the administrator of the husband must prosecute an action for her benefit.

The case shows a demand for support, and that she has had no support from that source. She was under no obligation to demand the support upon the premises; and, moreover, the evidence of the condition and habits of the defendant shows that she could not be suitably supported there, and that a demand of it at that place was therefore unnecessary.

Parker, C. J.—The defendant entered without any title to the premises, either in his own right, or in right of his wife. His wife it seems had a right of dower on the decease of her former husband, John Day, subject to the mortgage under which the plaintiff claims; but it does not appear that the dower had been assigned. If it had been, it could avail nothing against the mortgage.

He is guardian of three of the children of John Day, but their title is subject to the mortgage. If it were not so, a question might be raised, how far the defendant could avail himself of it under his plea.

But he is in possession, and may maintain that possession, against any one who cannot show a better right.

The plaintiff sues as administrator of Othniel Day, and makes his title under a mortgage from John Day to his intestate. He is the proper person to enforce the performance of the condition of the bond, by a suit upon the mortgage. His intestate alone could have brought the action in his lifetime.

The entry of Rebecca Bancroft into the land is therefore of no importance. She could not lawfully enter, because the mortgage was not made to her, and gave her no title to enter. Her entry and possession cannot avail to the benefit of the plaintiff. He claims nothing under any title from her.

In order to sustain this suit upon the mortgage, it must appear that the condition has been broken. The mortgagor, John Day, and his representatives, were entitled to possession until a breach of the condition occurred.—*Flanders* v. *Lamphear*, 9 *N. H.*, 201.

John Day performed the condition during the life of his father, and until the marriage of his mother with Bancroft. After the marriage, the mother lived with Bancroft, and no claim was made for any support during the lifetime of John Day. Under these circumstances it must be considered as voluntarily waived, for the time being; and the plaintiff does not contend that there was any breach up to the time of his death.

Upon his decease, the duty of performing the condition devolved upon his administrator and heirs.

In order to constitute a breach of the condition subsequent to this, there must be a demand of the support, and a refusal; and the question arises, whether there has been a sufficient demand.

A demand for support was made upon Parkhurst, the administrator of the estate of John Day, by Mrs. Bancroft, which he refused to comply with. It was not necessary to make a demand upon the heirs also, if this demand were well made.

We are of opinion that it was not essential that the demand should be made upon the mortgaged premises. The land mortgaged was not necessarily the place where the support was to be furnished.—*Flanders* v. *Lamphear*, before cited; *Fisher* v *Fiske*, 4 *Pick.*, 497.

Nor was it necessary that the demand should be made by the administrator of Othniel Day. The bond and mortgage were taken for the benefit of his wife as well as himself. Although she was not a party to it, she had an interest in the subject matter, and after his death she might well make a demand of what was secured for her use.

Prior to the time when it was made, she had married Bancroft, and had gone to live with him. This did not defeat her right to the support, or her right to ask for it. But it may have an influence upon the demand which was made. The condition of the bond was not to furnish her certain articles, or a sum sufficient for her support, but she was to be supported and maintained with clothing, lodging, washing, mending, and every necessary of life. She could not make this duty more onerous, by contracting another marriage. There was no obligation to furnish provisions or lodging, &c., in the use of which her husband should participate, nor did the bond require that she should be supported wherever she might live with him. She must have been ready, when she made the demand, to receive the support at a convenient place, none being designated, and in such a manner as the terms of the obligation required. Whether she could do this without seperating from her husband, may admit of question, and the circumstances under which the demand was made do not appear. A mere demand of support while living at a distance from the place, with her husband, may not have imposed any duty upon Parkhurst, the administrator of John Day, if he objected for that reason. But his refusal, if unqualified, or put upon the ground that she had no right under any circumstances, might perhaps obviate the objection.

And we are of opinion that there must be a further inquiry into the circumstances attending the demand and refusal; and for this purpose there must be a *New Trial.*

BOOK ACCOUNT.

A continuous running account, between the same parties, is an entire thing, not susceptible of division, the aggregate of all the items being the amount due, and therefore a recovery of a part by suit will bar an action for the residue. The rule applies to a physician's account, who having sued for and recovered a part, cannot maintain an action for the residue of the account.—*Oliver* v. *Holt*, 11 *Alabama R.*, p. 574. (1847.)

(*Martin* cited *Lock* v. *Miller*, 3 *Stew. & P.*, 14; *De Sylva* v. *Henry*, 3 *Porter*, 132; *Bendernagle* v. *Cocks*, 19 *Wend.*, 207; *Guernsey* v. *Carver*, 8 *Wend.*, 492; *Stevens* v. *Lockwood*, 13 *Wend.*, 644; *Colven* v. *Corwen*, 11 *Wend.*, 557; *Bunell* v. *Pinto*, 2 *Conn.*, 431; *Avery* v. *Fitch*, 4 *Conn.*, 362; *Lane* v. *Cook*, 3 *Day*, 255; *Markham* v. *Middleton*, 2 *Strange*, 1259; 3 *Phil. Ev.*, 642, *n.* 592.

Ormond, J, cited *Lock* v. *Miller*, 3 *Stew. & P.*, 14; *De Sylva* v. *Henry*, 3 *Porter*, 132; *Guernsey* v. *Carver*, 8 *Wend.*, 492; *Bendernagle* v. *Cocks*, 19 *Wend.*, 207; *Bunell* v. *Pinto*, 2 *Conn.*, 431; *Lana* v. *Cook*, 3 *Day*, 255; *Ingraham* v. *Hale*, 11 *S. & R.*, 78.)

A wife who keeps her husband's accounts is a competent witness for him, in a suit in which he introduces his book of original entries, to testify that she made the entries, by his direction and in his presence: and after she has so testified, he may be permitted to testify as to the times when the entries were made, and that the charges contained in them are just and true.—*Littlefield* v. *Rice*, 10 *Metcalf's R.*, p. 287. *Mass.* (1847.)

(*Mellen* cited *Foster* v. *Sinkler*, 1 *Bay*, 40; *Smith* v. *Sanford*, 12 *Pick.*, 139; *Hartley* v. *Brooks*, 6 *Whart.*, 189; *Stanton* v. *Willson*, 3 *Day*, 37; *Mather* v. *Robinson*, 8 *Metcalf*, 269.

Train, contra, cited 1 *Phil. Ev.* (*4th Amer. ed.*), 77; 2 *Ib.*, 683; *Carr* v. *Cornell*, 4 *Vermont*, 116.)

In order to recover for goods sold, in an action on book account, the plaintiff must prove an executed and perfected contract of *sale* of the property, completed by *delivery*.—*Bundy et al.* v. *Ayer*, 18 *Vermont R.*, *p.* 497. (1847.)

(Kellogg, J., cited *Read* v. *Barlow*, 1 *Aik.*, 145; 1 *Vt.*, 97; *Carpenter* v. *Dole*, 13 *Vt.*, 578.)

BREACH OF TRUST.

Continuing to carry on the business of the assignor, in the same way in which it was conducted prior to the assignment, retailing the goods, replenishing the stock from the proceeds of the sales, and keeping no account of the sales of the assigned property, amounts to a breach of trust, which will authorize the appointment of a receiver.—*Connah* v. *Sedgwick et als.*, 1 *Barbour's R.*, *p.* 210. *N. Y.* (1848.)

(Edmonds, J., cited, *Hart* v. *Crane*, 7 *Paige*, 37; *Reed* v. *Emory*, 8 *Paige*, 417.)

BROKER.

If a broker sell property to one, knowing it to be subject to the lien of a *fieri facias*, and conceal the fact; or if he direct an investigation about incumbrances on the property to be made in a direction whence he knows correct information cannot be obtained, his conduct is calculated to deceive and injure, and is therefore fraudulent.

False and fraudulent representations may be made by actions as well as by words.

He who makes use of another in a transaction calculated and intended to mislead, is himself guilty of the deception.

Any fraudulent conduct, injurious to another, is actionable.—*Chisholm* v. *Gadsden*, 1 *Strobhart's R.*, *p.* 120. *S. C.* (1847.)

(*Yeadon* cited *Culver* v. *Avery*, 7 *Wend.*, 380; *Allan* v. *Addington*, 7 *Wend.*, 9; *Ire* v. *Durnford*, 1 *East*, 318; *Hough* v. *Evans*, 4 *McCord*, 169; *Snider* v. *Heath*, 3 *Camp.*, 508; *Pickering et al.* v. ——, 4 *Taunt.*, 779.)

BURGLARY.

The offence of breaking is a violation of the security intended to exclude; and when coupled with an entrance into a store with a felonious intent, it may constitute the crime described in *Rev. Stat.*, *c.* 155, *sec.* 11.

But when the store is lighted up, and the doors are latched merely, in the ordinary manner, without any fastening to exclude others, and the clerks are in the store ready to attend upon customers; and before eight o'clock in the evening one carefully lifts the latch and enters the store by the door, with the intention to commit a larceny therein, and does so enter and commit a larceny, secretly, and without the knowledge of the attendants in the store; it does not amount to such breaking and entering as to constitute the crime intended to be punished under that section of the statute.—*The State* v. *Newbegin*, 25 *Maine R.*, *p.* 500. (1847.)

This was an indictment against Edward Newbegin and Samuel L. Barnes, for breaking and entering the store of Jeremiah Dow, in Portland, in the night-time, and stealing twenty yards of satinett, valued at ten dollars, and was tried at the District Court, Cumberland County, March Term, 1846. Barnes did not appear, and Newbegin was tried alone. There was evidence tending to show, that said Newbegin was seen coming out of the store between seven and eight of the clock in the evening of the day alleged in the indictment. The store was occupied by Mr. Dow, as a dry goods store, and was open in the evening for selling goods, till after said cloth was taken. There were two entrances to the store, one on Temple-street and one on Middle-street. The latter was the more frequented, but there was free access through either. There was a sign over each door. It was the door on Temple-street, into which the evidence tended to show that Newbegin entered. It was a door with two sides and a glass in the upper part, the right side was the part used, and it was, when shut, held by a common latch, when persons were in the store, and opened and shut by customers as store-doors are usually opened and shut; but when the store was left or closed for the night, it was secured by barring and locking. The evidence tended to show, that Newbegin and Barnes watched an opportunity to open the door, so as not to attract observation when they went in; but there was no other breaking than the lifting the latch and opening the door, as was usually done by persons entering the store. The store was lighted, and the clerks were in it, when the goods were taken, as alleged in the indictment. The store consisted of but one room extending from Middle to Temple streets, and there was a light on the counter where the cloth which was taken lay. No one saw Newbegin lift the latch.

Goodenow, District Judge, presiding at the trial, instructed the jury, that if said Newbegin opened the door on Temple-street, and entered into the store for an unlawful purpose, it was breaking and entering, within the meaning of the statute, and would support the indictment upon the facts aforesaid.

On the return of a verdict of guilty, the counsel for Newbegin filed exceptions to the instructions of the Judge.

Wells & Sweat, for Newbegin, said that the store was open for the sale of goods in the usual manner, and that there was no other breaking than every one commits who lifts the latch of the door, and enters to purchase goods. The store was lighted up, and three clerks were in it to attend to customers. Signs were up over each door, thus by universal custom inviting all to enter without asking permission. When the store was intended to be closed, the doors were fastened, so that there could be no admission without breaking. Whether the accused entered the store with the intention to commit a larceny or not, is entirely irrelevant to this question. There was no such breaking as is necessary to sustain an indictment under *Rev. Stat.*, c. 155, *sec.* 11; *Commonwealth* v. *Trimmer*, 1 *Mass.*, 476; 2 *C. & P.*, 628; 2 *Russ. on Cr.*, 4 & 5; 2 *Stark. Ev.*, 318; 2 *East's P. C.*, 487; *Commonwealth* v. *Stephenson*, 8 *Pick.*, 354.

Moor, Attorney General for the State, contended that the instruction of the District Judge was right. The accused opened the store-door with the felonious intent to steal goods from it, which custom did not warrant, and the entry, therefore, was not for a lawful purpose. It was a sufficient breaking and entering. The words, in this respect, are the same as in *Rev. Stat.* c. 156, *sec.* 2; one forbidding the breaking into a store, and the other into a dwelling-house. The authorities in relation to each, are therefore pertinent.—2 *East's P. C.*, 487; 2 *Russ. on Cr.*, 5, 9–12; *Rosc. on Cr. Ev.*, 253.

The opinion of the Court was delivered by

SHEPLEY, J.—The *Statute*, c. 155, *sec.* 11, provides, that if any person, with intent to commit a felony, shall at any time, break and enter any office, bank, shop, or warehouse, he shall be punished by imprisonment in the state prison. The prisoner was indicted with another person for breaking and entering the shop of Jeremiah Dow, in Portland. He was convicted, and the case is presented on exceptions taken to the instructions, as to what facts were sufficient to constitute the offence of breaking.

The facts essential to a decision of the question presented, appear to have been these. The shop had been occupied for the sale of goods, with two doors opening on different streets for the entrance of persons to trade. The prisoner entered between seven and eight o'clock in the evening by the door opening on the street least frequented, being aided by another person to watch and inform him, so that he did it when three clerks were seated by the fire, where they could not see that door. The shop was lighted and the clerks were there for trade. The doors and windows had not been closed to exclude persons, although the doors were shut. The prisoner, watching for a favorable opportunity, carefully lifted the latch, opened the door, took a piece of cloth, and escaped.

It was doubtless the design of the legislature to use the words, break and enter, when defining this offence, in the sense in which they are used to define the crime of burglary. To constitute that offence, there must be proof of an actual breaking, or of that which is equivalent to it. Proof of an illegal entrance merely, such as would enable the party injured to maintain trespass *quare clausum*, will not be sufficient. Nor will proof of an entrance merely, for a purpose ever so felonious and fault, accompanied by any conceivable stratagem, be sufficient, if there be no actual breaking. There must indeed be proof of a felonious intent; but however clearly that may be proved, and however full may be the proof of entrance, the offence is not proved until there be proof of an actual breaking, or its equivalent. It is immaterial by what kind of violence the breaking is effected. The gist of the offence consists not in the degree or kind of violence used. One, who had obtained an entrance by threats, causing the door to be opened for him; or by fraudulent misrepresentation and falsehood; or by conspiring with a servant within, was considered as guilty of the offence by the commission of acts equivalent to an actual breaking.—*Rex* v. *Brown*, 2 *East's P. C.*, 487. Yet Baron BOLLARD held that the lifting of such a door, while newly placed and without the fastenings intended to be made, was not a breaking. —*Rex* v. *Lawrence*, 4 *C. & P.*, 231. An entrance effected by cutting away a network placed around an opening for a glass window, which had been left open, was held to be a breaking.—*Commonwealth* v. *Stevenson*, 8 *Pick.*, 354. While the offence will not be committed by an entrance through an open door, window, or other open place usually closed, when others are intended to be excluded, it has been decided, that an entrance by a chimney open, when the intention is to exclude, will be a breaking.—*Rex* v. *Brice*, *Russ. & Ry. C. C.*, 450.

The offence of breaking is a violation of the security designed to exclude; and coupled with an entrance into a shop with a felonious intent, it constitutes the crime charged in the indictment. The opening of a shop door in the daytime, which had been closed only to exclude the dust or cold air, with a design that it should be opened by all who should be inclined to enter, could not be a violation of any security designed to exclude, and therefore not a breaking. It would not even be a trespass, for the custom of trade in it would be evidence of a general license to enter. The effect would not be different, if the entrance were made in the evening under like circumstances, while the shop continued to be lighted and prepared for trade. Our statute, in defining this offence, makes no distinction respecting the time of breaking and entrance. The same acts will constitute the offence irrespective of light or darkness.

In accordance with the principle stated, it was decided in the case of *Rex* v. *Smith*, *Ry. & Moo. C. C.*, 178, that an entrance through a window left a little open, by pushing it wide open, was not a breaking. The twelve judges appear to have been equally divided in opinion in the case of *Rex* v. *Callan*, *Russ. & Ry. C. C.*, 157, whether the offence of breaking out of a cellar was committed by lifting a flap floor, by which the cellar was closed, where the flap had bolts, by which it was usually fastened, and which were not bolted. If the proof had been, that the door had been closed to exclude, though not fastened by bolts, there would seem to have been a commission of the offence by the violation of that security. But when a door usually fastened for the purpose of exclusion, by a lock, bar, or bolt, is entered, when not fastened in that mode nor in any mode for the purpose of excluding others, one necessary element of the offence of breaking is wanting.

Exceptions sustained, and case remanded to the District Court.

CARRIER.

One who contracts to transport goods from one point to another, and deliver them in *good order and condition, unavoidable accidents only excepted*, is not a common carrier, but is responsible on his contract as one.

To make a person a *common carrier*, he must exercise it as a common employment; he must undertake to carry goods for persons generally, and he must hold himself out as ready to engage in the transportation of goods for hire as a business, and not as a casual occupation, *pro hac vice*.

Unavoidable is synonymous with *inevitable*, and *inevitable or unavoidable accidents* are the same with *the acts of God*, which mean any accident produced by physical causes which are inevitable; such as lightnings, storms, perils of the sea, earthquakes, inundations, sudden death or illness.

A common carrier is in the nature of an insurer of the goods intrusted to his care, and is responsible for every injury sustained by them, occasioned by any means whatever, except only the *act of God* and *the King's enemies*.

Nor can he vary his responsibility by notice or special acceptance, such being void as contravening the policy of the law; but he may require the nature and value of the goods to be made known to him, and may avail himself of any *fraudulent* acts or sayings of his employers.—*Fish* v. *Chapman et al.*, 2 *Kelly's R.*, *p.* 349. *Ga.* (1847.)

(NISBET, J., cited *Coggs* v. *Bernard*, 1 *Smith's Leading Cases*, 172, *Forward* v. *Pittard*, 1 *T. R.*, 27; *Morse* v. *Slew*, 2 *Lev.*, 69; 1 *Vent.*, 190, 238; *Rich* v. *Kneeland*, *Cro. Jac.*, 330; *Mavings* v. *Todd*, 1 *Stark.*, 72; *Brook* v. *Pickwick*, 1 *Bing.*, 218; *Palmer* v. *Grand Junction Canal Co.*, 4 *M. & W.*, 749; 2 *Kent*, 598; *Story on Bail.*, *sec.* 495; *Jackson* v. *Rogers*, 2 *Show.*, 327; *Riley* v. *Horne*, 5 *Bing.*, 217; *Lane* v. *Cotton*, 1 *Ld. Raym.*, 646; *Edwards* v. *Sheratt*, 1 *East*, 604; *Batson* v. *Donovan*, 1 *B. & A.*, 32; *Elsee* v. *Gatwood*, 5 *T. R.*, 143; 1 *Pick.*, 50; 2 *Sumner*, 221; *Story on Bail.*, 322, 323; *Dudley*, *S. C. Law & Eq.*, 159; 1 *Inst.*, 89; *Dale* v. *Hall*, 1 *Wils.*, 281; *Covington* v. *Willan*, *Gow.*, 115; *Davis* v. *Garret*, 6 *Bing.*, 716; 2 *Kent*, 597; *Coggs* v. *Bernard*, 2 *Ld. Raym.*, 918; 1 *T. R.*, 27; 3 *Esp.*, 127; 5 *Bing.*, 217; *Story on Bail.*, *secs.* 457, 495; *Bac. Abr.*, *Carrier*, *a*; 2 *Bos. & Pul.*, 417; 4 *Taunt.*, 787; *Jones Bail.*, 121; 1 *Wend.*, 272; 6 *Taunt.*, 577; *Story on Bail.*, *secs.* 25, 511; *McArthur & Hurlbut* v. *Sears*, 21 *Wend.*, 190; 1 *Murphy*, 173; 2 *Bailey*, 157; 2 *Bailey*, 421; 5 *East*, 507; 1 *H. Black.*, 298; 3 *Taunt.*, 264; 2 *M. & S.*, 1; 8 *Taunt.*, 146; 4 *B. & Ald.*, 39; 5 *Bing.*, 217; 4 *Price*, 34; 4 *Camp.*, 41; 2 *Kent*, 607; *Holister* v. *Nolan.* 19 *Wend.*, 234; *Camden and Amboy Transportation*

Co. v. *Belknap*, 21 *Wend.*, 355; *Cole* v. *Goodwin*, 19 *Wend.*, 251; *Gould* v. *Hill*, 2 *Hill* (*N. Y.*), 623; 3 *Hill*, 9, 20; *Story on Bailm.*, 4th *ed.*, 558, *note*; 9 *Watts*, 87; 4 *Harr. & Johns.*, 317; 10 *Ohio*, 145; 2 *Kent*, 608, *note*.)

When the plaintiff has a *prima facie* case, that must pass to the jury, and not be turned out of Court by a nonsuit.

Although the common law liability of carriers be controlled by the custom of excepting fire as a risk in the bill of lading, the carrier should be held to strict proof of diligence and care in avoiding loss to the owner by so dangerous an element.

Customs and usages should be plain and distinct, ancient and certain, before men should be required to know them, as constituting the law of their contracts.

He who would, by virtue of a special contract, derogate from his legal liability, is bound to give explicit information *to all*, of the precise limitation intended.

Without the concurrence, expressed or plainly implied by the words or conduct of a party, he cannot be bound by the acts of another apparently assuming to be his agent, nor by a mistaken conclusion drawn by a third party, of such agency.—*Singleton* v. *Hilliard et al.*, 1 *Strobhart's R.*, *p.* 203. *S. C.* (1847.)

(Richardson, J., cited 2 *T. R.*, 58; 1 *Roll. Ab.*, 565; *Wiggollsworth* v. *Dallison*, *Doug.*, 201; *and the collection of cases in* 1 *Smith's Leading Cases*, 401; *Coke Lit.*, 114.)

Proprietors of a railroad, who transport goods over their road, and deposit them in their warehouse without charge, until the owner or consignee has a reasonable time to take them away, are not liable, as common carriers, for the loss of the goods from the warehouse, but are liable, as depositaries, only for want of ordinary care.—*Thomas* v. *Boston and Providence Railroad Corp.*, 10 *Metcalf's R.*, *p.* 472. *Mass.* (1847.)

(*Hilliard* cited *Garside* v. *Proprietors of Trent and Mersey Navigation*, 4 *T. R.*, 581; *Young* v. *Smith*, 3 *Dana*, 92; *Rowe* v. *Pickford*, 1 *Moore*, 526, *and* 8 *Taunt.*, 83; *Foster* v. *Frampton*, 6 *Barn. & Cres.*, 107; *Allen* v. *Gripper*, 2 *Crompt. & Jerv.*, 218, *and* 2 *Tyrw.*, 217.)

CERTIFICATE OF NOTARY.

The certificate of a notary by whom a bill or note has been protested should state the day on which notice was given to the endorser. It is not necessary to mention the date of the letter containing the notice.

Where, after due diligence, a notary is unable to ascertain the residence of an endorser, notice of protest must be put in the nearest post-office to the place at which such protest was made, addressed to him at the place at which the note or bill appears, from its face, to have been drawn. Notice in a letter addressed to the endorser, and left at the domicil of a subsequent endorser, is insufficient.—*Act* 13 March, 1827, *sec.* 3.—*Palmer* v. *Lee et al.*, 7 *Robinson's La. R.*, *p.* 537. (1847.)

APPEAL from the Commercial Court of New-Orleans.—WATTS, J.

Grivot, for the appellant.
Lewis, contra.

MARTIN, J.—This is a suit against the maker and endorser of two promissory notes. There was judgment against the first, and a judgment as in case of nonsuit in favor of the second. The plaintiff appealed, the endorser alone being cited.

The certificate of the notary attests that, as to the first note, he put a notice to the endorser and appellee in the post-office, diligent inquiry having been vainly used to discover his residence. This was done on the 23d of December, 1839, the 22d being Sunday, and the note having been protested on the 21st.

As to the second note, the certificate attests that the notary gave notice of the protest to the endorser on the 22nd of June, 1839, (the protest having been made the preceding day,) in a letter addressed to him, which he left at the domicil of S. E. Forstall, a subsequent endorser; his diligent efforts to discover the domicil of the appellee having been fruitless.

The counsel for the endorser and appellee has urged, that it does not appear that the notary used proper diligence to discover his client's domicil; that the certificates do not state the dates of the notices to the endorser, and that the notice of the protest of the second note ought to have been put in the post-office.

The testimony shows, that the notary public made inquiries for the residence of the endorser, at the Merchants' Exchange, St. Charles Exchange, St. Louis Hotel, at Bishop's and the Verandah. This appears to us sufficient, especially as the Merchants' Exchange and the post-office are under the same roof. The certificates ought certainly to state the day on which the notice was given to the endorser; but nothing requires that it should state the date of the letter which contains that notice. The notice of protest of the second note was improperly given in a letter directed to endorser, but left at the domicil of Forstall, a subsequent endorser. The letter ought to have been lodged in the post-office. —*Bul. & Curry's Dig.*, 43.

The Court erred, in our opinion, in giving judgment of nonsuit on the second note.

It is, therefore, ordered, that the judgment be annulled and reversed; and the plaintiff recover from the endorser and appellee, the sum of two hundred and twenty dollars and fifty cents, with legal interest from the 21st day of December, 1839, until paid, with costs in both Courts; reserving to the plaintiff his right on the second note, if any he has.

CESTUI QUE TRUST.

A deed of trust executed to indemnify the *cestui que trust* as a surety for the grantor, the grantor being dead, the *cestui que trust* having executed a new note with endorsers and taken up the old one, and having assigned his interest in the trust deed to his endorsers to indemnify them, and such endorsers having been compelled to pay the debt, they may pursue the trust fund against the heirs of the original grantor, without making his personal representatives, or his widow, or the assignor of the trust deed, parties.

On a bill of review the Court will not reverse a decree taken *pro confesso*, and where there had been a reference to a master to state an account, merely because some irregularity may have occurred in not exhibiting in the record the whole proof upon which the master based his report, but to authorize a reversal of such decree, positive error must appear.

Notice of publication, if so specific as to advise the respondents of the nature of their interest sought to be affected by the proceeding, is sufficient.

Taxes paid by a *cestui que trust*, are a lien upon the land, and may be paid out of the trust fund.

A decree will not be reversed on bill of review, because a defence may have existed, of which the party neglected to avail himself.

If the debt is barred by the statute of limitations at law, the Court will not on that account deprive the *cestui que trust* of his equitable security, and refuse to compel an execution of the trust.—*Gary et al.* v. *May et al.*, 16 *Ohio R.*, *p.* 66. (1848.)

(*Swan & Andrews*, and *Wilcox*, cited *David* v. *Graham*, 2 *Har. & Gill*, 94; 3 *Barb. & Harring. Dig.*, 100; *Story's Eq. Pl.*, *secs.* 175, 179; 3 *P. Wms.*, 333, *note*; 2 *Brown's Ch.*, 276, 279; *Slaughter* v. *Foust et al.*, 4 *Blackf.*, 379; 3 *Pow. on Mort.*, *Rand's ed.*, 969; *Bradshaw* v. *Outram*, 13 *Ves.*, 239; *Daniel* v. *Skipwith*, 3 *Brown's C. C.*, 155; 3 *P. Wms.*, 311, *note*; 5 *Eq. Ab.*, 119; *Story's Eq. Pl.*, *secs.* 1, 281, 229, 212; *Thomas* v. *Harvey's Heirs*, 10 *Wheat.*, 146; *Whiting et al.* v. *Bank U. S.*, 13 *Pet.*, 14; *Dies* v. *Birchard*, 10 *Paige* 445; *Crane* v. *Deming*, 7 *Conn.*, 387; *Story's Eq. Pl.*, *sec.* 74 (*a*), *3d ed.*; *Ibid.*, *sec.* 237; *Sanford* v. *McLean*, 3 *Paige*, 117; *Niemcewitz* v. *Gahn*, 3 *Paige*, 614; *Capes* v. *Middleton*, *Tur. & Russ.*, 229; *King* v. *Baldwin*, 2 *Johns. Ch.*, 554; *Polk* v. *Gallant*, 2 *Dev. & Bat.*, 395; *Thompson* v. *McDonald*, *Ibid.*, 463; *Story's Eq. Pl.*, *sec.* 191; *Whitney* v.

M'Kinney, 7 *Johns. Ch.* 144; *Trecothick* v. *Austin*, 4 *Mason* 16; *Miller* v. *Bear*, 3 *Paige*, 468; *Fenton* v. *Hughes*, 7 *Ves.*, 287; *Whitworth* v. *Davis*, 1 *Ves. & Beame*, 545; *Lockwood et al.* v. *Wildman et al.*, 13 *Ohio*, 430; *Mitchell* v. *Gazzam et al.*, 12 *Ohio*, 315, 335; *Sheets* v. *Baldwin*, 12 *Ohio*, 120; *Knapp* v. *Alvord*, 10 *Paige*, 205; *Maddox* v. *Jackson*, 3 *Atk.*, 406; *Angerstein* v. *Clark*, 3 *Swanst.*, 147; *Cockburn* v. *Thompson*, 16 *Ves.*, 326; 11 *Conn.*, 160; 8 *Dana*, 284; 1 *Johns. Ch.*, 11; 1 *Hop. Ch.*, 471; *Mitford*, 130, *note* 1.

Ewing, and *Smythe & Sprague*, contra, cited *Story Eq. Pl.*, 1*st ed.*, 74; 7 *Cranch*, 69; *Story Eq. Pl.*, 66, 137, 155, 161, 162; *Powel on Mort.*, 815, 816, 824, 825; 1 *Atk.*, 487; 8 *Ohio*, 379; 4 *Porter*, 245; 5 *Ohio*, 204, 248; 6 *Ohio*, 555; *Story Eq. Pl.*, 148, *note*; 2 *Story Eq. Jur.*, 306; *Story Eq. Pl.*, 76, 77; 3 *Mumf.*, 29; 2 *Atk.*, 234; *Story Eq. Pl.*, 87, 168, *note* 2; 1 *Story Eq. Jur.*, 114; *Sug. on Vend.*, 66, 97, 393; 4 *Kent's Com.*, 319; *Sug. on Vend.*, 13, 21; 2 *Bl. Com.*, 154; 1 *Atk.*, 376; 1 *Ver.*, 83; *Sug. on Vend.*, 44, 267, 210, 213, 209, 228, 241, 242, 263, 264; 4 *Kent's Com.*, 333; *Ibid.*, 310, 311; 2 *Hen. & Mumf.*, 95; *Swan's Stat.*, 701; 1 *Cow.*, 711; 6 *Wheat.*, 119; 1 *Hill* (*N. Y.*), 141; *Bank of U. S.* v. *Ritchie et als.*, 7 *Pet.*, 128; 7 *Leigh*, 271; 4 *Hen. & Mumf.*, 476; 1 *Hopk.*, 471; 2 *Ohio*, 381; *Ibid.*, 415, 420, *Am. Ch. Dig.*, 205; 2 *Bligh*, 170; *Chit. Ind.*, 956; 1 *A. K. Marsh.*, 325; 3 *Johns. Ch.*, 595; 4 *Mad.*, 379; 5 *Johns. Ch.*, 449; *Halst. Dig.*, 173; 1 *Paige*, 648; 2 *Dess.*, 629; 3 *Johns. Ch.*, 115; 3 *Litt.*, 339; 10 *Wheat.*, 188; 3 *Stewart*, 243; 1 *Root*, 273, 466, 521; 10 *Yerg.*, 41; 2 *Bibb*, 4, 26; 4 *Ohio*, 321; 3 *Dana*, 179; *Story Eq. Pl.*, 210; 8 *Ves.*, 398, 401; *Story Eq. Pl.*, 206, *sec.* 241; *Story Eq. Pl.*, 24, 28, 206, 210, 218; 2 *Atk.*, 632; 16 *Wend.*, 460; 1 *Ver.*, 312; 10 *Mass.*, 458; 12 *Mass.*, 461; 4 *Day*, 395; 4 *Johns. Ch.*, 521; 1 *Rice Eq.*, 13; *Story Eq. Pl.*, 213, 214, 219, 220; 7 *Wheat.*, 522; 1 *Bland.*, 249, 255; 4 *Call*, 361; 22 *Pick.*, 55; 3 *Ohio*, 62; 6 *Cowen*, 37; 8 *Gill & Johns.*, 171; 2 *A. K. Marsh.*, 317; 10 *Wheat.*, 181; 3 *Ves.*, 343; 6 *Mumf.*, 20; 4 *Dana*, 624; 1 *Root*, 273, 466, 521; 10 *Yerg.*, 41; 3 *Yerg.*, 81; *Story Eq. Pl.*, 389, 378, 379, 390, 485, *note*; 3 *Atk.*, 225; 4 *Ves.*, 479; 19 *Ves.*, 180; 1 *Bibb*, 73; 7 *Paige*, 198, 373; 5 *Johns. Ch.*, 521, 551, 552; 7 *Johns. Ch.*, 283; 4 *Wash. C. C.*, 631; 3 *Brown*, 640; 9 *Peters*, 405, 416; 13 *Peters*, 381; 1 *McL.*, 105, 160; 10 *Peters*, 177; 10 *Ohio*, 24; 10 *Wheat.*, 152; 5 *Johns. Ch.*, 184; 2 *Story Eq. Jur.*, 735, 736, *and notes*; 7 *Yerg.*, 222; 8 *Yerg.*, 238; 1 *Hill* (*N. Y.*), 56; 3 *Ohio*, 276; 5 *Wend.*, 85; 3 *Cowen*, 272; 6 *Cowen*, 297; 11 *Johns.*, 409; 15 *Johns.*, 241; 1 *Johns.*, 580; 4 *Johns.*, 41; 11 *Ohio*, 341; 7 *Wend.*, 94; 9 *Dana*, 139; 10 *Yerg.*, 350; 8 *Porter*, 211; 8 *Paige*, 195; 3 *McCord's Ch.*, 429; 7 *Johns. Ch.*, 111; 3 *Johns. Ch. Cases*, 190; 1 *Bald.*, 394.)

CHALLENGE.

On a trial for murder, where one of the panels summoned by the sheriff, is excused on his own application, it is not error in the Court to refuse to order the sheriff to summon another in his place, before exhausting the panel.

The defendant is entitled to only twenty-three peremptory challenges.

The Attorney appointed by the Court to assist the Prosecuting Attorney need not be sworn, nor give bond.

When a juror states that he is on principle opposed to capital punishment, and that his opinion will influence his decision against the law and the evidence, he may be challenged by the State for cause.—*Martin* v. *The State of Ohio*, 16 *Ohio R.*, *p.* 364. (1848.)

CLAIM—PRESENTMENT OF.

An actual presentment of a claim against the estate of a deceased person, or something equivalent thereto, is necessary to prevent the operation of the statute of non-claim. Knowledge of the existence of the claim, on the part of the executor or administrator, no matter how full and complete, will not dispense with such presentation, and the rule is the same in Chancery as at law.—*Jones' Ex'rs* v. *Lightfoot*, 10 *Alabama R.*, *p.* 17. (1847.)

CLERK OF COURT.

A clerk of a Court is not subject to garnishment for moneys received by him. Such funds are subject to the control of the Court whilst in his hands as an officer of the Court.—*Drane* v. *McGavock*, 7 *Humphreys' R.*, *p.* 132. *Tenn.* (1847.)

COLLECTOR.

A collector of taxes, before he can proceed to sell real estate taxed to persons unknown, must ascertain whether the owner lives out of the State or not; if he lives within the State, then the collector must, before proceeding to sell his land for the payment of taxes, give him two months' previous notice in writing of his liability; or the sale will be unauthorized and viod.—*Brown* v. *Veazie*, 25, *Maine R.*, *p.* 359. (1847.)

COMMITTAL—ESCAPE.

If a creditor at whose suit one is committed to jail, by artifice or fraud induce him to escape, the sheriff is not responsible.

The principle is the same if another who is agent for the creditor for the purpose of commencing a suit in the event of an escape, for the benefit of the creditor, but without his knowledge, procure an escape by fraudulent device practised upon the prisoner, and the creditor seek to avail himself of it by prosecuting an action founded on the escape so procured.

So if the fraud be practised by one acting in concert with such agent.

The prosecuting of the action against the sheriff in such a case is a ratification of the fraudulent acts done under the assumed agency.

Accordingly, where the owner of a judgment rendered for a tort had caused the defendant to be committed to the liberties of the jail on a *ca. sa.*, and then procured a capias against the sheriff to be placed in the hands of an agent with instructions if the prisoner should be off the limits to hand it to a messenger to take to the coroner, and go with him and see it delivered, which was accordingly done, the prisoner at the moment of the delivery to the messenger having stepped beyond the limits in consequence of a fraudulent representation made to him by the person acting as a messenger, and there was evidence tending to show that the creditor's agent and the messenger were acting in concert—*held*, that the jury should have been advised that if the agent was a party to the fraudulent device, the plaintiff could not recover.—*Dexter et al.* v. *Adams*, 2 *Denio's R.*, *p.* 646 *N. Y.* (1847.)

Debt against the defendant, a sheriff of Albany county, for the escape of one John F. Jenkins from the jail limits, tried at the Albany Circuit in April, 1844, before Parker, C. J. Jenkins was committed to jail June 4, 1842, on a *ca. sa.* issued upon a judgment in favor of the plaintiff against him, rendered in the Mayor's Court in an action for a tort. The escape was alleged to have taken place on the 4th day of August, 1842, just before seven o'clock in the morning, and it consisted in the prisoner's stepping across the steamboat Columbia upon the boat Albany, which lay in the Hudson river, the Columbia lying between her and the pier. The eastern boundary of the jail liberties is a line running thirty feet east of the pier. Jenkins returned in a few minutes, but the plaintiff insists that the suit was duly commenced against the sheriff while he was thus absent from the liberties. W. J. Hadley, who at the time of the alleged escape was the assignee and owner of the judgment upon which the *ca. sa.* issued, and who is an attorney at law, about the 1st of August, 1842, issued the *capias* by which this suit was commenced, and delivered it to one Baker, with instructions that if he should see Jenkins off the limits to deliver the writ to a messenger, and instruct him to deliver it to Mr. Allen, the coroner; and the evidence tended to show that he told Baker to go with the messenger and see it so delivered. It appeared that another capias against the sheriff, issued by Hadley, was at the same time in the hands of another agent with similar instructions. The fact of Jenkins having stepped upon the steamboat Albany at the time above-mentioned was then proved, and it was shown that while he was there Baker gave the *capias* to C. Mink, and told him to deliver it to the coroner. They went together, and Mink handed it to the coroner after seven o'clock. On the part of the defendant it was shown that Mink, between six and seven o'clock that morning, sent a message to Jenkins, informing him that Mr. E. C. Delavan, for whom Jenkins was agent at Albany, was on board the steamboat Albany, which was to leave for New-York at seven o'clock, and wished to see him, Jenkins; which message was delivered at the door of Jenkins' house, who in consequence of it went upon the boat as above-mentioned, and found that Delavan was not there. The defendant offered to prove that Mink the next day admitted to the person by whom he sent the message that it was false, and was intended to get Jenkins off the limits, and exulted in the success of his plan. The plaintiff's counsel objecting, the Judge excluded the evidence, and the defendant's counsel excepted. The defendant then proved by other testimony that Mr. Delavan was not in Albany on the 4th of August, but was at his residence in Ballston. After the *capias* was delivered to the coroner, Mink and Baker went to Hadley's, and told him that it had been so delivered. It was also shown on the part of the defendant, that soon after Jenkins was committed, and in June preceding the alleged escape, Mink wrote a note, signing it with another name, asking Jenkins to call that evening at seven o'clock at Mr. G. V. S. Bleecker's, (whose residence was off the limits,) and delivered it at the door of Jenkins' house; and the evidence tended to show that Hadley and Mink, at the hour indicated, were at a store opposite Mr. Bleecker's, watching, but Jenkins did not go there. Hadley, who had parted with his interest, was examined as a witness for the plaintiff, and testified that he had never requested Baker or Mink to make an effort to get Jenkins off the limits. It appeared that Baker and Mink measured the width of the Columbia the evening before the alleged escape, to ascertain how far thirty feet east of the pier would extend. Baker was not called.

The defendant's counsel requested the Judge to charge the jury, among other things, 1st, that the delivery of the *capias* to Mink was not, under the circumstances of the case, a commencement of the suit, inasmuch as Baker accompanied him to the coroner, and being the agent of the plaintiff in interest, had power at any time to recall the capias and prevent its delivery, and that if Jenkins returned to the limits before it was delivered to the coroner, the defendant was entitled to the verdict; 2d, that if Jenkins was by any one fraudulently induced to leave the limits, in order to charge the sheriff with the debt, the plaintiff, by commencing this suit, adopted the fraudulent act, and therefore could not recover; 3d, that if Jenkins was induced to leave the limits by the fraud of the agent of the owner of the judgment, or of any one employed by such agent, although such owner did not authorize or assent to, and was not personally aware of such fraud; yet bringing the suit was in law an adoption of the fraudulent contrivance, and prevented the plaintiff from recovering; and, 4th, that if Baker had knowledge of the fraud, it was the same thing as though Hadley, for whom he was agent, knew it. The Judge charged the jury, that it was for them to say whether Baker retained any control over the *capias*, after delivering it to Mink; and if he did, the suit was not commenced until it was delivered to the coroner; and he declined to charge affirmatively as to either of the foregoing propositions. The defendant's counsel excepted to the instruction given, and to the refusal to charge as requested. The jury found a verdict for the plaintiff. The defendant moves for a new trial on a bill of exceptions.

Hill & Stevens for the defendant.—1. Jenkins was induced to go off the limits by a gross fraud, which the plaintiff, by bringing this action, has adopted. He cannot, therefore recover.—*Sweet* v. *Palmer*, 16 *Johns.*, 181; *Van Wormer* v. *Van Voast*, 10 *Wend.*, 356, 2. The plaintiff is chargeable with knowledge of the fraudulent device by which the escape was brought about. The knowledge of the agent is the knowledge of the principal.—*Bank of the U. S.* v. *Davis*, 2 *Hill*, 451. Where one adopts a part of what his agent has done, he is held to have adopted the whole.—*Paley on Agency*, 172; *Corning* v. *Southland*, 3 *Hill*, 552; *Moss* v. *The Rossie Lead Mining Co.*, 5 *Hill*, 137; *Sandford* v. *Handy*, 23 *Wend.*, 268; *Story on Agency*, 245, *sec.* 250; *Id. sec.* 452. Where one commits a trespass for the benefit of another, and that other accepts the goods taken by the trespass, he is a trespasser by adoption.—*Broom's Legal Maxims*, 383–4. 3. The suit was not commenced until the delivery of the *capias* to the coroner. When the *capias* is delivered to a messenger, to take to the officer, the intention to have it delivered must be absolute.—*Visscher* v. *Gansevoort*, 18 *John.*, 496; *Ross* v. *Luther*, 4 *Cowen*, 158.

Wheaton & Peckham for the plaintiff.—If the escape is without the assent of the party at whose suit the prisoner is committed, the sheriff is liable.—2 *R. S.*, 437, *sec.* 63. The only excuse which will avail the sheriff is the act of God, or the public enemy.—*Alsept* v. *Eyles*, 2 *H. Black.*, 108; *Cargill* v. *Taylor*, 10 *Mass.*, 206. Mink, who was a stranger to the controversy, alone practised the deception. This does not affect the plaintiff. Even the assent of the plaintiff's attorney to an escape will not protect the sheriff.—*Kellogg* v. *Gilbert*, 10 *John.*, 220; *Jackson* v. *Bartlett*, 8 *John.*, 361; *Crary* v. *Turner*, 6 *John.*, 51.

By the Court, Beardsley, J.—Passing by all other questions which arise in this case, I think it should have been put to the jury to determine whether Jenkins had been induced, by trick and fraud on the part of Baker alone, or in conjunction with Mink, to leave the limits: the trick and fraud having been resorted to for the benefit of Hadley, who owned the judgment, and with instruction to the jury, that if such were found to be the facts, the plaintiff could not recover. In substance the Judge was requested so to charge the jury, and it seems to me he erred in withholding the instruction. Although there was no direct evidence on the point, there were facts and circumstances upon which the jury might well have come to that conclusion.

Baker was the agent of Hadley to commence an action against the sheriff, if Jenkins should be seen off the limits. This was the character of his agency, and the extent of his power. But the evidence contained in the bill of exceptions, affords strong ground to believe that he did much more than his agency required or authorized, and that he and

Mink were acting in hearty concert in the base fraud by which Jenkins was decoyed beyond the limits. Whatever Baker and Mink did, was plainly enough designed to benefit Hadley. No other motive is suggested, and the object palpably was to create a cause of action against the sheriff by which Hadley might collect his debt. If Jenkins was thus entrapped into an act which, under other circumstances, might constitute a ground of action against the sheriff, such ought not to be its effects as to Hadley, if the fraud had been perpetrated for his benefit. If he sets up as constituting a ground of action in his favor, a departure from the limits which had been fraudulently induced and procured for his benefit, he must submit to all the legal consequences which follow from this his own voluntary act. And he cannot be allowed to separate the fact of passing beyond the limits from the cause which induced it, and rely upon the escape as an efficient ground of action in his behalf, while at the same time he repudiates the fraud by which the escape was procured. He must repudiate both or neither; he cannot reject one while he virtually affirms the other. If the escape was brought about by those who were acting to aid him and for his supposed benefit, and he now seeks to gain an advantage by this result of their efforts in his behalf, he necessarily thereby becomes a party to what they had done. As to others, this escape might give a good right of action against the sheriff; but not so as to him for whom the fraud was committed. I am not aware of any exception to the principle, that one who endeavors to turn to his own advantage, what others had assumed to do for his benefit, although without authority, is, as to such act, deemed to stand in their place; and if what the assumed agents had done, was fraudulent as to themselves, it is equally so as to him who thus adopts and assumes it. It is too plain to admit of question, that if Hadley, by artifice and trick, had induced Jenkins to quit the limits, the sheriff would not be responsible for the escape; and in principle the case is the same, where Hadley seeks to avail himself of the result of artifices and tricks which others had resorted to for his benefit. If in this case, then, there was evidence on which the jury should have found that the escape was caused by the fraud of Baker and Mink, while acting with a view to aid Hadley, the prosecution of this suit is an unqualified and absolute ratification of their fraudulent acts; and as to Hadley, here was in law no escape from the limits for which he can have redress. In effect he procured it, and therefore the action will not lie. There should be a new trial.

New trial granted.

COMPENSATION.

When the rate of compensation for attorneys and counsellors is changed by the Legislature during the progress of a suit, the costs of such suit are to be taxed according to the statute in force at its termination.—*The Supervisors of Onondaga* v. *Briggs*, 3 *Denio's R.*, *p.* 173. *N. Y.* (1848.)

CONCEALMENT.

In an action upon a policy of insurance, if it shall appear that any matter in reference to a description of the property, and which would increase the risk, is not made known by the insured, such concealment will avoid the policy. It is otherwise if the matter concealed, could in no way increase the risk.—*The Lexington Insurance Co.* v. *Paver*, 16 *Ohio R.*, *p.* 324. (1848.)

(*Fox & Lincoln*, and *Riddle*, cited 2 *Greenl. Ev.*, 328; 1 *Phil. Ins.*, 249—50; 4 *East*, 590; 7 *Ohio*, 284; 2 *Phil. Ins.*, 5, 40; 8 *Pick.*, 14; 11 *Pick.*, 227; 3 *Mass.*, 331; 8 *Mass.*, 322; 15 *East*, 208; 8 *Conn.*, 459; 1 *Phil. Ins.*, 214, 249—50, 309, 310, 316, 317, 632, 642.

Taft, Key & Mallon, contra, cited, 2 *Stev. N. P.*, 1798—1807; 3 *Ch. Gen. Prac.*, 872—875; 2 *Phil. Ev.*, *by C. & H.*, *notes*, 479; 1 *Greenl. Ev.*, sec. 74—6; 1 *Stark. Ev.*, 6*th Am. ed.*, 539; *Mercer* v. *Whall*, 48 *Eng. C. L.*, 464; *Heckman* v. *Ferrie*, 3 *Mees. & Wels.*, 517; *Barrell* v. *Wickham*, 25 *Eng. C. L.*, 354; *Smart* v. *Engal*, 14 *Mees. & Wells.*, 97; *Pearson* v. *Coles*, 1 *Mood. & Rob.*, 206; *Weidman* v. *Khor*, 13 *Serg. & Rawle*, 24.)

CONSIDERATION.

Where a deed purports to be executed for a *valuable* consideration, and is impeached by proving that no such consideration passed, it cannot be sustained by proving that it was executed in consideration of *natural love and affection.*—*Burrage's Lessee* v. *Beardsley*, 16 *Ohio R.*, *p.* 438. (1848.)

(*Hitchcock & Wilder* cited *Steele et al.* v. *Worthington*, 2 *Ohio*, 182; *Clarkson* v. *Harney*, 2 *P. Wms.*, 103; *Watts* v. *Grove*, 2 *Sch. & Lef.*, 500; 1 *Phil. Ev. by Cowen & Hill*, 549, 552; *Roberts* v. *Roberts*, 2 *Barn. & Ald.*, 368; 3 *Phil. Ev.*, 1451, *note*; *Betts* v. *Union Bank of Maryland*, 1 *Har. & Gil.*, 175; *Bullard* v. *Briggs*, 7 *Pick.*, 537; *Harvey* v. *Alexander*, 1 *Rand.*, 219; *Wilt* v. *Franklin*, 1 *Binn.*, 518.

Wade & Wood, contra, cited *Saxton* v. *Wheaton*, 8 *Wheat.*, 229; *Hinde's Lessee* v. *Longworth*, 11 *Wheat.*, 199; *Brice* v. *Myers et al.*, 5 *Ohio*, 121; *Seward* v. *Jackson*, 8 *Cowen*, 496; *Van Wick* v. *Seward*, 6 *Paige*, 526; *Bank of U. S.* v. *Houseman*, 6 *Paige*, 535; 1 *Con. R.*, 525; *Lush* v. *Wilkinson*, 5 *Ves.*, 384; *Gale* v. *Williamson*, 8 *Mees. & Wels.*, 404; 12 *Ves.* 236; *Russell* v. *Hammond*, 1 *Atk.*, 15; *Walker* v. *Barrows*, 1 *Atk.*, 93; *Townshend* v. *Windham*, 2 *Ves. Sr.*, 1; *Henderson* v. *Dodd*, 1 *Bailey*, 138; *Jackson* v. *Town*, 4 *Cowen*, 603; *Wilkes* v. *Clark*, 8 *Paige*, 161; 5 *Peters*, 264; 18 *Pick.*, 131; 14 *Mass.*, 139. 12 *Johns.*, 526; 1 *Story's Eq. Jur.*, 426–30.)

CONSTABLE.

The bonds of constables, who are reappointed from year to year, are not cumulative; and therefore sureties of a constable are only responsible for breaches committed during the official year for which they became his sureties, though at the expiration of the year, he may have been reappointed.—*Miller* v. *Davis*, 7 *Iredell's R.*, *p.* 198. *N. C.* (1847.)

(NASH, J., cited *Keck* v. *Coble*, 2 *Dev.* 491; *Governor to the use of Leisner* v. *Lee et als.*, 4 *Dev. & Bat.*, 467; *Goforth* v. *Lackey et als.*, 3 *Iredell*, 25.)

A constable, appointed by a justice of the peace to levy an execution on the goods of A, levied the same on the goods of B. A trial of the right of property was claimed by B, who gave bond, &c. But the constable refused to deliver the goods to B. *Held*, that for this misconduct of the constable, the justice was liable to B in an action on the case.

The jury in such case may, though the constable tender the property to the plantiff before suit brought, give the value of the property as the amount of the damages.—*Dugan* v. *Melogue*, 7 *Blackford's R.*, *p.* 144. *Ind.* (1847.)

APPEAL from the Hendricks Circuit Court.

SULLIVAN, J.—Case by Melogue against Dugan. The declaration contains three counts. The cause of action is substantially as follows: Dugan, who was an acting justice of the peace, rendered a judgment in favor of one Burnet, against Henry Burger, and there being no constable in the township, appointed Pemberton S. Dicken a special constable, to whom he directed an execution commanding him to levy the amount of the above-named judgment of the goods and chattels of Burger. The appointment was made under the 55th section of the justices' act. Dicken levied the execution on a buggy and harness, amongst other things, the property of Melogue. The latter claimed the buggy and harness, and demanded a trial of the right of property according to the statute. At the time of filing his claim to the property, he also filed a bond with security, which was approved by the justice, conditioned that his claim should be well and truly prosecuted to effect, or in default thereof that the property should be delivered to the person entitled to receive it. The justice of the peace, with whom the bond was filed, immediately informed the constable of it, and Melogue demanded the property, but the constable refused to deliver it. Plea not guilty; verdict and judgment for the plaintiff.

This suit is founded on the 55th section of the act regulating the duties and jurisdiction of justices of the peace, R. S., 1838, p. 376, which provides that in all cases where it shall be necessary to have process served, and there shall be no constable in the township legally authorized to act in such case, it shall be lawful for any justice of such township to appoint a person willing to serve as constable until one shall be legally appointed, &c., and the justice shall stand as security, and be also civilly liable for any neglect of duty, or any illegal proceedings, on the part of the constable so by him appointed.

Various exceptions were taken to the judgment of the Court in receiving and rejecting testimony, and to instructions given to the jury and refused to be given, but we discover no error in either for which the judgment ought to be reversed.

The points relied on for the reversal of the judgment by the counsel for the appellant are, that the action is misconceived, and that the damages are excessive.

It is not denied but that the constable was guilty of a trespass in seizing the property of Melogue, instead of the property of Burger, the execution defendant. For that act the constable might be sued as a trespasser, and his refusal to deliver the property to Melogue on demand, was a continuation of the trespass. But Dugan was not present aiding and assisting in the wrongful acts of the constable, nor were they done by his command. He, therefore, cannot be made liable for those acts, in an action of trespass. Even in the case of master and servant, the master is not considered as a trespasser for an act of his servant which was not done at his command. He may, however, in numerous cases, be made liable for the damage arising from the employment of negligent or unskilful servants, in an action on the case. We think there is no objection to the form of action adopted in this case. The statute, whatever may be the object intended to be gained by it, makes the justice responsible for any illegal proceeding on the part of the officer appointed by him. The appointment is his act, the breach of duty by the constable is the act of the latter, and for any damage sustained in consequence of such appointment, we think an action on the case is the appropriate remedy.—*McManus* v. *Bricket*, 1 *East*, 106; *Burnet* v. *Lynch*, 5 *B. & C.*, 589; *Morley* v. *Gaisford*, 2 *H. Bl.*, 442.

As to the second point, we think the jury were justifiable in giving the value of the property as the amount of the damages. The plaintiff in error contends, that as the constable tendered the property to Melogue before suit brought, the damages should have been only for the temporary deprivation of it. There are cases in which the Court will stay proceedings upon the restoration of the property, and payment to the plaintiff of such damages as he may have sustained by the temporary loss and deterioration of the property, and his costs. Admitting this to be such a case, and the property to be such as a Court would order the restoration of, no application was made to the Court for that purpose. The defendant should have followed up the tender made by Dicken with such an application, and an offer to pay to the plaintiff the damages he had sustained and the costs he had incurred.—*Shotwell* v. *Wendover*, 1 *Johns.*, 65; 2 *Selw. N. P.*, 1417; *Pickering* v. *Truste*, 7 *T. R.*, 49.

PER CURIAM.—*The judgment is affirmed, with five per cent. damages and costs.*

CONTRACT.

Where several persons agreed to do certain acts, such as to pay equal proportions of particular expenditures, if one advance more money than his proportion of those expenses, the excess will be regarded as so much money paid for the use of the other parties, and he will be entitled to interest thereon.—*Buckmaster* v. *Grundy et al.*, 3 *Gilman's R.*, *p.* 626. *Ills.* (1847.)

The plaintiff and defendant made an agreement in writing, that the plaintiff should convey to the defendant a certain farm, and that in consideration thereof the latter should pay the former the sum of four thousand dollars. The parties also agreed that each should pay to the other, should he neglect to perform his part of the contract, upon performance or tender of performance by the other, the sum of one thousand dollars. —*Held*, that this sum was liquidated damages, and that the plaintiff was entitled to recover it, with interest, of the defendant, upon a neglect by him to perform his part of the contract.—*Mead* v. *Wheeler*, 13 *New Hampshire R.*, *p.* 351. (1847.)

(*Handerson* cited *Stearns* v. *Barrett*, 1 *Pick.*, 451; *Curtis* v. *Brewer*, 17 *Pick.*, 513; *Heard* v. *Bowers*, 23 *Pick*, 455; *Slosson* v. *Beadle*, 7 *Johns.*, 72; *Knapp* v. *Maltby*, 13 *Wend.*, 587; *Dakin* v. *Williams*, 17 *Wend.*, 454; 2 *Story's Eq.*, 550; 5 *Cow.*, 151, *note*; *Astley* v. *Welden*, 2 *B. & P.*, 353; *Kemble* v. *Farren*, 6 *Bing.*, 141; *Crisdee* v. *Bolton*, 3 *C. & P.*, 240; 2 *Com. on Cont.*, 525.)

When a workman undertakes to do work, to be paid for in the notes of third persons, he cannot abandon the contract, and treat it as a money demand, unless the contract has been rescinded, or he has been prevented by the act of the opposite party, from performing it according to its terms. —*Aikin* v. *Bloodgood*, 12 *Alabama R.*, *p.* 221. (1848.)

(Ormond, J. cited *McVoy* v. *Wheeler*, 6 *Porter*, 201; *Livingdale* v. *Livingston*, 10 *Johns.*, 36.)

If one person bargains with another for the release and conveyance of a title, equally known to both to be a doubtful one, and takes such conveyance and gives his note for the price; he does not show a failure or want of consideration, by proof that the grantor had no valid title.—*Sawyer* v. *Vaughan*, 25 *Maine R.*, *p.* 337. (1847.)

CONTRACT—NOTE.

If a joint note be made by four, payable on time, and before it was payable two of the promissors pay "two-thids of the within note, principal and interest, being their part," and it is thus endorsed thereon, they are not thereby discharged from the payment of the sum still remaining unpaid.—*Coburn et al.* v. *Ware*, 25 *Maine R.*, p. 330. (1847.)

(*Hutchinson* cited *Tuckerman* v. *Newhall*, 17 *Mass.*, 581; *Houston* v. *Darling*, 16 *Maine*, 413; *Walker* v. *McCullock*, 4 *Greenl.*, 421.

(*Wells* and *Kidder*, contra-cited *Goodman* v. *Smith*, 18 *Pick.*, 414; *Shaw* v. *Pratt*, 22 *Pick.*, 305; *Berks* v. *White*, 2 *Metc.*, 283; *Walker* v. *McCullock*, 4 *Greenl.*, 421.)

CONTRIBUTION.

One of several co-sureties who pays the debt may call upon the other sureties for contribution, whether they were bound jointly or severally, and whether by the same or by different instruments.

And although they became sureties for the same debt at different times.

And a co-surety is liable, although the one who paid the debt, and who sues for contribution, did not know at the time he became such that the defendant was also a surety.

And where one wishing to borrow money made and signed a joint and several promissory note, which he procured to be signed by the plaintiffs, and afterwards—to satisfy the lender, but without the knowledge of the plaintiffs—by the defendant, and then obtained the money on the note, which the plaintiffs at its maturity were compelled to pay: *Held*, that the plaintiffs could maintain an action against the defendant for contribution; and that the defendant was holden, notwithstanding he signed under a representation by the principal that the plaintiffs would be primarily liable.

A second surety may qualify his obligation in such a manner as not to be liable to the first; but then if he has the debt to pay he cannot call upon the others.

Where there is a legal right to demand money, and no other remedy than an action *ex-contractu*, the law, for the purpose of the remedy, will imply a promise of payment.—*Norton* v. *Coons*, 3 *Denio's R.*, p. 130. *N. Y.* (1848.)

(Bronson, C. J., cited *Deering* v. *The Earl of Winchelsea*, 2 *B. & P.*, 270; 1 *Cox*, 318, *S. C.*; *Campbell* v. *Mesier*, 4 *Johns. Ch.*, 334; *Davies* v. *Humphreys*, 6 *Mees.*, *& Wels.*, 167; *Mayhew* v. *Cricket*, 2 *Swanst.*, 193; *Warner* v. *Price*, 3 *Wend.*, 397; *Lapham* v. *Barnes*, 2 *Vt.*, 213; *Harris* v. *Warner*, 13 *Wend.*, 400; *Craythorne* v. *Swinburne*, 14 *Ves.*, 160; *Story on Cont. sec.*, 584; *Pitman's Pr. & Sur.*, 147; 1 *East*, 220; 17 *Mass.*, 464; 2 *B. & P.*, 268.)

CONVERSION.

Where there is evidence of a conversion, by selling the property in controversy, proof of a demand and a refusal is unnecessary, and the rule is the same, although in the first instance the property came lawfully to the defendant.—*Kyle* v. *Gray*, 11 *Alabama R.*, *p.* 233. (1847.)

(*Huntington* and *Martin* cited *Tompkins* v. *Hart*, 3 *Wend.*, 406; *Earle* v. *Van Buren*, 2 *Halst.*, 344; *Newsum* v. *Newsum*, 1 *Leigh*, 76; *Jewet* v. *Partridge*, 3 *Farf.*, 243.)

CONVICTION.

A conviction before a justice of the peace is well sustained by a record which shows that the defendant, on being asked whether he was guilty or not of the offence alleged against him, fraudulently and wilfully stood mute, and that, after a due examination of witnesses and a full hearing of the case, he was adjudged to be guilty, and was sentenced to imprisonment.—*Ellenwood* v. *The Commonwealth*, 10 *Metcalf's R.*, *p.* 222. *Mass.* (1847.)

CORONER.

The coroner has no power to levy upon an execution directed to the sheriff, and if he does so, as he is a trespasser, he may return the goods so levied on, to the person from whose possession he took them.—*Gresham* v. *Leverett*, 10 *Alabama R.*, *p.* 384. (1847.)

(Ormond, J., cited *Pope & Hickman* v. *Stout*, 1 *Stew.*, 375; *Clay's Dig.*, 336; *sec.* 139; *Adamson* v. *Parker*, 3 *Ala.*, 727; *Mason* v. *White*, 7 *Ala.*, 705.)

CORPORATION.

The tangible property and estate of a corporation, are subject to sale under execution in the same manner that those of an individual are; where, therefore, by the charter of an incorporated railroad and banking company, the corporation was authorized to purchase the lands necessary for the site of the road and the requisite depots, stations and buildings, and to possess and hold the same in fee simple, it was *Held*, that the real estate of the corporation, so purchased for the site of the road and other purposes specified, was subject to sale under execution, and might be assigned by the corporation.—*Arthur* v. *The Commercial and Rail-*

road Bank of Vicksburgh, 9 *Smedes Marshall's R.*, p. 394. *Miss.* (1848.)

(Clayton, J., cited *Hopkins et al.* v. *Gallatin Ins. Co.*, 4 *Humph.*, 403; *Beckwith* v. *Windsor Manuf. Co.*, 14 *Conn.*, 594; *Union Bank of Tennessee* v. *Ellicott*, 6 *Gill & Johns.*, 363; *Nevitt* v. *Bank of Port Gibson*, 6 *Smedes & Marshall*, 513.)

A corporation, like a natural person, may have a special or constructive residence, so as to be charged with taxes and duties, or be subject to a special jurisdiction, but the legal residence of a corporation is not confined to the locality of its principal office of business; it extends to the territorial limits of the jurisdiction which granted its charter, which, for judicial purposes, defines its locality.—*Glaize* v. *The South Carolina Railroad Co.*, 1 *Strobhart's R.*, p. 70. *S. C.* (1847.)

Where the common council of a city passed a resolution directing a sum which had been reported by arbitrators to be due to a contractor for extra work in grading and paving a street, to be added to the assessment for grading and paving that street; *Held*, that such resolution was a substantial acknowledgment, on the part of the corporation, of the extent of the debt, and a promise to pay it. And that after such resolution had been assented to by the contractor, the claim became valid against the corporation to the extent specified therein; and that such resolution could not afterwards be rescinded except by the mutual agreement of the parties.—*Brady* v. *The Mayor &c. of Brooklyn*, 1 *Barbour's R.*, p. 584. *N. Y.* (1848.)

No express authority in the charter of a corporation is necessary to authorize it to make a promissory note, in the course of their legitimate business.—*Brode* v. *The Firemen's Ins. Co. of New Orleans.* 8 *Robinson's La. R.*, p. 244. (1847.)

CORPORATION—DAMAGES.

A municipal corporation is liable for injuries occasioned by the negligence, unskilfulness, or malfeasance, of its agents or contractors, engaged in the construction of its public works.

Accordingly the City of New York was held liable for damages by the breaking down of a vault, built by permission, under the street; the injury being occasioned by the negligent and improper act of a contractor, who was building a sewer in the street under a contract with the corporate authorities, in unduly piling the excavated earth, &c., over such vault.—*Delmonico* v. *The Mayor &c. of the City of New York*, 1 *Sandford's R.*, p. 222. *N. Y.* (1849.)

(*Cutting* cited *Burgess* v. *Gray*, 1 *M. Gr. & Scott*, 578; *Traver* v. *Chadwick*, 3 *Bing. N. C.*, 334; *Payton* v. *Mayor of London*, 9 *B.*

& C., 725; *Bridge* v. *Grand Junction Railway Co.*, 3 *M. & W.*, 246; *Goodloe* v. *City of Cincinnati*, 4 *Hamm.*, 500; *Smith* v. *Same Defendants*, 4 *Hamm.*, 514; *Rhodes* v. *City of Cleveland*, 10 *Ohio*, 160; *Bailey* v. *The City of New-York*, 3 *Hill*, 536; *Furze* v. *The Same*, 3 *Hill*, 612.)

CORPORATION—RECEIVER.

A receiver of an insolvent corporation, who is empowered by law to sue for and recover "all the estate, debts, and *things in action*," belonging to the corporation, may maintain *trover* for the conversion of the personal property of the corporation before the plaintiff was appointed receiver.

No assignment by the corporation to the receiver is necessary to enable him to maintain the action.—*Gilbert* v. *Fairchild*, 4 *Denio's R.*, *p.* 80. *N. Y.* (1849.)

COSTS.

Sentence to pay costs of prosecution may be passed, though there be a general pardon after the verdict.—*Playford* v. *The Commonwealth*, 4 *Barr's R.*, *p.* 144. *Pa.* (1847.)

COURTS—JURISDICTION OF.

A judgment rendered by a Court in one State, has no efficacy when it is sought to be enforced in another State, unless such Court had jurisdiction of the person against whom it is rendered, acquired by service of process on him, or actual notice to him, or by his appearance and submission to such jurisdiction.

Neither by the general principles of law, nor under the Constitution of the United States, is greater effect to be given to a judgment rendered in one State, when sought to be enforced in another State, than it would have in the State in which it was rendered.

By the laws of the State of New-York, the judgment rendered in an action on joint contract, where the process is against all the defendants, and is served on either of them, though in form it is against all, yet it is conclusive of the liability of those only who were personally served with process in the suit; as against every other defendant, it is evidence only of the extent of the plaintiff's demand after the liability of such defendant has been established by other evidence, and creates no debt of record or liability, on which an action of debt can be sustained in another State.

Nor is such judgment, as to a defendant not served with process, a merger of the original cause of action.

The forms of remedies and judicial proceedings are governed, exclusively, by the laws of the place where the action is instituted.—*Wood et als.* v. *Watkinson et als.*, 17 *Connecticut R.*, *p.* 500. (1847.)

This was an action of debt on judgment, in the usual form, brought by Wood, Johnson & Burritt, against Henry Wells, Peter Vandervoort and Edwin B. Watkinson, partners, under the firm of Wells, Vandervoort & Co. The plea by agreement, was *Nil debet.*

The cause was tried, at Hartford, January term, 1846, before Storrs, J., when the following facts were proved and admitted.

The judgment on which the action was brought, was rendered by the Superior Court of the City of New-York, at the term of that Court held in May, 1839, in a suit brought by Wood, Johnson & Burritt, the present plaintiffs, against the present defendants, upon five promissory notes, dated at different times in the years 1836 and 1837, made by Wells, Vandervoort & Co., in the city of New-York, in the regular course and within the scope of their partnership business, while all the plaintiffs and defendants were there domiciled. That suit was an action of *assumpsit*, the declaration being in the usual form, upon promissory notes, with the money counts. Vandervoort alone was served with process; the return stating, that Wells and Watkinson could not be found to be served therewith. Vandervoort appeared; but Wells and Watkinson did not. Judgment was rendered against all the defendants, for $14,643, (the amount of the notes,) and costs of suit. From the time that suit was instituted, until said judgment was rendered, Wells and Vandervoort resided in the City of New-York. In the month of April, 1837, before the commencement of that suit, Watkinson removed from the City of New-York into the county of Hartford in this State, (Connecticut,) where he has ever since resided and been domiciled. No dissolution of the copartnership of Wells, Vandervoort & Co. took place until the autumn of 1838, some time after the commencement of the suit in New-York.

The Superior Court of the City of New-York had, by the laws of the State of New-York, jurisdiction of the subject matter of said suit. The Legislature of the State of New-York, in the year 1830, passed a statute, which has ever since been in force, containing the following provisions: Sect. 1. In actions against two or more persons jointly indebted, upon any joint obligation, contract or liability, if the process is issued against all the defendants, and shall have been duly served upon either of them, the defendant so served shall answer to the plaintiff; and in such case, the judgment, if rendered in favor of plaintiff, shall be against all the defendants, in the same manner as if all had been served with process.

Sect. 2. Such judgment shall be conclusive evidence of the liability of the defendant who was personally served with process in the suit, and who appeared therein; but against every other defendant, it shall be evidence only of the extent of the plaintiff's demand, after the liability of such defendant shall have been established by other evidence. 2 *Rev. Stat. N. Y.*, 377.

By virtue of the statute and the laws of the State of New-York, the judgment so recovered before the Superior Court of the City of New-York, was a merger of the original cause of action, as to all the defendants, and conclusive, to all intents, upon such of the defendants as were served with notice of the suit, and also upon the other defendants, not actually served with such notice, except so far forth as the burden of proving the existence of the original cause of action; and the amount of the plaintiff's claim against the defendants rested upon the plaintiffs, in respect to such of the defendants as were not actually served with notice of the former suit, and did not appear therein.

By agreement of parties, the case was reserved for the advice of this Court as to what judgment should be rendered.

Hungerford & Cone for the plaintiffs contended—

1. That the Court in New-York had such jurisdiction as to render the judgment binding upon all the defendants, although they were not all personally served with notice, independently of the Constitution of the United States and the Act of Congress.—*Buchanan* v. *Rucker*, 9 *East*, 192; *Cavan* v. *Stuart*, 1 *Stark Ca.*, 525; *Douglas* v. *Forrest*, 4 *Bing.*, 670; 15 *Eng. C. L.*, 113; *Becquet* v. *McCarthy*, 2 *B. & Adol.*, 951; 22 *Eng. C. L.*, 220; *Green* v. *Sarmiento*, 1 *Pet. C. C. R.*, 74; *McRae* v. *Mattoon*, 13 *Pick.*, 53; *Phil. Ev. by Cow. & Hill*, 910 *et. seq.*

2. That the contract upon which the original judgment was founded, having been made by the defendants, while resident in New-York, and there to be carried into effect, any discharge or extinguishment of that contract in pursuance of the laws of that State, existing at the time it was made, will be effectual every where.—*Story's Conf.* 8, *sec*, 335, 6; 340, 1, 2, 3; 267; *Sherrills* v. *Hopkins*, 1 *Cowen*, 103, 108; *Towne* v. *Smith*, 9 *Law Rep.*, *No.* 1, (*May* 1846,) *p.* 12.

3. That by the laws of the State of New-York, the judgment in the original suit is a merger of the cause of action upon which that judgment was rendered, and an action of debt will lie on the judgment.—*Dando* v. *Doll*, 2 *J. R.*, 87; *Bank of Columbia* v. *Newcomb*, 6 *J. R.*, 98; *Taylor* v. *Pettibone*, 16 *J. R.*, 66; *Townsend* v. *Carman*, 6 *Cowen*, 695; *S. C.*, *in Err.*, 6 *Wend.*, 206; *Mervin* v. *Kumbull*, 23 *Wend.*, 293.

4. That by the 1st section of the 4th article of the Constitution of the United States, and the Act of Congress, passed in pursuance thereof, the judgment is to have the same effect in this State as in the State of New-York.

Bulkley and *Perkins*, for the defendant, insisted—

1. That no action will lie upon a judgment obtained in another State, on the face of which it appears, that the defendant was not a resident within the jurisdiction of such Court, and was neither served with process nor came to defend the action, although such judgment may have been obtained according to the course and practice of the Court in similar cases. To give validity to the judgment of any Court, it is necessary that it should have jurisdiction of the person, the subject matter and the pro-

cons.—1 *Sw. Dig.*, 754; *Kibbe* v. *Kibbe*, *Kirb.*, 126; *Aldrich* v. *Kinney*, 4 *Conn.*, 380; *Bartlett* v. *Knight*, 1 *Mass.*, 401; *Bissell* v. *Briggs*, 9 *Mass.*, 464; *Hall* v. *Williams*, 6 *Pick.*, 239; *Gleason* v. *Dodd*, 4 *Metc.*, 333; *Borden* v. *Fitch*, 15 *Johns.*, 121; *Harrod* v. *Barretto*, 1 *Hall*, 155.

2. That a suit upon the judgment rendered in New-York, could not be maintained against the present defendant, even in that State. Such a judgment is only evidence of the extent of the plaintiff's demand, after the liability of the defendant shall be established by other evidence.—2 *Rev. Stat. N. Y.*, 377.

3. That an action of debt on such judgment cannot be maintained against him in this State. An action would not lie on a judgment obtained in our own Courts, against one of our own citizens, who had had no notice of the suit: *a fortiori* it will not lie on a judgment so obtained in another State.

Storrs, J.—This is an action of debt on a judgment recovered in the Superior Court of the City of New-York, in the State of New-York, in favor of the plaintiffs, against Wells, Vandervoort & Watkinson, all of whom are named as defendants in the suit, but in which service of the writ has been made only upon Watkinson, who alone appears to defend.

It appears by the record, introduced by the plaintiffs, of the judgment on which they rely, and it is admitted, that service of the process in the suit in which it was rendered, was made on Vandervoort, but not on either Wells or Watkinson; and that neither of the two latter had any notice of, or appeared in, that suit; and it is also admitted, that at the time of the commencement of the suit, and ever since, Watkinson has resided in the State of Connecticut. On these facts it is very clear, that independent of the construction and effect which is to be given to the statute of New-York, which is made a part of this case, and to the proceedings of said Court under that statute in the suit in which that judgment was rendered, Watkinson is not to be held here to be personally bound or affected by that judgment; since the general principle is now well established, that a judgment rendered by a Court in one State has no effiacy when it is sought to be enforced in another State, unless such Court had jurisdiction of the person against whom it is rendered, acquired either by service upon him of the process in the suit, or actual notice to him of the suit, or at least by his having appeared in it, and thus submitting to the jurisdiction of the Court; and it is also settled, that it is competent for him to prove a want of jurisdiction in that respect. Whether the latter rule, by a just construction of the first section of the fourth article of the Constitution of the United States, and the laws passed by Congress in pursuance thereof, extends to the case of a judgment rendered in a Court of one of the States of this Union, and attempted to be enforced in a sister State, where the record of the judgment shows the existence of such facts as are requisite in order to confer jurisdiction, so that the defendant would be permitted to contradict that record, by disproving those facts, is a point perhaps not yet fully determined, and which we need not consider, because, as has been remarked, the record of the judgment here produced itself shows, that there was neither any service upon Watkinson of the process in the suit in which it was rendered, nor any notice to him of that suit, nor any appearance by him therein.—*Aldrich* v. *Kinney*, 4 *Conn.*, 380; *Denison* v. *Hyde*, 6 *Conn.*, 508; *Bartlett* v. *Knight*, 1 *Mass.*, 401; *Bissell* v. *Briggs*, 9 *Mass.*, 464; *Hall* v. *Williams*, 6 *Pick.*, 239; *Borden* v. *Fitch*, 15 *Johns.*, 121; *Starbuck* v. *Murray*, 5 *Wend.*, 148; *Phil. Ev. by Cowen & Hill, note* 551, 637, *and cases cited.*

The statute of the State of New-York, which has been mentioned, provides, in the first section, that "in actions against two or more persons jointly indebted upon any joint obligation, contract, or liability, if the process is issued against all the defendants, and shall have been duly served upon either of them, the defendant so served shall answer to the plaintiff;" and that "in such cases, the judgment so rendered in favor of the plaintiff shall be against all the defendants, in the same manner as if all had been served with process;" and in the second section, that "such judgment shall be conclusive evidence of the liability of the defendants, who were personally served with process in the suit, and who appeared therein; but that against every other defendant it shall be evidence only of the extent of the plaintiff's demand, after the liability of such defendant shall have been established by other evidence." It is admitted, that the judgment on which the present action is brought, was recovered on certain promissory notes, executed and delivered to the plaintiffs in the City of New-York, while the said statute was in force, by Wells, Vandervoort & Watkinson, who were then partners, and all of whom, together with the plaintiffs, then resided in that city; and that said notes were given in the regular course and scope of their co-partnership business. Under these circumstances, the plaintiffs claim that on general principles of public law, independent of the Constitution of the United States, and the laws of Congress in pursuance thereof, those of the defendants in the suit in which the judgment in question was rendered, upon whom the process in that suit was not served, and who had no notice of the suit, are personally bound by that judgment. This claim is urged, upon the ground that a sovereign State or Nation possesses a jurisdiction, which it may exercise, through the medium of its Courts, over its citizens, or persons residing within its limits, *in personam*, after they have become domiciled elsewhere, in respect to a transaction to which they were parties, taking place in that State under its existing laws, and while they were there domiciled. The construction which we put on the statute of New-York, and the proceedings there under it, upon which the plaintiffs rely, precludes the necessity of our determining the interesting and somewhat novel question which this claim presents.

Taking it for granted, that when a judgment recovered in the Court of a sovereign State, or of one of the States of this Union, is sought to be enforced in another State than that in which it was rendered, there is no objection to its validity, on the ground of a want of jurisdiction in that Court, it is well settled, that no greater effect is to be given to it than it would have in the State where it was rendered. It has no higher dignity in any other State than in the one where it was pronounced; and hence, if in the Courts of the State where the judgment was rendered, it is inconclusive, or if it is inquirable into there, during a particular period, or on certain conditions, it will be open to investigation, to the same extent, every where else.—*Armstrong* v. *Carson's Ex'rs*, 3 *Dall.*, 302; *Green* v. *Sarmiento*, 1 *Pet. C. C. R.*, 74; *Spencer* v. *Sloo*, 8 *La.*, 290; *Curtis* v. *Gibbs*, 1 *Pennington*, 399; *Baugh* v. *Baugh*, 4 *Bibb*, 556; *Rogers* v. *Coleman et ux.*, 1 *Hardin*, 413, 420; *Smith* v. *Nichols*, 5 *Bing. N. C.*, 208; 35 *Eng. C. L.*, 88. So, if a judgment operates in the State where it was rendered only *in rem*, it will not elsewhere be enforced *in personam*. It results conclusively from this principle, or is rather involved in it, that if a judgment in a State where it is recovered, has not the effect of binding personally the defendants, or any of them, in the suit in which it was rendered, no greater effect will be given to it in any other State where it is endeavored to be enforced. It derives its obligation only from the laws of the State in which it is pronounced. A judgment creates a debt, on the ground that a liability is ascertained and established, by the decision of a tribunal, which might rightfully adjudicate upon it; and such adjudication derives its whole force and effect from the laws of the State under whose authority it is made. In the case of *Milan* v. *Fitzjames*, 1 *Bos. & Pul.*, 138, where a bond given in France, where it was understood to bind the property, and not the person, of the obligor, was sued in England, where he was arrested; and the question was, whether he should be discharged from the arrest, *Lord Chief Justice* EYRE said: "If it appears that this contract creates no personal obligation, and that it could not be sued as such, by the laws of France, (on the principle of preventing arrests so vexatious as to be an abuse of the process of the Court,) there seems to be a fair ground on which the Court may interpose to prevent a proceeding which may be so oppressive as a personal arrest in a foreign country, at the commencement of a suit in a case, which, as far as we can judge at present, authorizes no proceeding against the person in the country in which the transaction passed. If there could be none in France, in my opinion there can be none here. I cannot conceive that what is no personal obligation in the country in which it arises, can ever be raised into a personal obligation by the laws of another. If it be a personal obligation there, it must be enforced here in the mode pointed out by the law of this country. But what the nature of the obligation is, must be determined by the law of the country where it was entered into; and then this country will apply its own law to enforce it." And the Court accordingly discharged the party from the arrest. The same course of reasoning applies both to a foreign judgment, and to the judgment of a State of this Union, between which there is not, in respect to the point we are now considering, any ground for a distinction. *Judge* STORY, speaking of the remarks first quoted, says: "There does not seem the least reason to doubt the entire correctness of the doctrine thus laid down. If the contract creates no personal obligation, but an obligation *in rem* only, it cannot be that its nature can be changed, or its obligation varied, by a mere change of domicile. That would be to contradict the principles maintained in all the authorities, that the validity, nature, obligation and interpretation of a contract are to be decided by the *lex loci contractus*. A suit in England could not be maintained, except upon some contract which bound the person. If it bound the property only, the proceeding should be *in rem*; and if, in express terms, the party bound his property and excepted himself from a personal liability, no one would doubt that a suit *in personam* would not be maintainable." *Conflict of Laws*, 569. He then distinguishes between a contract, which, by its very terms, excludes personal liability, and a contract made in a country, which binds the party personally, but where the laws do not enforce the contract *in personam*, but only *in rem*; in which last case it would be enforced according to the *lex fori*. It is impossible to distinguish between the effect of an obligation created by an express contract, made between the parties to it, and an obligation created by a judgment to which a specific effect is given by the laws of the State under which it was rendered. It is, moreover, to be observed, that by the general principles of public law, no law of a nation has, *proprio vigore*, any extra territorial operation; it is enforced in another only *ex comitate gentium*. But comity would never require that the law of a country should elsewhere receive a construction, which should give it a more extensive operation than it would have where it was enacted. Between the States of this Union, however, the effect to be given to their records and judicial proceedings, is regulated by the constitutional compact, and they therefore stand on higher ground than mere comity. But there is nothing in our national constitution, on this subject, which, according to any construction which has ever been claimed for it, gives the judgment of one of the States, when sought to be enforced in another, a greater effect than it would have in the State where it was rendered.

What effect, then, is given in the State of New-York, by the laws of that State, to the judgment in question, as it respects the defendant Watkinson, against whom personally it is here sought to be enforced? The statute of the State of New-York, which has been recited, most explicitly answers this inquiry. In the first place, it provides, that in an action against joint debtors, where the process is against all, and is served upon either of them, "the defendant so served shall answer to the plaintiffs;" implying that none of the others, unless at least they appeared as defendants in the suit, are to be deemed parties to the proceeding, except for the mere sake of form. In the next place, it prescribes the form of the judgment in such case, if rendered for the plaintiff: it "shall be against all the defendants, in the same manner as if all had been served with process." And lastly, it declares the effect of such judgment: "such judgment shall be conclusive evidence of the liability of the defendants, who were personally served with process in the suit, and who appeared to defend therein; but against every other defendant, it shall be evidence only of the extent of the plaintiff's demand, after the liability of such defendant shall be established by other evidence."

Hence it is perfectly clear, that it was the intention of the makers of this law, that the judgment, although in form against all the defendants, should not create any obligation, personal or otherwise, nor be any evidence of indebtedness, against those not served with process in the suit. As to them, therefore, it had only the form of a judgment, without any of its qualities, attributes, or consequences; it could not be enforced as a judgment usually is, by execution, nor by any action founded upon it, which would be sustained by any evidence that the record of it furnished; it did not, as an ordinary judgment does, create a debt of record, arising from and evidenced by matter of record, because it is expressly provided here, that the record shall be no evidence of their liability. We have then, before us, an action of debt, brought upon a judgment, which creates no obligation, and furnishes no evidence of liability; and is, therefore, as ineffectual, as a ground of recovery, as if it were rendered in a case where there was confessedly no jurisdiction. In this State, we have no such remedy as an action of debt on judgment, excepting where there has been a judgment rendered, which is evidence of a debt. It results, therefore, that in this action, the defendant, who appears before us, is not here liable.

It is urged as a reason why we should sustain this action in the present case, that by the laws of New-York, a similar action may be there sustained against all the defendants in the suit in which such a judgment is entered; and by the authorities cited from that State, such appears to be the case.—*Merwin & Goldsmith* v. *Kumbull*, 23 *Wend.*, 293. It also appears, that, after such a judgment is entered, the plaintiff is not at liberty there to recur to the original cause of action, but that his remedy on such cause of action is in the form of an action of debt on such judgment. It is very obvious, however, that that action is prescribed there, in such case, not because there is in fact any judgment which creates or furnishes evidence of any liability, but on the grounds of local policy, as a convenient mode of proceeding for the recovery of the original debt from those of the joint debtors who were not, as well as those who were, served with process in the first suit; because it is there held, in pursuance of the provisions of the statute on which that judgment was entered, that such judgment, in the action so brought upon it, furnishes no evidence of the liability of those defendants, who were not served with process in the suit in which it was entered, but that their liability must be established by other evidence. That it was competent for that State to prescribe that, or any other form of remedy, in such case, there is no doubt. But that regulation was only local in its operation, and had no effect elsewhere. It appertained merely to the remedy in the case, and not to its merits. In stating the principle on this subject, we take the language of *Judge* STORY: "It is universally admitted and established, that the forms of remedies, and the modes of proceeding and the execution of judgments, are to be regulated solely and exclusively, by the laws of the place where the action is instituted; or, as the civilians uniformly express it, according to the *lex fori*." And, after explaining the reasons for the doctrine, he adds: "The doctrine of the common law is so fully established on this point, that it would be useless to do more than state the universal principle which it has promulgated; that, in regard to the merits and rights involved in actions, the law of the place where they originated, is to govern; but that all forms of remedies and judicial proceedings are to be according to the law of the place where the action is instituted, without any regard to the domicil of the parties, the origin of the right, or the country of the act." The authorities cited by him on this point are numerous and decisive.—*Story's Conf. of Laws, p.* 467, 8; *sec.* 556, *p.* 469, 470; *sec.* 558. (2*d Ed.*)

The plaintiffs further claim, by the laws of New-York, the judgment in question merged the debt of the defendants on which it was rendered; —that therefore, that debt was thereby discharged; that what operates as a discharge of it there, must have the same effect here; and that, therefore, no action will lie upon it, either in that State or elsewhere. If it were a correct use of language, it would be more proper to say, that the remedy, which before existed in that State, for the recovery of the debt, rather than the debt itself. was merged by that judgment. Nothing was done by the statute of that State, except to take away the former remedy for the recovery of it, and provide a new one. That the original cause of action did not, by the formal judgment which was entered become *res adjudicata*, is admitted. The plaintiffs disclaim that ground of recovery; and if so, we do not perceive how the original nature of the debt is changed, or the cause of action upon it has become merged or extinguished in one of a higher nature. If the debt itself is merged or extinguished, and thus discharged, by the judgment, it surely would not be necessary to prove the existence of that debt, by other evidence than the record of the judgment, in order to recover in an action on that judgment. It could hardly be claimed, at least by the defendant who is now before us, in an appropriate suit brought upon the original cause of action, that it was barred by a judgment, which, as to him is entirely inoperative.

For these reasons, we are of opinion, that judgment should be rendered by the Superior Court in favor of the defendant.—In this opinion the other Judges concurred.

Judgment for defendant.

COVENANT.

A covenant not to sue one signer of a promissory note is no release of the others.—*Ferson* v. *Sanger et als.*, 1 *Woodbury & Minot's U. S. R.*, *p.* 138. (1847.)

CREDITOR'S BILL.

Where a person in the receipt of a monthly salary, as an officer in the custom-house, assigned the same to another before it became due and payable, and gave the assignee his draft upon the disbursing office of the custom-house, for the amount, payable when the salary should become due, and deposited the draft with the disbursing officer, with the understanding that when the salary should become due the assignor should endorse the check which was required by the regulations of the custom-house to be endorsed by him, and receive the draft from the officer and leave with him the check for the assignee; *Held*, that such salary could not be reached by a creditor's bill filed against the assignor subsequent to the assignment.

Held also, that the act of endorsing such check, by the assignor, after the filing of the creditor's bill and the service of an injunction, was not a violation of such injunction.—*Ireland* v. *Smith*, 1 *Barbour's R.*, p. 419. *N. Y.* (1848.)

In Equity. This was a motion for an attachment against the defendant, for the violation of an injunction. The defendant is a measurer connected with the custom-house in the city of New-York, and as such is entitled to a salary of $125 per month, payable on the last day of each month. On the first day of September, 1847, the plaintiff filed a creditor's bill against the defendant, with a view to reach the month's salary which had become payable the day previous, and served upon the defendant the usual injunction. In the early part of August, the defendant had applied to one Sharp to advance him the amount of his month's salary. He accordingly received from Sharp $125 and gave him a draft upon the paying officer of the custom-house for that amount, payable the last day of August. It was agreed between Sharp and the defendant, at the time, that the draft should be deposited with the paying officer, and that when the salary should become due the defendant should endorse the check, which according to the regulations of the custom-house was required, and receive the draft from the officer and leave with him the check for Sharp. In pursuance of this agreement, the defendant, after the injunction had been served on him, endorsed the check for his salary, which was left with the officer, and was afterwards delivered by him to Sharp.

Horn, for the plaintiff, contended that the fund belonged to the defendant at the time of serving the injunction. The draft was a mere request to pay money, and not being accepted it created no lien on the fund; and even had it been accepted it would not have done so, as there was, at that time, no fund in existence. Neither can the draft be considered as an assignment of the salary.—18 *Wend.*, 344; 2 *Edw. Ch.*, 438.

Wanmaker, for the defendant.

Harris, J.—The transaction between the defendant and Sharp amounted to an equitable appropriation, if not a legal transfer, of the defendant's salary for the month of August. The officer upon whom the draft was drawn had notice of such appropriation; and by receiving the draft from Sharp he must be deemed to have assented to the payment. If the endorsement of the check was necessary to put Sharp in possession of the fund to which he was already entitled, the defendant was bound to make such endorsement. If he had refused, he might have been compelled to do so. The defendant had no right to that portion of his salary. To have received it, would have been a gross fraud upon Sharp. Had it come into the hands of a receiver appointed in this suit, I think it would have been the duty of this Court to direct it to be paid to Sharp. The plaintiff has come to a Court of Equity for assistance in the collection of his debt. And the Court while extending its aid to him, will also see that the equitable rights of others are protected. Although the money then due had been earned by the defendant, and although his endorsement upon the check was required according to the regulations of the custom-house, before the money would be paid, yet at the time the injunction was served, the defendant had no right to collect the money, or if he had received it, to appropriate it to the payment of his debts or otherwise to his own use. There is nothing then in the act of endorsing the check which amounts, even constructively, to a violation of the injunction, *and the motion must be denied with costs.*

CREDITOR'S BILL—CHANCERY.

A party having elected to proceed at law, equity will not interpose until he has pursued his remedy to every available extent; neither will a Court of Chancery *anticipate* that the legal redress may not prove effectual.

A charge in a creditor's bill that he *fears* that his debtor, if he gets possession of funds which he is proceeding to collect under execution, will apply them to the payment of other liens, having no priority over his own, will not justify the interposition of a Court of Chancery. He must state the ground of his *fears*, or allege some *issuable fact*, such as a fraudulent combination between his debtor and other creditors, to entitle him to equitable relief.—*McGough et al.* v. *The Insurance Bank of Columbus et al.*, 2 *Kelly's R.*, *p.* 151. *Ga.* (1847)

CRIMINAL LAW.

It is a sound principle of criminal jurisprudence, that the intention to commit the crime is of the essence of the offence; and to hold that a man shall be held criminally responsible for an offence, of the commission of which he was ignorant at the time, would be intolerable tyranny. *Duncan* v. *The State*, 7 *Humphrey's R.*, *p.* 148. *Tenn.* (1847.)

Where one statute creates an offence, and another directs the penalty, the indictment must conclude against the form of the statutes. *The State* v. *Moses*, 7 *Blackford's R.*, *p.* 244. *Ind.* (1847.)

(SULLIVAN, J., cited 2 *Hale's P. C.*, 173; *Dingley* v. *Moore*, *Cro. Eliz.*, 750; *Broughton* v. *Moore*, *Cro. Jac.*, 142.)

CROSS NOTES.

Where cross notes are made and specifically exchanged by the makers, each note is the proper debt of the maker thereof, and each holder is a purchaser for value.

And if such notes are transferred at a discount beyond the legal rate of interest, the makers cannot set up usury against the endorsees.

Where one made a note for the accommodation of the payee, *who gave the maker security that it should be paid when due*, and then transferred it at a greater discount than the legal rate ; *Held* that such note had no inception until such transfer, and that it was void for usury.

Held also, that the maker could set up the defence of usury, although the payee, when he transferred the note, had represented to the holder that it was business paper.

And where upon such transfer the payee informed the holder that it was business paper, and guaranteed the payment of it, and the maker after it fell due took it up and gave his note directly to the holder ; *Held* that such second note was usurious.

But the payee, in a suit upon the guaranty, could not set up usury.

And if the maker had purchased of the holder his claim on the guaranty against the payee, a note given as the consideration of such purchase would not have been usurious.—*Dowe* v. *Schutt et al.*, 2 *Denio's R.*, *p.* 621. *N. Y.* (1847.)

Assumpsit on a promissory note, tried at the Tompkins Circuit in August, 1844, before Monell, late C Judge. The note declared on was made by the defendants, dated April 16, 1841, for $253,84, and was payable to the plaintiff or bearer in six months from date, with interest.

The defence was usury. In January, 1840, the defendants gave their note to one Southard or bearer for $250, payable in one year, with interest, which he transferred to the plaintiff, with his guaranty endorsed on it, at a large discount beyond the legal rate of interest. It was not paid up when it fell due, but the note in suit was afterwards given for the balance due upon it, in order to take it up. Evidence was given to show that before the defendants gave the first note to Southard, he agreed to turn out to them his books of account on which several hundred dollars were due, to *secure* the payment of that note ; but they were never in fact turned out. The plaintiff gave evidence to show that when Southard transferred the first note to him, he represented it to be a business note.

The Judge charged the Jury, that if Southard *sold* and transferred, or agreed to *sell* and transfer his books and accounts to the defendants *as a consideration* for the first note given by them, it was a business note valid in Southard's hands, and that the plaintiff in that case would be entitled to recover, although he had discounted it at a usurious rate of interest ; but if Southard only agreed to assign the books and accounts *as security*, then the note was accommodation and not business paper.

And if it was transferred at a discount beyond the legal rate of interest, the plaintiff could not recover. The plaintiff's counsel excepted to the last proposition of the charge. He requested the Judge to charge, that, even though the note were accommodation paper, if it was sold by Southard to the plaintiff as business paper and represented by him to be such, and was purchased as such by the plaintiff at an usurious rate, upon the faith of such representation, then the guaranty of Southard was a valid contract, and the defendants, by executing the note in suit and taking up Southard's guaranty, became liable to the plaintiff to the extent of Southard's liability, that is, for the amount advanced by the plaintiff on purchasing the first note. The Judge declined to charge as requested, but on the contrary instructed the Jury that upon the facts assumed the defendants would not be liable. The Jury found a verdict for the defendants, and the plaintiff moved for a new trial on a case.

Sandford & Beers, for the plaintiff.

1. Where negotiable paper is made and delivered to a party who makes an express agreement to indemnify the maker, this gives the paper a legal inception, and it is thenceforward business paper.—*Cameron* v. *Chappell*, 24 *Wend.*, 94 ; *Rose* v. *Simms*, 1 *Barn. & Ad.*, 521.

2. A party representing paper which he offers to transfer to be business paper, cannot set up usury against the purchaser of it at a discount. *Holmes* v. *Williams*, 10 *Paige* 326. The guaranty of Southard was therefore a valid contract not infected with usury. The purchase or extinguishment of that guaranty was the consideration of the note now sought to be recovered. The note therefore is free from usury, being given for a demand of which usury could not be predicated.

Spencer, for the defendants, was stopped by the Court.

By the Court, BEARDSLEY, J.—There was no error in the charge of the Judge. If the first note had been given in consideration of a sale and transfer, or an agreement to sell and transfer to the defendants, debts then due to Southard, it would have been business and not accommodation paper in his hands. It would have been but the common case of a note given on the purchase of property by the makers, and which, as between them and the seller, they would be bound to pay. Where cross notes are made and specifically exchanged by the makers, each note is the proper debt of the maker thereof, and each holder is a purchaser for value. As the note is a debt due to the holder and his property, he may sell it on such terms and at such price as he pleases. It is strictly business paper, and although discounted on usurious terms, that cannot affect its validity as respects the maker. *Cameron* v. *Chappell*, 24 *Wend.*, 94, *and authorities referred to ; Chitty on Bills*, [10*th Am. ed.*] 708. In such cases the relation of principal and surety does not exist ; and it is plain that a promise to indemnify the maker would not be implied. But where a note is made by one person for the benefit of another, a promise to indemnify the maker exists, for in every case of suretyship such a promise is implied by law where none has been expressly made. An accommodation note is invalid in the hands of the person for whose benefit it was made, and if discounted for him at an usurious rate, it is equally invalid in the hands of the person who thus receives it. The legal attributes of accommodation paper are not changed by a promise, performed or unperformed, to give security for its payment by the person for whose benefit it was made. It is still but accommodation paper. The person for whom it is made cannot collect it, as to him the maker is but a surety, and if the note is transferred on usurious terms, it is void in the hands of the person who thus receives it. These principles are too plain to require a reference to authority for their support. Upon this part of the case therefore, as indeed throughout, the charge was unobjectionable.

But although the first note may have been unavailable in the hands of Southard, having been made for his accommodation, still, if he represented it to be business paper, and it was purchased by the plaintiff as such, relying on the truth of that representation, then although the purchase may have been at an usurious rate, yet as between the plaintiff and Southard there would be no usury; and the latter would be bound by his guaranty that the notes should be paid. This, however, would not change the character of the note; it would, notwithstanding the false representations of Southard, be, as to the makers, usurious and void. *Holmes* v. *Williams*, 10 *Paige*, 326; *Dix* v. *Van Wyck*, 2 *Hill*, 522. And the note in suit having been given by the makers, for a part of the first note remaining unpaid, and in substitution for their liabilities on that note, is equally invalid with the first. Had these defendants gone to the plaintiff, and agreed to purchase of him, his claim upon Southard, which was then a valid debt to the extent of the money advanced; and had the note in suit been given upon such a purchase, it might have been obligatory within the principle of the case of *Holmes* v. *Williams*. But there is not a scintilla of evidence, nor the slightest reason to believe, that this note was given upon any such arrangement, or on any such consideration. The guaranty of Southard was not thought of by either party, and the note was a mere renewal of the former invalid security. The second note therefore, as well as the first, was, as between these parties, void.

New trial denied.

Where cross notes of equal amount are made and exchanged by the makers, each party is to pay the note made by himself. And there is no implied contract by the payee to indemnify the maker.

Accordingly, where one of the parties to such an exchange negotiated the note which he received, and at maturity paid and took it up, and also made payments on the note made by himself, and sued the other party to the exchange, *for the money thus paid on his own note*, HELD that he could not recover.—*Wooster* v. *Jenkins*, 3 *Denio's R.*, *p.* 187. *N. Y.* (1848.)

DAMAGES.

Where an action on the case was brought to recover damages for laying out a highway around a turnpike gate, so as to divert the travel from the turnpike, and damage was recovered for the loss of toll occasioned from the opening of the highway to the date of the plaintiff's writ —*Held*, that subsequent suits might thereafterwards be maintained, for farther damage accruing from time to time, as long as the highway was kept open.—*Cheshire Turnpike* v. *Stevens*, 13 *New Hampshire R.*, *p.* 28. (1847.)

DAMAGES—OFFICER.

Where goods are tortiously taken by an officer, he is liable to the owner for all the damages sustained thereby.—*Weston* v. *Dorr*, 25 *Maine R.*, *p.* 176. (1847.)

DAMAGES—WARRANTY.

The difference of value between the article in a sound or unsound state is the measure of damages for a breach of a warranty, without regard to the price given.—*Cothers* v. *Keever*, 4 *Barr's R.*, *p.* 168. *Pa.* (1847.)

DEBT.

If the amount sued for be not ascertained by an instrument of writing, nor a sum certain, a jury is necessary to inquire of damages.

C. sued S., in an action of debt on a bill single, a promissory note, and an open account, and a final judgment was rendered without a jury to inquire of damages. *Held*, to be erroneous.—*Sandford* v. *Campbell & Co.*, 7 *Smedes & Marshall's R.*, *p.* 127. *Miss.* (1847.)

ERROR from the Circuit Court of De Soto County; *Hon. James M.* HOWREY, *Judge.*

This was an action of debt brought by Erastus T. Collins and Andrew Campbell, partners, under the name and style of A. Campbell & Co., for the use of John R. Chester, against Robert J. Sandford, for $900, 81½, founded on two bills single, the one for $811 99, and the other for $53, 80; one promissory note for $25 62½, and an open account for goods sold amounting to $9 40.

On the first bill single, was the following endorsement, to wit: "$230, of the $560, is Hernando money, payable in New Orleans, which, if it cannot be used at par, Mr. Sandford is to redeem with par funds; also, $100, West Railroad bill, is to be redeemed if it is not passed at par." The defendant failed to appear and plead, and judgment by default was rendered against him for "$380 12½, the balance of the debt in the declaration mentioned, and $56 27, damages for the detention of the same." The defendant brought the case to this Court by writ of error.

Shelton, for plaintiff in error.

First. The judgment instead of being final should have been interlocutory with a writ of inquiry.

1. An account for goods, wares and merchandise, constituted a part of the demand sued on, and was the subject of one count in the declaration. Our statute enacts that where the sum due does not appear by any instrument of writing, if the defendant do not plead, &c., an interlocutory judgment may be taken, on which a writ of inquiry shall be awarded, &c., &c.—*H. & H.*, 616.

2. An action on an account for goods, wares, and merchandise, is not for a sum certain on which, at common law, judgment final might be recovered.

In debt upon a bond or promissory note for the payment of money, by the default, the defendant admits the promise in writing to pay the money as alleged. So in debt for so much money loaned, the defendant admits the loan of the amount of money alleged in the declaration, and since money was not to be valued by a jury, a computation by figures is all that is necessary to ascertain the amount due; so too, in an action for goods, wares, and merchandise, by the default, the defendant admits something to be due for goods, wares, and merchandise, but the amount and value thereof is not admitted, but is wholly uncertain, and can be ascertained only by proof, that must be made before a jury. The true rule is, that when the matter of inquiry depends exclusively upon figures, it may be computed by the clerk, and not otherwise; therefore when upon the inquiry, the defendant may admit the contract as stated in the declaration, and yet give evidence to reduce the verdict, a jury must be called.—4 *T. R.*, 275, 276; 4 *T. R.*, 493; 8 *T. R.*, 648; 2 *Saund.*, 107. *a. n. b.*; *Tidd's Prac.*, 514, 515; 1 *Ch. R.*, 619, 620, *b.*

3. The interest could not be ascertained in this case without a jury, because upon the account a jury might, and could properly have refused to allow interest by way of damages. In such a case the clerk cannot compute the interest, and a jury must find it by way of damages.—8 *T. R.*, 395.

Second. The sum of $380 12, being the pretended balance of the debt for which judgment was rendered, is not the true balance; unless the Hernando money, mentioned in the credit, was estimated at less than specie, it should be $340 82.

Without a jury no such discount could be made, because it must be ascertained upon proof of the value of the money.—1 *Ch. R.*, 619, 620, *b.*; 4 *T. R.*, 493.

Van Winkle and *Potter*, for defendants in error.

It is assigned for error that the judgment was final, when it should have been a judgment with an inquiry of damages.

1. This was not error. This Court has decided that a judgment by default final on an assessment of damages by the clerk is a "a judgment after inquiry of damages," within the meaning of the 91st section of the Circuit Court law.—*Rev. Code, p.* 124; *H. & H.*, 591, *sec.* 11; *Gridley* v. *Briggs, Lacoste & Co.*, 2 *How.*, 833. That section declares such a judgment shall not be reversed for any matter which would not be cause to reverse a judgment upon the verdict of a jury. If then the legal effect of this judgment is the same as if it had been rendered upon a verdict, can it be objected that a jury did not pass upon the account for $9 40? *The Stat. of* 4 *Ann, ch.* 16, *sec.* 2, is like our statute, and the English Courts hold that a want of inquiry of damages is aided by their statute.—1 *Tidd's Prac.*, 583; *Mallory* v. *Jenings*, 2 *Stra.*, 878; *Longman* v. *Fenn*, 1 *H. Black.*, 543, *n. a.*

Another statute provides for an assessment of damages by the clerk on any judgment by default "in actions of debt, for a sum certain."—*How. & H., p.* 616, *sec.* 9. This action is for a sum certain; the count for goods sold, is upon the contract to pay the very sum for the goods; "debt is upon the contract or sale, but *indebitatus assumpsit* is upon the promise;" the count is, in effect, for the very sum agreed to be paid for the goods, and the default admits the agreement.—*See cases cited in argument by Gibbs, in Emory* v. *Fell*, 2 *Durn. & East*, 28. "In debt the judgment (by default) is always final *quoad* the debt."—1 *Tidd's Prac.*, 573; 2 *Arch. Prac.*, 33 *et seq.*; *Fenton* v. *Garlick*, 6 *Johns.*, 287.

2. By his default, Sandford admitted that the amount of the three notes sued on was still due and unpaid. That amount was $890 81, with interest, and yet the judgment was for only $438 39. If Campbell & Co. are content with a judgment for less than one-half of what Sandford thus admitted to be due, can Sandford complain?—*Ward* v. *Haight*, 3 *Johns. Cas.*, 80.

The cases cited for plaintiff in error do not reach the question before the Court; they merely show when a Court will direct a reference and when direct an inquiry by a jury to ascertain the amount due on a default; they do not show that an assessment like this would be error. On the contrary, the English rule is, that the Court itself may in all cases assess the damages on a default.—2 *Saund.*, 107, *n.* 2; 2 *Arch. Prac.*, 32; *Collum* v. *Barker*, 3 *Johns.*, 153.

Mr. Justice CLAYTON delivered the opinion of the Court.

This was an action of debt founded upon a bill single, a promissory note, and an open account, for goods sold. There was a judgment by default, and a final judgment rendered without a jury to inquire of damages. This raises the sole question in the cause.

It was no doubt competent to the Court to enter up a final judgment, without the intervention of a jury, upon the bill single, and promissory note. This is authorized by the Statute—*H. & H.*, 616, *sec.* 9. But where the amount is not ascertained by an instrument of writing, nor is a sum certain, there a jury is necessary. This produces a reversal of the judgment below.

Judgment reversed.

DEBTOR AND CREDITOR.

A special action on the case may be sustained against a debtor, for fraudulently representing himself insolvent, and thereby inducing his creditors to discharge a promissory note for less than its value.

Proof of general representations, made at the time to others, by which they were defrauded, may be given in evidence to show the intention of the debtor in making the false representations complained of.

But it is error to instruct a jury that proof of false and fraudulent declarations, thus made, to other creditors, would sustain a declaration, counting upon representations made directly to the plaintiff.—*Edwards* v. *Owen*, 15 *Ohio R.*, *p.* 500. (1847.)

This is a writ of error to the Court of Common Pleas of Montgomery County.

The original action was case. The declarations averred in substance, that Owen held a note against Edwards for $278, due November 5, 1841. That on the 17th of June, 1841, Edwards fraudulently, &c. represented himself to Owen as insolvent and unable to pay his debts, and thereby induced him to give up said note and receive in satisfaction of it, certain property worth not over $75, by which he was defrauded and lost $203, when in fact Edwards was solvent.

To this declaration there was a general demurrer, which was overruled. The plea of the general issue was then filed, upon which was a trial by jury, and a verdict for plaintiff.

Motions for new trial, and in arrest of judgment, were made and overruled; and, finally, judgment was entered upon the verdict.

During the progress of the trial, five bills of exceptions were taken and made part of the record.

Several errors are assigned, which will be noticed in the opinion of the Court.

Crane & Davies, for plaintiff in error.

First. The declaration was bad, and the Court below erred in overruling the demurrer. It is subject to the following exceptions:

1. It contains no direct averment of the solvency of the defendant below at the time of the composition. The averment may relate to the time of the composition, or to the subsequent period when the note fell due.

2. It is repugnant and contradictory, in its averment, as to the time when the composition was made.

3. It is not alleged that the plaintiff was ignorant of the quality and value of the articles taken by him in satisfaction of his note, or that any fraud or deceit was practised him in such sale.

4. If it be urged that the ground of action is not fraud in the sale, but the delusion produced on the mind of the plaintiff by the misrepresentations of the defendant, as to his circumstances, by which the plaintiff was induced to incur a certain and known loss to avoid a greater, then no such *gravamen* is set out in the declaration, or fairly inferable from the facts there stated.

5. If such cause of action had been fully set forth in the declaration, still the action for deceit could not be sustained, the sale itself being uninfected by fraud or concealment.—*Butler* v. *Kent*, 19 *Johns.*, 225; *Patton* v. *Gurney*, 17 *Mass.*, 182; *Vicars* v. *Wilcocks*, 8 *East.*, 3; 1 *Chit. Pl.*, 387; *Bagley* v. *Morrell*, *Cro. Jac.*, 632; *Vernon* v. *Kays*, 12 *East.*, 632; *Dawes* v. *King*, 1 *Stark.*, 61; *Davis* v. *Meeker*, 5 *Johns.*, 354; 2 *Steph. N. P.*, 1283.

If it is urged that according to our view of the law, fraud and misrepresentation would go unpunished, and the deceived unredressed,—we answer, that if this transaction was so fraudulent as to vitiate it, the appropriate remedy is by assumpsit on the note, treating the composition as a nullity.—*Forsythe on Comp., with Cr.*, 27, *in* 1 *Lib. of Law and Eq.*; *Belden* v. *Davies*, 2 *Hall*, 448; *Stafford* v. *Bacon*, 1 *Hill*, 532; *Cooling* v. *Noyes*, 6 *T. R.*, 262; 1 *Com. Dig.* 362; *Lamb* v. *Stone*, 11 *Pick.*, 527.

Second. But the Court erred in admitting evidence of the general reputation of defendant's insolveney, in the spring of 1841. The declaration charges representations made by the defendant to the plaintiff. This averment is not sustained by proof of representations made to others, still less by proof of compositions, made with other creditors, without the knowledge of plaintiff.—*Peake's N. P.*, 226; *Allen* v. *Addington*, 7 *Wend.*, 10; *Snell* v. *Moses*, 1 *Johns.*, 96; *Perry* v. *Aaron*, 1 *Johns.*, 129; *Beach* v. *Catlin*, 4 *Day*, 284; *Smith* v. *Blake*, 1 *Conn.*, 262.

Third. The Court should have charged the jury as requested, that no representations were admissible under the declaration, unless made by the defendant to the plaintiff, or to the agent of the plaintiff, and communicated by him to his principal.—*Allen* v. *Addington*, 11 *Wend.*, 375, *and cases above cited.*

Lowe & M'Kinney, for defendant.

BIRCHARD, J.—The first assignment of error goes to the sufficiency of the declaration which it is said cannot be maintained, mainly because, if the note in question was given up by reason of the fraudulent inducement, without full payment, there is a plain remedy, by action of assumpsit upon the note, and that, in such a case, no special action upon the case can be resorted to. Of this opinion are two of the members of this Court, while the other members hold that, notwithstanding the action of assumpsit might be maintained, the special action upon the case will also lie; that the defrauded party may count directly upon the fraud, and avoid any notice of offset; that he may have his action for the deceit in this case, without returning the property, as well as he might have an action for the note, after an offer to return that for which he gave it up; and this upon general principles. The Court being equally divided in opinion, the objection to the declaration fails, and the decisions of the Court of Common Pleas, in overruling the demurrer, and disallowing the motion in arrest of judgment, are sustained.

By the first bill of exceptions, it appears an objection was taken to the admission of the testimony of D. A. Wareham, and an error is assigned upon this exception. The witness stated, that he was at Edwards' store on the 17th of June, endeavoring to collect a debt of $600, in goods, when Edwards told him he was as poor as a church mouse; that Owen was there on the same day making his arrangement to receive, out of the store, goods on the note set forth in the declaration; that he did not communicate the conversation to him; that on the same day, and before he received his goods of Edwards, the clerk of Edwards then being in the store and in the hearing of Edwards, told him he had better take goods, &c., for it was the only chance—that if he waited until after Court he would not give fifty cents for the claim, &c.

The next bill of exceptions on which errors are assigned presents no principle distinguishable from the above, and both may be considered together. It is proper to remark, that they do not set forth what particular ground of objection was taken to the evidence, and we are, therefore, under the necessity of considering whether, in any aspect of the case, such evidence was competent for any purpose. Several things were necessary to sustain the plaintiff's right of action, and whatever tended to prove any one of those several matters, was competent for that purpose. It is clear, that what was said to others, whether communicated to Owen or not, was incompetent to prove the fraudulent misrepresentations alleged to have been made directly to him. But upon the hypothesis that those charges of the declaration were specifically proved by other evidence, might not proof of this description tend to throw some light upon the question, whether they were made in good faith or with a fraudulent design, and with the intention that they should deceive? It was as important for Owen to satisfy the jury of the existence of a fraudulent purpose in making the false representations, as of their falsity, or that he was thereby defrauded. What passes in men's minds can, in general, only be gathered from their acts, and the attending circumstances, from what they were doing, causing and requiring to be done. As to what was said by the clerk, we know not that it was objected to. But is it to be supposed that a clerk in a store, his employer at home and daily supervising and directing him, will represent his principal as insolvent, and in a few days likely to be unable to pay fifty cents on a $600 note, without instruction to do so—and that his principal will retain him after such representation, make similar ones in his presence, profit by them at the expense of his creditor, and all w..t. honest and fair intentions? The necessary and legal inference from such conduct is, that the servant, thus acting in concert with the principal, but obeys the behests of the master, and that the latter intends and sanctions the commission of the imposition which so profits him.

Again—in this case, that part of the evidence which went to show that goods were received out of the store, was competent, for it was incumbent on Owen to satisfy the jury that he received on that day the goods, as averred in the pleadings. We are not prepared to say this evidence was incorrectly admitted.

The third bill of exceptions was taken to the admission of the testimony of R. C. Schenck and another, and the fourth to the admission of sundry other witnesses; and errors are assigned upon these. The specific ground of objection is not stated in either of these bills of exception, and, as has been said in remarking upon their predecessors, if the proof objected to tended to support the issue in any respect, it was not error to admit it. Mr. Schenck testified to sundry conversations of Edwards with him, as the agent of sundry of his creditors—that he said they must take what he offered them, or they would get nothing. The witness narrates the manner of his compromising the value of his property, and the price at which he induced creditors to take it. The other witness proved, that about that time Edwards was generally representing himself insolvent, and that he became generally so reputed about Dayton, and that the report, contrary to the truth, was believed to be well founded. Now, all this proof, connected with the fact that he made compromises of his debts greatly below their amount, admitting that he was then able to pay the full amount of each claim, would seem to furnish some evidence that he knew the falsity of the representations made by him to Owen, and which Owen says deceived him. Admitting that there was proof that those representations were made, and falsely made, one would hardly need more to bring his mind to the conclusion that the design was fraudulent. If it tended to support that part of the issue, it was proper to suffer it to go to the jury, whether, by itself and unaided, it was sufficient or not. Upon the fifth bill of exceptions two errors are assigned—First: In refusing to charge the jury as requested. Second: In the instructions given.

The Court were asked to instruct the jury that, to entitle Owen to recover, they must be satisfied that Edwards represented to him that he was insolvent, and unable to pay him and his other creditors, with intent to deceive and defraud him; that the representations were false and fraudulent, that they were relied on by him, and were the means by which he had been deceived, and had sustained the damage complained of; and that representations made to others, and by them communicated to Owen, would not sustain the action.

We think that this instruction should have been given. It is what the law required, and to us seems to have been all that the case required. The residue of the instructions requested, present questions that could not legitimately arise in the case, because they were foreign to the issue. It was not, therefore, error to refuse them.

In the instructions given we find no fault, save in the last clause, in these words: "Proof that Edwards made the false and fraudulent representations imputed to him, to other creditors, with intent to defraud his creditors generally, by inducing them to compound their claims at less than their value, and that the false representations so made to others came to the knowledge of Owen, and induced him to compound his debt at less than its value, will sustain the declaration." And Edwards would be liable to make good the difference between the value of the note and the property given in its discharge, although he did not warrant the property, and made no false representations as to its quality. To this there are objections. Proof that false representations were made to Owen's neighbors does not sustain an averment that they were made to himself. Parties must recover according to their *allegata* and *probata*. Both must correspond. Owen could not allege that Edwards had deceived him, by a misstatement made to him, and in which he had placed confidence, when none was made to him. The falsehoods imposed upon his neighbors was not a matter of his. He made no case of that kind in his declaration, and he could not be justified in relying upon what was said to them. Indeed, all that was thus said had nothing to do with this case, except so far as it tended to show with what intent Edwards made false statements to him directly, and upon which he did, and had a right to rely.

The Court erred in this, and the judgment must be reversed.

DECLARATION.

A suit was brought on four different writings obligatory, which were set forth in as many different counts in the declaration. Issue was joined on all; the cause was submitted to the Court for trial; the Court found the issues joined on the three first counts in favor of the plaintiffs, and assessed their damages accordingly. *Held*, that the judgment was erroneous, there being no finding on the fourth count of the declaration. —*Semple* v. *Hailman et al.* 3 *Gilman's R.*, *p.* 131. *Ills.* (1847.)

(Caton, J., cited *Miller* v. *Trets*, 1 *Lord Raym.*, 324; 2 *Salk.*, 374; *Van Benthuysen* v. *De Witt*, 4 *Johns.*, 213; *Patterson* v. *The United States*, 2 *Wheat.*, 221.)

In an action to recover the penalty for taking illegal fees, the declaration must set out the services for which the fees were taken, or judgment may be arrested after verdict.—*Ross* v. *Palmer*, 4 *Barr's R.*, *p.* 577. *Pa.* (1847.)

(Rogers, J., cited *Aechternacht* v. *Watmouth*, 8 *Watts & Serg.*, 162.)

DECREE.

A decree erroneous in allotting a portion of the property in controversy to one of the complainants, will not be disturbed on that account; unless the other parties complain of it.—*Newell* v. *Newell et al.*, 9 *Smedes & Marshall's R.*, *p.* 56. *Miss.* (1848.)

DEED.

The law is well settled, that for the advancement of a right, and the furtherance of justice, and where the rights of third persons are not to be injuriously affected, a deed will have relation to, and take effect from the time the grantee was entitled to receive it.—*Ferguson* v. *Miles*, 3 *Gillman's R.*, *p.* 358. *Ills.* (1847.)

(*Powell* cited *Jackson* v. *McMichael*, 3 *Cow.*, 75; *Jackson* v. *Bull*, 1 *Johns. Cas.*, 81, 85; 3 *Caine*, 262; *Jackson* v. *Bard*, 4 *Johns.*, 234; *Heath* v. *Ross*, 12 *Johns.*, 140; 15 *Johns.*, 309; *Jackson* v. *Dickenson*, 20 *Johns.*, 3; 2 *Wend.*, 404; *Klock* v. *Cronkhite*, 1 *Hill* (*N. Y.*), 107; *Scribner* v. *Lockwood*, 9 *Ohio*, 184; *Boyd's Lessee* v. *Longworth*, 11 *Ohio*, 235.

Treat, J., cited *Jackson* v. *Raymond*, 1 *Johns. Cas.*, 85; *Jackson* v. *Ball*, 1 *Johns. Cas.*, 81; *Heath* v. *Ross*, 12 *Johns.*, 140; *Boyd* v. *Longworth*, 11 *Ohio*, 235; *Case* v. *De Goes*, 3 *Caine*, 262; *Jackson* v. *Bard*, 4 *Johns.*, 234; *Jackson* v. *Dickenson*, 15 *Johns.*, 309; *Jackson* v. *Ramsey*, 3 *Cowen*, 75; *Evertson* v. *Sawyer*, 2 *Wend.*, 507; *Klock* v. *Cronkhite*, 1 *Hill* (*N. Y.*), 107.)

The delivery of a deed to the grantee after the same has been recorded is a good delivery, and the deed need not again be recorded.—*Kent et al.* v. *Walker et als.*, 16 *Ohio R.*, *p.* 168. (1848.)

An instrument purporting to be a deed, by which the grantor gives to his son certain property, after his death and the death of his wife, is not a deed, but a testamentary paper, and cannot be read to the jury in any case affecting the title to personality in a Court of Common Law, until it has passed to probate before the Ordinary.—*Hester, Ex'r*, v. *Young*, 2 *Kelly's R.*, *p.* 31. *Ga.* (1847.)

(*Lloyd* cited *Greenl. on Ev.*, 560; 1 *Starkie*, 194; 2 *Douglass*, 09; 12 *Wheaton*, 175; 4 *T. R.*, 258; 6 *Conn.*, 593; 2 *Wheat. Sel.*, 813, 8 *B. & C.*, 338; *Prince's Dig.*, 240, 010.

Nisbet, J., cited, 3 *Hagg.*, 221; *Carth.*, 38; *West's case*, *Moore*, 177; *Audley's case*, *Dyer*, 166, *a.*; *Greene* v. *Proude*, 1 *Mod.*, 117; *Finch*,

195; 1 *Peere Wms.*, 529; 8 *Viner's Ab.*, 45; 4 *Eng. Ec. R.*, 108; 4 *Hagg.*, 44; 2 *Hagg.*, 554; *Habergham* v. *Vincent*, 2 *Vesey Jr.*, 230; 2 *Bailey S. C.*, 588; *Kinard v. Kinard*, 1 *Speer's Ex.*, 256; *Crawford* v. *McElroy*, 2 *Speers*, 230; 1 *McCord*, 517; 1 *Will. Ex'rs*, 59; *Greenleaf's Ev. sec.*, 518; 2 *Doug.*, 707; 1 *Stark.*, 343; *Shumway* v. *Holbrook*, 1 *Pick.*, 115; 2 *Phil. Ev.*, 172; *Gordon* v. *Dyson*, 1 *B. & B.*, 221; *Pinney* v. *Pinney*, 8 *Barn. & Cres.*, 335; 1 *Will. Exr's*, 172; *Rex* v. *Netherseal*, 4 *T. R.*, 260.)

DEED—CANCELLATION OF.

A mere agreement to cancel a deed, without an actual cancelling, will not render it void.—*Barret* v. *Barron*, 13 *New Hampshire R.*, *p.* 150. (1847.)

(*Morrison* cited *Farrar* v. *Farrar*, 4 *N. H.*, 191; *Cross* v. *Powell*, *Cro. Eliz.*, 483.

Gilchrist, J., cited *Farrar* v. *Farrar*, 4 *N. H.*, 191; *Morse* v. *Child*, 6 *N. H.*, 521.)

DEED—RELIGIOUS SOCIETY.

Detinue will lie by the trustees and deacons of a religious society, to recover a deed which they had deposited with the defendant and which he refused to re-deliver.

One to whom, in common with others, a deed is made as a trustee of a religious society, is seized to the use of the society, and has not such an interest in the land as would authorize him to withhold the deed from those from whom he had received it.—*Stoker et al.* v. *Yerby*, 11 *Alabama R.*, *p.* 322. (1847.)

Error to the County Court of Tuscaloosa.

Detinue for a deed conveying land. The declaration states, the plaintiffs, as deacons of the Baptist Church, established at Bethel Meeting House, and successors, as such deacons, of Castleton Lyon, John Yerby, and Wiley McGee, formerly deacons and trustees of said church, complain of John Yerby, &c.—for that the said plaintiffs, on the 24th of April, 1845, at, &c., delivered to the defendant, a certain deed, to wit, &c. (describing the land therein conveyed), which conveyance it alleges, was made for the purpose of erecting a house of worship of Almighty God, of great value, &c., to wit, of the value of $1,000, to be delivered to the plaintiffs on request. Yet although often requested, &c., concluding with the common breach.

The second count differs from the first, only in alleging that they lost the deed out of their possession, and that it came to the possession of the defendant, and that he refuses to deliver it.

To this declaration the defendants demurred, and the Court sustained the demurrer. This is the error assigned.

Porter, for the plaintiff in error. The delivery was enough to sustain the action.—1 *Arch. N. P.*, 288, Or right of possession without delivery.—*Ib.* 287.

A grant to use of a church not incorporated, grantor stands seized to use. *D. Church* v. *Veder*, 4 *Wend.*, 494. And trustees *de facto* of a church, not incorporated, may maintain an action.—*Green* v. *Cady et al.*, 9 *Wend.*, 414; *People* v. *Russell*, 9 *Johns.*,147; 1 *Chitty's P.*, 8, *note* 10; *Jef. Ins. Co.* v. *Cotheral*, 7 *Wend.*, 72.

The power of a successor, in such a case, arises as incident *ex necessitate.*—1 *Cowen*, 679.

Martin & Huntington, contra. This suit was brought by the plaintiffs *as successors*, &c., to recover a deed, &c.

A demurrer was filed and sustained to the plaintiff's declaration, on the ground that the plaintiffs are not *incorporated*, and could not sue *as successors*, &c. To sustain the opinion of the Court below, we rely upon *Earnest* v. *Battle et als.*, 1 *Johns. Cas.*, 319; *Bumpass* v. *Richardson*, 1 *Stew.*, 16; *Ewing* v. *Matlock*, 5 *Porter*, 82; 2 *Ala.*, 699.

ORMOND, J.—To maintain detinue, it is not necessary that the plaintiff should have the absolute property in the thing sued for; a special, or qualified property, as that of a bailee, is sufficient against a wrong doer.—*Arch. N. P.*, 286.

We understand the declaration to allege, that the plaintiffs, as deacons and trustees of the Baptist Church, established at Bethel Meeting House, were possessed of a certain deed, for two acres of ground, on which the church has been erected, that they delivered the deed to the defendant, to be re-delivered to them on request, and that although requested, he refuses to re-deliver it. The second count varies from the first only in charging that the deed came to the possession of the defendant by finding.

It is obvious that no question of title is presented here; it is the case of a bailee against a wrong doer. It is however insisted, that the declaration shows that the defendant has the right to the possession of the deed. The deed is described as having been made by William H. Terrell, to Castleton Lyon, Wiley McGee, and the defendant, as deacons and trustees of the Baptist Church established at Bethel, in Tuscaloosa county, and their successors in office, upon trust, that the grantees should hold the land, for the purpose of erecting thereon houses suitable for the worship of Almighty God, for the accommodation of the Baptist society, &c. It is obvious that the title is merely vested in these persons, without any beneficial interest, and that they are seized to the use of the Baptist Society of Bethel Meeting House.—*Reformed Dutch Church* v. *Veder*, 4 *Wend.*, 494. The defendant, therefore had not such an interest in the property conveyed by the deed, as would authorize him to detain it against the acting trustees of the church, from whom he had received it, and who were entitled to the possession, as deacons and trustees of the church.

Whether the plaintiffs could maintain this action, as the present deacons and trustees, and successors of the defendant and others to whom the possession of the deed was delivered, and without ever having had possession themselves, is a question not presented on the record, by the declaration.

Let the judgment be reversed, and the cause remanded.

DEFAULT.

If the plaintiff amends his bill, by adding new parties, after the defendant's default for want of an appearance has been entered, he thereby waives the default.—*Scudder et als.* v. *Voorhis*, 1 *Barbour's R., p.* 55. *N. Y.* (1848.)

DEMAND OF PAYMENT.

The *dating* of a promissory note at a particular place does not make that the place of payment, or authorize a demand to be made at that place for the purpose of charging an endorser.

But it is presumptive evidence of the residence of the maker at that place.

Where no place of payment is mentioned in a note, the general rule is, that it must be demanded of the maker personally, or at his dwelling, or place of business, in order to charge the endorser.

But where the maker has absconded, or being a seaman without a domicil in the State is absent on a voyage, and also where he has no known residence or place of business at which a demand can be made, a presentment for payment is dispensed with, and the endorser will be liable on receiving notice of the facts constituting the excuse.

So where the maker being a resident of the State where the note is made, removes therefrom and takes up a permanent residence elsewhere, the holder need not follow him, but a demand at his former place of residence will suffice.

But to enable the holder to charge an endorser without a demand of the maker, the facts creating the exception must be distinctly proved.

Where the maker has a known residence when the note is given, which is not changed before it becomes payable, a regular demand must be made, though the note is given and dated at a different place from his residence.

Accordingly where one who resided in Florida made a note at Troy, dating it at the latter place, and continued to reside in Forida until it became due, which fact was known to the holder, who instead of causing a demand to be made of the maker, procured the note to be presented to the endorser residing at Troy, and then gave him notice of non-payment;

Held, that there was nothing in the case to dispense with a demand of the maker, and that the plaintiff could not recover.—*Taylor* v. *Snyder*, 3 *Denio's R.*, *p.* 145. *N. Y.* (1848.)

(Beardsley, J., cited *Anderson* v. *Drake*, 14 *Johns.*, 114; *Bank of America* v. *Woodworth*, 18 *Johns.*, 322; *Story on Prom. Notes*, *sec.* 235; 1 *Ld. Raym.*, 443, 743; 3 *Kent*, 5*th Ed.*, 96; *Putnam* v. *Sullivan*, 4 *Mass.*, 53; *Lehman* v. *Jones*, 1 *Watts & Serg.*, 126; *Chit. on Bills*, 10*th Am. Ed.*, 354, *n.* 1; *Barnett* v. *Wills*, 4 *Leigh*, 114; *Dennie* v. *Walker*, 4 *N. H.*, 199; *Whittier* v. *Graffam*, 3 *Greenl.*, 82; *Duncan* v. *McCullough*, 4 *S. & R.*, 480; *McGruder* v. *Bank of Washington*, 9 *Wheat.*, 598; *Gillespie* v. *Hannahan*, 4 *McCord*, 503; *Reid* v. *Morrison*, 2 *Watts & Serg.*, 401; *Lowery* v. *Scott*, 24 *Wend.*, 358; *Galpin* v. *Hard*, 3 *McCord*, 394.)

DESCENT.

A posthumous child may claim by descent as an heir of its father, and may join with its elder brothers and sisters in an action for the recovery of the possession of the lands descended.—*Bishop's Heirs* v *Hampton*, 11 *Alabama R.*, *p.* 254. (1847.)

DIVORCE.

The complainant, in a suit for a divorce, who asks for a decree declaring the children of the defendant illegitimate, must produce some further evidence of his non-access than the mere fact that his wife was living in adultery with another person.

The maxim, *pater est quem nuptiæ demonstrant*, is founded upon very strong reasons of policy as well as of law. And Courts should not unsettle the title to property, nor put the *status* of any one in jeopardy, by speculating upon the mere probabilities in favor of the illegitimacy of a child who may, or may not, have been begotten by the husband of its mother.

The ancient rule of the Common Law, that the husband must be presumed to be the father, if he was within the realm during any part of the period of gestation, has long since been repudiated by the Courts.

It is not necessary, in order to bastardize the issue, that the evidence should be such as to render it impossible that sexual intercourse should have taken place between the husband and wife. It is sufficient if it proves beyond a reasonable doubt, that no such intercourse did take place during the usual period of gestation, previous to the birth of the child.

The Court of Chancery, upon dissolving the marriage contract for the adultery of the wife, is not authorized to declare one of her children illegitimate, who must have been begotten before the commission of the adultery charged in the complainant's bill.

Where the wife of the complainant was for several years living in the same place with him, as the concubine or kept mistress of another person, the husband in the meantime making no exertions to break up the adulterous intercourse; *Held*, that in the absence of evidence of non-access, the complainant must be presumed to be the father of the children begotten upon his wife during that time; and that he was not entitled to a decree declaring such children to be illegitimate.—*Van Aerman* v. *Van Aerman*, 1 *Barbour's Ch. R.*, *p.* 375. *N. Y.* (1847.)

The bill in this case was filed by the husband to obtain a divorce from his wife, upon the ground of her adultery. It appeared from the bill that the defendant had two children; who, as the complainant charged, were illegitimate. And from the proofs it appeared that she had another child born a short time after the filing of the complainant's bill. The master to whom it was referred to take proofs of the facts and circumstances stated in the bill, reported that the defendant had been guilty of the adultery charged; and that all three of the children were illegitimate.

Fuller, for the complainant.

The Chancellor.—The adultery is sufficiently established, in this case, to entitle the complainant to a divorce, But the Master erred in supposing that the testimony before him was sufficient to authorize the Court to declare all the children illegitimate. The statute declares that when the husband is complainant, the legitimacy of the children, born or *begotten* before the commission of the offence charged, shall not be affected by the decree. And even as to children begotten after that time, and before the commencement of the suit for the divorce, their legitimacy shall be presumed until the contrary is shown. 2 *R. S.*, 145, *sec.* 42. The first offence of adultery charged in the complainant's bill, in this case, is stated therein as having occurred some time in the year 1841, but without stating at what particular time of the year. It cannot, however, be presumed to have occurred so as to have broken off sexual intercourse between the complainant and the defendant until the time when he says he first learned the fact, in July or August of that year. If the eldest child, therefore, was born within the usual period of gestation from the first of July, 1841, it must have been begotten before the time of the commission of the first offence charged in the bill. At least, such is the legal presumption, in the absence of any evidence of a premature birth. The time of the birth of such first child, however, is not stated either in the bill or in the proofs, so as to enable the Court to form an opinion whether it was, or was not begotten before the commission of the first offence charged in the bill. It is true, one of the witnesses, who was examined in December last, stated that the defendant had lived and cohabited with her paramour for the last five years, and that her eldest child was born more than one year after she commenced living with him. That, however, would extend the adulterous intercourse back into 1840, and would not show that the child was begotten after the commission of the first offence charged in this bill. The time of the birth of that child should at least have been ascertained, to enable the Court to see whether it was probably begotten after the first offence charged. For if it was begotten before that time, the Court has no jurisdiction to declare it illegitimate; even if the fact of the non-access of the husband was fully established. 2 *R. S.*, 145, *sec.* 44. Again, the mere fact that the wife of the complainant was living in the same place with him as the mistress or concubine of another man, for several years, the husband in the meantime making no exertions to break up such adulterous intercourse, and taking no steps to obtain a divorce, is not sufficient evidence from which the non-access of the husband can be legally presumed; so as to entitle him to a decree bastardizing the children of his wife. The bill states the residence of the complainant to be in Schenectady, where the defendant and her paramour are proved to have also openly cohabited together. And the husband, in substance, admits that he was acquainted with their adulterous intercourse more than four years previous to the filing of his bill. Some further evidence, therefore, should have been produced by him to prove his non-access in the meantime. In a case in the Year Books, 1 *Hen.*, 6, 3' 7, *Justice* ROLFE says, "Although the wife leaves her husband and lives with an adulterer, her son is legitimate and shall inherit, unless his adversary can show some special matter." In other words, the party insisting upon the illegitimacy of the son born in wedlock, must give some farther evidence of the non-access of the husband, than the mere fact that the wife was living in adultery with another. The legal maxim, *pater est quem nuptiæ demonstrant*, is founded upon very strong reasons of policy, as well as of law. And Courts should not be permitted to unsettle the title to property, or to put the *status* of any one in jeopardy, by speculating upon the mere probabilities in favor of the illegitimacy of a child, who might or might not have been begotten by the husband of its mother. In the strong language of *Lord President* BLAIR, in *Routledge* v. *Carruthers*, *Nichol. Adult. Bast.*, 161, "This legal maxim, that he is the father whom the nuptials show to be so, is the foundation of every man's birth and status. It is a plain and sensible maxim, which is the corner stone, the very foundation on which rests the whole fabric of human society; and if you allow it once to be shaken, there is no saying what consequences may follow." The ancient rule of the common law was, that the husband must be presumed to be the father, if he was within the realm, during any part of the time, within the extreme limits of the period allowed for gestation. This rule has long since been repudiated by the Courts, as not consistent either with reason or common sense. For, other evidence of the non-access of the husband, is frequently as strong and satisfactory to show the actual impossibility that the husband could have been the father of the child. Nor is it necessary, that the evidence should be such as to render it impossible that sexual intercourse should have taken place between the husband and wife. It is sufficient if it proves, beyond a reasonable doubt, that no such intercourse did take place. But, though I utterly reject the ancient strictness of the rule on this subject, and with it the coarse elucidation of the rule adopted by *Judge* RICKHILL, in *Flattsham and Julian's Year Book*, 7 *Hen.*, 4*th*, 9, 13, which the great dramatist afterwards put in the mouth of King John, I cannot consent to relax the settled rule of the law on this subject beyond what was done by this Court, in the case of *Cross* v. *Cross*, 3 *Paige*, 139.

The usual decree for a divorce must be entered in this case, but without bastardizing the children; unless the complainant prefers to have the case referred back to the Master, to enable the latter to receive evidence of the actual non-access of the husband; or proof that he was residing at such a distance from her at the time these children must have been begotten, or such of them as were not begotten previous to the adultery charged in the bill, as fully to rebut the presumption that they are his children. If he prefers to have a further inquiry on that subject, the matter will be referred back to the Master to review his report, and to take further testimony; and the entry of the decree in the meantime will in that case be suspended.

DOWER.

Where the legal title to real estate was vested as a security for the payment of the purchase money, and the equitable owner died, his widow cannot have dower assigned to her without a discharge of the sum charged on the estate, and if the money be not paid, she is entitled to have the land sold for its payment, and to be endowed of one-third of the surplus.—*Thompson* v. *Cochran et als.*, 7 *Humphrey's R.*, *p.* 72. *Tenn.* (1847.)

If a married woman unite with her husband in the granting part of a deed conveying his land, she is thereby barred of her right of dower, as against all those who claim under such deed.—*Smith et ux.* v. *Handy*, 16 *Ohio R.*, *p.* 191. (1848.)

DRAFT.

Where a draft was drawn by a consignor of cotton, upon the consignee thereof, on account of such consignment, and was discounted by a [illegible]k, upon the faith of representations made by the payee and the drawer that such draft was drawn against the consignment, and would be paid out of the proceeds thereof; which draft was accepted by the drawee, but before the cotton was received by him, he executed a general assignment of his property, for the benefit of his creditors, and his assignee claimed the cotton as a part of the assigned estate; *Held*, that the proceeds of the cotton, in the hands of such assignee, was a trust fund, applicable to the payment of the draft drawn against such proceeds.—*The Marine and Fire Insurance Bank of Georgia* v. *Jaucey*, 1 *Barbour's R.*, *p.* 486. *N. Y.* (1848.)

(HARRIS, J., cited *Curtis v. Tyler Paige*, 434; *Pratt* v. *Adams*, 7 *Paige*, 626.)

DYING DECLARATIONS.

The dying declarations of one who has been killed are admissible in testimony against the slayer, notwithstanding the constitutional provision that the accused "shall be confronted with the witnesses against him;" their admissibility is confined to cases of homicide only.—*M'Daniel* v. *The State*, 8 *Smedes & Marshall's R.*, *p.* 401. *Miss.* (1847.)

EASEMENT.

He who owns the land on both banks of a navigable river, owns the entire river, subject only to the easement of navigation; and he who owns the land upon one bank only, owns to the middle of the main channel, subject to the same easement.—*Walker et al.* v. *Board of Public Works*, 16 *Ohio R.*, *p.* 540. (1848.)

EJECTMENT.

When a person is in possession of land, in pursuance of a contract of purchase, and fails to comply with his part of the agreement, an action of ejectment will lie against him at the suit of the vendor, without a previous notice to quit.—*Baker* v. *Lessee of Gittings et als.*, 16 *Ohio R.*, *p.* 485. (1848.)

(HITCHCOCK, J., cited 7 *Cowen.*, 747; 5 *Wend.*, 26; 1 *Wend.*, 418; 21 *Wend.*, 233.)

ENDORSEMENT.

A writing upon the back of a negotiable promissory note, signed by the payee and directed to a third person in these words—"Please pay the bearer the within without recourse to the endorser"—is a sufficient endorsement of the note, to enable such third person to maintain an action upon the note in his own name.—*Keyes* v. *Waters*, 18 *Vermont R.*, *p.* 479. (1847.)

ENDORSER.

A firm in this State, (Mass.,) made a note payable to their own order, and endorsed it to a firm in New-York. *Held*, that a discharge of the makers and endorsers under the insolvent laws of this State, was not a bar to an action against them, on the note, by the endorsees, who had not proved their claim thereon, under those laws.—*Savoye et als.* v. *Marsh et als.*, 10 *Metcalf's R.*, *p.* 594. *Mass.* (1847.)

(Dewey, J., cited *Shaw* v. *Robbins*, 12 *Wheat.*, 369, *note* ; *Ogden* v. *Saunders*, 12 *Wheat.*, 213 ; *Boyle* v. *Zacharie*, 6 *Pet.*, 348, 635 ; *Woodhull* v. *Wagner*, 1 *Bald.*, 296 ; *Frey* v. *Kirk*, 4 *Gill & Johns.*, 509.)

If the endorsee of a bill of exchange give time to the drawer, for a valuable consideration, he thereby discharges the endorser.—*The State Bank* v. *Wymoud et al.*, 7 *Blackford's R.*, *p.* 363. *Ind.* (1847.)

Appeal from the Dearborn Circuit Court.

Dewey, J.—Assumpsit by the State Bank, as the endorsee, against Wymoud and Faris, as the endorsers, of a bill of exchange. The bill, which is dated December 2nd, 1841, was drawn by Isaac Dunn on N. N. John, at New Orleans, in favor of the defendants, for $4,500, at four months. Plea, the general issue. Cause submitted to the Court. Judgment for the defendants.

The plaintiff having made out a *prima facie* case, in which it appeared that the bill was drawn and endorsed for the benefit of the drawee, the defendants proved the following facts: On the 25th of September, 1842, the plaintiff entered into an agreement with Dunn, the drawer, by which it was stipulated that Dunn should give a *cognovit* for a judgment on the bill in favor of the plaintiff, at the then next term of the Dearborn Circuit Court; that he should deliver to the bank, and place under its control, certain mortgages, as collateral security; that there should be a stay of execution on the judgment confessed for eighteen months; and that a suit in favor of the bank against Dunn on the bill, then pending in the Marion Circuit Court, should be dismissed. In pursuance of the agreement, the mortgages were delivered to the bank, the *cognovit* given, the judgment confessed at the October term of the Dearborn Circuit Court, 1842, and a stay of execution for eighteen months entered on record. The mortgages were executed by E. D. John, to N. N. John, and assigned by the latter to Dunn. The object of the mortgages was to secure the drawer and endorser of the bill against loss. The defendants had no knowledge of the mortgages, nor of the arrangement between the plaintiff and Dunn.

The counsel for the bank contends that, inasmuch as the collateral security afforded by the mortgages was advantageous to the defendants, the giving time by the plaintiff to the drawer did not discharge them.

This is not, however, as we conceive, putting the cause on the true ground. The relief which, in some instances, is extended to sureties in Courts of law, in consequence of giving time to the principal, is a doctrine borrowed from a rule in equity. The rule is this, that the surety has the right, so soon as the debt for which he is bound becomes payable, to require the creditor to enforce his legal remedy, or to pay the money himself and resort immediately to the principal for reimbursement. Whatever impairs this right discharges the surety. A creditor, by suspending his rightful power to coerce the principal, undertakes that he will not, during the suspension, receive the money from the surety; for should he receive it from him, the surety would be entitled immediately to take his recourse against the principal, who would consequently lose the benefit of the further time given him by the creditor; this, if the principal has given a consideration for the delay, would be unjust to him. On the other hand, it would be equally wrong to compel the surety to submit to the delay, and run the hazard, in the meantime, of an unfavorable change in the circumstances of the principal.

This equitable doctrine has been applied by Courts of law to actions founded on bills of exchange. *English* v. *Darley*, 3 *Esp.*, 49; 2 *B. & P.*, 61, was assumpsit by the endorsee against the endorser of a bill of exchange. The plaintiff had obtained judgment and sued out execution against the acceptor; he compromised the matter by receiving from the acceptor part of the debt, and taking a new security for the remainder payable by instalments, and by withdrawing the execution. It was held that the endorser was discharged, on the ground that the holder of the bill had given time to the acceptor. *Gould et al.* v. *Robson et al.*, 8 *East*, 576, was also an action by the endorsees again the endorsers of a bill of exchange. At the maturity of the bill, the holders made an arrangement with the acceptor, by which they agreed to receive from him a portion of the money due, and for the residue to draw on him at a short future period. This was done, and the new bill accepted, the holders agreeing to retain the first bill until the other was payable, as a security. The second bill not having been paid at maturity, suit was brought upon the first. It was argued that the endorsers were benefited by that part of the transaction by which a part of the debt was paid, and could not, therefore, with propriety complain of the postponement of the time for the payment of the remainder. But the Court decided otherwise, and held that the giving of time for a part of the debt discharged the endorsers.

In the foregoing cases the acceptor was considered as the principal, and the parties to the bill, subsequently liable, as the sureties. But the equitable rule above stated is, in general, equally applicable to all cases founded on bills of exchange, where the holder has given time to any of the parties to the instrument who would be liable to any other party, upon such other party's taking up the bill. The effect of giving time is to discharge the party having the right of recourse. *Story on Bills*, 501. The case of the *Bank of the United States* v. *Hatch*, 6 *Pet.*, 250, was an action by the endorsee against the endorser of a bill of exchange. It appeared that the bank had previously commenced an action against the drawer, which stood for trial at a certain term of the C. C. of the United States for the district of Ohio; and that the bank agreed with the drawer, for a valuable consideration, to continue the cause for judgment until the next succeeding term, which was accordingly done. It was held that the endorser was discharged. See also *Hall* v. *Cole*, 4 *Ad. & Ell.*, 577; 6 *Nev. & Mann.*, 124; *English* v. *Darley*, *Supra*, *per Ld.* Eldon. The rule probably does not apply to a case in which the holder of a bill having given time to a mere accommodation party, afterwards seeks to recover the debt from the party for whose benefit the bill was drawn, endorsed, or accepted. *Story on Bills*, 501; *Lambert* v. *Sandford*, 2 *Blackf.*, 137. But this exception to the rule cannot avail the present plaintiff. The bill of exchange in question was not drawn or endorsed for the benefit of the defendants, but for the use and accommodation of the acceptor; and the defendants have been affected by the time given to the drawer, precisely as they would have been had the bill been drawn and transferred in the regular course of a business transaction.

It should be remarked, that when the time of payment is *agreed* by the holder of a bill to be postponed, the agreement, to operate as a discharge of a party otherwise liable, must be made without the consent of that party, and be founded upon a good and valuable consideration. A mere voluntary delay in suing any of the parties to a bill does not exonerate any other party. *Philpot* v. *Bryant*, 4 *Bing.*, 717; *Clark* v. *Devlin*, 3 *B. & P.*, 363. Nor does the taking collateral security have that effect. *Pring* v. *Clarkson*, 1 *B. & C.*, 14; *Bedford* v. *Deakin*, 2 *Stark.*, 178.

In the cause under consideration, the agreement of the plaintiff to give a stay of execution of eighteen months, on the judgment confessed by the drawer of the bill, was not only founded on a valid consideration—the delivery of the mortgages as collateral security,—but it was actually carried into effect by an entry of record; and it was made without the knowledge or consent of the defendants. Thus, the plaintiff was effectually prevented from collecting the debt from the drawer, until the lapse of a year and a half. It can make no difference as to the rights of the parties, whether the time given was in the form of a stay of execution, or by an agreement not to sue. The result was the same; the defendants were deprived of their right to have the plaintiff collect the money from the drawer without delay, or of paying it themselves and taking their remedy immediately against him. This is the injury of which they complain; and it is no answer to their complaint to tell them that the collateral security taken by the plaintiff was designed for, and might enure to, their benefit; the plaintiff had no right to deprive them of a privilege given them by the law, and to substitute for it something else, which, in the opinion of the plaintiff, might be equally advantageous. Of that matter, the defendants had a right to judge for themselves; and having been deprived of that right by the unauthorized act of the plaintiff, they stand discharged from all liability to the bank on the bill of exchange on which this suit is founded.

We think the decision of the Circuit Court is clearly right.

Per Curiam.

The judgment is affirmed with costs.

Where a promissory note was payable to the order of several persons, the name of one of whom was inserted by mistake, or inadvertently left on when the note was endorsed and delivered by the real payees, one of whom was also the maker of the note, the endorsee had a right to recover upon the note, although the names of all the payees were not upon the endorsement, and had a right also, to prove the facts by evidence.—*Pease* v. *Dwight*, 6 *Howard's U. S. R.*, *p.* 190. (1848.)

The endorser of a draft, who has paid or secured the amount thereof to the endorsee, and has taken a transfer of the draft, has a right to sue the acceptor, and to recover, for his own use, the same amount which the endorsee could have recovered in a suit upon the acceptance.

It is immaterial, in such a case, whether the endorser, on procuring the transfer of the draft and acceptance, has paid the endorsee the amount thereof, or has given him security for such payment.

So if the endorsee has relinquished his claim upon such acceptance, to the endorser, for a mere nominal consideration, that circumstance will not vary the amount of the recovery in an action brought by the endorser against the acceptor.—*Deas* v. *Harvie*, 2 *Barbour's Ch. R.*, *p.* 448. *N. Y.* (1848.)

Parol evidence of statements made by the endorser at the time of a blank endorsement of a promissory note, is not to be received to contradict or vary the legal contract implied by such endorsement; but such evidence is admissible for the purpose of showing a waiver of the necessity of making a demand or giving notice.

If a note is endorsed when overdue, a demand is sufficient, if made within a reasonable time after the endorsement.—*Sanborn* v. *Southard*, 25 *Maine R.*, *p.* 409. (1847.)

ENDORSER—BLANK.

A party wishing to raise money drew a note, leaving a blank for the name of the payee, and the defendant endorsed it. The note was afterwards transferred by the drawer for his benefit, and the transferee filled up the blank with the name of the defendant. *Held*, that the defendant was liable on the note as endorser.—*Aiken* v. *Cathcart*, 3 *Richardson's R.*, *p.* 133. *S. C.* (1847.)

Before Frost, J., *at Fairfield, Spring term*, 1846.

This was an action by the last endorser, who had taken up the note, against the first endorser. The note was made by J. J. Myers, dated 9th March, 1842, for $5000, and the name of the payee left in blank. It was endorsed first by the defendant, and by W. J. Woodward, and then by the plaintiff. James R. Aiken testified that Myers had applied to the plaintiff to endorse this note, which, at first, he refused to do; but after some persuasion by Myers, and being assured that the prior endorsers were abundantly good, and his name only important to give the note greater credit in bank, he consented to endorse it. This witness also said it was not an accommodation note. Myers transferred the note, with the name of the payee still in blank, to Robinson & Caldwell in payment of a balance of account due to them, and also for future advances to be made by them for him. The name of the defendant was inserted in the note by Robinson & Caldwell, after it was transferred to them, and it was by them discounted in bank; at maturity they took it up; afterwards it was repaid to them by the plaintiff. At this time Robinson proposed to the plaintiff to pay one-third of the note; he refused to do so, saying he was not to pay any part, and if Robinson sued he might sue all the parties to the note.

The case was submitted to the jury, without argument, who were instructed by his honor, the presiding Judge, that the plaintiff was entitled to recover; they found a verdict accordingly.

The defendant appealed, and now moved this Court for a new trial, on the following grounds:

1. That the note of John J. Myers, on which the action was brought, having no payee inserted in its body until after it was put into circulation, the insertion of a payee, after that time, was such an alteration, in a material part, as vitiated the note.

2. That no payee having been inserted in the note at the time it was drawn and endorsed, it was not a note, under the law merchant, capable of being endorsed, but was payable, upon general principles, to a fictitious payee or to bearer, and that each endorser was a guarantor, and equally liable as a guarantor.

McCall, for the motion, cited 1 *Hill*, 74; 2 *N. & Mc. C.*, 102; *McM.*, 76; *Bail. on Bills*, 30; 3 *McC.*, 482; 1 *N. & McC.*, 128; 2 *McM.*, 320.

McDowel, contra.

Curia per Frost, J.—The questions presented by the grounds of appeal have been decided in *Carson* v. *Hill & Jones*, 1 *McM.*, 76. In that case, a note in blank, except that $5000 was written at the top, was signed by several parties, and delivered to one of them, to be used for his benefit, who delivered it in blank to the plaintiff, as collateral security for advances. The plaintiff, long after the delivery of the blank to him, filled it up in the terms of a promissory note for the payment of the sum expressed on the paper. It was held that the defendants, who had signed the note as sureties, were liable as makers. In *Russell* v. *Longstaffe*, *Doug.*, 515, *Lord* MANSFIELD held, that the endorsement of a blank note is a letter of credit for an indefinite sum. Many cases concur to establish that when the endorser of a note commits it to the maker in blank, either in whole or in part, the note carries on the face of it an implied authority to the maker to fill up the blank. As between the endorser and third persons the maker must, under such circumstances, be deemed to be the agent of the endorser, and as acting under his authority, and with his approbation.—*Collins* v. *Emmet*, 1 *H. Bl.*, 313; *Snaith* v. *Mingay*, 1 *M. & S.*, 87; *Crouchley* v. *Clarence*, 2 *M. & S.*, 90.

The insertion of the name of the first endorser in the blank left for the name of the payee, was not an alteration, but the completion of the note. It gave effect to the note consistently with the liabilities of the parties, expressed by their endorsements. The note might thus be perfected after a transfer. When the blank was filled up in pursuance of the authority implied by the delivery of the note to the maker, it had relation back to the endorsement, and took effect as if the note were then perfect; for the cases show that when a signature is written to a paper which is intended to have the operation of a negotiable instrument, it becomes such, when perfected, from the time when it was signed, so as to support the allegation that the party made or endorsed the note or bill.

The motion is refused.

EQUITABLE ASSIGNMENT.

Where a debtor gives to his creditor an order upon one indebted to him, requesting him to pay his creditor the amount of his debt, such order will be construed as an equitable assignment of the debt, even though the drawee had never assented thereto.—*Dickenson* v. *Phillips*, 1 *Barbour's R.*, *p.* 454. *N. Y.* (1848.)

(HARRIS, J., cited *Rogers* v. *Hosack's Ex'rs*, 18 *Wend.*, 319; *Clayton* v. *Fawcett*, 2 *Leigh's Va. R.*, 19; *Yeates* v. *Grover*, 1 *Ves. Jr.*, 280.)

EQUITY.

A Court of Equity will not grant relief against a judgment at law, on the ground of its being unconscientious, unless the defendant in the judgment was entirely ignorant of his defence pending the suit, or unless without any default or neglect on his part, he was prevented by fraud, or accident, or the act of the opposite party, from availing himself of his defence, or by some *unavoidable* necessity.—*Stroup* v. *Sullivan et al.*, 2 *Kelly's R.*, *p.* 275. *Ga.* (1847.)

(WARNER, J., cited 1 *Story's Eq.*, 178, *secs.* 894, 895; *Foster* v. *Wood*, 6 *Johns. Ch.*, 87; *Dodge* v. *Strong*, 2 *Johns. Ch.*, 228; *Marine*

Ins. Co. of Alexandria v. *Hodgson*, 7 *Cranch*, 332; *Bostwick* v. *Perkins et al.*, 1 *Kelly*, 136; *Maxwell* v. *Connor*, 1 *Hill's Ch.*, 22.)

ERROR.

Where the Court has permitted improper testimony to go the jury, it is not an error to permit it afterwards to be withdrawn.—*Carvilla* v. *Stout et al.*, 10 *Alabama R.*, *p.* 796. (1847.)

EVIDENCE.

The presumption of innocence may be overthrown, and a presumption of guilt be raised by the misconduct of a party in suppressing or destroying evidence which he ought to produce, or to which the other party is entitled.

The rule is, when a party refuses to produce books and papers, his opponent may give secondary or parol proof of their contents, if they are shown to be in possession of the opposite party; and if such secondary evidence is imperfect, vague and uncertain as to dates, sums, boundaries, &c., every intendment and presumption shall be against the party who might remove all doubt by producing the higher evidence.—*Rector* v. *Rector et al.*, 3 *Gilman's R.*, *p.* 105. *Ills.* (1847.)

(*Logan* and *Bledsoe* cited 1 *Stra.*, 505; 1 *Camp.*, 8; *Life & Fire Ins. Co.* v. *Mech. Ins. Co.*, 7 *Wend.*, 31; 1 *Greenl. Ev.*, 43; 2 *Vesey*, 155; *Story's Eq. Jur.*, *secs.* 187-8, 192, 254.)

The declarations or statements of persons are admitted as evidence in many cases, where they appear to have been made against their interest; but in all such cases the persons must be shown to be deceased at the time of the trial.—*Lowry* v. *Moss*, 1 *Strobhart's R.*, *p.* 63. S. C. (1847.)

(Frost, J., cited 1 *Phil. Ev.*, 255–260.)

On a prosecution for larceny in stealing bank bills of another State, the prosecution must show the existence of the bank, and the genuineness of the bills.—*Johnson* v. *The People*, 4 *Denio's R.*, *p.* 364. *N. Y.* (1849.)

(Beardsley, J., cited *The People* v. *Caryl*, 12 *Wend.*, 547.)

EVIDENCE—NOTE.

The evidence to prove the making of a promissory note, purporting to be signed by the defendant and payable to the bearer, was that the plaintiff's agent called on the defendant with the alleged note in his pocket, but which he did not exhibit, and told him he had a note for that amount against him, which he wanted the payment of for the plaintiff; and the defendant said he had given such a note, and would pay it if the plaintiff would make a small deduction and indulge him as to time; *Held*, that the note produced on the trial was not identified with that to which the admission referred, and that the proof was insufficient.—*Palmer* v. *Manning*, 4 *Denio's R.*, p. 131. *N. Y.* (1849.)

(*Church & Davis* cited *Cowen & Hill's notes*, 1263, 1265; *Shaver* v. *Ehle*, 16 *Johns.*, 201.)

EXECUTION.

An *alias* execution, issued by a justice of the peace, after the death of the defendant, is an absolute nullity, and no rights can be acquired under it.—*Henderson et al.* v. *Gandy's Adm'r*, 11 *Alabama R.*, p. 431. (1847.)

Payment of an execution to a sheriff, in any thing but constitutional currency, is no satisfaction thereof, except by the consent of the plaintiff; but such consent may be implied, as well as express, and may be inferred from long acquiescence.—*Prewett* v. *Standifer*, 8 *Smedes & Marshall's R.*, p. 493. *Miss.* (1847.)

(Clayton, J., cited *Anketel* v. *Torry et al.*, 7 *Smedes & Mar.*, 467; *Buchanan* v. *Tinnan et al.*, 2 *How.*, (*S. C.*,) 258.)

An execution cannot be enjoined, on grounds which might have been pleaded in defence before judgment.—*De Lizardi et als.* v. *Hardaway et als.*, 8 *Robinson's La. R.*, p. 22. (1847.)

(Simon, J., cited *Lafon's Ex'r* v. *Dessessart*, 1 *Mart. N. S.*, 135; *Monroe* v. *McMicken*, 8 *Mart. N. S.*, 513; *McMicken* v. *Millaudon*, 2 *La.*, 181; *Benton* v. *Roberts*, 3 *La.*, 224.)

EXECUTION—ASSIGNMENT.

A person not a party to an execution may advance money upon it, and by agreement have it assigned to himself, and thus keep it in force; but if he pay the execution, in whole or in part, without an agreement that it is not to operate as a discharge, or without taking an assignment, the execution will be *pro tanto* satisfied and cannot be afterwards enforced.

When, therefore, a sheriff having an execution in his hands against a principal and surety, pays to the attorney for the plaintiff therein a portion of such execution, expecting to reimburse himself out of a fund in his possession; and subsequently, when that fund fails, takes an assignment of so much of the execution from the attorney, the sheriff cannot enforce the execution for such sum so paid; but the execution will be *pro tanto* satisfied.—*Morris* v. *Lake*, 9 *Smedes & Marshall's R.*, *p.* 521. *Miss.* (1848.)

(CLAYTON, J., cited *Reed* v. *Pruyn et al*, 7 *Johns.*, 426; *Sherman* v. *Boyce*, 15 *Johns.*, 443; *Harwell* v. *Worsham*, 2 *Humph*, 525.)

EXECUTION—TESTE.

An execution, the *teste* of which bears date after the death of the defendant, should be quashed upon motion. Yet, if a sale take place under such execution, as the execution is not void but only voidable, the sale will be valid as to third persons who purchase under it, and will be protected; the purchaser's rights will not be affected by subsequent acts over which he had no control.—*Harrington* v. *O'Reilly et al.*, 9 *Smedes & Marshall's R.*, *p.* 216. *Miss.* (1848.)

(CLAYTON, J., cited *Davis* v. *Helm*, 3 *Smedes & Mar.*, 1; *Woodcock* v. *Bennett*, 1 *Conn.*, 737; *Jackson* v. *Robins*, 16 *Johns.*, 537; *Jordan* v. *Pool*, 6 *Iredell*, 288.)

EXECUTOR.

Where slaves are left by will to minor children, the executor is not discharged by delivering them to the children's father, but is accountable on their attaining majority, if the slaves are removed from the State and converted.—*Lang et al.* v. *Pettus*, 11 *Alabama R.*, *p.* 37. (1847.)

(*Robinson* cited *Isaacs* v. *Boyd*, 5 *Porter*, 388; *Chappel* v. *McMullen*, 8 *Porter*, 198; *Garrett* v. *Talmadge*, 1 *Johns. Ch.*, 3; *Merrill* v. *Dickey*, 1 *Johns. Ch.*, 153; *Williams* v. *Storrs*, 6 *Johns. Ch.*, 353; *Miles* v. *Bayden*, 3 *Pick.*, 213; *Hyde* v. *Stone*, 7 *Wend.*, 354; *Kline* v. *Beebe*, 6 *Conn.*, 494; *Fonda* v. *Van Horne*, 15 *Wend.*, 631; *Daily* v. *Tolferry*, 1 *P. Wms.*, 285; *Rotherham* v. *Fanshawe*, 3 *Atk.*, 629; *Cooper* v. *Thornton*, 3 *Bro. Ch.*, 96.)

An executor may be charged with interest on the balance in his hands found to be due the estate on settlement, from the date of such settlement.—*Smith* v. *Hurd et al.*, 8 *Smedes & Marshall's R.*, *p.* 682. *Miss.* (1847.)

(*Smith* cited *Davies* v. *Eden*, 3 *Dessaus.*, 241; *Shefflein* v. *Stewart*, 1 *Johns. Ch.*, 620.)

An executor who trades for a note, and in payment of it gives a note which he had taken for moneys of the estate loaned to another, will not be allowed to charge the estate, if the note traded for prove valueless, as he has no right to mix the funds of the estate with his own.—*Key* v. *Boyd*, 10 *Alabama R.*, *p.* 154. (1847.)

(*Williams* cited 2 *Story's Eq.*, 515, *sec.* 1274; *Powell* v. *Evans*, 5 *Vesey*, 839; *Langford* v. *Gascoigne*, 11 *Ves.* 333; *Tabbs* v. *Carpenter*, 1 *Mad.*, 290; *Underwood* v. *Stevens*, 1 *Merriv.*, 712; *Hanbury v. Kirkland*, 3 *Sim.*, 263.)

EXECUTORS.

Where there were four joint executors upon an estate, who gave a joint bond for faithful administration, and two of them ultimately became insolvent, and one of the remaining two was compelled, under a decree of the Court of Chancery, to pay for property, which, without fault or negligence on his part, had been wasted by one of the insolvent executors, prior to the time of his becoming insolvent, it was *held*, that the executor making such payment might recover from the other solvent executor one half of the amount so paid by him, and of all expenses incurred by him in defending the suit in Chancery, in which the decision was made.

And it was *held*, that it made no difference, in this respect, that it was agreed between the executors, prior to the execution of the bond, that the executor, who subsequently made such payment, should have the control of the estate, and that he in fact transacted most of the business of settling the estate,—it also appearing that the other executors did participate in the management of the estate. Such contract would only make the acting executor the agent of the other executors.—*Marsh* v. *Harrington*, 18 *Vermont R.*, *p.* 150. (1847.)

It is the duty of executors and administrators to retain sufficient of the personal estate of the decedent in their hands, to pay the expenses of the administration. And they cannot apply to the surrogate for the sale of the real estate of the decedent, to pay such expenses, after the lapse of three years from the time of granting letters testamentary, or of administration to them.—*Fitch* v. *Witbeck*, 2 *Barbour's Ch. R.*, *p.* 161. *N. Y.* (1848.)

EXEMPTION.

The law exempting certain articles from levy and sale, for the use of families, applies, whether the family is stationary, or moving from place to place. Nor would an intention on the part of the head of the family, to abscond from one part of the State to another, deprive the family of this privilege.—*Davis* v. *Allen*, 11 *Alabama R.*, *p.* 164 (1847.)

The articles exempted by law from sale by execution, are not rendered subject to such sale, in consequence of the husband making a fraudulent sale of all the rest of his property—*Calloway* v. *Carpenter*, 10 *Alabama R.*, *p.* 500. (1847.)

FACTOR.

A factor who makes advances on goods consigned to him for sale with a limit as to price, cannot sell below such price to cover his advances, without timely notice to his principal to return the same.

The measure of damages, in an action against a factor for selling goods in violation of instructions, is the difference between the price obtained on the sale, and the minimum price limited by the instructions.—*Blôt* v. *Boiceau et al.*, 1 *Sandford's R.*, *p.* 111. *N. Y.* (1849.)

(Vanderpoel, J., cited *Bell* v. *Palmer et al.*, 6 *Cowen*, 128; *La-Farge* v. *Kneeland*, 7 *Cowen*, 456.)

When a factor accepts a planter's order, payable "when in funds," it amounts to a promise to pay out of the first funds of the planter which shall come into his hands; and he cannot defend himself against an action on the acceptance, by showing that he has never been in funds over and above the amount of a debt due him by the planter, at the time of the acceptance.

It is no longer an open question, whether a conditional acceptance be binding. When the condition is performed, the acceptance becomes absolute.—*Hunton* v. *Ingraham et al.*, 1 *Strobhart's R.*, *p.* 271. *S. C.* (1847.)

FALSE IMPRISONMENT.

No actual force is necessary to constitute a false imprisonment. If a man is restrained of his personal liberty by fear of a personal difficulty, that amounts to a false imprisonment.—*Smith* v. *The State*, 7 *Humphreys' R.*, *p.* 43. *Tenn.* (1847.)

FALSE PRETENCES.

The offence of cheating by false pretences is, in judgment of law, committed where the false pretences are successfully used and where the money or property is obtained, although the fraud originated and was contrived elsewhere.—*The People* v. *Adams*, 3 *Denio's R.*, *p.* 190. *N. Y.* (1848.)

(*Whiting* cited *The King* v. *Brisac*, 4 *East*, 164; *The People* v. *Rathbun*, 21 *Wend.*, 509, 539; *Town of Barkhamsted* v. *Parsons*, 3 *Conn.*, 1; *Commonwealth* v. *Gillespie*, 7 *Serg. & Rawle*, 579; *Rex* v. *Johnson*, 6 *East*, 583; *S. C.*, 7 *East*, 68; *Commonwealth* v. *Harvey*, 8 *Amer. Jur.*, 69.)

FALSE REPRESENTATIONS.

Where a person about to purchase a farm was ignorant of the actual character and capabilities of the land, and had no means of obtaining such knowledge except by information to be derived from others; and the owner, with a knowledge that the purchaser's object was to obtain an early farm, and that his farm was not as early as the lands lying in the neighborhood, represented to such purchaser "that there was no earlier land any where about there," and the latter, relying upon the truth of that representation, made the purchase; and after ascertaining by actual experiment, that the land was not what it had been represented to be, he applied to the vendor, within a reasonable time, to rescind the bargain, who refused to do so; *Held*, that this furnished a sufficient ground for the interference of a Court of Equity, to rescind the contract; even though there was no intention on the part of the vendor to deceive the purchaser.

Whatever may have been the motive of a vendor in making erroneous representations respecting land about to be sold by him, it is enough to entitle the purchaser to relief, that there was a misrepresentation of a matter of fact, material to the subject of negotiation, and which constituted the very basis of the contract.—*Taylor* v. *Fleet*, 1 *Barbour's R.*, *p.* 471. *N. Y.* (1848.)

(HARRIS, J., cited *Doggett* v. *Everson*, 3 *Story's R.*, 733; 1 *Story's Eq. Jur.*, *sec.* 193; *Hough* v. *Richardson*, 3 *Story's R.*, 659.)

If a purchaser of goods make at the time material statements as to his debts and means, which are relied on, and turn out to have been false, the sale is voidable.

In such case, the articles may be recovered back by the vendor, though mortgaged to a third person to secure an existing debt, if the mortgage has not been foreclosed, or the third person has advanced no new consideration and will not be placed in a worse position than he occupied before the mortgage, by his security anticipated from it failing. But if the title has absolutely passed to a third person without notice, and for a new consideration, the goods cannot be recovered back by the original vendor.—*Johnson* v. *Peck*, 1 *Woodbury & Minot's R.*, *p.* 334. *U. S.* (1847.)

This was an action of trover for a certain quantity of merchandise, mostly English goods, valued at $722, and alleged to have been converted, March 28th, 1846.

The defendant pleaded not guilty.

It appeared in evidence, that the plaintiffs were merchants in Boston, (Mass.,) and early in March last, were applied to by one Wheelock, of Bristol, Rhode Island, to purchase of them a quantity of goods. Wheelock alleged that he was then worth $1200 surplus, after paying all debts, and owed nobody except one Briggs, for some goods he had lately purchased of him. The plaintiffs caused Wheelock to sign a written statement containing the above representations, and relying on their truth, made sale to him of about $750 worth of merchandise, which Wheelock took and carried to Rhode Island.

In a few days after, April 17th, 1846, he gave a mortgage of them and his other goods to Briggs, to secure him for the purchase money of his stock that had been sold to Wheelock in the January previous, and a mortgage of them then taken by Briggs from Wheelock, dated January 28th, 1846. On the 20th April, 1846, Wheelock executed another mortgage of them to Hutchings & Anthony, to secure a debt to them; and 22d April, 1847, assigned the whole to the defendant Peck, in trust to be sold, and first pay Briggs, then Hutchings & Co., then other creditors, and the surplus to Wheelock.

It further appeared in evidence, that $300 of the purchase money had been paid to Briggs in January, and some $200 or $300 since, by sales of the goods; and that in the assignment were contained sundry book accounts, to the amount of $700, a part of which had been collected by the defendant.

It was now contended by the defendant, that all the property assigned would not more than pay the two original mortgages, and it was not shown that Wheelock in fact had any other estate, though his wife was reported to be worth some money.

It was further shown, that when Wheelock bought of the plaintiffs, he owed other persons than Briggs, as follows, viz., Hutchings & Anthony, about $450; John A. Corcey, $396; and Whitcomb, $185.

Waters and *Carpenter*, counsel for the plaintiffs.

Bullock, for the defendant.

WOODBURY, J., instructed the jury, that if the representations made by Wheelock to the plaintiffs, at the time of the purchase, were false and fraudulent, and were relied on by the plaintiffs, and were so material that the sale would not probably have been made without them, the sale was voidable as between the parties to it.

One party had obtained credit by means not justifiable, and the other had parted with his property under false pretences and averments, which were material and untrue.

It was right, then, in law as well as equity, that such a purchaser should not profit by his own wrong, and that the seller and purchaser should in such case stand as if nothing had occurred between them.

But when rights of third persons intervene in this class of cases, they are to be upheld; if those persons purchased the property absolutely, and parted with a new and valuable consideration for it without notice of any fraud. Because, unlike the case of theft, the vendor here voluntarily parts with the possession of his property, and thus enables the purchaser to gain a credit, or to appear to be the owner, and thus he bought of honestly. And though in the case of theft, it is otherwise, and the owner may recover the property of third persons, yet he cannot in cases of fraudulent sales, else the community would be deceived and defrauded as much as the vendor.—*Parker* v. *Patrick*, 5 *D. & E.*, 175; *Somes* v. *Brewer*, 2 *Pick.*, 184; *Rowley* v. *Bigelow*, 12 *Pick.*, 307; *Story on Bailm.*, *secs.* 124, 125; 8 *Cow.*, 238; *Lloyd* v. *Brewster*, 4 *Paige*, 537.

The true tests, then, as to third persons, are these:

If they buy absolutely, and for a new and full consideration, and without notice of the fraud in procuring the goods, they are to be protected in holding them.

But if they have notice of the fraud, or give no new valuable consideration, or are mere mortgagees, pawnees, or assignees in trust for the debtor, or for him and others, such third persons are to be regarded as holding the goods open to the same equities and exceptions as to title, as they were open to in the hands of the mortgager, pawner, or assigner.

The latter is still interested in them; has a residuary title; has taken no new consideration for them; and his assignee or mortgagee has parted with nothing new for the goods; has not bought them; and, if he loses them, is in no worse condition than he stood before they were purchased and assigned or mortgaged him.

If the defendant then stood in this attitude, or the mortgagees for whom he acted; the plaintiffs should recover against him.

He would lose nothing by such a recovery, as he held other goods sufficient to defray his expenses, and had no debt against Wheelock to be secured or paid.

Nor would the mortgagees lose any thing, looking to this transaction as a whole. They stood better than before it took place, as they had been partly paid by sales of some of these goods before a demand on the defendant, and these last sales are not to be computed in the damages recovered against him.

They could stand no worse, as neither of them had given any new credit, or parted with any new consideration, on account of the morgages or assignment of this property.

The Court then called the attention of the jury to the evidence which bore upon the facts, that the representations made were not true, and were at the same time material in the trade.

The jury returned a verdict for the plaintiffs.

If A agrees to buy a plantation for B, and B agrees to pay A what he gives for it, and A should represent to B that he gave three thousand dollars for it, when in fact he paid a less sum, and B pays him three thousand dollars, an action on the case will lie in favor of B against A for the deceitful and false representation.—*Green* v. *Bryant*, 2 *Kelly's R.*, *p.* 66. *Ga.* (1847.)

(NISBET, J., cited 1 *East*, 318; 2 *East*, 92; 3 *Ves. & Bea.*, 110; 5 *Bos. & Pull.*, 241; 1 *Day*, 22; 7 *Cranch*, 92; 17 *Mass.*, 182; 6 *Johns.*, 181; 6 *Cowen*, 346; 2 *Wend.*, 385; 7 *Wend.*, 1.)

If a party makes a false representation to another person, who is about to act upon the faith of that representation, the former must make the representation good, if he knows it to be false.

Where a party intentionally misrepresents a material fact, or produces a false impression, in order to mislead another, or to entrap or cheat him, or to obtain an undue advantage of him; in every such case there is a positive fraud, in the truest sense of the term.—*Willink* v. *Vandeveer*, 1 *Barbour's R.*, *p.* 559. *N.Y.* (1848.)

(BARCULO, J., cited *Story Eq.*, *sec.* 181; *Evans* v. *Bicknell*, 6 *Ves.*, 173; *Story Eq. sec.* 192.)

One who designedly represents another as solvent when he knew that he was not so, and thereby induces a third person to give him a credit, in consequence of which the latter sustains a loss, will be bound to indemnify the party injured by such representations.—*Parrish* v. *Cirode*, 8 *Robinson's La. R.*, *p.* 117. (1847.)

APPEAL from the Commercial Court of New Orleans, WATTS, J.

Benjamin, for the plaintiff.—In actions like this the questions for consideration, are: 1. Were false representations made? 2. Was the person making such representations aware of their falsehood, or in a position in which he was bound to know the real facts? 3. Was there damage to the plaintiff? *Pasley* v. *Freeman*, 1 *Durnf. & East*, 61; *Eyre* v. *Dunsford*, 1 *East*, 325, 6; *Russell* v. *Clark*. 7 *Cranch*, 67; *Upton* v. *Vail*, 6 *Johnson*, 182; *Allen* v. *Addington*, 7 *Wendell*, 18, 19.

Schmidt, for the appellant.

BULLARD, J.—This is an action by which the plaintiff seeks to recover damages from the defendant for falsely representing his son and son-in-law, composing the firm of Cirode & White, of Mobile, as solvent and worthy of credit; by reason of which false representations he was induced to sell them merchandise to the amount of about $1700, which he lost by their insolvency. The plaintiff recovered a judgment for the amount of the goods sold, and the defendant has appealed.

In cases turning principally, if not altogether, upon mere matters of fact. we do not feel it to be our duty to enter minutely into an analysis of the evidence. In the present case, we are far from being ready to say that the Court below erred in the conclusion that the conduct of the defendant was designed to deceive the plaintiff, and others who had dealt with the firm of Cirode & White. He represented them to the plaintiff's clerk as dealing altogether for cash, and as having no bills due, while, at the same time, he had claims against them for a large amount for advances, to secure which, he soon after levied an attachment which broke up their establishment.

But it is contended that the plaintiff has failed to show that he has lost any thing, not having prosecuted his principal debtors, and exhausted his remedies against them. It is true, that however fraudulent the conduct of the defendant may be shown to have been, the plaintiff cannot recover without showing that he has really sustained damage. The record shows that Cirode & White are insolvent, and have been declared bankrupts. It further shows that the defendant levied an attachment on the property of Cirode & White, having previously made oath that they were about to remove themselves and their property out of the State of Alabama; and that the property which they had been enabled to purchase of the plaintiff went partly to pay the debt to the defendant, he knowing that the goods had been purchased on a credit.

It is ordered that the judgment of the Commercial Court be affirmed, with costs.

FEME COVERT.

An infant feme covert cannot bind herself by deed so as to bar her right of dower.—*Cunningham* v. *Knight*, 1 *Barbour's R.*, *p.* 399. *N. Y.* (1848.)

(*Jones* cited *Jones* v. *Todd.* 2 *J. J. Marsh.*, 361*; *Sandford* v. *McLean*, 3 *Paige*, 117, 121.)

FRAUD.

Where a fraudulent combination is entered into to defeat the claims of creditors of a judgment debtor, there is no difference between those who form the design and those who afterwards enter into it with a knowledge of its character, and aid in carrying it out; all are equally affected by the fraud.—*Stovall* v. *The Farmers' and Merchants' Bank of Memphis*, 8 *Smedes & Marshall's R.*, *p.* 305. *Miss.* (1847.)

Where the master of a steamer, for the fraudulent purpose of aiding a debtor in removing his property into a foreign country beyond the reach of a creditor, conceals from the latter the fact of his having entered into an arrangement with the debtor for its removal, and, with a full knowledge of the rights of the creditor, transports the property out of the United States, thereby preventing the creditor levying an attachment and saving his debt, he will be liable to the creditor for the amount of the debt, where it does not exceed the value of the property so removed.—*Irish* v. *Wright et als.*, 8 *Robinson's La. R.*, *p.* 428. (1847.)

When a party by fraud obtains possession of property, under a contract which he had not complied with on his part, an offer by the defrauded party, to make a new contract which is not acceded to, is not a waiver of any right he had against the other for the fraud practised. —*Adams* v. *Shelby*, 10 *Alabama*, *R.*, *p.* 478. (1847.)

FRAUDLENT CONVEYANCE.

Where the consideration of a conveyance is paid by one person, and the conveyance is taken in the name of another, for the purpose of defrauding the creditors of the person advancing the money, although such conveyance is valid as between the parties, and vests the whole legal and equitable title in the grantee, it is fraudulent as to creditors. And a creditor having a judgment against the person advancing the money, may file his bill against the fraudulent grantee, to set the deed aside; so far as to have his judgment satisfied out of the land. But the administrator of the person advancing the money upon the purchase of the land, is not a proper party to such a bill.—*Jackson* v. *Forrest*, 2 *Barbour's*, *Ch. R.*, *p*, 576. *N. Y.* (1848.)

FREIGHT—INSURANCE.

There is an interest in the freight of a ship whenever freight is engaged by a valid contract, and the ship is at the proper place to receive the cargo, which may be insured, though the goods be not laden on board.—*Gordon* v. *The American Ins. Co. of N. Y.*, 4 *Denio's R.*, *p.* 360. *N. Y.* (1849.)

(*Emerson & O'Connor* cited, 6 *T. R.*, 478; 7 *East*, 700; 2 *Wash. C. C.*, 346; 5 *Bing. N. C.*, 519; 1 *Moody & Rob.*, 88; 8 *Bing.*, 79, *note*, *S. C.*; 1 *B. & Ad.*, 45; 4 *B. & C.*, 538; 3 *Johns.*, 49; 2 *Conn.*, 368; 1 *Rawle*, 97; 3 *T. R.*, 368; 13 *East*, 323; 1 *M. & Sel.*, 313; 10 *Johns.*, 127, 201; 4 *Camp.*, 297; 1 *B. & P.*, 364; 2 *Archb.*, *N. P.*, 149; 3 *Steph. N. P.*, 2099; 2 *Brod. & Bing.*, 320; 3 *Chit. Com. Law*, 451, 326; 1 *Phil. on Ins.*, 132, 43; 3 *Kent*, 207; 2 *Burr.*, 1216; 2 *Johns.*, 335; 4 *Howard*, 326; 10 *Mass.*, 26; 1 *Duer on Ins.*, 168; *Hughes on Ins.*, 110, 11; *Miller on Ins.*, 15; 1 *Magens Lex Mer.*, 106; *Weskett on Ins.*, 244, 426; 1 *Marsh. on Ins.*, 97, 111; 2 *East*, 548; *Park on Ins.*, 28; 4 *Johns.*, 445; 4 *T. R.*, 210; 4 *B. & P.*, 33; 1 *Mason*, 127; 2 *Caine*, 14.

Bronson, C. J., cited Warre v. Miller, 4 B. & C., 538; Devaux v. J'Anson, 5 Bing. N. C., 519; Flint v. Fleming, 1 B. & Ad., 45; Hart v. The Delaware Ins. Co., 2 Wash. C. C., 349.)

GRAND JURORS.

Grand Jurors are competent witnesses to prove facts which came to their knowledge while acting in such capacity.—*Granger* v. *Warrington*, 3 *Gilman's R.*, p. 299. *Ills.* (1847.)

(*Tracy* cited, 2 *Wheat. Selw.*, 1091; 1 *Greenl. Ev.*, 300, *note*; *Freeman* v. *Arkill*, 2 *Barn. & Cres.*, 494; 3 *Stephen's N. P.*, 2286; *Lowe's case*, 4 *Greenl.*, 439; *Rogers* v. *Hall*, 3 *Scam.*, 45; 3 *Johns.*, 234; 4 *C. & P.*, 444.)

GUARDIAN AND WARD.

Where a guardian sold land of his ward for maintenance and education under an order of the Orphan's Court, and the ward married and died under twenty-one, leaving a child, who also died in infancy, the husband suing as administrator of the wife is entitled to the surplus of the proceeds of the sale, received by the guardian during the life of the wife, either in right of his wife, or of his child.—*Dyer* v. *Cornell*, 4 *Barr's R.*, p. 359. *Pa.* (1847.)

HIGHWAY.

A surveyor of highways is a competent witness for the town, in an action against the town to recover damages for an injury received by reason of a defect or want of repair in a highway within the surveyor's district, he not being liable to the town for the amount of the damages that may be recovered in such action.—*White* v. *Inhabitants of Philipston*, 10 *Metcalf's R.*, p. 108. *Mass.* (1847.)

HUSBAND AND WIFE.

A conveyance of real estate executed and acknowledged by husband and wife, but in the body of which the wife's name is not inserted, does not convey the interest of he wife in the premises.—*Cox et al.* v. *Wells*, 7 *Blackford's R.*, p. 410. *Ind.* (1847.)

Error to the Rush Circuit Court.

Blackford, J.—Assumpsit brought by Wells, as assignee of one James Conell, against Cox and Morrow on a promissory note. The note was dated on the 1st of December, 1836, and was payable to Conwell or order, three years after date.

Pleas.—1. Non-assumpsit. 2. That the note was given in part consideration of lots numbered 19 and 20 in the town of Laurel; that upon the execution of the note, the payee gave to the defendants his title-bond, the condition of which (after reciting that he had received one-third of the purchase-money, and the defendant's note for the residue payable in three years) was, that he would execute to the defendant a deed for said lots with relinquishment of dower, upon payment of the residue of the purchase-money; that the note sued on was for said residue of the purchase-money; and that the payee did not on the 1st of December, 1839, or at any time previously, make, or offer to make to the defendants, a deed for said lots, nor at any time afterwards, until the 18th of September, 1840; wherefore the consideration of the note had failed.

Replication to the special plea, that on the 15th September, 1840, the plaintiff tendered to the defendants a deed for said lots with relinquishment of dower, executed by said James Conwell and his wife, which tender was prior to the commencement of this suit; wherefore the consideration of the note had not failed.

The defendants craved and obtained *oyer* of the deed mentioned in the replication, the substance of which deed is as follows:—This indenture witnesseth that the parties to this agreement having considered, etc., do mutually agree, as follows, viz., James Conwell, the party of the first part, agrees, etc.; and we Robert S. Cox and Charles W. Morrow, the party of the second part, etc., have purchased of the said party of the first part lots numbered 19 and 20 in the town of Laurel, and have paid to the party of the first part the sum of, etc. The party of the first part hath granted, bargained, and sold, and by these presents doth grant, bargain, and sell to the said party of the second part, and to their heirs and assigns, the above-described premises, etc. The party of the first part binds himself, etc., to the said party of the second part, etc., to defend said lots against the claims of all persons, etc. In testimony whereof, the said James Conwell and Wineford Conwell his wife, have hereunto set their hands and seals this 5th of September, 1840.—James Conwell, [seal]. Wineford Conwell, [seal.]

There is a certificate of a justice of the peace in the usual form endorsed on the deed, stating the acknowledgment of the deed by the said Conwell and wife, the wife being examined separately, etc.

Oyer as aforesaid of the deed having been obtained by the defendants, they demurred generally to the replication; but the demurrer was overruled.

The cause was submitted to the Court on the general issue, and judgment rendered for the plaintiff.

On the trial the plaintiff proved the execution of the note and of Conwell's title-bond. He also proved that on the 15th of September 1840, he tendered to the defendants a deed for the lots aforesaid, the substance of which deed we have already stated, *oyer* of it having been given to the defendants. The deed was objected to by the defendants, but the objection was overruled.

The replication to the special plea is bad, because, as we shall presently show, the deed alleged to have been tendered is insufficient. The special plea is also bad.—*Cox et al.* v. *Hazard*, decided at this term. The deed offered in evidence by the plaintiff, and shown on *oyer*, does not convey the interest of Conwell's wife in the premises; her name not being inserted in the body of the deed.—*Catlin* v. *Ware*, 9 *Mass.*, 209; *Lufkin* v. *Curtis*, 13 *Mass.*, 223. The conveyance tendered, therefore, was not such a one as the defendants were entitled to, under their contract with Conwell.

Per Curiam. *The judgment is reversed, with costs. Cause remanded, &c.*

A husband may maintain replevin for personal chattels belonging to his wife at the time of the coverture, without joining her in the suit.—*Brown* v. *Fitz*, 13 *New Hampshire R.*, *p.* 283. (1847.)

(Gilchrist, J., cited *Bull. N. P.*, 50-53; *Powes* v. *Marshall*, 1 *Sid.*, 172; *Bourn* v. *Mattaire*, 1 *Bacon's Ab.*, 501; *Selw. N. P.*, 280.)

A conveyance being made of land and slaves, to a husband in trust for his wife and children, his possession of the property will be referred to the deed, and that he holds it as trustee merely, unless he does some act, demonstrating his intention to assert his marital rights over it. If he dies without manifesting such intention, and before any creditor has in his name asserted such right, the interest of the wife in the property will survive to her.—*Terrell et als.* v. *Green et als.*, 11 *Alabama R.*, *p.* 207. (1847.)

(Ormond, J., cited *Honnor* v. *Morton*, 3 *Russ.*, 68; *Johnson* v. *Johnson*, 1 *Jac. & W.*, 450; *Kenney* v. *Udall*, 5 *Johns. Ch.*, 573; *Elliott* v. *Cordell*, 5 *Madd.*, 150; *Andrews* v. *Jones*, 10 *Ala.*, 400; *Spear* v. *Walkeley*, 10 *Ala.*, 328; *Fellowes & Co.* v. *Tann*, 9 *Ala.*, 1002.)

Where in a suit against husband and wife, to foreclose a mortgage upon the separate estate of the wife, given to secure a debt of the husband, a decree *pro confesso* is rendered, it will not be sufficient ground to sustain a bill of review, at the instance of the wife, to set aside the decree, that her husband fraudulently concealed from her the extent and character of the mortgage, kept her ignorant of the nature of the suit against her, and told her it was mere form, and would not affect her rights; to affect the validity of the decree, the other party to the suit must have participated in these frauds.—*James* v. *Fisk et al.*, 9 *Smedes & Marshall's R.*, *p.* 144 *Miss.* (1848.)

If the husband merely expends his personal labor in the improvement of his wife's estate, the estate is not thereby made a debtor to the husband, nor can the creditors of the latter charge it with the value of the labor.—*Hoot et al.* v. *Sorrell et al.* 11 *Alabama R.*, *p.* 386. (1847.)

HUSBAND AND WIFE—BEQUEST.

A bequest of slaves to a husband, to be held and worked by him for the use of his wife and children, but subject in no way to his debts, contracts, or judgment, and at his death to be equally divided among his children, then living, does not create a legal estate in the husband, which can be sold under execution at law.—*Spear* v. *Walkley*, 10 *Alabama R.*, *p.* 328. (1847.)

Writ of error to the Circuit Court of Barbour.

Claim of property interposed by Spear, as trustee for his wife and children, to a certain slave levied on as his individual property, by virtue of a writ of *fi. fa*, in favor of Walkley.

At the trial, the claimant made title to the slave under the following bequest, in the will of Mrs. Hampton, to wit: "I give and bequeath to Anderson Spear, Letty, Becky and her children, Joe and Leonora, and their future increase, to be held and worked by him, for the use of his wife and children, but subject in no way to his debts, contracts, or judgments, and at his death, to be equally divided among his children, then living, and the issue of such as may be dead, taking together the part that would have fallen to their parent."

The claimant also proved that the debt for which the levy was made, was due at the time the will above stated was made, and that he was insolvent. It was also in proof that the wife and children of the claimant, living with him at the time of the levy, were the same as at the time when the will was made, and that he did not have possession of the slaves until after the death of the testatrix.

On this state of proof, the Circuit Court charged the jury, that the slave was subject to the plaintiff's execution.

This charge is the only error assigned.

Belser, for the plaintiff in error, insisted, that the claimant was a mere trustee for his wife and children, under the will, and took no beneficial interest by the devise.—*Hunt* v. *Booth*, 1 *Free.*, 215; *O'Neal* v. *Teague*, 8 *Ala.*, 345; *Lamb* v. *Wragg*, 8 *Porter*, 73; *Johnson* v. *Thompson*, 4 *Dess.*, 458; 2 *R. & M.*, 197; *Anderson* v. *Anderson*, 2 *M. & R.*, 427; *Bennet* v. *Davis*, 2 *P. Wms.*, 316; *Jarman* v. *Bridget*, 6 *S. & R.*, 467.

Burford, contra, argued, that goods given to the joint use of husband and wife, are subject to the husband's debts. *Harkins* v. *Coaller*, 2 *Porter*, 463. To make a separate estate to the wife, there must be words to exclude the interest of the husband. *Lamb* v. *Wragg*, 8 *Porter*, 72. So a bequest to wife and children makes the interest of the wife subject to the husband's debts. *Dunn* v. *Bank of Mobile*, 2 *Ala.*, 152; *Inge* v. *Forrester*, 6 *Ala.*, 418; *Br. Bank* v. *Williams*, 7 *Ala.*, 589. As the use for the benefit of the wife passed to the husband absolutely, the restriction upon the right of disposition is void.

Goldthwaite, J.—Without, at this time, undertaking to decide whether the husband has, or has not, an interest in the profits of the slaves bequeathed by Mrs. Hampton, we are clear he has no such interest in the slaves themselves, as is the subject of levy and sale under execution. The title to the slaves is vested in him for a special purpose, and his control over them is, to work them for the use of his wife and children. If they can be taken from his possession by a creditor, the trust that they shall be worked *by him*, cannot be carried into effect, but will be certainly defeated. On the other hand, if the profits of these slaves, when worked, constitutes a fund to be divided between the wife and children, then the wife's share of that devolves on the husband, and can only be separated and ascertained by a Court of Equity. This case has a very remote resemblance, if any, to *Banks* v. *Charlton*, 7 *Ala.*, 32, or *Branch Bank* v. *Williams*, 7 *Ala.*, 589, for in both these cases the use was a general one, for the benefit of his wife; whilst here, the slaves are to be used in a particular mode, and by a particular person.

The judgment, for the error in the charge, is reversed and the cause remanded.

IDIOT—CONTRACT.

The contracts of persons *non compos mentis*, are, if not wholly void, at all events voidable, unless when they relate to necessaries suited to their condition in life.

When the fact of an incapacity to make a legal contract is established, the contract, unless in certain excepted cases, is avoided. That is a legal consequence depending on the discretion of no Court or Judge.—*Fitzgerald* v. *Reed*, 9 *Smedes & Marshall's R.*, *p.* 94. *Miss.* (1848.)

(Clayton, J., cited *Comyn's Dig.*, *D.* 1, 2; *Chitty Con.*, 110.)

INDICTMENT.

The only mode of preferring an indictment is through the medium of a grand jury, and it is their imperative duty to make their present-ments in open Court. The indictment being the foundation of all subsequent proceedings in the cause, the record ought to show affirmatively the returning of the indictment into Court by the grand jury. This is a necessary part of the record, and can no more be dispensed with than the verdict of the jury.—*Rainey* v. *The People*, 3 *Gilman's R.*, *p.* 71. *Ills.* (1847.)

(*Trumbull & Bond* cited *Rev. Stat.*, 309, *sec.* 3; 1 *Chitty's Crim. Law*, 324; *Gardner* v. *The People*, 3 *Scam.*, 85; *McKinney* v. *The People*, 2 *Gilman*, 540.)

In an indictment for a misdemeanor, a substantial description of an offence is all that is required.—*Bilbro* v. *The State*, 7 *Humphreys' R.*, *p.* 534. *Tenn.* (1847.)

If on an indictment against two persons, one of them be tried separately, the record, by showing that the prisoner was separately tried, necessarily shows that the Court directed the trial.

If the record of a criminal case show that in the course of the trial, the Court had, on an adjournment from one day till the next, placed the jury in the charge of a bailiff, it will be presumed that the jury was committed to his care in a legal manner, whatever that may be.

A count in an indictment for murder stated, that the defendant made an assault on one G. B., and that the defendant with a certain axe, &c., the said G. B., in and upon the *left* side of the head and over the *left* temple of him the said G. B., then and there feloniously and wilfully and of his malice aforethought, did strike and beat, giving to the said G. B., then and there with the axe aforesaid, in and upon the *right* side of the head of him the said G. B., and over the *right* temple of him the said G. B., one mortal wound, &c., of which said mortal wound the said G. B., &c., on, &c., died, and so the jurors aforesaid, upon their oath aforesaid, do say, &c. *Held*, that the count, in the description of the offence, was repugnant and inconsistent with itself in a material part, and was void.

Such count must state the part of the body to which the violence was applied; but the proof need not correspond with the statement.

If an allegation in such count be sensible and consistent in the place where it occurs, and be not repugnant to *antecedent* matter, it cannot be rejected as surplusage, although it be repugnant to a *subsequent* allegation.

An objection to such count for repugnancy in the description of the offence, cannot be removed by striking out the allegation which is inconsistent with a previous one, unless, after striking out the subsequent allegation, a legal description of the offence will still remain.

In an indictment for murder, where the death is alleged to have been caused by a wound, it is not necessary to describe the depth or breadth of the wound.

An indictment in such case concluded as follows: "And so the jurors aforesaid upon their oath aforesaid do say, that the said S. D. (the prisoner), in manner and form aforesaid, feloniously and wilfully, and of his malice aforethought, did kill and murder, contrary to the form of the statute," &c. *Held*, that this conclusion was insufficient, for not designating the person murdered.

Although an indictment charge that the defendant feloniously and wilfully, and of his malice aforethought, did strike the deceased, &c., giving him, &c., a mortal wound, &c., yet if it do not contain the technical allegation that the defendant feloniously *murdered* the deceased, it is an indictment for manslaughter only and not for murder—the word *murder* being a term of art which cannot be supplied in an indictment by any other word.

A verdict against the defendant in manslaughter must fix the punishment.—*Dias* v. *The State*, 7 *Blackford's R.*, *p.* 20. *Ind.* (1847.)

Error to the Vigo Circuit Court.

Blackford, J.—This was an indictment against Samuel Dias and Hannah Gillman for the murder of one George Brock. There are two counts in the indictment. The said Dias being arraigned, pleaded not guilty, and a jury was sworn to try the issue. The examination of the cause not being finished on the day it was commenced, the jury were placed under the charge of a bailiff, to be returned into Court the next morning. The trial was not concluded on the second day, and the jury were again put in charge of a bailiff who was sworn to attend them, to be returned into Court the following morning. On the third day, the cause was submitted to the jury, who returned a verdict of *Guilty*. Motions for a new trial and in arrest of judgment were made and overruled, and judgment rendered that the prisoner *Dias* be executed.

The first error assigned is, that the record does not show an order of the Court for the separate trial of the prisoner. There is nothing in this objection. The record, by showing that the prisoner was tried separately, necessarily shows that the Court directed the trial.

It is also assigned for error, that the record does not show that the bailiff, to whose care the jury was intrusted on the first adjournment of the court, was sworn. In support of this objection, we are referred to the case of *The King* v. *Stone*, 6 *T. R.*, 527. There the entry of adjournment states that the bailiffs who took charge of the jury were sworn; but the case does not show that it would have been error had the oath been omitted, or had the record not shown that it was administered. This Court reversed a judgment against a prisoner in a capital case, because there was no entry of record from which it could be implied that the jury had been legally disposed of during an adjournment of the court. *Jones* v. *The State*, 2 *Blackford*, 475. But that was a different case from the present. There is here an entry of record, that on the adjournment the jury is placed in charge of a bailiff, to be returned into Court the next morning; and we must presume from that entry that the jury was committed to the care of the bailiff in a legal manner, whatever that may be.

The last error assigned is, that both the counts in the indictment are insufficient.

The first count, so far as it is necessary to state it, is as follows: That Samuel Dias, late of, &c., and Hannah Gillman, late of, &c., on, &c., with force and arms, at, &c., in and upon one George Brock, &c., did make an assault, and that the said Samuel Dias and the said Hannah Gillman, with a certain axe, &c., the said George Brock in and upon the *left* side of the head and over the *left* temple of him the said George Brock, then and there feloniously and wilfully, and of their malice aforethought, did strike and beat, giving to the said George Brock then and there, with the axe aforesaid, in and upon the *right* side of the head and over the *right* temple of him the said George Brock, one mortal wound, of the depth of three inches and of the breadth of six inches, of which said mortal wound the said George Brock, &c., on, &c., died; and so the jurors aforesaid, upon their oath aforesaid, do say, &c. The objection made to this count is, that, in the description of the offence, it is repugnant and inconsistent with itself. The charge is, that the persons indicted struck the deceased with an axe on the *left* side of the head and over the *left* temple, giving to him then and there, with said axe, on the *right* side of the head and over the *right* temple, a mortal wound.

There is in this part of the count a manifest repugnancy in the description of the offence as to the place of the wound; the first part of the sentence, viz., that the persons indicted struck the deceased with an axe on the *left* side of the head, &c., being inconsistent with what follows, viz., their giving him then and there with said axe on the *right* side of the head, &c., a mortal wound. And this repugnancy occurs, as it must occur to be fatal, in a material part of the count, for the part of the body to which the violence was applied must be stated; and even if the wound be alleged to have been on the arm, hand, &c., without saying whether the right or left, the indictment is bad. The proof, to be sure, need not correspond in this respect with the allegation, but the allegation itself cannot be dispensed with in the indictment. 3 *Chitt. Cr. Law*, 735; *Arch. Cr. Pl.*, 334. The defect cannot be remedied by treating the first statement as to the part of the head of the deceased which was struck as superfluous, because that statement is sensible and consistent in the place where it occurs, and is not repugnant to *antecedent* matter. *Chit. Cr. Law*, 224. *The King* v. *Stevens et al.*, 5 *East*, 244. Nor can the difficulty be removed by considering as superfluous the subsequent allegation, as to the persons indicted giving to the deceased on the opposite side of his head the mortal wound. If this latter allegation were left out, the count, as to the matter in question, would read as follows: That the said Samuel Dias and the said Hannah Gillman, with a certain axe, &c., the said George Brock in and upon the *left* side of the head and over the *left* temple of him the said George Brock, then and there feloniously, &c., did strike and beat, giving to the said George Brock, then and there, with the axe aforesaid, one mortal wound. In that case, the necessary allegation relative to the giving of the deceased a mortal wound, would be defective for not setting out the part of his person on which such wound was given, the word "there" in the sentence having reference only to the venue. There being then a repugnancy in a material charge of the count in question, which cannot be avoided by striking out a part as superfluous, the count cannot be sustained.—2 *Hawk. Pl. Cr.*, 228; 1 *Chitt.*, *Cr. Law*, 227; *Arch. Cr. Pl.*, 51; *Rex* v. *Stevens*, 5 *East*, 244.

The second count is objected to on account of an alleged defect in its conclusion. This count is similar to the first until it comes to the conclusion commencing with the words, "And so the jurors aforesaid," &c., except that it does not state the length and breadth of the wound, which it was not necessary to state. *Rex* v. *Tomlinson*, 6 *Carr. & Payne*, 370; and except that it is not subject to any objection for repugnancy. The conclusion objected to is as follows: "And so the jurors aforesaid, upon their oath aforesaid, do say, that the said Samuel Dias and the said Hannah Gillman, in manner and form aforesaid, feloniously and wilfully, and of their malice aforethought, did kill and murder, contrary to the form of the statute," &c. The defect here complained of is, that the person murdered is not designated. This defect is believed to be fatal. The averment that the persons indicted, feloniously and wilfully, and of their malice aforethought, did kill and murder, without any thing more, does not amount to any charge against them which the law can recognize. The consequence is, that the count is left without the techincal allegation, that the persons indicted feloniously, &c., *murdered* the deceased. It is true, that the previous part of the count charges that the persons indicted, feloniously and wilfully, and of their malice aforethought, did strike the said George Brock, &c., giving him, &c., three mortal wounds, &c.; but the law is well settled, whether wisely or otherwise we need not stop to inquire, that such description of the offence is not sufficient in a count of an indictment for murder. There must be in such count an express allegation, that the prisoner feloniously, &c., *murdered* the deceased, the word murder being a term of art which cannot be supplied by any other word. The language of *Hawkins* on the subject is as follows: "No periphrasis or circumlocution whatsoever will supply those words of art, which the law has appropriated for the description of this offence, as *murdravit*, in an indictment for murder; *cepit*, in an indictment for larceny; *mayhemiavit*, in an indictment for maim; *felonice*, in an indictment for any felony whatever," &c. 2 *Hawk. Pl. C.*, 244. The same doctrine is laid down in *Long's case*, 5 *Cooke* 245; 1 *Chitt. Cr. Law*, 239-244; 4 *Blacks. Com.*, 306, 307; 3 *Bac. Abr.*, 554.

The conclusion to the second count, as before noticed, being a nullity, and there being no techinical allegation in the count that the persons indicted feloniously, &c., *murdered* the deceased, the following authority is applicable to the case: "An indictment was removed into B. R.'s "That of malice aforethought, A. B. made an assault on C. D., and the same C. D. feloniously struck, giving him one mortal stroke of which he languished for seven days, and on the eighth day of the stroke aforesaid died; without saying 'And so the aforesaid A. B, the said C. D. feloniously did kill and murder.' Therefore this word *murder* is wanting in the indictment. And whether this shall be adjudged *murder* or only manslaughter, was doubted on account of the general pardon passed in the late parliament, in which murder is excepted. And at length is was resolved by the justices of B. R. and others, that without this word *murder* it is only manslaughter;" *Anon.*, 3 *Dyer*, 305. That case, which is directly against the count in question, occurred as early as the time of Elizabeth, and has been ever since adhered to.

We are of opinion, therefore, that the second Count does not contain a valid charge of murder, but that it is a good count for manslaughter.

As the first count of the indictment is bad, and the second contains a charge of manslaughter only, the judgment that the prisoner Dias be executed is erroneous; and for the same reason the verdict is wrong for not fixing the punishment.—*R. S.*, 1838, *p.* 519, *sec.* 78.

Per Curiam.—*The judgment is reversed and the verdict set aside. Cause remanded, etc.*

Where an indictment contains four counts, and the jury find the defendant guilty on three of them, without any express finding on the other, such finding is sufficient to warrant a judgment, and is tantamount to an acquittal as to the count upon which there was no express finding.

Where a party, charged in four counts in an indictment, is tried and found guilty on three, and acquitted on one of them, and a new trial is granted, the new trial should be confined to the three counts on which he was found guilty.—*Morris* v. *The State of Mississippi*, 8 *Smedes & Marshall's R.*, *p.* 762. *Miss.* (1847.)

(Thacher, J., cited *Campbell* v. *The State*, 9 *Yerg.*, 333; 1 *Chitty's Criminal Law*, 637.)

On the trial of an indictment against a slave for a capital offence, it is good cause of challenge on the part of the State to one called as a juror, that he is nearly related to the owner of the slave, as it would be on the part of the prisoner that a juror was a near relative of the prosecutor.

An indictment for highway robbery may charge either that the robbery was committed in the highway or that it was committed *near* the highway.—*The State* v. *Anthony*, 7 *Iredell's R.*, *p.* 234. *N. C.* (1847.)

(Ruffin, C. J., cited *The King* v. *Stone*, 1 *Tremaine*, 288; *Cr. Cir. Com.*, 682; *Fowler's case, East's Pl. C.*, 785.)

INDICTMENT—HUSBAND AND WIFE.

A wife may be indicted, convicted, and punished in conjunction with her husband. For although coercion is to be presumed from his presence, still, it is clear that this is only one of those presumptions, or influences, classed as *prima facie*, that may be rebutted by testimony, and hence presents a question for the jury.—*The State v. Parkerson et ux.*, 1 *Strobhart's R.*, p. 169. *S. C.* (1847.)

Tried before the RECORDER in the City Court of Charleston, July Term, 1846.

This was an indictment for assault and battery upon one Mary Jane Adams. The indictment charges: "John Parkerson and Mary Parkerson, residents, &c., on the 7th of January, 1846, with force and arms, &c., at, &c., in and upon one Mary Jane Adams, &c., did make an assault, and her, the said Mary Jane Adams, then and there did beat, bruise, wound and ill-treat, &c. The defendants plead not guilty, and Parkerson, the husband, conducted the defence in person, aided by Mr. Pressley, as his counsel.

After much testimony had been introduced on both sides, the case was argued before the jury by the Attorney General and Mr. Parkerson, and finally submitted to them as one of mere fact.

They found a verdict of guilty. When sentence was about being pronounced, the defendant, Parkerson, made the objections now taken as the grounds for a motion in arrest of judgment, viz.:

1. That the husband and wife cannot be joined for an assault and battery committed in his presence.

2. That the indictment in this case does not set forth whether the assault and battery were committed by the husband, or wife, but charges it upon both; whereas it is respectfully submitted, that the indictment should have set forth whether the husband was charged with an offence committed by himself, or by the wife, in his presence.

Pressley, for the motion.
Bailey, Attorney General, contra.

WITHERS, J., delivered the opinion of the Court.

It is a mistake to affirm that a wife may not be indicted, convicted, and punished in conjunction with her husband; while it is true, that if she committed a bare theft or even a burglary by the coercion of her husband, she shall not suffer punishment; and while it is also laid down that coercion is to be presumed from his presence, still it is quite as clear that this is only one of those presumptions or inferences classed as *prima facie*, that may be rebutted by testimony, and hence presents a question for the jury, which in this case has been resolved against the defendants, and certainly not without foundation. All here said is well supported by what may be found in *Russell on Crimes, from page* 23 *to* 25 *inclusive.*

The motion is therefore dismissed.

INFANT.

Where an infant purchased land and gave his note for the purchase money, and after he became of age, continued in possession of the land, and promised to pay the note, *Held*, that this was a confirmation of the contract by the infant, after he became of age, and he and his representatives were bound by it.—*Armfield* v. *Tate*, 7 *Iredell's R., p.* 258. *N. C.* (1847.)

An infant defendant, on attaining twenty-one, discharged the solicitor who had acted for her in the suit. Afterwards, that solicitor was served with a subpœna, for her to hear judgment. He returned the subpœna to the plaintiff's solicitor, and stated at the same time, that the defendant had come of age, and that he was no longer employed for her. Some months afterwards the cause was heard, but without the defendant having been served with a subpœna to hear judgment, or any one appearing for her at the hearing; and a decree was made in which she was described as an infant. *Held*, that she was entitled to put in a new answer to the bill.—*Snow* v. *Hole*, 15 *Simons' R., p.* 161. *Eng.* (1848.)

Where one of several brothers and sisters, having title to personal property, dies in infancy, the remaining brothers cannot sue at law, to recover the property, until administration is taken out on the estate of the infant.—*Miller* v. *Eatman et al.*, 11 *Alabama R., p.* 609. (1847.)

INJUNCTION.

Where an appeal has been taken from the dissolution of an injunction and the decree below affirmed, and another injunction is granted by the Chancellor upon an amended bill, from a refusal to dissolve which the defendant has in turn appealed, on the hearing of the last appeal the Court cannot go into the questions decided by the first: they are matters adjudicated.—*McDonald* v. *Green*, 9 *Smedes & Marshall's R., p.* 138. *Miss.* (1848.)

The jurisdiction of the Court to restrain by injunction an act which the defendant is by contract bound to abstain from, is not confined to cases in which there are either no other executory terms in the contract or none which a Court of Equity has not the means of enforcing.

If a bill states a right or a title in the plaintiff to the benefit of a negative agreement on the part of the defendant, or of his abstaining from a given act, the Court will equally interfere by injunction, whether the right be at law or under an agreement, which cannot be otherwise brought under its jurisdiction.—*Dietrichsen* v. *Cabburn*, 2 *Phillips' Ch. R.*, *p.* 52. *Eng.* (1848.)

(*Parker* and *Glasse* cited *Clark* v. *Price*, 2 *Wils.*, 157; *Morris* v. *Colman*, 18 *Ves.*, 437; *Rankin* v. *Huskisson*, 4 *Sim.*, 13; *Williams* v. *Williams*, 2 *Swanst.*, 253; *Barrit* v. *Blagrave*, 5 *Ves.*, 555.)

INSANITY.

Insanity to constitute a proper ground of defence to a criminal accusation, must be shown to exist to such an extent as to blind its subject to the consequences of his acts, and to deprive him of all freedom of agency.—*Commonwealth* v. *Mosler*, 4 *Barr's R.*, *p.* 264. *Pa.* (1847.)

Insanity, is shown by the proof of acts, declarations, and conduct, inconsistent with the character and previous habits of the party. The mere opinions of witnesses, of the sanity or insanity, of a person, are not competent testimony, unless they are medical men, acquainted with the facts.—*McCurry* v. *Hooper*, 12 *Alabama R.*, *p.* 823. (1848.)

INSTRUCTION OF COURT.

On the trial of a prisoner indicted for murder, the prisoner's counsel asked the Court to instruct the jury, "that unless they find from the evidence that the prisoner, with a premeditated design, or in some act dangerous to others, evincing a depraved mind regardless of human life, killed the deceased, they cannot find a verdict of guilty for murder;" this charge was refused: *Held*, that the instructions being couched in the language of the statute, was improperly refused.

Nor was the error refusing it cured by the fact, that the Court below had, at the instance of the State, instructed the jury that if they believed the act of killing was committed without sufficient legal provocation, and without reasonable ground to believe himself in imminent danger of death, or great bodily harm, they must find the prisoner guilty of murder.

In criminal trials, the Circuit Judge is not bound to give or refuse the instructions asked by counsel on either side, in the precise terms in which they are framed. He may modify the charges asked on both sides, so as to make them conformable to his own views of the law.—*Boles* v. *The State of Mississippi*, 9 *Smedes & Marshall's R.*, *p.* 284. *Miss.* (1848.)

INSURANCE.

Where a policy of Insurance prohibited an assignment of the interest of the assured "unless by the consent of the company manifested in writing," and the Secretary, on an application to him at the office of the company, endorsed upon the policy and subscribed a consent to an assignment; *Held*, that his authority to do so, in the absence of evidence to the contrary, should be presumed.

Held also, that if it were necessary to prove his authority, evidence that he had often given such written consent in other cases would be sufficient to carry the case to the jury.—*Conover* v. *The Mutual Ins. Co. of Albany*, 3 *Denio's R.*, *p.* 254. *N. Y.* (1848.)

INSURANCE—FIRE.

Policies of insurance against fire are personal contracts with the assured, and do not pass to an assignee or purchaser without the consent of the insurers. The transfer of the policy is equivalent to a new contract of insurance with the transferee.

Where a policy of insurance provides that, "in case the insured have already any other insurance against loss by fire on the property thereby insured, not notified to this corporation, and mentioned in, or endorsed on this instrument, or otherwise acknowledged by them in writing, this insurance shall be void;" and a third person, to whom the property insured had been assigned and to whom the policy was transferred with the assent of the insurers fails to notify the latter at the time of the transfer of another policy previously taken out by him on the same property, the insurers will be discharged. A declaration of the first insurance made after the loss, in compliance with a condition of the policy requiring all persons insured sustaining any loss, to declare on oath whether any and what other insurance has been made on the same property, will be too late.—*Leavitt et als.* v. *The Western Marine and Fire Insurance Company*, 7 *Robinson's La R.*, *p.* 351. (1847.)

Appeal from the Commercial Court of New Orleans, Watts, J.

Duncan for the appellants cited 8 *Johnston*, 245; 11 *Johnston*, 275; 6 *Cowen*, 404; 4 *Dallas*, 35; 2 *Phillips on Ins.*, 350.

Eustis, on the same side.

Maybin and *Grimes*, for the defendants.

Murphy, J.—This is an action brought upon a policy of insurance against fire, executed by the defendants on the 25th of June, 1839, in favor of Viles & Company, of New Orleans, but admitted to have been made for the account of George G. Henry, on a house, stable and furniture, at Mobile. The policy was for one year, and insured $8000 on the house, $500 on the stable, and $1500 on the furniture. On the 17th of September, 1839, Henry being in New-York, made an assignment of property to the petitioners, in trust for his creditors, which assignment included the insured premises. On the 27th of the same month, the trustees effected an insurance on the same house for $8500, for one month from the 17th, the day of the assignment of the property to them, in the office of the North American Insurance Company, at New-York. Vles & Co., in pursuance of instructions from the plaintiffs, obtained the consent of the underwriters in New Orleans to have Henry's policy transferred to them, which transfer was accordingly made on the 7th of October. The property insured was destroyed by fire two days after, to wit, on the 9th of October. At the time the consent of the company was obtained, and the transfer or assignment of the policy sued on was made to the trustees, no notice was given of the existence of the New-York policy; and it is admitted, that the defendants had no intimation of any such policy having been taken out, until the 13th of December following. The preliminary proof required by the conditions of the policy was not regularly made, until November, 1841. The defendants paid the loss on the furniture in March, 1840, but refused to settle for that on the house and stable assigned to the plaintiffs, on the ground that they had received no notice of the insurance effected in New-York on the same property. The claim of the petitioners on the New-York company was submitted to the arbitration of distinguished jurists of that city, who decided that the loss should be apportioned between the two offices, according to a stipulation to that effect contained in each of the policies. Their award has been laid before us. In relation to the liability of the defendants, which it was necessary to establish to authorize this apportionment, they reason at some length on difficulties supposed to result from the policy having been made out through error in the name of Vles & Co., instead of George G. Henry, and but slightly touch on what we conceive to be the true and only difficulty in the case. The New-York company having settled with the plaintiffs in compliance with this award, the latter now claim of the defendants their proportion of the loss.

The defence set up is: *First*, the want of early notice of the loss, and of the preliminary proof required by the conditions of the policy: *Secondly*, the failure of the insured to give notice to the company of the New-York policy, which they had taken out on the same property. We have found it unnecessary to inquire into the sufficiency of the preliminary proof, or its waiver on the part of the company, as, in our opinion, the second ground of defence on which they rely, must prevail.

The policy sued on provides that, "in case the insured have already any other insurance against loss by fire on the property hereby insured, not notified to this corporation, and mentioned in or endorsed on this instrument, or otherwise acknowledged by them in writing, then this insurance shall be void and of no effect; and if the insured, or their assigns, shall hereafter make any other insurance, on the same property, and shall not, with all reasonable diligence, give notice thereof to this corporation, and have the same endorsed on this instrument, or otherwise acknowledged by them in writing, this policy shall cease, and be of no further effect."

Policies against fire are personal contracts with the assured, and they do not pass to an assignee or purchaser, without the consent of the underwriters. Between the 17th of September, 1839, when the insured property was assigned to the plaintiffs, and the 7th of October following, when the policy was transferred to them with the approbation of the company, it did not cover the property. Had a loss occurred during that time, the defendants would clearly have been discharged. Henry could not have claimed, having parted with all his interest by the assignment; and petitioners could not have recovered, because they were not parties to the contract of insurance. The transfer of Henry's policy to the plaintiffs, with the consent of the company, on the 7th of October, was equivalent to a new insurance, or contract with them. Before, or at the time of receiving such transfer, they were bound to notify the defendants of the prior policy made in New-York, and at that time covering the property. When the assignees or trustees sent out orders to obtain a transfer of the New Orleans policy, which they appear to have done on the very day they had effected an insurance in New-York on the same property, there was nothing to prevent them from directing their correspondents, Vles & Co., to notify the underwriters of such insurance, and to have it endorsed on the policy transferred to them. By their neglect to do this, the transfer of the policy, if viewed as a new insurance, never took effect so as to protect them from loss. If, although the policy sued on was at an end on the 17th of September, 1839, by the assignment of the property insured, it be considered as a prior policy, and the New-York policy as a subsequent one, the obligation to give notice of the latter policy with reasonable diligence, was the same, and they had ample time to do it between the 27th of September and the 9th of October, when the fire occurred; but no notice whatever was given until the 12th of December following. This difficulty was not in the way of a settlement with the New-York company, as at the time they insured there was no available policy in existence to be declared; and only two days elapsed between the transfer of Henry's policy in New Orleans to the plaintiffs, and the fire which destroyed the premises insured. In relation to the ninth condition of the policy, to which our attention has been called, it is clear, that the declaration to be made by the insured of other insurances existing on the property is a part of the preliminary proof, and does not relate to the notice to be given of prior or subsequent policies. The insurance offices generally require it, to secure themselves the means of ascertaining, after the fire, whether other insurances existed on the property. This knowledge, in most cases, they can obtain only from the insured himself; until this declaration is made, they have a right to withhold payment; but if it appears from such declarations, when made, that other policies existed, not notified to them, they can absolutely refuse to pay. This declaration cannot surely supply the notice not previously given in accordance with the conditions of the policy. These conditions are clear and explicit; by failing to comply with them, the petitioners have forfeited their right to recover. 3 *Robinson*, 384; 1 *Philips*, 420; 16 *Wendell*, 400; 5 *Hammond's Ohio R.*, 466; 16 *Peters*, 510. The present case is one of some hardship, as the plaintiffs, no doubt, acted in good faith. Their object was clearly to effect a temporary insurance until they could obtain a transfer of the assignor's policy, or be apprised whether it was granted or refused. But they can blame only themselves, or their agents in New Orleans, as it was easy for them to comply with the conditions of the policy. If notice of a prior policy for a period of one month can be withheld, notice of a policy for one year might also be dispensed with. In the case of *Carpenter* v. *The Providence and Washington Insurance Company*, the Supreme Court of the United States, in speaking of these conditions of the policy, say: "We see no reason why, as these clauses are a known part of the stipulations of the policy, they ought not to receive a fair and reasonable interpretation, according to their terms and obvious import. The insured has no right to complain, for he assents to comply with all the stipulations on his side, in order to entitle himself to the benefit of the contract. Upon reason or principle he has no right to ask the Court to dispense with the performance of his own part of the agreement, and yet to bind the other party to obligations, which, but for those stipulations, would not have been entered into."—16 *Peters*, 511.

Judgment affirmed.

INSURANCE—LIFE.

Where a married woman procured a policy of insurance, upon the life of her husband, in her own name, and for her sole use, as authorized by the act of April, 1840, the insurance money being made payable to her children in case she should die before her husband, and subsequently both husband and wife, and their only child, perished at sea, by the same disaster, and probably at the same moment; *Held*, that the act of April, 1840, did not extend to the case; and that this contract of insurance stood upon the same footing as any other contract made by a feme covert, in her own name, in the lifetime of her husband, and without the intervention of a trustee.

Where the mother and daughter perished at sea, and by the same disaster, and there was no evidence of survivorship; *Held*, that there was no legal presumption that the daughter survived the mother.

It seems that where the husband and wife perish together, at sea, and where there is no evidence to authorize a different conclusion, it will be presumed that the husband survived his wife.

At common law, the husband may sue upon bonds, notes, and other contracts for the payment of money, given to the wife during coverture, either in his own name, or in the name of himself and wife jointly, at his election.

When he elects to treat them as his own, by bringing a suit in his own name only, the judgment will belong to his personal representatives, although his wife survives him. But if he sues in their joint names, the judgment will belong to her by survivorship, if he dies first.

And where the consideration of the bond, or other security, has proceeded from the wife, or her estate, or where it was the gift of a third person, if the husband does not dispose of such security, or collect the money due thereon, or proceed to judgment thereon in his own name during his lifetime, it seems the debt will belong to her, by survivorship, if she outlives him.

A feme covert cannot, under the provisions of the Revised Statutes, make a will of her general personal estate, during coverture, founded upon the mere assent of the husband to the making of such will.

And it seems that she cannot dispose of her separate estate by will, unless such will is made in pursuance of a power, either beneficial or in trust, to dispose of her separate estate by will, or by a testamentary instrument in the nature of a will.

But a feme covert having personal estate conveyed to her separate use, with an express power to dispose of it by will at her death, may make a will, or an instrument in the nature of a will, for the purpose of appointing, or disposing of such property, in pursuance of such power.—*Mœhring* v. *Mitchell*, 1 *Barbour's Ch. R.*, *p.* 264. *N. Y.* (1847.)

This was an appeal from a decision of the Circuit Judge of the first circuit, affirming a sentence and decree of the Surrogate of New-York, refusing to admit to probate, as a will of personal estate, an instrument in writing propounded by the proctor of the appellant, as the will of Isabella Leo Wolf, deceased.

The following opinion was delivered by the Circuit Judge:

Kent, C. J.—I agree with the Surrogate in his conclusion, as to the invalidity of the will of Mrs. Leo Wolf. The right of making a will of real property, a married woman never had, by the law of England or America, at least since the conquest. As to personal property, before our Revised Statutes, the capacity of a married woman was less restricted. She could not devise lands, because, by the feudal law, none could devise; and the Statute of Wills, 32 *and* 34 *Henry* 8, did not relieve her from this restriction. But she was prevented from exercising the power of testamentary disposition of personal effects, which power, by imperceptible degrees, freeing itself from ecclesiastical usurpation, became common to all persons except married women, by the rights acquired by her husband in her personal property; and with which rights, a power in the wife of bequeathing that personal property would have been inconsistent. 2 *Black.*, 98. The license of the husband gave her the power of testamentary disposition, because it removed the reason for restricting the power.

But the Revised Statutes, 2 *R. S.* 60, it seems to me most clearly, put an end, by positive and unequivocal prohibition, to the remnant of testamentary power remaining in married women. "Every person of the age of eighteen years, or upwards, and every female, not being a married woman, of the age of sixteen years, or upwards, of sound mind and memory, and no others, may give and bequeath his, or her personal estate, by will in writing." There is no reservation of pre-existing rights, as in a recent English statute on this subject. 1 *Vict. c.* 26. What was a common law right has become statutory; and a positive prohibition is enacted against the exercise of the right by any other than those mentioned in the statute. A married woman may not, then, give and bequeath her personal estate, by will, in writing. The disposition of personal estate by will appears to me to be forbidden to married women, by language even stronger than that which prevents her devising real estate. The consent of the husband could not authorize a devise of lands; and I cannot see how it can, under our laws, authorize a testament of chattels.

This doctrine will not exclude a disposition of personal property, testamentary in its nature, or akin to a testament, if made by a married woman under a power. For as we have observed in an early case, *Southby* v. *Stonehouse*, 2 *Ves. sen.*, 610, such disposition is not a proper will; but merely a direction of the use or trust, arising under the instrument creating the power, and depending for its efficacy wholly upon the validity of that instrument. Neither do I pretend to say it would limit, or affect, the power of a Court of Equity to carry into effect a wife's disposition of her separate estate. All I mean to say is that, in the present case, I cannot see how the Surrogate, in the exercise of his duties in recording and granting probate of wills, could, under our existing laws, permit the paper propounded to be proved as the last will and testament of Isabella Leo Wolf. The decree of the Surrogate is therefore affirmed.

Allen, for the appellant.

1. The policy of Insurance was the separate property of Isabella Leo Wolf. Such is the tenor and effect of the policy. The consideration is sixty-five dollars, and forty-one cents, to them in hand paid by Isabella Leo Wolf. It assures the life of Joseph for the sole use of the said Isabella Leo Wolf. The company contract with her, her executors, administrators and assigns, in case of loss, to pay the sum insured to her, her executors, administrators and assigns, for her sole use. *Adamson* v. *Armittage*, 19 *Ves.*, 415; *Ex parte Ray*, 1 *Mad.*, 199. The provisions in the act, and in the policy, relative to the children, only apply where the wife has not disposed of her interest; at all events, they have no application in the present case, because, 1, the contingency has not happened. Mrs. Wolf and her husband having sailed in the same ship, and never having been heard of, they will be held to have died at the same instant; *Taylor* v. *Diplock*, 2 *Phil.*, 261; *Wright* v. *Saunders*, 2 *Phil.*, 266, *note c*; *Satterthwaite* v. *Powell*, 1 *Curt. Ecc. R.*, 705; and 2, their only child died with them. Isabella Leo Wolf was fully empowered to become a party to such a contract, and to acquire such rights, by the law of 1840.—*Laws of* 1840, *p.* 59.

2. The policy being thus the separate property of Isabella Leo Wolf,

she is regarded, in Equity, as to that property, as a feme sole; and as an incident to that property, she had the power of disposing of it, either by will or otherwise.—*Peacock* v. *Monk*, 2 *Ves. jr*, 190; *Rich* v. *Cockell*, 9 *Ves.*, 369; *Fettiplace* v. *Gorges*, 1 *Ves.*, 47; *Whistler* v. *Neuman*, 4 *Ves.*, 135; *Clancy, Husb. & Wife*, 308; *Methodist Ep. Ch.* v. *Jaques*, 17 *Johns.*, 578; *Powell* v. *Murray*, 2 *Edw. R.*, 643; *N. Am. Coal Co.* v. *Dyett*, 7 *Paige*, 9; 20 *Wend.* 570; *S. C.*, *Gardner* v. *Gardner*, 7 *Paige*, 112.

3. So far as its form goes, the instrument endorsed on the policy, is a will, and is entitled to probate.—*Glynn* v. *Ostrander*, 2 *Hagg.* 432; *Masterman* v. *Maberley*, 2 *Hagg.*, 247; *In the goods of Joseph Knight*, 2 *Hagg.* 554; *Lovelass on Wills*, 317.

4. Being made by a married woman, it may not be, strictly, and at law, a will; but being of a testamentary nature, its testamentary character must be established by being proved as wills are proved, before Courts either of law or equity will take cognizance of it.—2 *Roper, Husb. and Wife*, 188, *and note m*; *Stevens* v. *Bagwell*, 15 *Vesey*, 152; *Picquet* v. *Swan*, 4 *Mass.*, 60.

5. The provisions of the Revised Statutes have not changed, in any respect, the rights of married women to separate estates, or their powers over such estates. 1. The statute relative to wills of personal property, 2 *R. S.* 60, *sec.* 21, was not intended to change the position of married women, in equity, as to their separate property, but to regulate the manner of making wills. 2. It makes no change in the law, but is merely declaratory of what was before the law. 2 *Black. Com.*, 498; *Toller on Ex'rs*, 9, 10; *Lovelass on Wills*, 266. 3. The Legislature only intended to declare what was the law. *Reviser's Notes*, 3 *R. S. 2d Ed.*, 629; *Hyer* v. *Bergen*, 1 *Hoffm.*, 2. The statutory provision in reference to wills of personal property, is identical, in effect, with what has been a statutory provision in reference to wills of real property for over three hundred years; under which Courts of Equity have always sustained the testamentary disposition of their separate real estate made by married women. *See cases cited under the second point.* *Bradish* v. *Gibbs*, 3 *John. Ch.*, 523. The two provisions are in *pari materia*, and should both receive the same construction.

Wilson, for the respondent.

The Chancellor.—The facts in this case, so far as the same can be ascertained from the proceedings returned by the Surrogate, are substantially these: In May, 1840, Isabella Leo Wolf, the wife of Joseph Leo Wolf, procured a policy of insurance, from the New-York Life Insurance and Trust Company, upon the life of her husband, for $5000, for the term of five years. The policy was in her own name, and for her sole use; as authorized by the first section of the act of April, 1840, in respect to insurances for lives for the benefit of married women. *Laws of* 1840, *p.* 59. And the amount was made payable to the assured, or her executors, administrators and assigns, for her sole use, within sixty days after due notice and proof of the death of her husband; and in case of her death before his decease, the same was made payable to her children, for their use, or to their guardian, if they were under age; as authorized by the second section of that act. In March, 1841, the assured and her husband, and as the counsel for the appellant states, their only child, sailed for Europe in the steam-ship President, and have never since been heard of; and there is no doubt that such ship was lost, and that all on board perished. A few days before they sailed for Europe, Mrs. Leo Wolf executed the paper propounded as her will, in the presence of two subscribing witnesses, on the back of the policy of insurance, in the following words: "In the event of the within policy, No. 1321, of the New-York Life Assurance and Trust Company, becoming payable, by said company, in consequence of the death of my husband, Joseph Leo Wolf, and in the event of my being, at the time when the within policy becomes payable, not among the living, it is my wish and will, and I hereby order and direct that the amount insured in said policy, on the life of my husband, shall be paid over to Doctor Gottlief Mœhring, of the city of Philadelphia, in trust; to be held by him for my daughter, Mary Jane Leo Wolf, until her becoming of age; and in the event of her death, before coming of age, without issue, I hereby direct that the whole amount thus held in trust by the said Gottlief Mœhring, shall be divided into equal parts, and shall be paid over to the children of the brothers and sisters of my husband, Joseph Leo Wolf, living at the time when such division shall take effect. Given under my hand and seal, in the city of New-York, this 6th day of March, 1841. Isabella Leo Wolf," [L. S.] And her husband, at the same time, and in presence of two subscribing witnesses, wrote the following consent under the same: "I consent to the above, and ratify the same. New York, 6th March, 1841. Joseph Leo Wolf."

In April, 1842, G. F. Allen, as proctor for the appellant, who was the trustee, or executor, named in the instrument propounded as a will, presented a petition to the Surrogate of New-York, stating that the decedent left assets, or personal estate in the city and county of New-York; and praying that the instrument propounded might be admitted to probate, and that letters testamentary thereon might be granted. The next of kin of the decedent were duly cited to attend before the Surrogate, and the public administrator, having taken out administration on the estate of Joseph Leo Wolf, was also cited; and they resisted the probate of the instrument propounded, upon the ground that a married woman could not, under the provisions of the Revised Statutes, make a will of personal estate, even with the consent of her husband. The Surrogate sustained the objection, and rejected the instrument propounded as a will, upon that ground alone. And the Circuit Judge, upon appeal to him, arrived at the same conclusion; as appears by his written opinion.

The insurance money in this case, by the terms of the policy, was made payable to the children of the assured, in case she died before her husband. If her daughter had survived her, therefore, it would have been necessary, perhaps, to inquire whether there is any legal presumption that the husband survived his wife; when they have both perished by the same disaster, and when there is no extrinsic evidence to guide the judgment of the Court upon this matter of fact. In the cases of *Taylor* v. *Diplock*, 2 *Phil. R.*, 267; *Colvin* v. *The King's Proctor*, 1 *Hagg. Eccl. R.*, 92; *and in Selwyn's case*, 3 *Hagg.*, 748, it appears to have been supposed, in the absence of any evidence to justify a different conclusion, that the Court would be bound to presume a survivorship of the husband, where the husband and wife perished together at sea; upon the ground, I presume, that the greater strength of the male would probably enable him to sustain life the longest, in such a calamity. But as there is no presumption of the survivorship of the daughter, in this case, after the death of the mother, and the probability is that they both perished at the same moment, it becomes immaterial to inquire whether it must be presumed that the husband survived his wife. It is sufficient for this case, that there is no legal presumption that she survived him. For if she did not survive him I am of opinion that the act of April, 1840, does not extend to the case; and that, in the event which has occurred, this contract of insurance stands upon the same footing as any other contract made by a feme covert, in her own name, in the lifetime of her husband, and without the intervention of a trustee. By referring to the first section of that act it will be seen that the insurance money is only payable to her, to and for her own use, free from the claims of the representatives of the husband, and of his creditors, in case she survives her husband; but not where they both die at the same instant, or where he survives her. The second section of the statute provides for the case of survivorship of the husband, where the wife has left children; by authorizing the insurance money to be made payable to such children, or to their legal guardians, for their use. But no provision is made, by the statute, for this case; where there are no children, and where the husband survived the wife; or where they both perished at the same instant, so that neither survived the other.

In regard to bonds, notes, and other contracts, for the payment of money, given to the wife during coverture, the common law rule appears to be, that the husband may sue upon them in his own name, or in the name of himself and wife jointly, at his election. Where he elects to treat them as his own, by bringing a suit and proceeding to judgment in his own name, the judgment will belong to his personal representatives, although his wife survives him. But if he sues in their joint names, the judgment will belong to her survivorship. And where the consideration of the bond, or the security, given to the wife in her own name, during coverture, has proceeded from her, or her estate, or where it was the gift of a third person, it seems that if the husband does not dispose of such security, or collect the money thereon, or proceed to judgment in his own name, during his lifetime, it will belong to her by survivorship if she outlives him. *Nash v. Nash*, 2 *Mad.*, 133; *Hilliere et ux. v. Hambridge, Alleyn*, 36; *Searing v. Searing*, 9 *Paige*, 283. In cases of this kind, as well as in cases of choses in action given to the wife before coverture, or other property of the wife not reduced to possession by the husband, the wife was permitted, previous to the Revised Statutes, to dispose of the same by will, with the written authority and consent of her husband, in case he survived her. The principle upon which such wills were originally sustained in Equity, and afterwards at law, probably was that as the husband, if he outlived the wife, would be entitled to the property by survivorship, and had also the right to reduce it to possession immediately during coverture, he might waive such right. He could, therefore, allow her to appoint it to whom she pleased, by an instrument in the nature of a will; although such will was, in fact, nothing but an appointment with his assent. The provisions of the Revised Statutes, however, have somewhat changed the husband's rights to the property of his wife, by survivorship; by refusing him the right to administer thereon without giving security for the payment of her debts, to the amount of the assets which may come to his hands. 2 *R. S.* 75, *sec.* 29. And as he is entitled to all his wife's personal estate by survivorship, and even during her life subject to her equity to a support out of the same, he ought not to be permitted to deprive his own creditors of the benefit thereof, in case of her death, by permitting her to dispose of it by will, during coverture. The provision of the Revised Statutes which declares that males of the age of eighteen years and upwards, and unmarried females of the age of sixteen and upwards, *and no others*, may dispose of his or her personal estate by will, 2 *R. S.* 60, *sec.* 21, is, as I think, sufficient to deprive a feme covert of the right to make a will of personal estate, of the character above described, founded upon the mere assent of the husband to the making of the same. And I am also inclined to think, it likewise deprives her of the right to dispose even of her separate estate by will; where it is not so disposed of in pursuance of a power, either beneficial or in trust, to dispose of such separate estate by a will, or by a testamentary instrument in the nature of a will.

The Revised Statutes, however, have expressly provided for the execution of beneficial powers, as well as powers in trust, by femes covert, in relation to the real estate and chattels real. 1 *R. S.* 732, *secs.* 78, 80, 87; 1 *R. S.* 735, *secs.* 105, 106, 110, 115; 1 *R. S.* 737, *sec.* 130; 1 *R. S.* 750, *sec.* 10. I cannot, therefore, believe that it was intended, by the legislature, to deprive a feme covert, who has personal estate conveyed to her separate use, with an express power to dispose of it by will at her death, of the right to make a will, or an instrument in the nature of a will; for the purpose of appointing or disposing of her separate estate, in pursuance of such power. That question, however, is not necessary to be settled at this time; as there was no power reserved in the policy, in this case, authorizing the wife to dispose of the insurance money, by will or otherwise, in the event which has occurred. Nor had the interest of the husband, or of the wife, in this policy, been conveyed to a trustee, subject to such a power of appointment by the wife. For these reasons, I think the insurance money belongs to the personal representatives of the husband, to be disposed of as a part of his personal estate; and that the instrument propounded as the will of Isabella Leo Wolf, ought not to be admitted to probate.

The order of the Circuit Judge affirming the sentence and decree of the Surrogate must, therefore, be affirmed. As this, however, was a new and somewhat difficult question, arising for the first time under the provisions of the Revised Statutes, and of the Act of April, 1840, I shall not charge the appellant with the costs of the respondent on this appeal; but shall direct such costs to be paid out of the insurance money which is in controversy in this suit.

INSURANCE—TENANT.

A tenant for a year has an insurable interest in buildings demised to him, but he cannot recover the value of such buildings in case of loss.

On an insurance against loss or damage by fire, on a building which is destroyed by fire during the policy, the assured cannot recover for his loss occasioned by the interruption or destruction of his business, carried on in such building; nor for any gains or profits, which were morally certain to enure to him, if the building had remained uninjured to the expiration of the policy.—*Niblo v. North American Fire Ins. Co. 1 Sandford's R., p.* 551. *N. Y.* (1849.)

INSURANCE—VESSEL.

If the master of a vessel, which has been insured, in departing from the usual course of the voyage from necessity, acts *bona fide* and according to his best judgment, and has no other view but to conduct the vessel by the safest and shortest course to her port of destination, what he does is within the spirit of the contract of assurance, and the voyage will be protected by it.

The primary purpose of the owner of a vessel and of the cargo, and of others interested, is to have the voyage completed without unnecessary delay. This is known to the insurer when he takes the risk. And if the vessel suffer such injury during the voyage, that she cannot safely proceed to her port of discharge without repair, the master is not compelled to proceed directly to the nearest port, geographically, to make the repair in, or that the voyage should be protected by the policy. So long as she can be expected by an intelligent and faithful master to pursue her voyage in safety, she will be entitled so to do.

When a vessel has sustained damage, the interest of the insurer is not the controlling consideration, that should influence the master to depart from the course of his voyage. That consideration is the safety of life; and next to that is the preservation of the property intrusted to his care. And the pursuit and accomplishment of the voyage can be forsaken or delayed only so far, as it may become necessary for the security of life and property.

When the safety of life and property requires an instant and entire departure from the course of the contemplated voyage, it is the duty of the master to seek the nearest land which he can hope to reach, if the peril be so great as to outweigh all other considerations; and he should proceed directly upon his new course without delay or deviation, unless prevented by some unforeseen obstacle. But if the state of the weather be such that, in the judgment of the master, it would be more safe to seek another port, it would then become his duty to attempt to reach it. —*Turner* v. *The Protection Insurance Company,* 25 *Maine R., p.* 515. (1847.)

(*Fessenden* and *Goodenow* cited *Park on Ins.* 294; *Marsh. on Ins.* 408; 1 *Phil. on Ins.* (2*d ed.*), 516, 520; 11 *Johns.*, 352; 2 *Strange*, 1264; *Cowp.*, 601; 7 *Mass.*, 349, 368.

Deblois, contra, cited 1 *Phil. on Ins.*, 193, *Matteaux* v. *London Ins. Co.*, 1 *Atk.*, 556; *Clark* v. *U. F. & M. Ins. Co.*, 7 *Mass.*, 365; *Guibert* v. *Redshaw, cited in Marsh. on Ins.*, 411, *and in Park on Ins.*, 301; 1 *Marshall*, 413; *Neilson* v. *Columb. Ins. Co.*, 3 *Caines*, 108; *Lavabre* v. *Wilson* 1 *Dougl.*, 284; 1 *Phil. Ins.* (2*d ed.*), 537; *Kittel* v. *Wiggin*, 13 *Mass.*, 72; *Robertson* v. *Col. Ins. Co.*, 8 *Johns.*, 491; *Maryland Ins. Co.* v. *LeRoy*, 7 *Cranch*, 26; *Phelps* v. *Auldjo*, 2 *Camp.*, 350; *Marshall*, 522; 1 *Phil. Ins.*, 514, 516; *Stocker* v. *Harris*, 3 *Mass.*, 409; *Kittell* v. *Wiggin*, 13 *Mass.*, 68; *Brazier* v. *Clapp*, 5 *Mass.*, 1; *Curtis' Treatise on Maritime Law*, 236.)

INTEREST.

Interest is not recoverable on a running or unliquidated account, unless there is an agreement, either express or implied, to pay interest. —*Esterley* v. *Cole*, 1 *Barbour's R., p.* 235. *N. Y.* (1848.)

(Parker, J., cited *Newall* v. *Griswold*, 6 *Johns. Ch.*, 45; *Trotter* v. *Grant*, 2 *Wend.*, 413; *Wood* v. *Hickok*, 2 *Wend.*, 501.)

Interest upon interest cannot be collected by law, except upon an agreement to pay it, made after the day of payment has passed. But if it be paid voluntarily it is not usury. And it may be lawfully included in a note, by the agreement of the parties; without rendering such note usurious.

But a reservation, in a new security, of compound interest which had accrued upon a sum previously due, made against the will of the debtor, and as condition of forbearance upon the new security, affects the new security with usury, and renders it void.—*Townsend* v. *Corning*, 1 *Barbour's R., p.* 627. *N. Y.* (1848.)

(Gridley, J. cited *Kellog* v. *Hickok*, 1 *Wend.*, 521.)

JUDGE—DEATH OF.

Where a party has lost the benefit of a bill of exceptions tendered to the ruling of a judge at nisi prius, or at the assizes, by the death of the judge, and without any default on his own part, it is not competent to another judge of the Court out of which the record issues, to seal the bill of exceptions.

But in such a case the Court will, where the circumstances warrant it, allow the party to move for a new trial, notwithstanding the proper time for so doing has elapsed.—*Newton* v. *Boodle*, 3 *Common Bench R.*, *p.* 795. *Eng.* (1848.)

JUDGMENT.

A judgment of a Court of competent jurisdiction upon a point sought to be litigated between the same parties in another suit, is *res judicata*.

It is not necessary that the plaintiff's claim in both suits should be identical. If they arise out of the same transaction, and the defence is equally applicable to each suit, the first judgment will be conclusive.

And a judgment upon demurrer is equally conclusive with one rendered upon a verdict.—*Bouchard* v. *Dias*, 3 *Denio's R.*, *p.* 238. *N. Y.* (1848.)

Where the lien of a judgment upon slaves has once attached in one county, the removal of the slaves to another county, by the defendant, without the knowledge of the plaintiff, cannot defeat the lien of the judgment; such removal by the judgment debtor being a fraud upon the judgment creditor.

A forthcoming bond after forfeiture, becomes, by operation of law, a judgment, which extinguishes the original judgment, and also all liens created by that judgment.—*Chilton* v. *Cox*, 7 *Smedes & Marshall's R.*, *p.* 791. *Miss.* (1847.)

(*Tompkins* cited 1 *How.*, 64 ; 3 *How.*, 60 ; 5 *How.*, 200, 566 ; 6 *How.*, 518 ; 1 *S. & M.*, 386 ; 2 *S. & M.*, 457.)

Where a summons has been served upon a part only, of several named as defendants, and judgment is rendered against all, the judgment is erroneous and voidable, but not void.

If land be sold by virtue of an execution upon such judgment, a title to a proportion, if not the whole, will pass to a purchaser at the sheriff's sale.

Lands, on the death of the ancestor, intestate, descend to the heirs, and may be sold on execution against the heirs, but subject to the rights of the administrator, in case they are needed for the payment of the ancestor's debts.—*Douglass' Lessee* v. *Massie*, 16 *Ohio R.*, *p.* 271. (1848.)

A case heard and decided in vacation before one judge, by agreement of the parties, is to be considered as if heard and decided before and by the Court.

If the decree be not actually entered till after the judge dies who drew it up and announced it, an entry of it may be made at the next term.

The intervening death of the judge, in such a case, is no objection, and no ground, for a rehearing, if an opinion was actually delivered; but otherwise, if only prepared. To justify a rehearing, it is not sufficient to satisfy the Court, that the opinion may have been erroneous in law, if there was no mistake as to the law or fact when it was given.

A Court may alter its judgment at any time before it is entered up; or, if entered, before it is made final to be carried into effect. But it should not be altered without notice to both parties, if it has before been announced, nor without full hearing and adequate causes which take place and justify rehearings usually in Chancery.—*Daggett* v. *Emerson et al.*, 1 *Woodbury & Minots' U. S. R.*, p. 1. (1847.)

(WOODBURY, J., cited *Plowden*, 501; 4 *Bingh.*, 628; *Gould* v. *Oliver*, 2 *Scotts' N. R.*, 241; *Hudson* v. *Guestier*, 7 *Cranch*, 1.)

JUDGMENT—REVERSAL OF.

It is a general rule, that any one who seeks to reverse a judgment, must put his finger on the error, as every presumption is in favor of the correctness of judgments.

In an action at law on an administrator's bond, the bond is but inducement to the action, and no recovery can be had on it without proof of damages.

An administrator's bond, without proof of damages, is not a valid claim against an insolvent estate, or against any one.—*Green* v. *Creighton*, 7 *Smedes & Marshall's R.*, p. 197. *Miss.* (1847.)

JUDGMENT DEBTOR.

The right and title of a judgment debtor to real estate, belonging to him which has been sold by the sheriff upon execution, is not divested, by the sale, until the expiration of the fifteen months allowed for redeeming.

And the deed given by the sheriff to the purchaser at a sale upon an execution, will not relate back, so as to give to the purchaser a legal estate which will merge a mortgage previously given to him by the judgment debtor, upon the land sold.

Even after the time for redemption has expired, the naked legal estate continues in the judgment debtor. And the purchaser's interest, before deed is but a lien, or a conditional right.

The doctrine of merger applies only when there is a legal estate; as where the title and a lien, or a legal and an equitable, or a larger and a lesser estate meet.—*Schermerhorn* v. *Merrill*, 1 *Barbour's R.*, *p.* 511 *N. Y.* (1848.)

JUDGMENT LIEN.

The lien of a senior judgment which has not been levied within the year will not be defeated by a decree of foreclosure of a junior mortgage, ordering a sale, and a sale and confirmation within the year from the rendition of the decree.

A judgment creditor may file a bill after levy, to clear away the cloud cast upon the title by such sale, and subject the land again to sale, or he may charge the fund arising from such sale in satisfaction of his judgment.

Although a decree upon foreclosure of a mortgage may be so framed as to permit execution to issue as upon judgment at law, to collect any balance which may remain after exhausting the mortgaged premises, yet such decree creates no lien upon other land.

The only decrees which give liens under the statute, are decrees for the payment of money generally.—*Myers et als.* v. *Hewit et als.*, 16 *Ohio R.*, *p.* 449. (1848.)

(*Brazee* cited *Norton* v. *Beaver*, 5 *Ohio*, 178; *Jackson* v. *Mills*, 13 *John.*, 463; *Minor* v. *Wallace*, 10 *Ohio*, 403; *Walpole* v. *Inks*, 9 *Ohio*, 142; *Rankin et al.* v. *Scott*, 6 *U. S. Cond. R.*, 504.

Welch, contra, cited 2 *Ohio*, 395, 366; 9 *Ohio*, 142; 10 *Ohio*, 208; 8 *Ohio*, 120, 377; 3 *Ohio*, 337, 541; 8 *Ohio*, 52.)

JUNIOR JUDGMENT.

It is well settled that a sale under a junior judgment is void as against an elder one, and the property may still be seized and sold in satisfaction of the prior judgment; but if the prior judgment creditor be guilty of gross negligence or delay, as by giving time to the defendant, he may lose his lien; the showing, however, for the purpose of defeating the prior lien, must come from the party who wishes to defeat it.—*Talbert* v. *Melton*, 9 *Smedes & Marshall's R.*, *p.* 9. *Miss.* (1848.)

(Thacher, J., cited *Michie* v. *The Planters' Bank*, 4 *How.*, 130; *Robinson et al.* v. *Green et al.*, 6 *Howard*, 223)

JURISDICTION.

There is nothing in the Constitution of the United States to deprive the Courts of one of the States, of the jurisdiction which they previously possessed, as to suits against a State, brought by citizens of another State, or by citizens or subjects of a foreign State.

The Courts of the United States have not even a concurrent jurisdiction with the State Courts of Chancery, in suits brought by individuals against a State.

The principle upon which the Court of Chancery assumes jurisdiction, in a suit to which a sovereign State is a party defendant, is not for the purpose of compelling such State to perform any decree which may be made against it; but to enable the State to appear and protect its rights, if it has any, in the suit.—*Garr* v. *Bright*, 1 *Barbour's Ch. R.*, *p.* 157. *N. Y.* (1847.)

JURY.

The incompetency of any one member of a grand jury by whom an indictment has been found, will vitiate the whole proceeding, no matter how many unexceptionable jurors joined with him in finding it.—*The State* v. *Jones*, 8 *Robinson's La. R.*, *p.* 616. (1847.)

(Boyle, J., cited *Hawkins' Pleas of the Crown, book 2d, chap.* 25, *secs.* 26, 27, 28.)

JURY—DISCHARGE OF.

If a person has been once put on his defence on a legal indictment before a competent jury, and the jury has been unnecessarily discharged, such discharge is equivalent to an acquittal of the defendant.

A verdict finding the defendant guilty on one of several counts of an indictment, and saying nothing of the other counts, is, as to such other counts, equivalent to an express finding of not guilty. A judgment may be rendered on such verdict; and the proceedings will be a bar to a future prosecution for any of the offences charged in the indictment.

The entry, after such judgment, of a *nolle prosequi* of the counts concerning which the verdict is silent, is a nullity.

If the description of rape in an indictment leave out the word "unlawfully," but be in accordance with the common law definition of the offence, it is sufficient.—*Weinzorpflin* v. *The State*, 7 *Blackford's R.*, *p.* 186. *Ind.* (1847.)

(Dewey, J., cited *Commonwealth* v. *Cook*, 6 *Serg. & R.*, 576; *Commonwealth* v. *Clue*, 3 *Rawle*, 501; *State* v. *Garrigues*, 1 *Hayw.*, 241; *In*

R. Spier, 1 *Dever.* 491; *United States* v. *Shoemaker*, 2 *McLean*, 114; *The People* v. *Barrett*, 1 *Johns.*, 66; 1 *Chit. C. L.*, 641; *Jerry* v. *The State*, 1 *Blackf*, 395; *The United States* v. *Bachelder*, 2 *Gall.*, 15; *People* v. *Enoch*, 13 *Wend.*, 159.)

JURY—VERDICT.

The Court may inquire of the jury respecting their verdict, and the grounds upon which they proceeded, for the purpose of ascertaining whether the case has been thoroughly tried.—*Walker* v. *Sawyer*, 13 *New Hampshire R.*, *p.* 191. (1847.)

(Parker, C. J., cited *Hix* v. *Drury*, 5 *Pick.*, 296; *Pierce* v. *Woodward*, 6 *Pick.*, 206; *Parrott* v. *Thatcher*, 9 *Pick.*, 426; *Dorr* v. *Fenno*, 12 *Pick*, 521; *Smith* v. *Putney*, 6 *Shepley*, 87.)

LAND—DIVISION OF.

If a division line between adjoining lots of land is agreed upon by the owners, and is so designated as to be clear and distinct, and is acquiesced in by the respective owners of the lots for more than fifteen years, they will be held bound by such line.—*Ackley* v. *Buck*, 18 *Vermont R.*, *p.* 395. (1847.)

(*Coolidge* cited *Mitchell* v. *Walker*, 2 *Aik.*, 266; *Shumway* v. *Simons*, 1 *Vt.*, 53; *White* v. *Everest*, 1 *Vt.*, 181; *Hazard* v. *Martin*, 2 *Vt.*, 77; *Univ. of Vt.* v. *Reynolds*, 3 *Vt.*, 542; *Stephens Adm'r* v. *Griffith et al.*, 3 *Vt.*, 448; *Beecher* v. *Parmelee et al.*, 9 *Vt.*, 352; *Jackson* v. *Ogden*, 4 *Johns.*, 143; *Jackson* v. *Van Cortland et als*, 11 *Johns.*, 123; *Burton* v. *Lazell et al.*, 16 *Vt.*, 158.)

LANDLORD AND TENANT.

A promise by landlord to pay tenant for repairs, does not include improvements to the soil, or other matters which were only good husbandry. Nor does it include new erections of any kind, but simply a restoration of old or dilapidated buildings, &c.—*Cornell* v. *Vanartsdalen*, 4 *Barr's R.*, *p.* 334. *Pa.* (1847.)

(Rogers, J., cited *Long* v. *Fitzimmons*, 1 *Watts & Serg.*, 532; 3 *Kent's Com.*, 468; 4 *Kent's Com.*, 110.)

In case for a nuisance in obstructing the lights of the plaintiff's tenement, brought by a tenant for a year against his landlord, during the term, damages can only be given for the time which had elapsed when the suit was commenced, and not for the whole term.—*Blunt* v. *McCormick*, 3 *Denio's R.*, p. 283. *N. Y.* (1848.)

In a suit by landlord against tenant to recover rent for demised premises, destroyed by fire during tenancy; evidence that the property was insured, and landlord received insurance money, or that the landlord received a sum of money for loss of said property, out of a general relief fund, is immaterial to the issue, and cannot be used as a defence.

If a landlord take possession of the ruins of his premises destroyed by fire for the purpose of rebuilding, without the consent of his tenant, it is an eviction; if with his assent, it is a rescission of the lease, and in either case the rent is suspended.—*Magaw* v. *Lambert*, 3 *Barr's R.*, p. 444. *Pa.* (1847.)

Error to the Common Pleas of Alleghany County.

This was an appeal from a justice of the peace, in a suit brought by Wm. H. V. Magaw, plaintiff below and in error, against Henry Lambert, to recover rent for demised premises. The plaintiff filed a declaration in case, to which the defendant pleaded defalcation, and payment with leave to give special matter in evidence. It appeared from the testimony, that plaintiff rented to defendant a lot of ground and building, in Pittsburgh, from March 1, 1845, until April 1, 1846, at the rate of $300 per annum. The rent for March, to be paid April 1, 1845, and the balance in quarterly payments. The plaintiff on the trial claimed $100, rent for four months, from March to July, 1845, and admitted payments to the amount of $51 25.

Evidence was offered by the defendant on the trial, and admitted by the Court, that the building was destroyed in the great fire of April 10, 1845: to be followed up by evidence of various acts done by the plaintiff, shortly after the fire, viz.: cleaning off the pavement in pursuance of a city ordinance, requiring the owners of lots to clear the side-walks; bargaining for the cleaning of the cellar, and offering to sell the property and give immediate possession. To this evidence plaintiff excepted, that there was no notice of this ground of defence, and that under the pleadings it was inadmissible.

This was plaintiff's first bill of exception.

The defendant further gave in evidence proof that the building was insured by the plaintiff in a large amount; and that nearly the whole insurance money was paid to the plaintiff. Also, that plaintiff received a considerable sum of money on account of the loss of his building out of the Pittsburgh Relief Fire Fund, created by general contribution. There was some evidence that this payment was a misapplication of the fund, because the plaintiff's property was insured. To the admission of all which evidence, the plaintiff excepted: that there was no notice of these grounds of defence, and that the evidence was inadmissible under the pleadings; and the Court sealed plaintiff's second and third bill of exceptions.

A number of points were submitted by plaintiff and defendant to the

Court for instructions to the jury, which were answered in the charge; but as these points, and the answers of the Court, are not necessary to elucidate the points decided, they are omitted. The jury found for the defendant; and the plaintiff, among other assignments for error, made the following:

The Court erred in receiving testimony under plaintiff's first, second and third bills of exceptions.

Selden and *Biddle*, for plaintiff in error.
Kuhns, contra.

Per Curiam.—It is impossible to see what payment of the loss by the insurance company had to do with the payment of the rent by the tenant. It was not the rent which was insured, but the premises out of which it issued; and the tenant could not say the company had paid it for him. Nor was the misapplication of the charity fund for the relief of indigent sufferers by the fire, a better ground of defence. The committee of distribution ought possibly to have relieved the tenants of rented property in preference to their landlords; but that is a matter which, resting as it did in their discretion, cannot be drawn into view. The evidence of these matters, therefore, ought to have been excluded. The question on the merits is one of fact, and not of law. If the landlord took possession of the ruins for the purpose of rebuilding without the consent of the tenant, it was an eviction of him; if with his assent, it was a rescission of the lease; and in either case, the rent was suspended. On this plain ground the point ought to have been submitted.

Judgment reversed, and venire de novo awarded.

LEASE—ALTERATION OF.

If a lessee fraudulently alter his lease in a material part, subsequent to its execution, he thereby destroys all his future right under the lease, either to retain the possession of the premises, or to preclude the lessor from re-entering upon them.

And if the lessor, in such case, enter upon the premises and demand possession, and he is afterwards forcibly prevented by the lessee, or those who act under him, from exercising acts of ownership upon the premises, he may sustain therefor an action of trespass *quare clausum fregit.*

And whether such alteration of the lease has been made by the lessee is a question of fact, to be determined by the jury.—*Bliss* v. *McInyre et al.*, 18 *Vermont R.*, *p.* 466. (1847.)

Trespass, *quare clausum fregit.* Plea, the general issue, and trial by jury.—Redfield, J., presiding.

On the trial it appeared, that the plaintiff, on the first day of May, 1844, was the owner of the premises described in his declaration, consisting of a clothier's shop, dwelling-house and out-buildings, and that on that day he conveyed them by deed to one Johnson, and delivered to him the possession; that Johnson continued to occupy the premises under the deed until the fourteenth day of August, 1844, when he re-conveyed the premises to the plaintiff, and took from him a lease of the premises for the term of nine years, reserving rent, and continued in possession of the premises, under the lease, until the twenty-first day of October, 1844. The plaintiff claimed, that the lease, as executed, contained a clause, securing to him the right of re-entry upon the premises, in case of non-performance by Johnson of certain stipulations in the lease, and that that clause had been erased by Johnson, without the knowledge or consent of the plaintiff. The erasure was apparent upon the lease; but it was claimed by the defendant, that it was made before the lease was executed. At the time Johnson purchased the premises, there was a quantity of wood in the shed, fitted for the fire, which he was to have, and which he continued to use, until the time last named. About that time (October 21, 1844,) a controversy arose between the plaintiff and Johnson in regard to the wood and the erasure in the lease; and the plaintiff made an entry upon the premises and demanded possession, on the ground of the alleged erasure, and also for the alleged reason, that he had been denied the rights secured to him by the stipulations contained in the erased clause; but Johnson refused to surrender the possession. The plaintiff then demanded the wood, on the ground that it was resold to him with the premises; but Johnson refused to surrender it, claiming that it was agreed that he should retain it, notwithstanding the re-conveyance of the premises. The plaintiff then entered upon the premises, for the purpose of obtaining the wood, and succeeded, after some resistance, in carrying away one load; but, while he was gone, Johnson and others, among whom were the defendants, fastened the gates, so as to prevent the plaintiff from coming again upon the premises, and in so doing necessarily dug up the soil and destroyed some of the shrubbery; and this was the trespass of which the plaintiff complained. Johnson had been, and then was, in exclusive possession of the premises, except as above mentioned in regard to the plaintiff's entry.

Upon these facts the County Court instructed the jury, that the plaintiff was not entitled to maintain this action; to which decision the plaintiff excepted.

Heaton & Reed and *Prentiss*, for plaintiff.

1. A deed, or any other written instrument, becomes void by a fraudulent erasure by the party claiming the benefit of it.—4 *Com. Dig.*, 294; *Shep. Touch.*, 69; *Masters et al.* v. *Miller*, 4 *T. R.*, 320; *Hunt* v. *Adams*, 5 *Mass.*, 358; *Martendale* v. *Follet*, 1 *N. H.*, 95, and cases cited.

2. If the deed was made void by Johnson's alteration of it, he can show no legal title to the premises. He cannot offer in evidence his forged lease. He becomes a mere tenant at will, or sufferance.—*Chesley* v. *Frost*, 1 *N. H.*, 145; *Babb* v. *Clemson*, 10 *S. & R.*, 419; *Wethers* v.

Atkinson, 1 *Watts*, 236; *Newell* v. *Maybury*, 2 *Leigh*, 250; *Dyer*, 262, *a*.

3. Then the plaintiff's entry for that purpose deprived Johnson of even the right of possession, and gained an actual possession for himself. And, after that, Johnson was upon the premises but as a trespasser, and all his acts upon the premises were trespasses.—*Butcher* v. *Butcher*, 14 *E. C. L.*, 59; *Campbell* v. *Proctor*, 6 *Greenl.*, 12.

Smith and *Peck* for defendants.

1. The plaintiff did not offer to prove that the alteration, or erasure was made in fact after the execution and delivery of the lease; and if it had been fully proved, we insist, that it would not have given the plaintiff a right to re-enter. If Johnson had destroyed the lease, it would have been good for one year.—23 *Pick.*, 231.

2. Admitting that the plaintiff would have a right to treat the lease as void, and the tenant as a mere tenant at will, still, if he treated the lease as in force, and claimed to enter by virtue of stipulations therein contained, (as it appears he did,) the latter proceedings would amount to a waiver of the former; and in that case it would be incumbent upon the plaintiff to show that Johnson had failed to perform the stipulations.—*Chit. on Cont.*, 741, (*n.*)

3. We deny, that it is a legal presumption, from the mere fact that there is an apparent erasure, that the erasure was made after the execution of the instrument. It is a question for the jury, whether the alteration was made before or after the execution of the instrument, and whether made with or without the assent of the adverse party.—*Cumberland Bank* v. *Hall*, 1 *Halst.*, 215; *Bayley* v. *Taylor*, 11 *Conn.*, 531; *Hefflefinger* v. *Shute*, 16 *S. & R.*, 44; 1 *Nott & McCord*, 554; *Barrington* v. *Bank of Washington*, 14 *S. & R.*, 405; *Wilkins* v. *Caulks*, 5 *Har. & J.*, 36; *Smith* v. *Farmer*, 1 *Gal.*, 170; *Penny* v. *Corwith*, 18 *Johns.*, 499; *Nazro* v. *Fuller*, 24 *Wend.*, 374.

4. Even if the lease were rendered void, by reason of the erasure, and the plaintiff had a right to the possession of the premises, still, as it appears that Johnson refused to surrender the possession under a claim of right, his possession would thereby become adverse, and the plaintiff's only remedy would be by action of ejectment.—*Bakersfield Cong. Soc.* v. *Baker*, 15 *Vt.*, 119; *Chit. on Cont.*, 786; *Robinson* v. *Douglass*, 2 *Aik.*, 364.

The opinion of the Court was delivered by

Williams, C. J. In this case, the Court decided, upon the evidence, that the plaintiff was not entitled to recover. It appears to us, that the case should have been submitted to the jury; and, if the facts were as claimed by the plaintiff, he was entitled to recover. There was apparent, on the lease executed by the plaintiff to Johnson, a material alteration and erasure, by which the estate of Johnson was enlarged. The right of the plaintiff to re-enter, was erased, and the situation of the grantor and grantee was materially changed. If this alteration and erasure were made by Johnson, under whom the defendants acted, the plaintiff had a right to recover; and whether it was so altered by him is a question which should have been submitted to the jury.

The plaintiff claimed a right to re-enter, on being denied the rights secured to him by the stipulations in the lease. These rights were secured to him by that clause in the lease, which is erased. In this view, alone, it was important to have that fact passed upon by the jury.

But, moreover, if this erasure was made by Johnson, it destroyed all his future rights under that lease. And although it might not divest an estate already vested, and might not have operated on his acts committed before the alteration was made (questions, however, which are not now to be decided,) *in odium spoliatoris*, he must be considered as having destroyed the evidence of his title fraudulently, and thereby lost all his subsequent claim under and by virtue of the same, either to retain the possession, or preclude the plaintiff from entering on the premises leased.

In the case of *Chesley* v. *Frost*, 1 *N. H.*, 145, it was decided, that if a grantee in possession fraudulently make a material alteration in a deed, he cannot avail himself of such deed in evidence, nor supply it by parol proof,—limiting its effect prospectively, so as not to divest an estate already vested. In *Withers* v. *Akinson*, 1 *Watts*, 236, such an alteration was held to destroy the deed, as to the party altering it, and to deprive him of all benefit from the covenants,—treating it as in the case in New Hampshire. And in *Lewis* v. *Paine*, 8 *Cow.*, 71, it was said, that, if a party have no other evidence but an altered deed, he cannot recover thereon, having by his own act destroyed the evidence of his demand. The principle recognized in these cases we think is correct, and would have had a decisive effect in this case against the defendants, if it had been established by the evidence.

Again, the plaintiff had a right to enter and take away the wood, if it was sold to him by Johnson, as he contended. If the plaintiff had a right to enter in consequence of Johnson having failed to perform the stipulations in the lease, as it apparently was before the alteration, or to take the wood, if it was sold to him, or if Johnson had destroyed the evidence, under which he first entered into possession, so that the defendants could not avail themselves of it, the defendants were trespassers in turning the plaintiff out of possession and fastening gates and doors against him. These facts could alone be found by the jury; and the Court erred in deciding that the plaintiff was not entitled to recover, without submitting the question to the jury.

The judgment of the County Court is therefore reversed.

LEGATEE.

Where a legatee or distributee of an estate owes a debt to the testator, so much of such debt as can be collected by the executor, including the interest due at the testator's death, is to be considered and treated as a part of the capital of the estate; and must be apportioned and distributed accordingly.

If the whole amount of such debt, and interest, can be collected or received, by the retainer of the income, by the administrator, the interest which has accrued upon the amount which was due at the death of the testator is properly distributable among those who have present interests in the personal estate of the testator; and the sum due at the death of the testator is to be considered and treated as a part of the capital of the personal estate.

The right of retainer depends upon the principle that the legatee or distributee is not entitled to his legacy, or distributive share, while he retains in his own hands a part of the funds out of which that and other legacies or distributive shares ought to be paid, or which is necessary to extinguish other claims on those funds. And it is against conscience that he should receive any thing out of such funds, without deducting therefrom the amount of the funds which is already in his hands, as a debtor to the estate. And the assignee of the legatee, or distributee in such a case, takes the legacy or distributive share subject to the equity which existed against it in the hands of the assignor.—*Smith V. Kearney*, 2 *Barbour's Ch. R., p.* 533. *N. Y.* (1848.)

(THE CHANCELLOR cited *Melland* v. *Grey*, 2 *Coll. Ch.*, 296; *Jeff* v. *Wood*, 2 *P. Wms.*, 128; *Sims* v. *Doughty*, 5 *Ves.*, 243; *Lady Elibank* v. *Montelieu*, 5 *Ves.*, 737; *Carr* v. *Taylor*, 10 *Ves.*, 574; *In Re Gordon*, 1 *Glyn & Jam.*, 347; *Rankin* v. *Barnard*, 5 *Mad.*, 32; *Courtenay* v. *Williams*, 3 *Hare Ch.*, 539.)

A sole legatee has no right to the possession of the personal estate, until the personal representative has assented to it, and if in possession, it may be recovered by the personal representative when appointed.—*Upchurch* v. *Norsworthy*, 12 *Alabama R., p.* 532. (1848.)

LIBEL.

In an indictment for a libel, charging that the prosecutor "was called a murderer and forsworn," it is not competent for the defendant to justify by proving that there was and long had been a general report in the neighborhood that the prosecutor was a murderer and forsworn.—*The State* v. *White*, 7 *Iredell's R., p.* 180. *N. C.* (1847.)

(RUFFIN, C. J., cited *The Earl of Northampton's case*, 12 *Rep.*, 134; *Hampton* v. *Wilson*, 4 *Dev.*, 468.)

In case for libel, the declaration alleged the libel to be, that plaintiff sought admission to a club in the town of P., and gave an entertainment a few days before he was to be elected, as he thought; that three days after he stood the ballot and was black-balled; that next morning he *bolted*, and some of the poor tradesmen had to lament the fashionable character of his entertainment. Plea, that plaintiff did suddenly leave and quit the town of P., without paying every one and all of the debts contracted by him with *divers* persons in the said town, and without notice to them, and with intent to defraud and delay *some* of the last-mentioned persons, whereby the said persons remained unpaid and defrauded:—*Held*, bad on special demurrer, for not stating the names of the persons alleged to have been defrauded.—*O'Brien* v. *Clement*, 16 *Meeson & Welsby's R.*, p. 159. *Eng.* (1848.)

(*Lush* cited *Janson* v. *Stuart*, 1 *T. R.*, 748; *Newman* v. *Bailey*, 2 *Chit.*, 665.)

LIBEL—HUSBAND AND WIFE.

A suit cannot be sustained by husband and wife for a libel on them both.

In the case of such libel there should be two actions, one by the husband for the injury to him, and the other by husband and wife for the injury to the wife.—*Hart* v. *Crow et ux.*, 7 *Blackford's R.*, p. 351. *Ind.* (1847.)

Error to the Warrick Circuit Court.

Sullivan, J.—This was an action on the case by Crow and wife against Hart for a libel on the plaintiffs, written and posted up by the defendant in a place of public resort. The declaration alleges that the defendant, wickedly and maliciously intending to injure the plaintiffs in their good name, &c., and to cause it to be believed by their neighbors and others that they had been and were guilty of the crimes of lying and stealing, and to subject them to the scorn of their neighbors, &c., did, on, &c., at, &c., falsely, wickedly and maliciously, compose and publish of and concerning the plaintiffs, a certain false, scandalous, malicious, and defamatory libel, &c. The alleged libel is then set out, and charges that John Crow and his wife are liars, rogues, &c. By means whereof the plaintiffs have been greatly injured, &c. Demurrer to the declaration overruled, and joint damages assessed upon a writ of inquiry.

There are some questions raised on the admissibility of certain testimony that was objected to on the execution of the writ of inquiry, but the case does not require that we should decide them. The Court erred in overruling the demurrer to the declaration. The suit is brought not only for the injury sustained by the wife, but for the wrong done to the husband also. The action is joint, and joint damages are sought to be recovered. Two separate causes of action are shown, accruing to different persons that cannot be united in the same suit. For the injury done to the wife, the husband must join in the suit; but the declaration must show that it is for the wrong done to the wife that the suit is prosecuted. For the injury done to the husband, he alone should sue. 1 *Selw. N. P.*, 297; *Saville et ux.* v. *Sweeney*, 4 *Barn. & Ad.*, 514. In *Newton et ux.* v. *Hatter*, 2 *Ld. Raym.*, 1208, the suit was brought for a battery, committed on both. There was a judgment by default, and a writ of inquiry was executed. On the return of the writ, judgment was arrested, because the wife could not be joined in an action with the husband for a battery on the latter. If the defendant had pleaded to the declaration, and the cause had gone to a jury, and separate damages had been given for the injury to the wife, it may be that the verdict might have been sustained.—*Bull. N. P.*, 21; *Cro. Jac.*, 655; 3 *Binney*, 555.

PER CURIAM.—*The judgment is reversed with costs. Cause remanded, &c.*

LICENSE.

A license to keep a grocery is not transferable. It attaches to the person and cannot be used by others, even with the consent of the Court which granted it.—*Munsell* v. *Temple*, 3 *Gilman's R.*, *p.* 93. *Ills.* (1847.)

(KOERNER, J., cited *Wheeler* v. *Russell*, 17 *Mass.*, 257, *and cases there cited.*)

LIFE INSURANCE—SUICIDE.

Where a policy of insurance on life contained a condition, that the policy should be void if the assured should "commit suicide;" and it was proved that the assured had died from the effects of poison taken by himself:—*Held*, that, in order to avoid the policy, it must be shown that the assured, at the time he committed that act, could distinguish between right and wrong, so as to be able to understand and appreciate the nature and quality of the act he was doing.—*Schwabe* v. *Clift*, 2 *Carrington & Kirwan's R.*, *p.* 134. *Eng.* (1848.)

This was an action of assumpsit on a policy of insurance on life.

The policy contained a condition to the effect, that, if the person should "*commit suicide*, or die by duelling, or by the hands of justice," then such policy should be void. The assured, Mr. Schwabe, had, it appeared, died from the effects of sulphuric acid taken by himself; but evidence was gone into at considerable length on the part of the plaintiff, to show, that, at the time the deceased took the said sulphuric acid, he was, in fact, of unsound mind.

Kelly, S. G., in stating the defendant's case, contended, that, in the present instance, the soundness or unsoundness of mind of Mr. Schwabe formed no part of the question; and that the insurance office, in framing such a clause as the one now under consideration, must be taken to have intended to include within the exception contained in that clause every act of voluntary self-destruction; and he referred, in support of his position, to the judgment of COLTMAN, J., in *Borradaile* v. *Hunter*, 5 *Man. & G.*, 639, 662.

Knowles, in reply.—The question in this case is, did the deceased commit suicide? This term imports a felonious act; and hence it follows, that, unless the party who destroys himself be a responsible agent at the time he destroys himself, he is not, in the eye of the law, guilty of that act. In *Borradaile* v. *Hunter*, it was assumed, that, if the terms of the policy had been the same as they are in this case, the decision would have been different. The words of the policy in that case were, that, if the assured should "die by his own hands," the policy should be void; and speaking with reference to those words, ERSKINE, J., in delivering his judgment, makes the following observations: "When I find the terms 'shall commit suicide,' that have been popularly understood, and judicially considered, as importing a criminal act of self-destruction, exchanged for terms not hitherto so construed, it may, I think, be fairly inferred, that the terms adopted were intended to embrace all cases of intentional self-destruction, unless it can be collected from the immediate context that the parties used them in a more limited sense." And to the like effect TINDAL, C. J., says: "The expression 'dying by his own hands' is, in fact, no more than the translation into English of the word of Latin origin 'suicide.' But, if the exception had run in the terms, 'shall die by suicide, or by the hands of justice, or in consequence of a duel,' surely no doubt could have arisen that a felonious suicide was intended thereby."—5 *Man. & Gr.*, 668. The case of *Borradaile* v. *Hunter*, therefore, is in favor of the plaintiff; and there are, besides, several cases referred to in the report of that case, in which the terms of the policies were the same as they are in the present case. *Garrell* v. *Barclay*, 5 *Man. & Gr.*, 643; *Kinnear* v. *Borradaile*, 5 *Man. & Gr.*, 644; and in which, the juries being satisfied of the insanity of the parties assured, found for the plaintiffs. The question then is, did Mr. Schwabe, when he took the poison which caused his death, commit a criminal act of self-destruction? Because, if he did not, it is submitted that the plaintiff is entitled to recover in this action, according to the evident meaning of the words of the policy. Moreover, the words of the contract are those of the insurers; and, therefore, if these words are doubtful in their meaning, they must be construed most strictly as against them. But it is submitted, that here there is no doubt that those words were intended by the insurers to import the commission of a criminal act; and this is shown, not only by the words themselves, but by the terms in connexion with which they are found in the policy. To adopt the language of *Lord Chief Justice* TINDAL in the case referred to: "The dying in consequence of a duel, is a dying in consequence of a felony then in the very act or course of being committed by the assured. The dying by the hands of justice is dying in consequence of a felony previously committed by him. And it appears to me, upon the acknowledged rule of construction, viz: *noscitur à sociis*, that the dying by his own hands should, if left in doubt as to its meaning, be governed by the same condition as the other two, and be taken to mean a felonious killing of himself, that is, self-murder." The same rule of construction must prevail in this case; and it is therefore submitted, that, unless the jury are of opinion that Mr. Schwabe was, at the time of his death, in such a state of mind as that he would have been held criminally responsible, if, instead of taking his own life, he had taken that of another person, they must find for the plaintiff.

Cresswell, J.—The policy of insurance in question is subject to this condition, namely, that if the person assured, "commit suicide, or die by duelling, or by the hands of justice, then such policy shall be void;" and the defendant says, that the contract in the present instance is void, because Mr. Schwabe, the assured, did commit suicide. In order, however, to make that out, it must, I think, be made to appear that the deceased died by his own voluntary act, that, at the time he committed that act, he could distinguish between right and wrong, so as to be able to understand and appreciate the nature and quality of the act he was doing; and that, therefore, he was at that time a responsible moral agent. If *Borradaile* v. *Hunter* had been like this case, I should have felt myself bound by it. But that is not so. There the words of the policy were, "that, in case the assured shall die by his own hands, or by the hands of justice, or in consequence of a duel, this policy shall be void;" and from the remarks made by Erskine, J., on these words in the course of his judgment, I take it for granted that, if that learned judge had been considering a policy like the present, his opinion would have been different from that which was expressed by him in the case referred to. I draw the same conclusion from the judgment delivered by *Lord Chief Justice* Tindal in that case, who says, in the passage already referred to by Mr. *Knowles*, that, "if the exception had run in the terms 'shall die by suicide, or by the hands of justice, or in consequence of a duel,' surely no doubt could have arisen that a felonious suicide was intended thereby." Now I do not find that the other judges who delivered their judgments in that case say any thing in contravention of this; and I am therefore at liberty to act in the present case on my own opinion, which is, that it must appear that the deceased was a responsible moral agent at the time of his death, in order to make the act committed by him amount to suicide; it being borne in mind, however, that the jury must assume that he was a responsible moral agent, unless the plaintiff prove the contrary. You will therefore say, whether Mr. Schwabe died of his own act, committed for the purpose of destroying life; and whether he could, at the time, distinguish and understand the nature and quality of the act he was doing. If you are of opinion that he could not, you will find for the plaintiff; if you are of opinion that he could, you will find for the defendant.

Verdict for the plaintiff.

LOST NOTE.

An action may be brought on a lost negotiable note, which had not been negotiated at the time of the loss.—*Branch Bank at Mobile* v. *Tillman*, 12 *Alabama R.*, *p.* 214. (1848.)

LUNACY.

A person proceeded against as a lunatic, except in cases of confirmed and dangerous madness, is entitled to reasonable notice of the time and place of executing the commission, and a reasonable time to produce his witnesses before the jury. But it is not necessary that notice should be served on him personally where it is evident he keeps out of the way to avoid service of the notice.

The jury upon the execution of a commission of lunacy, have a right to inspect and examine the lunatic; and they should do so, in every case of doubt, when practicable.

In such cases they should direct the person in whose custody the lunatic is, to produce him, or permit him to attend before them. And when such an order is made, either by the Court or by the commissioners, the person who prevents the attendance of the lunatic before the commissioners and jury will do it at his peril.

This Court has a right to discharge an inquisition of lunacy, upon a mere examination of the alleged lunatic, in connexion with the evidence produced before the jury; without subjecting him to the expense of an issue or a traverse, where upon such an examination and evidence it is evident that the jury erred.

But where no change has taken place in the situation of the lunatic, since the execution of the commission, it must be a very clear case of mistake, or of undue prejudice, on the part of the jury, to authorize the Court to do so.

The Court will not discharge an inquisition upon *ex parte* affidavits, contradicting the finding of the jury, without any excuse being given for neglecting to produce the deponents as witnesses before the commissioners.

Although it is not a matter of course to allow a feigned issue in a lunacy case, when asked for, it is proper to allow it whenever the Court entertains a reasonable doubt as to the justice of the finding of the jury, upon the execution of the commission.—*In Re Russell a Lunatic*, 1 *Barbour's Ch. R.*, *p.* 38. *N. Y.* (1847.)

This case came before the Chancellor upon an inquisition finding P. Russell to be a lunatic, and upon the petition of one of his sons, on whose application the commission was issued, to have a committee of his person and estate appointed. A counter-application was made on the part of Russell to have the inquisition set aside for irregularity, or for leave to traverse, or for a feigned issue to try the question of lunacy.

Holmes, for the original petitioner.
Willard, for the alleged lunatic.

The Chancellor.—There is no irregularity in the proceedings which can justify the Court in setting aside the inquisition on that ground. The alleged lunatic, except in cases of confirmed and dangerous madness, to be judged of and provided for by the Court, in the order for the commission, is entitled to reasonable notice of the time and place of the execution of the commission, and a reasonable time to produce his witnesses before the jury, to rebut the charge of lunacy. It is not necessary, however, that the notice should be served on him personally, where it is evident he keeps out of the way to prevent the service of notice of the execution of the commission. Here the notice was served at the place where Russell made it his home, and also at the several places where he would be most likely to receive it. And the evidence produced before the commissioners was sufficient to establish the fact that he must have been aware of the existence of the notices which had been left at those places for him, or of some of them. The jury also have the right to inspect and examine the lunatic; and they should do so in every case of doubt, where such an examination can be had. And in such cases the commissioners should direct the person in whose custody the lunatic is, to produce him, or to permit him to attend upon the execution of the commission. Where such an order is made, either by the Court, or by the commissioners without a previous direction of this Court, the person who prevents the attendance of the lunatic before the commissioners and jury will do it at his peril.

I have no doubt of the right of the Court to discharge an inquisition of lunacy upon the mere examination of the supposed lunatic, in connexion with the evidence produced before the jury, without subjecting him to the expense of an issue or a traverse; where upon such examination and proof it is perfectly evident that the jury erred in finding him to be a lunatic. *In Re Heli*, 3 *Atk.*, 635. But to authorize the Court to dispose of the case thus summarily, where there has been no change in the situation of the alleged lunatic subsequent to the finding of the inquisition, it must be a very clear case of mistake or undue prejudice on the part of the jury. It is also improper, in a case of this kind, to discharge the inquisition upon *ex parte* affidavits contradicting the finding of the jury; where there is no reasonable excuse given for neglect to produce the deponents before the commissioners, and the jury, for examination as witnesses. The present is therefore not a proper case for the discharge of the inquisition upon this hearing, and without a traverse.

The only remaining questions, therefore, are, whether the alleged lunatic should be permitted to traverse the inquisition, and if so, upon what terms and conditions; or rather, whether a feigned issue should be awarded to try the question of insanity, which is the form in which the question is tried, in a Court of law, by our practice. Although it is not a matter of course to allow a feigned issue if it is asked for, it is proper to allow it wherever the Court entertains a reasonable doubt as to the justice of the finding of the jury upon the execution of the commission. In the case under consideration, I have not only read the testimony upon which the inquisition was founded, but have also examined the party proceeded against, in relation to the particular subject upon which he is supposed to be insane. For it is admitted by the counsel for the petitioners, that the testimony produced upon the execution of the commission did not establish a case of general insanity. The mental alienation, if any, in this case, is of that character to which Professor Esquirol has given the modern name of *monomania*, or partial insanity, as distinguished from *polymania*, or general mental alienation. In this species of insanity, the delusion of the mind is confined to a particular subject, or an isolated train of ideas, and which some medical writers suppose leaves the intellect unaffected in other respects. Because persons thus afflicted frequently appear perfectly rational on all other subjects, both in their conversation and actions. But persons in this situation frequently become passionate, and even dangerous, when the train of their particular delusion has been touched; so that for a time they may exhibit all the fury and violence of raving maniacs. It is very difficult, therefore, as *Sir Matthew* HALE very justly observes, to define the invisible line which divides perfect from partial insanity. Where the particular subject of the insane delusion, or monomania, connects itself however with the disposition or management of the property of the person who is thus afflicted, he is a proper subject of a commission of lunacy. For his unsoundness of mind renders him incompetent to manage or dispose of his property with reason and judgment.—*Dew* v. *Clark*, 3 *Addams' Eccl. R.*, 79; 1 *Hagg. Eccl. R.*, 311; 5 *Russ.* 163, S. C.

In the case under consideration, the monomania or insane delusion, if it be such, assumes the form of a fixed and abiding idea, in the mind of Mr. Russell, that his wife, who has nearly reached the age of sixty, and who is the mother of a large family of grown up children, has for the last two or three years been carrying on a criminal intercourse with a member of the church to which she belongs. And the effect of this strange and unaccountable delusion has been to sever the ties of affection and of nature which once attached him to his wife and children, and to cause him to sell his homestead, and other property, with a view to the final abandonment of his family and his home. The evidence upon the execution of the commission, if the facts there stated were the only grounds upon which his settled conclusion of his wife's guilt was based, showed that such a conclusion was not only unfounded, but was so clearly absurd and irrational as to be attributable only to the insane delusion of a diseased intellect. In my private examination, therefore, I have endeavored to ascertain the origin of his delusion on this subject, and to trace down the consecutive series of his actions and associations of ideas on the particular subject of his supposed mental alienation; but without arriving at a satisfactory conclusion, whether the opinion which has fixed itself in his mind is merely the result of false reasoning from facts which could not justify such a conclusion, or whether the supposed facts, as well as the erroneous and absurd conclusions based thereon, were not the mere creations of an impaired intellect. It is, therefore, a proper case for the awarding of a feigned issue.

An issue must be made up and tried, at the Circuit in Rensselaer County, to determine the question whether Mr. Russell is of unsound mind, so as to be mentally incapable of governing himself or of managing his property and affairs. And the only condition which I shall annex to the order is, that he shall attend personally upon the trial of the issue, and submit to such examination before the jury as the judge who tries the issue shall think proper to direct. In the meantime, it may be referred to Master Kellogg, to report a proper person as the committee, to take charge of such parts of Mr. Russell's estate as it is necessary to preserve from loss. And such committee is to take charge of the monies now in possession of the alleged lunatic, and pay out of the same what is necessary for his board and clothing, and such reasonable sums as may be requisite to procure the attendance of witnesses upon the trial, and for the employment of proper counsel for him before the Court and jury.

LUNATIC—EXECUTOR OF.

Executor of a lunatic is liable for necessaries furnished to his testator, while *non compos mentis*, before a commission is issued, and after the issuing of the commission and before the appointment of a committee.—*La Rue* v. *Gilkeson*, 4 *Barr's R.*, p. 375. *Pa.* (1847.)

(GIBSON, C. J., cited *Stiles and West, cited in Manby* v. *Scott*, 1 *Sid.*, 109; *Baxter* v. *The Earl of Portsmouth*, 2 *Car. & Payne*, 178; 12 *Eng. Com. Law*; S. C. 5 *Barn. and Cres.*, 170.)

MANDAMUS.

A private individual can apply to the Supreme Judicial Court for a writ of *mandamus* to Courts of inferior jurisdiction in those cases only, where he has some private or particular interest to be subserved, or some particular right to be pursued or protected by the aid of this process, independent of that which he holds in common with the public at large. It is for the public officers exclusively to apply for such writ, where the public rights are to be subserved.—*Sanger* v. *The County Commissioners of Kennebec*, 25 *Maine R.*, p. 291. (1847.)

MARRIAGE CONTRACT—FOREIGN LAW.

By a marriage contract executed in France by parties domiciled there, on the eve of their marriage, the wife under the provisions of the French law, put one-third of her fortune into *community*, and excluded the residue therefrom, which residue was to belong to her and be retaken by her. The parties removed to New-York, and the husband died there twenty years afterwards. He had taken and used in his business, the whole residue of his wife's property, as well as that of the community. At his death, he was in equity seized of and entitled to real estate in New-York.

On a bill filed by his widow, claiming that the marriage settlement operated as a *mortgage* on his whole estate, and that she was entitled to priority of payment of all her demands arising under the settlement—

Held, 1. That according to the laws of France, if the parties had remained there, she would have had no preference over other creditors of the husband in respect of his movables, nor any lien by way of *privilege* over his immovables. She would have had a *mortgage* upon his immovables. 2. That although the Courts here, construing the settlement according to the *lex loci contractus*, will give to her the same right as a creditor, that the French law would confer; they cannot and ought not to yield to her over real estate situated here, a lien or priority unknown and repugnant to the laws and regulations of the country *rei sitæ*. 3. Creditors here are entitled to rely upon those laws for the administration of their debtors' estates. 4. The French Civil Code refuses to contracts made in a foreign country, the force of a mortgage in France; and international comity does not require us to pursue a different course. 5. That therefore the complainant, whatever was the extent of her rights as a creditor by reason of the contract of marriage, had no lien upon her husband's estate, nor priority over his other creditors.—*Ordronaux* v. *Rey*, 2 *Sandford's Ch. R., p.* 33. *N. Y.* (1847.)

MARRIAGE SETTLEMENT.

When a husband, by virtue of a marriage settlement, gets into his possession the estate of the wife, which did not pass by virtue of the marital right, under a promise to secure it to the wife, creditors of the husband cannot reach such estate because the deed of settlement was unregistered.. The Court of Chancery will protect her rights.—*Embry et al.*, v. *Robinson et ux.*, 7 *Humphreys' R., p.* 444. *Tenn.* (1847.)

By a marriage settlement, real estates were conveyed to trustees in trust, to sell and to hold the proceeds in trust for the husband and wife for their lives successively, remainder in trust for their children, remainder in trust for the survivor of the husband and wife absolutely.

There was no child of the marriage. The husband survived his wife, and after her death consulted his solicitors upon his rights under the settlement, and they having advised him that he was entitled to the whole beneficial interest in the estates, he got possession of the settlement, and of the title-deeds, and remained in possession of them, and also of the estates, until his death. *Held*, that thereby he declared his election to take the estates as land.—*Davies* v. *Ashford*, 15 *Simon's R.*, *p.* 42. *Eng.* (1848.)

MARRIED WOMAN—SEPARATE ESTATE.

To make the separate estate of a married woman liable for her debt, where it is not charged upon the estate pursuant to the deed of settlement, it must be shown that the debt was contracted either for the benefit of her separate estate, or for her own benefit upon the credit of the same.

A general debt incurred by a married woman is not a charge upon her separate estate, nor is such estate chargeable upon any implied undertaking of hers.—*Curtis et al.* v. *Engel et al.*, 2 *Sandford's Ch. R.*, *p.* 287. *N. Y.* (1847.)

(THE ASSISTANT VICE CHANCELLOR cited *North American Coal Co.* v. *Dyett*, 7 *Paige*, 9; *S. C. on Appeal*, 20 *Wend.*, 570; 2 *Story's Eq. Jur.*, *sec.* 1398, 1400; *Gardner* v. *Gardner*, 7 *Paige*, 112; *Murray* v. *Barlee*, 4 *Simons*, 82; *Tullet* v. *Armstrong*, 4 *Beav.*, 319; *S. C. London Jurist*, 601.)

MASTER AND SERVANT.

The hiring of a person of full age, for wages, by the year, creates the relation of master and servant between the parties, and will enable the employer to maintain *case*, against one who imprisons the person employed, for the loss of his service.

The officers of a Bank cannot justify the imprisonment of a person on the ground that he remained in their office after the usual time for shutting the same, and was detained by their locking the outer door, though he knew the hour at which the Bank was usually closed.—*Woodward* v. *Washburn*, 3 *Denio's R.*, *p.* 369. *N. Y.* (1848.)

MASTER OF VESSEL.

Where a whaling vessel has been lost abroad, and the cargo sent home to the owners, a seaman cannot recover wages of the captain, but must resort to the owners for his share in "the catchings," in conformity with the contract.

A captain of a vessel is not justified in imprisoning a seaman merely on suspicion that he is a dangerous man, or on the request of the crew, unless some facts are shown, rendering the truth of the charge probable; and if he detain him in custody till his effects on board are lost or sold, the captain is answerable for their value.—*Jay* v. *Almy*, 1 *Woodbury & Minot's U. S. R.*, *p.* 262. (1847.)

MEMORANDUM.

A witness may use a memorandum to refresh his recollection. But it is not evidence to go to the jury; even though he swears he thinks it correct. He may refresh his memory, and then, if his recollection recalls the transaction, that recollection is testimony to go to the jury. The witness must be conscious of the reality of the matters he swears to at the time he testifies. It is not sufficient that his mind recurs to the memorandum, and that he himself believes that true.—*Butler* v. *Benson*, 1 *Barbour's R.*, *p.* 526. *N. Y.* (1848.)

MINING COMPANY—AGENT.

By the deed of association of a mining company, it was provided, that the affairs of the company should be managed by a committee of seven shareholders, called managing directors; and they were empowered, at their meetings, to vote by proxy; and B. was appointed the resident director or manager, to superintend the mine and the local concerns thereof, hire workmen, provide machinery, &c., but subject to the instructions he might from time to time receive from the managing directors, to whom he was to transmit monthly accounts of the ore raised, wages paid, &c., and a full statement of all the debts and liabilities due from the company; with a proviso that he should not expend or engage the credit of the company for any sum exceeding £50, in any one month, without the express authority in writing of three of the managing directors:—*Held*, that this deed did not authorize B. to draw or accept bills of exchange in the name of the company, even for the necessary purposes of the mine, without the express authority of the managing directors. *Held*, also, that a managing director who was represented at a meeting of directors by proxy, was not bound by a resolution of the directors present at such meeting, authorizing the resident director to accept bills for the company.—*Brown* v. *Byers*, 16 *Meeson & Welsby's R.*, *p.* 252. *Eng.* (1848.)

MISTAKE.

A mistake as to the value of the consideration given for the conveyance of land, is not a sufficient ground for setting aside the conveyance, where the vendor had means of avoiding the mistake by inquiry, and no fraud or falsehood was used to influence his judgment.—*Warner* v. *Daniels et al.*, 1 *Woodbury & Minot's U. S. R.*, *p.* 90. (1847.)

(WOODBURY, J., cited *Daniel* v. *Mitchel*, 1 *Story*, 172; *Hough* v. *Richardson*, 3 *Story*, 659; *Attwood* v. *Small*, 6 *Clark & Finn.*, 523, *note*; *Moffat* v. *Winslow*, 7 *Paige*, 124.)

Wherever a written contract contains, by mistake, less than the parties intended, or more, and the mistake is clearly established, a Court of Equity will reform it, so as to conform to the precise intentions of the parties.—*The State* v. *George*, 7 *Iredell's R.*, *p.* 430. *N. C.* (1847.)

(NASH, J., cited *Durant* v. *Durant*, 1 *Cox*, 58; *Calverly* v. *Williams*, 1 *Ves.*, 210; *Harrison* v. *Howard*, 1 *Iredell's Eq.*, 409.)

A mistake made by the clerk, in the date of a probate of a deed, cannot prejudice the party, or prevent him from proving the true date of the probate.—*Jordan* v. *Mead*, 12 *Alabama R.*, *p.* 247. (1848.)

MORTGAGE.

If the mortgagor of personal property be in the actual possession, and makes an illegal sale thereof to a third person, a servant of the purchaser, who merely carries the goods from one shop to the other, without any knowledge of the mortgage, or of any claims upon the property but those of the seller and purchaser, is not liable to the mortgagee in an action of trover.—*Burditt et al.* v. *Hunt et al.*, 25 *Maine R.*, *p.* 419. (1847.)

E. advanced money to one who held a bond and mortgage against his mother, H., paying its full amount. There was no assignment executed; the securities were lost, and it did not appear that they ever left the possession of their mutual attorney; but E. had the possession of H.'s deed for the premises mortgaged, and retained it till his death. It did not appear how he came by the deed.

Held, that the son had an equitable lien on the premises for the amount of his advance with interest.

If there had been no deposit of the deed, but he advanced the money on an agreement to have the mortgage assigned, equity would substitute him in the place of the mortgagee.

In the absence of other proof, evidence of an advance of money, and the finding of title-deeds of the borrower in possession of the lender, establishes an equitable mortgage.—*Rockwell* v. *Hobby*, 2 *Sandford's Ch. R.*, *p.* 9. *N. Y.* (1847.)

(THE ASSISTANT VICE-CHANCELLOR cited *Ex parte Corning*, 9 *Ves.*,

115; *Ex parte Wetherell*, 12 *Ves.*, 401; *Ex parte Haigh*, 12 *Ves.*, 403; *Ex parte Langton*, 17 *Ves.*, 230; *Featherstone* v. *Fenwick*, 2 *Bro. C. C.*, 279, *n.*; *Harford* v. *Carpenter*, 1 *Bro. C. C.*, 370, *n.*; 2 *Hovendon's Supplement to Vesey, Jr.*, 104; *Ex parte Kensington*, 2 *V. & B.*, 79, 83; *Ex parte Wright*, 19 *Ves.*, 258; *Hockley* v. *Bantock*, 1 *Russel*, 141, 145.)

A mortgagee, claiming title against a purchaser under a judgment creditor of the mortgage, must prove the consideration of the mortgage.—*Doe ex dem. McGintry & McCarty* v. *Reeves*, 10 *Alabama R.*, *p.* 137. (1847.)

(*Belser* cited *McCown* v. *Wood*, 4 *Ala.*, 258; *Branch Bank* v. *Kinsley*, 5 *Ala.*, 9; *Graham* v. *Lockhart*, 8 *Ala.*, 23.)

If a mortgagor of chattels makes a new and distinct contract with the mortgagee to deliver to him the mortgaged chattels, and also other chattels, to be held as security for payment of the debt which the mortgage was made to secure, and delivers them accordingly, and the mortgagee takes and holds possession of them under such new contract, he thereby becomes pawnee of all the chattels so delivered.—*Rowley* v. *Rice*, 10 *Metcalf's R.*, *p.* 7. *Mass.* (1847.)

A mortgage of goods which the mortgagor does not own when the mortgage is made, though he afterwards acquires them, is void as against his attaching creditors.—*Jones* v. *Richardson*, 10 *Metcalf's R.*, *p.* 481. *Mass.* (1847.)

MORTGAGE—PERSONAL PROPERTY.

A mortgage of personal property, where the mortgagor retains possession of the property mortgaged, with the power of sale, is void as against subsequent purchasers and execution creditors.—*Collins et al.* v. *Myers et als.*, 16 *Ohio R.*, *p.* 547. (1848.)

MURDER.

An indictment for murder charged A. with giving a mortal wound to B. G., on the 27th of May, of which wound, B. G. died on the 29th of May; and that Y. and Z., "on the day and year *first* aforesaid were present, aiding and abetting A. the felony aforesaid" to do and commit. The jury found all the prisoners guilty of manslaughter; and it was objected for Y. and Z., that the felony of A. was not complete until the death of B. G., but the judges held the conviction right.

In one count of an indictment for murder, the death was stated to be by a blow of a stick, and in another by the throwing of a stone. The jury found the prisoners guilty of manslaughter generally on both counts, and the judges held the conviction right, and that judgment could be given upon it; and *semble*, that these are not inconsistent statements of the modes of death, but that, if they had been so, no judgment could have been given on this verdict.—*Regina* v. *O'Brien et als.*, 2 *Carrington & Kirwan's R.*, *p.* 115. *Eng.* (1848.)

MURDER—DISCHARGE OF JURY.

In a prosecution for murder where the Court is satisfied that the jury cannot agree in a verdict, it may discharge them, though the prisoner oppose it, and may direct a trial before another jury.—*The State* v. *Ferguson*, 8 *Robinson's La. R.*, *p.* 613. (1847.)

Appeal from the District Court of East Baton Rouge, Boyle, J.

Preston, Attorney General for the State, cited 4 *Black.*, 355; *Chitty*, 376; *United States* v. *Coolidge*, 2 *Gallison*, 364; *The People* v. *Goodwin*, 18 *Johns.*, 200; *The People* v. *Green*, 13 *Wend.*, 56; *Commonwealth* v. *Bowden*, 9 *Mass.*, 494; *United States* v. *Perez*, 9 *Wheat.*, 580; *State* v. *Brown*, *Ante*, *p.* 566.

Burk, for the appellant.

Nicholls, J.—The accused, charged with the crime of murder, invokes the aid of this Court to release him from all further prosecution in consequence of the Court, *a qua*, having discharged the jury empannelled to try him; the said jury not having been able to agree upon a verdict.

The record shows, that on Saturday, the 24th of January last, upon the trial of this case, the jury having come into Court and stated the impossibility of their agreeing upon a verdict, it was ordered by the Court, the prisoner dissenting, that a juror be withdrawn and a mis-trial entered. This dismissal of the jury, in opposition to the wishes of the accused, is considered by his counsel as equivalent to an acquittal, and that he cannot be legally called upon to answer to the charge, before another jury.

To deny to Courts, in *all* cases, the right to discharge a jury, when no verdict can be had, would lead to consequences so calamitous and unjust, and would tend so frequently to defeat the ends for which Courts are instituted, that we should hesitate long before adopting such conclusion. Nothing short of the most imperative, positive, and unequivocal mandate of the law, could constrain us to sanction a doctrine, where the law would be on the one side and reason on the other. Aware of this result from the consideration of the principle *in extenso*, the right to discharge the jury, in certain excepted cases, is conceded to the Court; but is to be confined and restricted, according to the argument of the counsel of the accused, to cases of *absolute necessity*. This concession or partial adoption of the principle, which was too palpably self-evident not to be admitted, covers the whole ground; and reduces the matter to the simple question, *necessitas vel non?* Of the existence of this necessity the Court must *necessarily* be the judge—an authority to be exercised in *all*, particularly in *capital* cases, within the limits of a sound legal discretion. The power to apply the remedy, *must* be lodged *somewhere*, else Courts would be converted as often into snares for the innocent, as engines for the punishment of the guilty; and it can be lodged only with the *Court*, before whom the trial is had.

Without straining the imagination in search of cases illustrative of the principles involved in this investigation, the books furnish ample materials to guide the Courts in the exercise of this delicate power. In the case of *The King* v *Edwards*, 4 *Taunt.*, 309, the words of the Court are as follows; "One of the jurors fell down in a fit, and was pronounced by a physician, under oath, incapable of proceeding on the trial, on that day, whereupon the jury was discharged. The point being argued before all the judges in England, (except Mansfield,) the judges, without hearing the counsel for the Crown, said, that it had been decided in so many cases, it was now the settled law of the country," and gave judgment accordingly. So in the case of *The King* v. *Stephenson*, *Leach's C. C.*, 618, the *prisoner* fell down in a fit during the trial, and the jury was discharged; and upon his recovery, he was tried and convicted by another jury. In the case of the *United States* v. *Coolidge*, 2 *Gallison*, 364, a witness refusing to be sworn, the trial was suspended during the imprisonment of the witness for contempt; and *Mr. Justice* STORY held, that the discretion to discharge a jury existed in all cases, but that it was to be exercised only in very extraordinary and striking circumstances.

These citations are considered sufficient to point out to the Court which tries a prisoner, the limits beyond which it should not go, in the exercise of its discretion. The sessions of the District Court in the parish of Ascension, (and probably some other parishes in the State may be in a like situation,) are limited by law to *a single week*, and the Judge who there presides is likewise the Judge of the District Court of the adjoining parish of St. James, whose sessions commence on the following Monday. Granting to the accused in a capital case in the *former* parish, the delays necessary to furnish him a copy of the indictment and the panel of the jury, (and of these delays he cannot be deprived,) it is manifest, that in almost every instance, it would be equivalent to a verdict of acquittal, if you withhold from the Court the power to discharge the jury, in case of disagreement. It would be a proclamation to the guilty, that impunity was certain, and secured by the mere employment of counsel for the purpose of speaking against time, of spinning out the argument, and occupying the time of the Court until the clock struck the fatal hour of twelve on Saturday night, when Court and jury, Judge and jurymen, would all vanish by the fiat of the law, leaving the guilty one alone, washed from the consequences of his crime, reintegrated in his privileges as a citizen, and let loose upon society to repeat similar atrocities, with a similar result; for it should not be forgotten, that in the United States, the Judges are not clothed with the same authority (which the exigencies of an age of barbarism formerly conferred upon the Judges in England,) of trundling the jury after them, from county to county, and from circuit to circuit, until they could agree, in hampers or baskets made expressly for the purpose—a happy invention truly, and wonderfully well adapted to insure unanimity, and to afford an unerring and certain test of innocence or guilt. These absurdities have disappeared before the advancing light of reason and of law; and the boast of English jurists, that the common law of England is the perfection of reason, is vindicated and approved by rejecting and repudiating them as having never constituted part or parcel of the same.

Error, however sanctified by authority, or hoary by time, cannot be permitted to invoke the antiquity of its existence as a justification of its aberrations, but, on the contrary, should be renounced whenever and wherever it is discovered to lurk. *Malus usus abolendus est*, says the same common law, with regard to *customs;* a like sentence should be pronounced against error when detected.

Many of the early, *all* of the modern decisions in England and the United States, accord to Courts the power exercised in the present instance. Justice could not be administered *without it*. The amount of *fancied* evils flowing, as it is alleged from the concession of such power to courts of justice, would be more than compensated by the possible, probable, nay, positive infliction of wrong upon the unhappy class of persons themselves, for whose benefit and protection the rejection of the power is now invoked. In fine, we adopt the language of *Judge Story*, in the case of the *United States* v. *Perez*, 9 *Wheat.*, 580, as comprehending all the law on the subject. "We think that in all cases of this nature, the law has invested courts of justice with the authority to discharge a jury from giving any verdict, whenever, in their opinion, taking all the circumstances into consideration, there is a manifest necessity for the act, or the ends of public justice would otherwise be defeated; they are to exercise a sound discretion on the subject, and it is impossible to define all the circumstances which would render it proper to interfere; to be sure the power ought to be exercised with the greatest caution, under urgent circumstances, and for very plain and obvious causes; and, in capital cases especially, Courts should be extremely careful how they interfere with any of the chances of life, in favor of the prisoner; but after all, they have the right to order the discharge, and the security which the public have for the faithful, sound, and conscientious exercise of this discretion rests, in this, as in other cases, upon the responsibility of the judges, under their oaths of office."

Wherefore it is ordered that this case be remanded, that a *venire de novo* be awarded, and that the Court *a qua*, proceed in the premises according to law, and agreeably to the principles herein established.

NEW SECURITY.

Where the creditor recovers judgment against principal and surety, they are thenceforth principal debtors, and the taking of a new security from the one who was the principal, with an extension of the time of payment, does not discharge the other.—*La Farge* v. *Hester et al.*, 3 *Denio's R.*, *p.* 157. *N. Y.* (1848.)

(BEARDSLEY, J., cited *Bay* v. *Talmadge*, 5 *Johns. Ch.*, 305; *Lenox* v. *Prout*, 3 *Wheat.*, 520; *Pole* v. *Ford*, 2 *Chit. R.*, 125; *Findlay* v *Bank U. S.*, 2 *McLean*, 44.)

NEW TRIAL.

Where, on a trial of a prisoner for murder, who was found guilty, the jury were, during the progress of the trial and after their retirement, under the charge of an *unsworn* officer, it was *held*, that that circumstance, though ground for a new trial, was not technically ground for a motion in arrest of judgment.—*McCann* v. *The State of Mississippi.*, 9 *Smedes and Marshall's R.*, *p.* 465. *Miss.* (1848.)

A new trial will not be granted on account of newly discovered evidence, which is only material to contradict or impeach witnesses who were sworn on the trial.—*Harrington* v. *Bigelow*, 2 *Denio's R.*, *p.* 109. *N. Y.* (1847.)

(BEARDSLEY, J., cited *Graham on New Trials*, 463, 496; *Halsey* v. *Watson*, 1 *Caine*, 25; *Bunn* v. *Hoyt*, 3 *Johns.*, 256; *Shumway* v. *Fowler*, 4 *Johns.*, 425; *Duryee* v. *Dennison*, 5 *Johns.*, 248; *Jackson* v. *Kinney*, 14 *Johns.*, 186; *Den* v. *Geiger*, 4 *Halst.*, 239; *Den* v. *Wintermute*, 1 *Green*, 182.)

NON-RESIDENT.

When the residence of a non-resident is known, a copy of the order posted up at the Court-house door, must be enclosed to him, otherwise no decree *pro confesso* can be rendered.—*Butler* v. *Butler*, 11 *Alabama R.*, *p.* 668. (1847.)

NOTARY—WITNESS.

A notary cannot be examined as a witness to contradict a statement made by him in a protest. *Per Curiam*: a public officer, who has given a certificate in his official character, cannot be listened to as a witness to prove it false.—*Peet* v. *Dougherty*, 7 *Robinson's La. R.*, *p.* 85. (1847.)

NOTE.

A note payable to a third person, will not support a claim unless the affidavit shows the claimant has either a legal or equitable interest in it.—*Cook* v. *Davis*, 12 *Alabama R.*, *p.* 551. (1848.)

A suit was brought on the following note: "On or before the fifth day of April, A. D. 1843, we jointly and severally promise to pay to A. S. Barnum or bearer, the sum of five hundred and eigthy-three dollars—the said Barnum is to take all the flour he may want for his family use, and such other articles that he may need previous to the day of payment." The declaration alleged the promise to pay the money by the time specified in the note, omitting the conclusion in relation to the flour, &c. *Held*, that the note was a positive undertaking to pay the money therein mentioned at maturity, and that the legal import of the memorandum was, that the payee might, if he chose, take what flour, &c., he might need; that it was a condition inserted for his benefit, and that no obligation was imposed upon the makers to pay in that manner, unless the payee, in his judgment, should need the property.—*Owen* v. *Barnum*, 2 *Gilman's R.*, *p.* 461. *Ills.* (1847.)

Assumpsit in the McHenry Circuit Court, brought by the defendant in error, against the plaintiffs in error. The cause was heard before the *Hon. Richard M.* Young, at the April term, 1844, when a judgment was rendered for the plaintiff below for $620 89.

The material facts in the case are sufficiently stated in the opinion of the Court. The cause was submitted by

Thomas and *Morris*, for the plaintiffs in error, on the following brief.

In actions upon contract, if any part of the contract proved should vary materially from that stated in the pleading, it will be fatal, for a contract is an entire thing and indivisible.—1 *Greenl. Ev.*, 79, *sec.* 66.

The entire consideration must be stated, and the entire act to be done in virtue thereof, together with the time, manner, and circumstances, and with all parts of the proposition, as stated, the proof must agree.

It (variance) may be defined to be a disagreement between the allegation and proof.—1 *Greenl. Ev.*, 74, *sec.* 63. The following authorities are also referred to: 6 *East*, 464, 567; 3 *T. R.*, 643, 646; 2 *A. K. Marsh.*, 287; 4 *B. & A.*, 765; 2 *Starkie's Ev.*, 401; 3 *Caine*, 286; 3 *Wend.*, 374.

If the allegation be of absolute contract, and the proof be of a contract in the alternative at the option of the defendant, &c., in these and the like cases the variance will be fatal.—1 *Greenl. Ev.*, 80. *sec.* 66. *See note to* 3 *Greenl., on this point at same page.* 2 *East*, 2; 2 *Doug.*, 665; 6 *Greenl.*, 109; 1 *Camp.*, 361; *Cro. Eliz.*, 79.

The note is set forth as if payable in money, when by the writing on the end of the note, it was to be paid in notes on the Bank of Kentucky, &c. *Osborne* v. *Fulton*, 1 *Blackford*, 234. The variance was held to be fatal.

The opinion of the Court was delivered by

PURPLE, J.—The defendant in error sued the plaintiffs in error in the McHenry County Circuit Court, in an action of trespass on the case upon promises. The declaration charges that the defendants below made their promissory note in writing, dated the 5th day of April, 1839, and thereby then and there jointly and severally promised to pay the plaintiff below, on or before the 5th day of April, A. D. 1843, the sum of five hundred and eighty-three dollars, and then and there delivered the said note to the said plaintiff.

Herman N. Owen pleaded his discharge under the bankrupt laws of the United States, which plea was confessed by the defendant in error, and judgment rendered in his favor.

Daniel Owen pleaded the general issue upon which the parties proceeded to trial.

The plaintiff below offered in evidence a note of which the following is a copy:

"On or before the fifth day of April, A. D. 1843, we jointly and severally promise to pay A. S. Barnum or bearer, the sum of five hundred and eighty-three dollars—the said Barnum is to take all the flour that he may want for family use, and such other articles as he may need previous to the day of payment.

(Signed,) H. N. OWEN.
DANIEL OWEN."

"*McHenry, April 5th*, 1839."

The defendant below objected to the introduction of the note in evidence upon the ground of variance between it and the note described in the declaration.

The Court overruled the objection and admitted the evidence. And this decision of the Court is now assigned for error.

This note is a positive undertaking on the part of the makers to pay the sum of money therein mentioned at its maturity; and the legal import of the memorandum at the bottom is, that the payee may, if he chooses, take what flour and other articles he may need for the use of his family previous to the day of payment. It is a condition inserted for his benefit. There is no duty or obligation imposed upon the makers to pay in this manner, unless the payee, in his judgment, should need the property. The defendant below could not have tendered the same and thereby, against the wish of the plaintiff below, have discharged the note. In a declaration, it is not necessary to state all the parts of a contract which consists of several distinct and collateral provisions. The *gravamen* is, that a certain act which the defendant engaged to do has not been done, and the legal proposition to be maintained is, that for such a consideration he became bound to do such an act, including the time, manner and other circumstances of its performance. If the allegation be of an absolute contract, and the proof be of a contract in the alternative, at the option of the defendant, the variance would be fatal.—1 *Greenl. Ev.*, 75–6.

In the case of *Osborne* v. *Fulton*, 1 *Blackf.*, 234, a note was drawn for the sum of $137, dated 6th July, 1821, and payable on the 1st of November next ensuing. Across the end of the note was written: "The amount of this note to be paid in notes on the Bank of Kentucky, or the Branch Bank at Lawrenceburg." The Court held this memorandum to be a part of the contract, and a necessary portion of the description of the note in the declaration, and the variance on account of the omission, fatal.

Admitting the correctness of this decision, there is a marked distinction between this case and the one now under consideration. In the one cited the contract was in the alternative, and at the option of the defendant to pay in money, in notes on the Bank of Kentucky, or the Branch Bank at Lawrenceburg. In this case there is no such alternative.

The judgment of the Circuit Court is affirmed with costs.

Judgment affirmed.

If two persons make a promissory note, and one of them afterwards obtain possession of the note as his property from the payee, the note is discharged.—*Cox et als.* v. *Hodge*, 7 *Blackford's R.*, p. 146. *Ind.* (1847.)

NOTE—ENDORSER.

A promissory note was payable to two persons not partners, and endorsed by them. *Held*, that notice by the holder of the maker's nonpayment should be given to each of the endorsers.—*The State Bank* v. *Slaughter, Adm'r*, 7 *Blackford's R.*, p. 133. *Ind.* (1847.)

Appeal from the Tippecanoe Circuit Court.

Blackford, J.—This was an action of assumpsit brought by the administrator of Chamberlin against the State Bank, for certain dividends on bank stock belonging to the intestate's estate. Plea, non assumpsit. The cause was submitted to the Court, and judgment rendered for the plaintiff.

On the trial, the defendant's possession of the dividends was admitted; and the defence was, that the intestate's estate was indebted to the defendant, and that the latter therefore was not liable, by a provision of the bank charter, to pay the dividends, whilst that indebtedness of the estate continued.

To prove the alleged debt to the bank, the following promissory note and endorsements were introduced: "$200. Lafayette, Ind., Sept. 11, 1839. Ninety days after date, I promise to pay to Edward Barroll and John C. Chamberlin, or order, 200 dollars, negotiable and payable at the branch at Lafayette, of the State bank of Indiana, for value received.

James White. Credit the drawer. E. Barroll." Endorsed, "Pay the State Bank of Indiana. Edward Barroll. J. C. Chamberlin." The maker's non-payment of this note, and due notice of the default to the plaintiff, (Chamberlin being dead,) were also proved. Barroll, the other endorser, resided at Lafayette, where the default occurred, and had there a place of business.

The only notice for him of the maker's default was deposited in the post-office at Lafayette, which was not a legal notice—*Curtis* v. *The State Bank*, 6 *Blackf.*, 312; *Story on Bills*, 451.

We are of opinion that, according to these facts, the bank had no claim against the plaintiff. The note was payable to two persons not partners, each of whom had endorsed it. The contract created by the endorsement being joint only, the endorsers, if liable at all, could be only jointly liable; and to render them so liable, the notice of the non-payment should have been given to them both. The following is the language of Justice STORY as to bills of exchange: "Where there are several persons, who are joint drawers or endorsers, entitled to notice, who are not partners, each is entitled to notice, and therefore, notice should be directed to his own proper domicil or place of business. Where they are partners, notice to either of the partners will suffice, at the domicil of either of them, or at their usual place of business." *Story on Bills*, 335. The law as to notice to joint endorsers must be the same, whether the endorsement be of a promissory note or bill of exchange; and the endorsers in the present case, therefore, according to the authority cited, were discharged for want of legal notice to each of them.

PER CURIAM.—*The judgment is affirmed, with three per cent. damages and costs.*

NOTE—MUTILATED.

If a person sue as payee on a promissory note so mutilated that the payee's name is illegible, he must prove that the note was made to him, that he had possession of it when he commenced the suit, and that it was mutilated under circumstances not affecting its validity.—*Hatch* v. *Dickinson's*, 7 *Blackford's R.*, *p.* 48. *Ind.* (1847.)

NOTE—PRESENTMENT.

A notice of the dishonor of a note, given to the executor of an endorser, before he has qualified as such, is not such a presentment, as will take the case out of the statute of non-claim.—*Branch Bank at Mobile* v. *Hallett et al.*, 12 *Alabama R.*, *p.* 671. (1848.)

NOTE—SIGNATURE.

Where a promissory note has been legibly signed and sealed by one person, and another signs his name *under* that of the first signer, but not opposite to his seal, (making no seal of his own, and nothing being on the face of the paper sufficiently indicative of the intention to seal, nor evidence of it *aliunde*) the seal of the second person cannot be inferred from his signature.—*O'Cain* v. *O'Cain*, 1 *Strobhart's R.*, *p.* 402. *S. C.* (1847.)

NOTICE.

If a notice of dishonor of a bill of exchange be *posted* by the holder in due time, he is not prejudiced if, through mistake or delay of the post-office, it be not delivered in due time.—*Woodcock* v. *Houldsworth*, 16 *Meeson & Welsby's R.*, *p.* 124. *Eng.* (1848.)

(*Bovill* cited *Dobree* v. *Eastman*, 3 *Car. & Payne*, 250.)

On a question of priority of incumbrances on shares, notice to one of a Joint Stock Company is not notice to the company.

A. held shares as trustee and executed a declaration of trust, but no notice was given at the office of the company. A. afterwards mortgaged his shares to secure his private debt. Notice of this mortgage was given to the company, and was entered in their books. *Held*, that the mortgagee had priority over the *cestui que trust*.—*Martin* v. *Sedgwick*, 9 *Beavan's R.*, *p.* 333. *Eng.* (1848.)

NOTICE—NEWSPAPER.

A party cannot be charged with notice of an advertisement, in a newspaper, merely because he is a subscriber to the paper.—*Watkins* v. *Peck*, 13 *New Hampshire R.*, *p.* 360. (1847.)

NUMERICAL FIGURES.

The Arabic numerical figures are, for some purposes, a part of the English language; but of themselves they signify mere numbers; and words, or signs, are therefore necessary to predicate the number signified of any particular subject, or thing.

The mark commonly used to denote dollars ($) is not part of the English language, within the statute of this State, which requires declarations and other pleadings to be drawn in the English language; and a declaration in assumpsit upon a promissory note, in which the amount for which the note was given was only expressed in figures with the mark for dollars prefixed, (thus $226 17) was held insufficient on demurrer.—*Clark* v. *Stoughton et al.*, 18 *Vermont R.*, p, 50. (1847.)

ASSUMPSIT. The defendants were attached to answer unto the plaintiff "in a plea of the case, for that the said Delancey Stoughton, Jr., Frederick Hazen, Henry Brayton, and Albert S. Matthews, all of Alburgh aforesaid, at Alburgh, on the 26th day of June, 1841, by their note under their hands of that date, for value received, jointly and severally promised to pay the said William A. Clark $226 17 by the first day of May, 1842, with interest, and then and there, to wit, on the 26th day of June, 1841, delivered said note to the plaintiff. Yet the said defendants not regarding said undertaking, have not paid said sum of money mentioned in said note, or any part thereof, though often requested," &c.

The defendants demurred, and assigned for cause "that the plaintiff's declaration does not allege for what thing the defendants promised, or for what said promise, in said declaration mentioned, was made." The County Court, BENNETT, J., presiding,—adjudged the declaration insufficient; to which decision the plaintiff excepted.

—— for defendants.
Harrington, for plaintiff.

The opinion of the Court was delivered by

ROYCE, J.—It would doubtless be going too far to assert that the Arabic numerical figures in universal use, are not, to some purposes, a part of the English language. To similar purposes they are also part of most other languages, throughout the civilized world. Of themselves, however, they signify mere numbers; and words, or signs, are therefore necessary to predicate the number signified of any particular subject, or thing. And how far a mark, point, or other sign, prefixed, or added to the figures, to show the application and sense of the number expressed, should also be recognized as English language, must depend much on usage and custom. The capitals A. D., as part of a date, having been adjudged to be English language by use, though in fact being the initials of two Latin words. *State* v. *Hodgeden*, 3 *Vt.*, 481. So the usual marks expressive of dollars and cents, when employed according to general and long practice, (as in stating accounts and the like,) may, to that extent, be treated as part of our language by adoption and use.

But the question upon this declaration is, whether figures with such attendant marks were properly employed within the meaning of the statute, as the only language by which to state the amount of the note in suit; in other words, to allege the only matter which gave validity or importance to the promise declared on. And we think, that the statute, in requiring declarations and other pleadings to be drawn in the English language, must have contemplated the use of English letters and words, allowing customary abbreviations, which would not obscure the sense, and figures for the purpose of expressing numbers merely. Without insisting on the greater liability to mistakes, or the increased facilities for committing fraud, or forgery, under a more lax interpretation of the statute, it is sufficient to say, that this is the more obvious and natural construction.

The present is a very novel mode of declaring, at least in this State. This is even the first attempt that I have noticed in the higher Courts, to set forth an essential part of a promise, or other engagement, without the use of words. *We think the innovation should not be countenanced, and that the judgment below should be affirmed.*

After this opinion was pronounced the plaintiff's counsel moved that the judgment below be reversed *pro forma*, that he might then move for liberty to amend. The judgment was accordingly reversed for that purpose, and a motion to amend was granted, upon payment of costs in this Court.

OBSTRUCTING PROCESS.

To constitute the offence of obstructing process, in a criminal point of view, there must be an active opposition; not merely taking charge of a debtor's property, keeping it out of view, and refusing when called on by an officer to place it within his reach.—*Crampton* v. *Newman*, 12 *Alabama R.*, *p.* 199. (1848.)

OFFICER.

An officer will not be held liable for the non return of an execution, when his failure has been produced by the instruction or intermeddling of plaintiff.—*Robinson* v. *Harrison*, 7 *Humphreys' R.*, *p.* 189. *Tenn.* (1847.)

The acts of an officer *de facto*, whether judicial or ministerial, are valid, so far as the rights of the public, or third persons having an interest in such acts, are concerned; and neither the title of such an officer, nor the validity of his acts as such, can be indirectly called in question, in a proceeding to which he is not a party.

An officer *de facto*, is one who exercises the duties of an office under color of right, by virtue of an appointment or election to that office; being distinguished, on the one hand, from a mere usurper of an office, and on the other, from an officer *de jure*.

Therefore, where a person eligible to the office of grand-juror, was in the month of *October*, duly chosen a grand-juror for the town, for the ensuing year; he refused to take the oath prescribed for grand-jurors, and was fined according to law for such refusal; this fine he paid; in the month of *May* afterwards, he took the oath, and the next day, exercised the functions of a grand-juror, by making a presentment for an offence, and prosecuting it; in a suit between third persons, in which the validity of his official acts came in question, it was *held*, that such person was an officer *de facto*, and his acts, as such, were to be regarded as valid.—*Town of Plymouth* v. *Painter*, 17 *Connecticut R.*, *p.* 585. (1847.)

This was an action of debt, brought by Allen Painter against the town of Plymouth, to recover of the defendants the sum of one dollar twenty cents, which the plaintiff claimed as due to him as his fees, as a witness, in a public prosecution, before a justice of the peace in that town, against John C. Calhoun and Lucius P. Porter, for a matter of delinquency.

On the trial of the cause before the justice, on the general issue, the following facts were proved.

At a town meeting of the town of Plymouth, legally warned, and held on the 7th of October, 1844, Sylvester Matthews was one of six persons who were duly chosen grand-jurors for that town. On the 21st of February, 1845, a suit was commenced against him, in favor of Edward Langdon, the town treasurer, to recover the penalty of five dollars, for refusing to accept the office of grand-juror, returnable before a justice of the peace, on the 1st of March, 1845; in which suit a judgment and execution were obtained against him. On the 19th of May, 1845, he paid the amount of such execution to the attorney of the town; which was by him paid into the town treasury. It did not appear, that the town of Plymouth had ever appointed another grand-juror in the place of Matthews; but it was proved, that on the 16th of May, 1845, the oath prescribed by law for grand-jurors was duly administered to him.

On the 17th of May, 1845, Matthews, as grand-juror, preferred his complaint against Calhoun and Porter, for violations of the law regulating the sale of spirituous liquors, which complaint was returned to Heman Welton, Esq., justice of the peace; and on the trial of the cause, Painter, the plaintiff, was duly summoned to appear as a witness in support of the complaint. He accordingly appeared before justice Welton, and testified on the part of the prosecution. Calhoun and Porter were acquitted of the offences charged against them, and the justice taxed the costs accruing in the suit, against the town of Plymouth, including the sum of one dollar twenty cents, in favor of Painter, as his fee as a witness. The record of this judgment counted upon the complaint as "the complaint of Sylvester Matthews, grand-juror," &c. On the 3rd of December, 1845, justice Welton issued his order to the town treasurer of that town for the payment of the costs so taxed. The plaintiff, on the 4th of December, 1845, presented said order to Edward Langdon, the treasurer of said town, and demanded of him the said sum of one dollar twenty cents, as the plaintiff's fees as such witness, which he neglected and refused to pay.

On these facts the defendants claimed, that Matthews was not, at the time of making said complaint, a grand-juror of the town of Plymouth. But the Court was of opinion and decided, that it sufficiently appeared from the records of justice Welton, that Matthews was a lawful grand-juror; that it was not competent for the defendants to go back of said record to inquire whether Matthews was, or was not, a lawful grand-juror; and if such inquiry was proper, the Court was of opinion, from the facts proved, that Matthews was a lawful grand-juror at the time of making and hearing said complaint. And therefore the Court found the issue in favor of the plaintiff, and rendered judgment accordingly. To reverse this judgment, the defendants thereupon brought a writ of error in the Superior Court; which was reserved for the advice of this Court, as to what judgment should be rendered thereon.

Hollister and *Graves*, for the plaintiffs in error, after remarking that Painter, the plaintiff in the suit, was bound to show the existence of such law and such facts, as would warrant the Court to find that the defendants were *indebted* to him,—the burden of such proof lying wholly upon him,—contended:

1. That a legal presentment must be made, by a legal officer, to authorize the magistrate to draw on the town treasurer for costs.—*Stat.* 328., *title* 45, *sec.* 2, *p.* 174; *tit.* 10, *sec.* 131, *p.* 179; *tit.* 20, *sec.* 151. (*Ed.* 1838.)

2. That Matthews, who assumed the functions of a grand-juror, in the presentment and prosecution of the complaint against Calhoun and Porter, was not such legal officer. In the first place, by the common law, irrespective of any Statute provision, where the appointment of an officer is not by *deed*, he may accept or decline the office *by parol*. *Rex* v. *Mayor of Rippon*, 1 *Ld. Raym.*, 563; *S. C.*, 2 *Salk.*, 433; *Regina* v. *Lane*, 2 *Ld. Raym.*, 1304; *S. C.*, 11 *Mod.*, 270; *Regina* v. *Gloucester*, *Holt's R.*, 450; *Van Orsdall* v. *Hazard*, 3 *Hill*, 243, 248. Secondly, by our statute, the acceptance and qualification, by taking the oath, must be *immediate*.—*Stat.* 328, *tit.* 45, *sec.* 3, 5.

3. That if the person chosen does not so accept and qualify, the office becomes *vacant*. Such neglect is equivalent to a positive refusal to accept. That a vacancy may be *implied*, see *The People ex rel. Whiting* v. *Carrique*, 2 *Hill*, 93, 97.

4. That the issuing of the order upon the town, had no effect upon its rights. In the first place, it was a mere *ministerial act*. Secondly, if otherwise, the town was not a party to the proceeding, and had no opportunity to be heard.

5. That the town was not estopped, by the record of justice Welton, from denying that Matthews was a legal grand-juror. In the first place, this point was not in issue. Secondly, it was not decided or passed upon by the Court. Thirdly, the town was not a party, and had no notice of the suit until the order came.

Seymour and *Johnson*, for the defendant in error, were stopped by the Court.

STORRS, J.—On the facts, in this case, the plaintiff in error claims, that there was a refusal by Matthews to accept the office, and that he could not, by subsequently taking the oath, become competent to exercise it; and that, therefore, not being legally a grand-juror, when said complaint was made, the town of Plymouth were not bound by the proceedings of the Court, before which it was tried, and could not be subjected for the fees of the defendant in error, as a witness in that cause. The main question made by the plaintiffs in error before us, is, whether Matthews, by taking the oath, under these circumstances, became lawfully entitled to exercise the office of grand-juror. We do not think that that question necessarily or properly arises in this case; for we are clearly of opinion, that, however it might be decided, Matthews, when he preferred the criminal complaint, was what is termed an officer *de facto*; and that his acts, as such, which are attempted here to be drawn in question, were therefore valid and binding, as to the parties in this case, and all other third persons, to the same extent as if he were an officer *de jure*.

An officer *de facto*, is one who exercises the duties of an office, under color of an appointment or election to that office. He differs, on the one hand, from a mere usurper of an office, who undertakes to act as an officer without any color of right; and, on the other, from an officer *de jure*, who is, in all respects, legally appointed and qualified to exercise the office. These distinctions are very obvious, and have always been recognized. It is not, in all cases, easy to determine what ought to be considered as constituting a colorable right to an office, so as to determine whether one is a mere usurper; *The King* v. *The Corporation of Bedford Level*, 6 *East*, 368; but it is not necessary, in the present instance, to examine the cases on that point, since, according to all the authorities, here was undoubtedly a fair color of right in the person acting as a grand-juror, to exercise that office, whether he was legally qualified to do so, or not. He was plainly more than a mere usurper; he was legally appointed by the town to the office, and was eligible to such appointment, and claiming a right to act under it, took, in due form, the oath prescribed by law for the office. These would, confessedly, be sufficient to confer on him a perfect legal title to the office, but for what intervened between the appointment and the taking of the oath. Whatever may be the effect of what thus intervened upon the question whether he could afterwards rightfully become qualified for the office, by taking the oath, it is clear, that the administration of it, in connexion with his previous appointment, gave him at least a color, pretence, or show of right to exercise the office; which is all that is necessary, in order to constitute him an officer *de facto*. Even if his previous refusal to take the oath, legally disqualified him from subsequently doing so, this effect was not so palpable and obvious as to deprive him of a fair color of right to exercise the office. There was an observance of all the legal forms requisite to enable him to act as such officer; and this clearly constituted a colorable title, or apparent right.

It is a well settled principle, that the acts of an officer *de facto*, are valid, so far as the rights of the public or third persons who have an interest in the acts done, are concerned; and that the title of such an officer, or the validity of his acts as such, cannot be indirectly called in question, in a suit to which he is not a party; and this principle applies as well to judicial as ministerial officers. This doctrine has been established from the earliest period, and repeatedly confirmed, by an unbroken current of decisions, down to the present time.

In the case of *The Abbot of Fonntane, Year-Book*, 9 *Henry* 6, 33, it was held, that an obligation for goods sold for the use of a religious house, made by one as abbot of the house, who held his office under color of an election, by only a minor part of the votes, was not voidable by the true abbot, who was elected by a majority of the votes after he recovered the possession of the office, because the former had a color of title when he made the obligation, and he who sold the goods was not bound to examine his title to the office.

In *Leech* v. *Howel, Cro. Eliz.*, 533, which was the case of an information for bringing certain merchandise into the country, without paying, or agreeing for the payment of, the custom and subsidy due for them to the collector of the custom in London, or in any other port, or to his deputy, it was held, that an agreement made at the custom-house in a particular port, with a person who had there exercised the office of deputy of one who was a deputy of the collector of the customs there, was valid, although the person with whom such agreement was made, was a deputy *de facto* only, and not *de jure;* for that it would be mischievous to the merchants to require them to examine by what authority the officers of the customs make their compositions.

In *Harris* v. *Jays, Cro. Eliz.*, 699, it was conceded by the Court, that if one being created bishop, the former bishop not being deprived or removed, admits one to a benefice upon a presentation, or collates by lapse, these are good, and not avoidable; for that the law favors one in a reputed authority.

In *Knight* v. *The Corporation of Wells, Lutw.*, 508, it was held, that if one elected mayor of a corporation, without being legally qualified to be chosen to that office, after such election puts the seal of the corporation to a bond, this obligation is good, because, by coming into the office by color of an election, he was thereby mayor *de facto;* and all judicial and ministerial acts done by him, are good.

In *Knowles* v. *L——, Moor*, 112, and *Harris* v. *Jays, Cro. Eliz.*, 699, a distinction was taken, by the Court, between copy-holds granted by a steward of a manor, who had color, but no right to hold a Court, and those granted by one who had neither color nor right, and who therefore was a mere usurper; the former being deemed valid, but the latter void.

In *King* v. *Lisle, Andrews*, 163; *S. C.* 2 *Stra.*, 1090, which has been considered a leading case, the same distinction was made between an officer *de facto*, acting *colore* officii, and an officer *de jure*.

The same principle has been uniformly adopted in the modern English cases. It was distinctly acted upon, in *The King* v. *The Corporation of Bedford Level*, 6 *East*, 366; and in the more recent case of *The Margate Pier* v. *Hannam*, 3 *B. & A.*, 266, (5 *E. C. L.*, 278,) where a statute provided for the appointment of justices of the peace in a certain place, and declared, that no person should be authorized to act as justice, unless he had taken certain oaths; it was decided that the acts of a justice appointed under that law were valid, although he had not taken the oaths; and although he might be punished for so acting; and that, therefore, persons seizing goods under a warrant of distress, signed by such justice, were not trespassers. Indeed the doctrine in these cases is universally applied in England to officers *de facto*, from the lowest officer up to the King.—1 *Black. Com.*, 204, 371; 1 *Hale's P. C.*, 60; *Foster*, 397, 398; *Hawk. P. C.*, *b.* 1, *ch*, 8, *sec.* 1, 3.

The same principles have been repeatedly adopted by the Courts of this country.

In *The People* v. *Collins*, 7 *Johns.*, 549, a peremptory *mandamus* was issued to the defendant, who was a town clerk, to record a highway laid out and established, by the commissioners of highways, in the town, although it appeared by the return of the clerk to the alternative *mandamus*, that the commissioners had not taken the oath of their office, and a certificate of such oath had not been filed in the clerk's office, as required by law. The Court said, that the commissioners were liable to a penalty; but that they were commissioners *de facto*, as they came into office by color of title, and that their acts, as such, were valid as far as the rights of third persons, and of the public were concerned; and KENT, *C. J.*, observed on the argument, that the point was too well settled to be discussed.

In *Tucker* v. *Aiken et al.*, 4 *N. H.*, 113, where the subject was elaborately examined, the Court adopted the same general principle as to the validity of the acts of officers *de facto*, and decided, that it was applicable to those officers of towns, whose duty it is to assess and collect taxes. Therefore, where the office of collector was set up at auction, and struck off to the lowest bidder, who was afterwards chosen collector by the town, it was held, that, although the proceeding was illegal, the collector coming into office by color of an election, was to be considered an officer *de facto*; and that the objection could not be taken in action against the select-men, for an illegal assessment and collection of taxes. It was also decided, in the same case, that where the moderator of the town-meeting at which the collector was chosen, had neglected to take the oath required by the statute, the select-men were not liable for committing the collection of the taxes to such a collector.

In *Mason* v. *Dillingham*, 15 *Mass.*, 170, a levy of an execution on a pew in a meeting-house, made by a coroner who had not given bond for the faithful execution of his office; and in *Bucknam* v. *Ruggles*, 15 *Mass.*, 180, an extent of an execution upon real estate, made by a deputy-sheriff, who had not taken the oath required by law, were held to be valid; the Court saying, in the latter case, that such a rule was necessary to prevent a failure of justice, and great public mischief. The following cases also fully sustain the same rule: *Fowler* v. *Beebee et al.*, 9 *Mass.*, 231; *Moore* v. *Graves*, 3 *N. H.*, 408; *Morse* v. *Culley*, 5 *N H.*, 222; *Baird* v. *Bank of Washington*, 11 *S. & R.*, 411; *Cocke* v. *Halsee*, 16 *Pet.*, 85; *McInstry* v. *Tanner*, 9 *Johns.*, 125; *Wilcox* v. *Smith*, 5 *Wend.*, 231; *The People* v. *Bartlett*, 6 *Wend.*, 422; *The People* v. *Covert*, 1 *Hill*,

674; *Trustees of Vernon Society* v. *Hills*, 6 *Cow.*, 23; *The People* v. *The Corporation of N. Y.*, 3 *Johns. Cas.*, 79; *McKim* v. *Somers*, 1 *Pa.*, 297; *The People* v. *Hopson*, 1 *Denio*, 174.

In the case last cited, it was held, that on the trial of an indictment for resisting a constable while engaged in executing process against the defendant's property, the defendant is not entitled to show, that the officer had not taken the oath of office, or given the security required by law; it being sufficient, in such a case, that the party resisted was an officer *de facto*.

The principle established by these cases, in regard to the proceedings of officers *de facto*, acting under color of title, is one founded in policy and convenience, is most salutary in its operation; and is, indeed, necessary for the protection of the rights of individuals, and the security of the public peace. The rights of no person claiming a title or interest under or through the proceedings of officers having an apparent authority to act, would be safe, if he were obliged to examine the legality of the title of such officer up to its original source, and the title or interest of such person were held to be invalidated, by some accidental defect or flaw in the appointment, election or qualifications of such officer, or in the rights of those from whom his appointment or election emanated; nor could the supremacy of the laws be maintained, or their execution enforced, if the acts of officers having a colorable, but not a legal title, were to be deemed invalid. The remarks of ABBOT, C. J., in the case of *Margate Pier Co.* v. *Hannam*, before cited, presents this subject in a strong light. He says that if the act of the justice issuing a warrant be invalid, on the ground of the objection there made, all persons who should act in the execution of the warrant, would act without any authority; a constable who arrests, and a jailer who receives a felon, would each be a trespasser; resistance to them would be lawful; every thing done by either of them would be unlawful; and a constable, or person aiding him, might, in some possible instance, become amenable even to a charge of murder, for acting under an authority, which they reasonably considered themselves bound to obey, and of the invalidity whereof they were wholly ignorant.

The acts of a mere usurper of an office, without any color of title, are undoubtedly wholly void, both as to individuals and the public. But where there is a color of lawful title, the doings of an officer, as it respects third persons and the public, must be respected, until he is ousted on a *quo warranto*, which is the appropriate proceeding to try the validity of a title to an office, and in which it would be necessary for him to show a complete title in all respects; although in a suit against a person for acts which he would have an authority to do only as an officer, he must, in order to make out a justification, show that he is an officer *de jure*; because the title to the office, being directly drawn in question, in a suit to which he is a party,—may be regularly decided: so where he sues for fees, or sets up a title to property, by virtue of his office, he must show himself to be an officer *de jure*.—*Fowler* v. *Beebee*, 9 *Mass.*, 231; *The People* v.

The Corporation of New-York, 3 *Johns. Cas.*, 79; *The People* v. *Hopson*, 1 *Denio*, 574.

This view of the case renders it unnecessary to consider the other points made in the case.

The Superior Court is therefore advised to affirm the judgment complained of.—In this opinion the other Judges concurred.

Judgment affirmed.

ORDER.

If a petition for an *ex parte* order suppresses any fact which, whether really material or not, would, if communicated to the officer whose duty it is to draw up the order, prevent him from doing so without mentioning the matter to the Court, the order will be discharged for irregularity. —*Cooper* v. *Lewis*, 2 *Philips' Ch. R.*, *p.* 178. *Eng.* (1848.)

(*Rolt* cited *Cartwright* v. *Smith*, 6 *Beav.*, 21.)

OVERSEER.

If an overseer so acts in the business of his employer as to authorize his dismissal, yet if the employer, with a knowledge of the fact, overlook the impropriety, and retain the overseer in his service for months, he cannot then make such misconduct an excuse for discharging him, in the absence of a cause subsequently occurring.—*Martin* v. *Everett*, 11 *Alabama R.*, *p.* 375. (1847.)

PARENT AND CHILD.

Where a father conveyed land to his son for services and affection, and took back a lease for life, but did not wish to have them recorded till after his death, in order to keep them from the knowledge of his wife and the public, the deed was held to be well delivered, though lodged with a third person under the above arrangement.

If that third person falls sick, and the grantor takes back the deed for safety, and dies leaving it among his papers, from which it is taken by the grantee and recorded, the original delivery still continues to be valid.—*Brown* v. *Brown et al.*, 1 *Woodbury & Minot's U. S. R.*, *p.* 325. (1847.)

(WOODBURY, J., cited *Dyer*, 167; 2 *Leonard*, 110; *Garnons* v. *Knight*, 5 *Barn. & Cres.*, 671; 12 *Com. Law*, 351; *Souverbye* v. *Arden*, 1 *Johns. Ch.*, 240; 2 *Mass.*, 447; 3 *Metc.*, 414; *Belden* v *Carter*, 4 *Day*, 66; *Bickford* v. *Daniels*, 2 *N. H.*, 71; 1 *N. H.*, 357; 4 *Cranch*, 219.)

A voluntary conveyance by a parent to a child, made in good faith, by way of advancement, will be sustained, although the parent may have been at the time, indebted; provided the property left in the parent is clearly and abundantly sufficient to satisfy all subsisting debts.

To entitle a widow to dower, it is necessary that her husband should have had a legal estate of inheritance in the premises in which dower is claimed, during the coverture, or that he should have had an equitable interest in the same at the time of his death.—*Miller et als.* v. *Wilson et als.*, 15 *Ohio R.*, *p.* 108. (1847.)

This is a suit in Chancery, reserved in the County of Franklin.

The bill and amended bill in this case, are filed by Thomas Miller and others, creditors of John Wilson, deceased, against the widow, heir and personal representatives of said Wilson. It is charged that said Wilson, in his lifetime, being involved in debt, with a view to defraud his creditors caused certain real estate, described in the bill, for which he had paid, or was liable to pay, to be conveyed to his wife and children, and afterwards died greatly insolvent. The prayer of the bill is, that the real estate so fraudulently conveyed may be sold, with the other real estate of the decedent, and that the avails may be appropriated in the discharge of debts, &c.

The allegations of fraud are denied in the answers of Margaret Wilson, the widow, and Ann Wilson, the only surviving heir of John Wilson.

Much testimony has been taken, which it is unnecessary to recapitulate, as a more full statement of the case, and facts of the case, are given in the opinion of the Court.

Andrews & Wilcox, for complainants, contended—

That the testimony showed clearly that, at the time the property in controversy was conveyed to the heirs of John Wilson, he was largely indebted, and therefore the deed was fraudulent as to creditors, even though there was no *actual* fraudulent intent. They also insisted that the facts of the case warranted the Court in coming to the conclusion that it was the design of Wilson—knowing that he was in embarrassed circumstances—to place a portion of his property beyond the reach of his creditors—to commit actual fraud upon them; and that his retaining possession of the property himself, withholding for years the deed from record—taking, subsequently to the date of the deed to his children, a deed to himself for the same property, and making valuable improvements thereon, were among the badges of fraud which the case presented, and which authorized the interference of a Court of Chancery to set aside the conveyance.

They referred the Court to the following authorities:—1 *Atk.*, 15; 2 *Atk.*, 600; 3 *Johns. Ch.*, 481; *Wright*, 213, 214; 5 *Ohio*, 122; 9 *Pet.*, 204; 11 *Wheat.*, 103; 2 *Leigh*, 52; 10 *Mass.*, 462; 12 *Johns.*, 418; 3 *N. H.*, 304; 4 *Blackf.*, 141.

Ewing, and *Swayne & Bates*, for defendants.

The whole case, in our view, resolves itself into this: When the conveyance was made to his children, Wilson was in easy circumstances. He had, *in any fair view of the testimony*, a large excess of means over his liabilities, exclusive of the property in question. Under these circumstances he made an advancement to his two children of property worth, according to the complainants' proof, $2,000, or at most not exceeding $2,500. Some years afterward he became involved, embarrassed and insolvent, and while in that condition died.

Does the after insolvency affect the prior advancement? What does the law say on this subject?

"Where a parent makes an advancement to a child, and honestly and fairly retains in his hands sufficient property to pay all his debts, such child will not be bound to refund such advancement for the benefit of creditors, although it should happen that the parent does not pay his debts which existed at the time of making such advancement."—*Van Wick* v. *Seward*, 6 *Paige*, 62.

"I presume it cannot be seriously urged that where a parent makes an advancement to his child, honestly and fairly retaining in his own hands, at the same time, property sufficient to pay all his debts, such child will be bound to refund the advancement for the benefit of creditors, if it afterwards happens that the parent, either by misfortune or fraud, does not actually pay all his debts which existed at the time of the advancement."—*Same case*, 6 *Paige*, 67.

"To impeach a settlement made after marriage, the husband must be proved to have been indebted at the time *to the extent of the insolvency.*"—*Lusk* v. *Wilkinson*, 5 *Vesey*, 384; *Sugden on Vendors*, 447.

This doctrine was also recognized in a late law case in Westminster Hall.—*Sears* v. *Rodgers*, 3 *Barn. & Adolph.*, 362.

"The judge was also right in deciding that the deed from T. Merrick to C. Merrick, was not void in law, as made in fraud of creditors; because although the grantor was indebted, there was property enough left to pay her debts."—*Jackson* v. *Post*, 15 *Wend.*, 593; *Hends. Lessee* v. *Longworth*, 11 *Wheat.*, 199.

"A voluntary gift of a solvent parent to his child, is good against existing creditors."—*Howard* v. *Williams*, 1 *Bailey*, 575.

"A voluntary conveyance in consideration of natural love and affection to grantor's daughter, leaving amply sufficient to meet all his debts, is valid against a subsequent mortgage to secure *a previous debt; and if valid at the time of its execution, it is not rendered fraudulent by subsequent embarrassments of the grantor.*"—*Brackett* v. *Weight*, 4 *Verm.*, 389.

"Strictly speaking, there is no such thing as *fraud in law. Fraud or no fraud, is, and ever must be, a fact.*"—*Spencer's Opinion, Jackson* v. *Seward*, 8 *Cowen*, 435.

This fact must be proved like any other.—*Ibid.; Jackson* v. *Peek*, 4 *Wend.*, 305; *Jackson* v. *Zimmerman*, 7 *Wend.*, 436.

"There is nothing to impeach this transaction but the simple circumstance that the *grantor remained in possession* after the deed was given. In relation to real estate, *that is not even a badge of fraud.*"—*Every* v. *Edgerton*, 8 *Wend.*, 263.

Reception of profits and possession by the father during the infancy of his children, does not repel the presumption of advancement, nor tend to raise a trust in favor of the father; nor does the making of repairs during the same period.—*Sugden on Vendors*, 445.

If the children reside with the parent, it repels any presumption arising from his receiving the income of the property.—*Stileman* v. *Ashdown*, 2 *Atk.*, 480; 2 *Swanst.*, 600.

If the conveyance should be set aside, we claim that the widow is entitled to dower in the property in controversy. This point was contested by the complainant's counsel in the argument in the Supreme Court. We have since understood from him that he abandons the position then taken. We shall therefore merely cite authorities on this point, relied upon by us, without further argument or comment: *Coke Litt.* 35, *a.*; 1 *Pick.* 191; 1 *Cowen*, 80; 3 *Metc.*, 42, 43; 1 *Hill Ab.*, 79.

Hitchcock, J.—This bill and amended bill are filed by complainants, as creditors of John Wilson, of Columbus, late deceased, to set aside conveyances of certain parcels of land, and to have the lands sold and the avails applied toward the payment of debts due from the estate of said Wilson. The particular lands in controversy are in lots 440 and 493 in Columbus. It is, perhaps, improper to say that there is any controversy with respect to this latter lot. The facts relative to it are, that it was purchased by Wilson in 1838, and by his direction conveyed to his wife. She does not, however, pretend to claim it, and if she did, the claim could not be sustained, as at the time of the purchase and conveyance, Wilson was hopelessly insolvent.

It is claimed, however, that lot number 440 was never the property of Wilson; that it was, by his direction, conveyed by the former owner to his two children, Thomas and Ann; that it was intended by him as an advancement, and that the son, after his arrival at full age, conveyed his undivided half of the property to his mother, the defendant Margaret

The leading facts, as to this property, are the following:

John Wilson, the decedent, some time before 1819, removed from Pennsylvania to Ohio, and took up his residence at or near Chillicothe. He was a man of small means, and was a tanner by trade. His father, whose name was Thomas, was a resident of the State of Pennsylvania, and had little or no property. Thomas Wilson had two brothers, Charles and John. John resided in Baltimore, and became wealthy. About the year 1819, he died, leaving his brothers Charles and Thomas his heirs. The amount of the estate of this John Wilson, of Baltimore, is not accurately ascertained. After his death, an arrangement was made between John Wilson, of Ohio, and his father Thomas, by which John was to administer on the estate of his deceased uncle, and was to have, in consideration thereof, the one equal half of his father's share in that uncle's estate. In pursuance of this arrangement, John proceeded to Baltimore, and, in connexion with one Sterritt, took letters of administration on his uncle's estate. At this time he was somewhat, although not very deeply, involved. John T. Barr, of Baltimore, a man of wealth, and an old schoolmate and friend of John, was instrumental in procuring for him letters of administration, and was one of his securities—it being the understanding that Sterritt and Barr were to have the principal control in the settlement of the estate.

This John T. Barr was the owner of a farm in the neighborhood of Columbus, containing two hundred and seventy-five acres of land, and also of several lots in the town of Columbus. During the time that Wilson was in Baltimore, an arrangement was made between him and Barr, by which Barr agreed to sell to him this property at and near Columbus, and to receive compensation, as is supposed, from the estate of the deceased John Wilson, of Baltimore. A part of this property was the lot number 440, now in controversy, upon which there was at the time a dwelling house and some other improvements.

John Wilson returned to Ohio, and took up his residence at Columbus, occupying the house upon lot 440, and continued in possession until his death, in 1841. While in Columbus, he owned a tannery, and carried on the business of tanning.

The estate of the uncle was not finally settled until April, 1829. In that month John Wilson, the decedent, was in Baltimore, for the purpose of making settlement. On the 27th day of the same month, he had a settlement with Barr, and gave him a note for $1,952 99, and procured Barr to make a deed to his two children, Thomas and Ann Wilson, for in-lot 440. At this time his son Thomas was eleven, and his daughter Ann five years of age.

The question arises, as to this deed, whether it was made in good faith, as an advancement of to these children, or whether the object was to defraud creditors. It is claimed by the complainants, that a voluntary conveyance, for the consideration of natural love and affection, cannot be sustained, if, at the time, the grantor is involved in debt. Decisions to this effect have unquestionably been made in England, and probably such is the law in that country; and such seems to have been the decision of *Chancellor* KENT, in a case decided by him in the State of New-York, 3 *Johns. Ch.*, 481. We do not, however, conceive this to be the correct rule, as generally established in this country. A man may make an advancement to his child, although at the time in debt, provided he has sufficient property remaining to satisfy such subsisting debts. And if the advancement is made under such circumstances, it cannot be impeached by subsequent creditors, merely because it is voluntary. A person claiming under such advancement, must be prepared, however, clearly and conclusively to show that there was other property sufficient to pay all subsisting debts.

Testimony has been taken in this case to show the extent of the indebtedness of John Wilson in April, 1829, and also as to the value of his property. This evidence is not very satisfactory. It is admitted, that he was indebted as trustee to his father's estate, and which is one of the claims attempted to be set up in this bill, in the sum of $1,805 14, and to John T. Barr in the sum of $1,952 99, making in the whole $3,758 13. It is claimed by the complainants, that there were other debts which would swell the amount to nearly $7,000. These were all eastern debts. There is no evidence as to any other.

The witnesses differ much as to the value of his property. It consisted of the property purchased of Barr, and of a tannery with the stock therein. In estimating the entire value, witnesses vary from seven or eight, to twelve or fifteen thousand dollars. This is including the lot in controversy. Exclusive of that lot, it is at least doubtful whether the other property would have been sufficient, under a forced sale, to have paid all the debts. We are not prepared, however, to say, absolutely, that it would not have been sufficient.

But, although an advancement may be made as before stated, which, if done in good faith, cannot be impeached by subsequent creditors, yet if, in taking all the circumstances into consideration, the mind is brought to the conclusion, that there was a fraudulent design, either as to subsisting or subsequent creditors, such advancement cannot be sustained.

The evidence in this case shows, that upon a settlement with the Orphans' Court, as trustee of his father's estate, which was made in April, 1829, Wilson was found in debt $1,805 14. On the 27th day of the same month, he settled with the Probate Court in Baltimore, and was found in debt; and on the same day, upon settlement, he was found indebted to Barr $1,952 99. In ten years from the time of undertaking to administer upon his uncle's estate, from which wealth was expected, he found himself indebted to the amount of more than $3,700, to say nothing of further indebtedness. And on this day he received from Barr the deed conveying to his two young children lot number 440. But this deed, although delivered by Barr to Wilson, was not, by him, handed over to the children, nor was it immediately placed upon record. He retained it in his own possession, and continued in possession of the lot. In 1834, this deed to the children still remaining unrecorded, he received a deed from Barr, conveying to him, together with other property, this identical lot. This deed, it is true, so far as this lot is concerned, was inoperative. At length in January, 1835, he placed the deed to the children upon record, and the next ensuing year put improvements upon the lot to the value of more than three thousand dollars.

Under these circumstances, we canhot but conclude that Wilson, finding himself thus in debt, in 1829, when he had expected to be wealthy, became apprehensive of eventual failure; and for the purpose of securing to himself and wife a home, as expressed to one or more of the witnesses, procured the conveyance to be made as it was. But still hoping to extricate himself from embarrassment, he kept the deed from record until 1835, when it was delivered and recorded; and from this time he spared no expense to render his house comfortable and convenient.

That his apprehensions were not without foundation, is manifest from the fact that, although during his life his credit was good, yet at his death he was found to be involved to the amount of more than eighteen thousand dollars.

But it is contended by the counsel for the defendant, Margaret, that if in the opinion of the Court this deed was fraudulent as to creditors, still that she is entitled to dower in the premises. The act relating to dower, *Swanst. Stat.*, 296, provides: that the widow shall be endowed "of one full and equal third part of all the lands, tenements and real estate of which her husband was seized during the coverture," and also of "one third part of all the right, title, or interest that her husband, at the time of his decease, had in any lands or tenements held by bond, article, lease or other evidence of claim." In other words, she shall be endowed of one third of the legal estate of inheritance of which the husband was seized during the coverture, and of one third of any equitable interests he may have in lands at the time of his death.

That Wilson had an equitable interest in this lot previous to 1829, there can be no doubt. He was in possession under a purchase from Barr. But, in 1829, he procured it to be conveyed to his children. Now this deed, although fraudulent and void as to creditors, was good as to Wilson. He could not controvert it. So far as he was concerned, and so far as his wife was concerned, it vested a legal estate of inheritance in the children. Wilson, then, had not, at any time during his life, a legal estate of inheritance in this lot. Had he any equitable interest in it at the time of his death? We think not. As to him, both the legal and equitable interest was vested in the children by the deed of 1829.

A number of authorities have been cited, which are claimed to be inconsistent with this opinion. Of these authorities the case of *Robinson* v. *Bates*, 3 *Metcalf*, 40, is the only one which has a direct bearing upon the case under consideration. In that case Robinson and wife joined in a deed conveying certain lands, she releasing her right of dower. Subsequently, a creditor of Robinson, having obtained judgment and levied upon the land, recovered the same, thereby avoiding the deed, on the ground that it was fraudulent as to creditors. After the death of Robinson, his widow prosecuted her suit for dower. The tenant attempted a defence, on the ground that she had, by the deed before referred to, released her right of dower. But the defence was not allowed, the Court holding that the tenant having avoided the deed for fraud, should not afterwards be permitted to set it up as a bar to the widow's right of dower. The substance of the decision is, that if husband and wife unite in the conveyance of his land for the purpose of defrauding creditors, and the deed is avoided for the fraud, the wife is not thereby barred of her dower.

The case differs from the one now before the Court in this: Robinson had, during the coverture, a legal estate of inheritance in the land *then* in controversy, whereas Wilson had not, during the coverture, such legal estate in the land *now* in controversy. Without such legal estate, his widow cannot be endowed, unless, at the time of his death, he had an equitable interest. To the Court, it seems clear, that he had no such interest.

Decree for Complainants.

PARTITION.

A decree for a partition cannot be made unless all the persons interested in the premises are made parties to the suit.—*Burhans* v. *Burhans*, 2 *Barbour's Ch. R.*, p. 398. *N. Y.* (1848.)

PARTNER—WITNESS.

In a suit by several partners, one of the plaintiffs consenting to be sworn as a witness is competent for the defendant, although his co-partners may object to him.—*Cunningham* v. *Carpenter et al.*, 10 *Alabama R.*, p. 109. (1847.)

(*White* cited, *Cowan & Hill's Notes*, 1563; *Ib.*, 134; *Duffee* v. *Pennington*, 1 *Ala. N. S.*, 506; *Pruitt* v. *Marsh*, 1 *S. & P.*, 17; 2 *H. & M.*, 603.)

PARTNERS.

The admissions of one member of a firm, who is not a party to the suit when the Court is *satisfied that the partnership has been established*, may be given in evidence to charge the other members, but not otherwise.—*McCutchin* v. *Bankston*, 2 *Kelly's R.*, p. 244. *Ga.* (1847.)

(Nisbet, J., cited 2 *Starkie on Ev.*, 45*; *Ib. part 4, page* 1074; *Nicholls* v. *Dowding et al.*, 1 *Starkie R.*, 81; *Grant* v. *Jackson et al.*, *Peake's Cases*, 204; *Burgess* v. *Lane et al.*, 3 *Greenleaf*, 165; *Whitney* v. *Ferriss*, 10 *Johns.*, 66; *Wood* v. *Braddick*, 1 *Taunt.*, 104; *Sangster* v. *Mazzerodo et al.*, 1 *Stark. R.*, 128; *Van Reimsdyk* v. *Kane*, 1 *Gall.*, 635; *Harris* v. *Wilson*, 7 *Wend.*, 57; *Whitcomb* v. *Whitington*, 2 *Doug.*, 652; 2 *Bingham*, 306; 8 *B. & C.*, 36; 8 *Bingh.*, 309; 1 *B. & A.*, 467; 3 *Pick.*, 291; 17 *Mass.*, 222; 2 *Pick.*, 581; 4 *Pick.*, 382; 1 *McCord*, 541; 4 *Conn.*, 336; 8 *Conn.*, 268, 276, 277; 5 *Gill & John.*, 144; 7 *Wend.*, 441; 2 *Hawk.*, 209.)

In an action against several persons as partners, the declarations of one of them, who admits himself to be a partner, are not admissible to prove that another is a member of the firm.—*Grafton Bank* v. *Moore*, 13 *New Hampshire R.*, p. 99. (1847.)

(Gilchrist, J., cited *Whitney* v. *Ferris*, 10 *Johns.*, 66; *Sweeting* v. *Turner*, 10 *Johns*, 216; *Whitney* v. *Sterling*, 14 *Johns.*, 215; *Harris* v. *Wilson*, 7 *Wend.*, 57; *Tuttle* v. *Cooper*, 5 *Pick.*, 414; *Robbins* v. *Willard*, 6 *Pick.*, 464; *Jennings* v. *Estes*, 4 *Shepley*, 323; *Van Reimsdyk* v. *Kane*, 1 *Gall.*, 635; *Sangster* v. *Mazzerado*, 1 *Stark. R.*, 161; *Woods* v. *Braddick*, 1 *Taunt.*, 104; *Dolman* v. *Orchard*, 2 *C. & P.*, 104.)

PARTNERSHIP.

Where one of two partners subscribes the partnership name to a note as sureties for a third person, without the authority or consent of the other partner, the latter is not bound; and it lies upon the plaintiff to prove the consent or authority of the other partner; such authority or consent may be presumed from sufficient circumstances.—*Andrews* v. *The Planter's Bank of Mississippi*, 7 *Smedes & Marshall's R.*, p 192. *Miss.* (1847.)

(*Yerger* cited *Foot* v. *Sabin*, 19 *Johns.*, 154; *Wilson* v. *Williams*, 14 *Wend.*, 146; *Williams* v. *Wolridge*, 8 *Wend.*, 415; *Bank of Rochester* v. *Beman*, 7 *Wend.*, 158.)

It is a settled principle of the law of partnership, that the partnership effects are to be first applied to the payment of the debts of the firm, and to equalize the claims upon the different co-partners in relation to the fund. In other words, the separate estate or interest of a co-partner in any of the co-partnership property, is only his share of that part of the co-partnership effects, or of the proceeds thereof, which remains after the debts of the firm, and the demands of his co-partners, as such, are satisfied.

The separate creditors, of individual partners, have no equitable right to any part of the partnership property until the debts of the firm are provided for, and the rights of the partners, as between themselves, are fully protected.—*Buchan* v. *Sumner*, 2 *Barbour's Ch. R.*, p. 165. *N. Y.* (1848.)

(The Chancellor cited *Nicoll* v. *Mumford*, 4 *Johns. Ch.*, 522; *Christian* v. *Ellis*, 1 *Grat.*, 396; *Cammack* v. *Johnson*, 1 *Green's Ch.*, 163; *Pierce* v. *Tierman*, 10 *Gill & Johns.*, 253.)

When partners execute several notes, in their individual names, for work done for the firm, if there is a total failure of the consideration, the defence may be made by either, when sued upon the note executed by him.—*Emanuel* v. *Martin*, 12 *Alabama R.*, p. 283. (1848.)

A person cannot claim to be a member of a partnership composed of a number of persons, unless all the persons composing said firm have agreed to accept him as such.—*Channell et al.* v. *Fassitt et als.*, 16 *Ohio R.*, p. 166. (1848.)

Although a new member cannot be admitted into a partnership without the consent of all parties, yet a person who has obtained a share in the concern can, after the partnership has expired, maintain a suit in Chancery for his share of the profits.—*Matthewson* v. *Clarke*, 6 *Howard's U. S. R.*, p. 122. (1848.)

A., the proprietor of a newspaper, agreed to sell all the plant of the office to B. for £1500, to be paid with interest, by instalments running over a period of seven years; A. undertaking to guarantee to B. during the seven years a clear profit of £150, over and above the annual payment of principal and interest: and B. in consideration of such guarantee, agreed *to pay all such surplus profits to A. until such surplus profits should amount to* £500, if they should amount to that sum during the seven years; and that if such surplus profits should, during the seven years, amount to £500, then B. should pay—over and above the purchase-money and interest, and the £500—the existing liabilities of the newspaper, not exceeding £250.

Held, that A. was liable as a (*quasi*) partner, for the price of goods supplied to B.'s order for the use of the newspaper.—*Barry* v. *Nesham*, 3 *Common Bench R.*, *p.* 641. *Eng.* (1848.)

(*Channel* and *Smith* cited *Waugh* v. *Carver*, 2 *H. Bl.*, 235; *Grace* v. *Smith*, 2 *W. Bl.*, 998; 1 *Smith's Leading Cases*, 504; *Bond* v. *Pittard*, 3 *M. & W.*, 357; *Ex parte Wheeler*, *Buck B. C.*, 25; *Ex parte Todd*, *Buck B. C.*, 48; *Smith* v. *Watson*, 2 *B. & C.*, 401; *Cheap* v. *Cramond*, 4 *B. & Ald.*, 668; *Pott* v. *Eyton*, *Ante*, p. 82; *Dry* v. *Boswell*, 1 *Camp.*, 329; *Benjamin* v. *Porteus*, 2 *H. Bl.*, 590; *Ex parte Hamper*, 17 *Ves.*, 404; *Ex parte Watson*, 19 *Ves.*, 459.)

A surviving partner cannot bind the firm, nor transfer the partnership effects to pay a debt of his own, nor pay the debt of one firm of which he is the survivor with the debt of another firm of which he is a survivor; but he may transfer the assets of a firm of which he is a survivor to pay the debts of that firm.—*Scott* v. *Tupper et al.*, 8 *Smedes & Marshall's R.*, *p.* 280. *Miss.* (1847.)

A partner, who after dissolution remains in possession of the store or place of business, and attends to the collection of the debts due to the firm, may give a note in the name of the firm for a debt due by the partnership, which will bind all the parties, although he may have no express authority to settle the business.—*Robinson* v. *Taylor*, 4 *Barr's R.*, *p.* 242. *Pa.* (1847.)

(*Harrison* cited 5 *Whart.*, 530; *Houser* v. *Irvine*, 3 *Watts & Serg.*, 345; *Griswold* v. *Waddington*, 15 *Johns.*, 83.)

Where two or more persons enter into an agreement to purchase cotton jointly, to advance equal portions of the purchase-money, to pay equal portions of the expense of the transportation of the same, and to share in the loss and profits, it is in judgment of law a copartnership for a single adventure.

When one, through a mistake of the law, acknowledges himself under an obligation which the law will not impose upon him, he shall not be bound thereby.—*Solomon* v. *Solomon*, 2 *Kelly's R.*, *p.* 18. *Ga.* (1847.)

(WARNER, J., cited *Warder et al.* v. *Tucker*, 7 *Mass.*, 449; *Garland* v. *Salem Bank*, 9 *Mass.*, 389; *Goodal et als.* v. *Dolley*, 1 *T. R.*, 712; *Lawrence* v. *Beaubien*, 2 *Bailey*, 623.)

The active partner of a mercantile partnership may transfer its funds.

Real estate purchased by the partnership is liable for its debts.

But the acting partner cannot transfer the real estate of the partnership, the same as personal.—*Piatt* v. *Oliver et als.*, 3 *McLean's U. S. R.*, *p.* 27. (1847.)

Where a partner sells his interest in a partnership concern, he has no lien on the partnership property for the payment of partnership debts for which he is liable. When he retired, he trusted to the personal covenant of his assignees.—*Smith* v. *Edwards et al.*, 7 *Humphreys' R.*; *p.* 106. *Tenn.* (1847.)

PARTNERSHIP—PART PROFITS.

One who takes a share of *the profits*, as such, of a trading concern, thereby becomes a partner as to third persons, on the ground of those profits forming a portion of the fund upon which creditors have a right to rely for payment.

Yet the receipt of a per centage upon the gross amount of sales made to certain customers, by the person who recommended such customers, does not constitute him a partner as against third persons.

A., who was concerned in a colliery, in the year 1830, built and stocked a general shop in its neighborhood, for the purpose of supplying goods to the workpeople, placing B. there to conduct the business; A. receiving for his own use 7 *per cent.* upon the amount of the gross sales made to the miners; and B. taking all the rest of the profits of the concern, from whatever source derived. A.'s name appeared over the shop-door, and in the excise licenses; and down to the year 1834, all the goods supplied to the shop were purchased and paid for by or in the name of A. In that year it was agreed between A. and B., that the latter should thenceforward buy all goods that were required for the shop, and that the former should receive only 5 *per cent.* upon the amount of sales to the miners. After this new arrangement had been come to, B., who had several other shops, opened an account with a bank at Holywell, and on the failure of the bank in 1839, there was a balance due to the bankers on that account exceeding £2000. There was no evidence to show that credit was in fact given to A. by the bank, or that they were aware that his name had been placed over the shop-door, or that they supposed him to be a partner at the time the debt was contracted.

In an action by the assignees of the bankers against A. and B., to recover the balance, the jury having negatived the existence of an actual partnership between A. and B., or that A. had, with his own permission, been held out as a partner, the Court refused to disturb the verdict.—*Pott et als.* v. *Eyton et al.*, 3 *Common Bench R.*, p. 32. *Eng.* (1848.)

Assumpsit for money paid, &c., by the bankrupts before their bankruptcy. The defendant *Jones* suffered judgment by default; and the defendant *Eyton* pleaded non-assumpsit, and several special pleas, which it is unnecessary to notice.

At the trial before Tindal, C. J., at the sittings in London after last Michaelmas term, it appeared, that, in 1828, the defendant, *Eyton*, was concerned in a colliery at Mostyn, in Flintshire; and an agreement was entered into between him and *Jones* for opening a tally-shop at Mostyn Quay (not far from the colliery), principally with a view of supplying goods to the workmen at the colliery. *Eyton* built the shop, and his name was placed over the door; licenses to sell tea, &c., were taken out in his name; and the invoices for goods that were supplied to the shop, were made out in *Eyton's* name, who paid for the same. *Jones* managed the shop. The workmen at *Eyton's* colliery were supplied with goods from it, for which they settled at the colliery when their wages were paid, until the truck system was abolished in 1831. From that time *Eyton's* workmen made their payments at the shop, once a fortnight. *Jones* paid over to *Eyton* the principal part of the money taken at the shop, as he paid for the goods, but reserved sufficient for such small payments as were usually made at the shop. *Eyton* received for his own use £7 per cent. on the amount of all sales to his workmen; and *Jones* had all the rest of the profits of the concern, from whatever source derived. In 1834, a change was made in the arrangements between *Eyton* and *Jones*. The latter was thenceforth to buy in his own name all goods supplied to the shop, and to receive payment for all goods sold; and *Eyton* was to receive £5 *per cent.*, instead of £7 *per cent.*, on the amount of sales to his workmen. *Eyton* objected to his name remaining over the door; but *Jones* said that if he was not allowed to retain it, he could not pay the £5 *per cent.*; and the name remained over the door till October, 1840, when a fire occurred, which put an end to the business. In 1834, when *Jones* began to buy goods, he opened an account with the bankrupts, who were bankers at Holywell. The bank failed in 1839, and at that time there was a balance exceeding £2000 due to it on that account. Besides the shop at Mostyn Quay, *Jones*, after 1834, opened three others at other places, which he carried on in his own name, and on his own account; and he supplied them with goods from the shop at Mostyn Quay.

There was no evidence to show that credit was in fact given to *Eyton* by the bankers, or that they knew that his name had appeared over the door of the shop at Mostyn Quay, or in the licenses, or that they ever supposed him to be a partner. Two individuals were in Court who had been in the employ of the bank during the currency of the account, the one as manager, the other as clerk; but they were not called as witnesses, the plaintiffs resting their case solely upon the evidence of *Jones*.

On the part of the plaintiffs, it was insisted that they were entitled to recover against *Eyton* the balance due to the bankrupts at the time of their bankruptcy, on the ground that he was either an actual partner with *Jones* in the shop at Mostyn Quay, by taking a share of the proceeds, or had been so held out as a partner, with his own permission, as to enable *Jones* to pledge his credit.

The learned Judge left it to the jury to say—first, whether there had been a sharing of profit and loss between *Eyton* and *Jones* after the account was opened with the bank in 1834, so as to constitute an actual partnership between them; secondly, whether *Eyton* had been, by his own permission, held out as a partner, and his credit pledged to the bank.

The jury answering both these questions in the negative, returned a verdict for the defendants.

Wilde, in Hilary term last, obtained a rule *nisi* for a new trial, on the ground that the verdict was against the evidence.

Channel, in Easter term, showed cause. The defendant, *Eyton*, had no such direct interest in the proceeds of the trade, as to make him liable as a partner with *Jones*. In *Ex parte Hamper*, 17 *Ves.*, 404, 412, *Lord* ELDON says: "It is clearly settled,—though I regret it,—that, if a man stipulates that, as the reward of his labor, he shall have, not a specific interest in the business, but a given sum of money, even in proportion to a given *quantum* of the profits, that will not make him a partner." [ERLE, J.—*Lord* ELDON there draws a distinction between a payment of a fixed sum and a per centage: he goes on—"But if he agrees for part of the profits, *as such*, giving him a right to an account—though having no property in the capital—he is, as to third persons, a partner; and, in a question with third persons, no stipulation can protect him from loss."] *Eyton* had no participation in the profits as such. But, in consideration of his advancing money to set the concern going, and of his supposed influence over the workpeople at the mine, it was agreed that he should receive, at first £7 *per cent.*, and afterwards £5 *per cent.*, upon the gross sales to them. Before the opening of the account with the bankrupts, in 1834, an important change took place in the arrangements between *Eyton* and *Jones*. The goods were no longer purchased for the shop at Mostyn Quay by *Eyton*, but were purchased and paid for by *Jones* in his own name. [ERLE, J.—Was the banking account a separate account for the shop at Mostyn Quay? or was it a general account kept by *Jones* for the various shops opened by him?] That did not distinctly appear. [ERLE, J.—In order to charge *Eyton* in respect of a participation of profits, it should have been shown, affirmatively, that credit was given to that concern in the profits of which he was to share.]

Wilde and *Archbold*, in support of the rule. The effect of the agreement between *Eyton* and *Jones* was, to constitute a partnership between them, *quoad* third persons having dealings with the concern at Mostyn

Quay. The facts proved bring the case precisely within *Waugh* v. *Carver*, 2 *H. Bl.*, 235. There A. and B., ship-agents at different ports, entered into an agreement to share, in certain proportions, the profits of their respective commissions, and the discount on the bills of tradesmen employed by them in repairing the ships consigned to them, &c.: and it was held, that by this agreement, they became liable to all persons with whom either contracted as such agent, though the agreement provided that neither should be answerable for the acts or losses of the other, but each only for his own. EYRE, C. J., there says: "A case may be stated, in which it is the clear sense of the parties to the contract, that they shall not be partners; that A. is to contribute neither labor nor money, and to go still further, not to receive any profits. But, if he will lend his name as a partner, he becomes, as against all the rest of the world, a partner; not upon the ground of the real transaction between them, but upon the principles of general policy, to prevent the frauds to which creditors would be liable, if they were to suppose that they lend their money upon the apparent credit of three or four persons, when in fact they lent it only to two of them, to whom, without the others, they would have lent nothing." And referring to *Grace* v. *Smith*, 2 *W. Bl.*, 998, the learned Judge says: "He who takes a moiety of all the profits indefinitely, shall, by operation of law, be made liable to losses, if losses arise, upon the principle that, by taking a part of the profits, he takes from the creditors a part of that fund which is the proper security to them for the payment of their debts." *Eyton's* participation in the profits, according to the doctrine of *Lord* ELDEN in *Ex parte Hamper*, 17 *Ves.*, 404, clearly rendered him liable as a partner. His *Lordship* there says: "The question whether the joint commission can be supported, turns upon two or three circumstances; first, whether *Thomas* and *Rogers* were partners; not upon the present state of the agreement between them; as they may clearly agree that all the property which is the subject of that agreement shall be the property of the one exclusively, but that the other shall participate in the profit arising from it. The cases have gone further, to this nicety—upon a distinction so thin that I cannot state it as established upon due consideration,—that, if a trader agrees to pay another person for his labor in the concern a sum of money, even in proportion to the profits, equal to a certain share, that will not make him a partner; but if he has a specific interest in the profits themselves, as profits, he is a partner." Here, the defendant *Eyton* had a specific interest in the profits. The facts are simple. The shop at Mostyn Quay was built and stocked by *Eyton*, whose name was inserted in the excise licenses, and appeared over the shop-door. The business was to be conducted by *Jones*, he paying to *Eyton* £7 *per cent.* originally, and afterwards £5 per cent., upon the sales to the workpeople employed at a mine in which *Eyton* was interested. Down to the year 1834, the goods that were sold at the shop were either sent there from another shop belonging to *Eyton*, or, were purchased and paid for by *Eyton*. Down to this period, at all events, there clearly was such a division of profits between *Eyton* and *Jones* as to constitute them partners; and their relative position was not altered by any thing that occurred subsequently. On the failure of the bank in 1839, *Eyton* furnished money for the purpose of opening an account with another bank; and when the fire happened in October, 1840, *Eyton* took the whole of the property that remained on the premises unconsumed, and agreed to pay the debts. *Eyton's* liability to be charged as a partner with the debt due to the bank, is wholly unaffected by Jones's appropriation of part of the goods to the other shops, in which *Eyton* had no interest. [Erle, J., referred to *Hawtayne* v. *Bourne*, 7 *M. & W.*, 595, where it was held that the resident agent appointed by the directors of a mining company to manage the mine, has not an *implied* authority from the shareholders of the company, to borrow money upon their credit in order to pay the arrears of wages due to the laborers in the mine, who have obtained warrants of distress upon the materials belonging thereto, for the satisfaction of such arrears—nor in the case of any other necessity, however pressing.] That is altogether distinguishable from the case of partners, who have a general authority to open a banking account. [Coltman, J. The opening of a banking account does not necessarily imply that there was a loan of money by the bank.] It is by no maens a departure from the usual course of dealing.

Cur. adv. vult.

Tindal, C. J., now delivered the judgment of the Court—recapitulating the facts.

On this state of facts, it was contended for the plaintiffs, that they were entitled to recover the balance against *Eyton*, as having been in partnership with *Jones*. I left it to the jury to say whether there was a sharing of profit and loss between *Eyton* and *Jones* after the account was opened; and, if not, whether *Eyton* was, by his own permission, held out as a partner, and credit given to him by the bankrupts. The jury answered both questions in the negative, and returned a verdict for the defendant. In Hilary term, a rule *nisi* for a new trial, on the ground that the verdict was against the evidence, was granted; which rule in the course of the last term was fully argued. Our judgment was deferred, in order that we might carefully examine the evidence given at the trial, and, having done so, we cannot find any ground for disturbing the verdict.

There was no evidence to show that credit was in fact given to *Eyton*, or that the Bankers knew that his name was over the door of the shop at Mostyn Quay, or that they supposed him to be a partner. One person who had been manager, and anothor who had been a clerk in the bank, were in Court; and, if they could have given such evidence, they would no doubt have been called as witnesses. We must assume, therefore, that credit was given to *Jones* alone; and, if *Eyton* is to be made liable, that must be on the ground of an *actual* partnership between himself and *Jones*.

It was contended that an actual partnership was proved; for, that *Eyton*, by taking £5 *per cent.* on the sales to his workmen, received a share of the profits, and was therefore, in point of law, a partner as to third persons. But we are of opinion that the taking of that money was not sufficient to make him a partner. Traders become partners between themselves by a mutual participation of profit and loss: but, as to third persons, they are partners if they share the profits of a concern; for, he who receives a share of the profits, receives a part of that fund upon which the creditors of the concern have a right to rely for payment, and is therefore to be made liable to losses, although he may have expressly stipulated for exemption from them: *Grace* v. *Smith*, 2 *W. Bl.*, 998; *Waugh* v. *Carver*, 2 *H. Bl.*, 235. But in the former of those cases, *Lord Chief Justice* De Grey, after laying down the rule of law in the terms which I have mentioned, proceeds: "If any one advances or lends money to a trader, it is lent on his general personal security. It is no specific lien upon the profits of the trade; and yet the lender is generally interested in those profits; he relies on them for repayment." Afterwards, he says: "I think the true criterion is, to inquire whether *Smith* agreed to share the profits of the trade with *Robinson*, or whether he only relied on those profits as a fund of payment—a distinction not more nice than usually occurs in questions of trade and usury. The jury have said that this is not payable out of the profits." So, in the present case, the jury have said there was no agreement to share the profits. This distinction has been recognized in many cases; of which it may suffice to mention *Dry* v. *Boswell*, 1 *Camp.*, 329; *Benjamin* v. *Porteus*, 2 *H. Bl.*, 590. And although in *Ex parte Hamper*, 17 *Ves.*, 404, *Lord* Eldon said the distinction was so thin that he could not state it as established upon due consideration, yet he acted upon it in that case, and again in *Ex parte Watson*, 19 *Ves.*, 459, where he said—"One who receives a salary, not charged upon profits—according to a known, though nice distinction—is not by that a partner." Nor does it appear to make any difference whether the money is received by way of interest on money lent, or wages, or salary as agent, or commission on sales. And it appears to us, that, in the present case, the payment to *Eyton* was in the nature of commission on certain sales supposed to be effected through his influence over his workmen, and was not sufficient to render him, as a matter of legal inference, liable as a partner; and in so far as it was a question of fact, it was disposed of by the jury.

This view of the subject renders it unnecessary to consider whether *Eyton*, if a partner in the shop at Mostyn Quay, would have been liable on the banking account.

Upon the whole, we are of opinion that the verdict was right, and the rule for a new trial must be discharged.

Rule discharged.

PARTNERSHIP—REAL ESTATE.

Where real estate was purchased by two partners, with the funds and for the business of the co-partnership, and one of them died leaving the firm without personal property sufficient to pay its debts; it was *held*, that the real estate was in equity to be treated as personal property, and the surviving partner had an absolute right to dispose of it as such, for the payment of the debts of the firm.

As it respects the partners and their creditors, real estate belonging to the partnership, is in equity subjected to the same general rules as personal property.

A farm was purchased by two partners, in their joint names, for the partnership business, was used in that business, and paid for out of the funds of the firm. At the dissolution by the death of one of the partners, the debts of the firm exceeded its personal assets, and the survivor entered into a contract to sell a part of the farm. On a bill filed by him against the purchaser, for a specific performance, to which the heir of the deceased partner was a party, it was *held* that the survivor was entitled to sell the property, and the performance was decreed with a direction that the heir should join in the conveyance.—*Delmonico* v. *Guillaume*, 2 *Sandford's Ch. R.*, *p.* 366. *N. Y.* (1847.)

(The Assistant Vice Chancellor, cited *Fereday* v. *Wightwick*, 1 *R. & Mylne*, 45; 1 *M. & Keen*, 663; *Phillips* v. *Phillips*, 1 *M. & K.*, 649; *Broom* v. *Broom*, 3 *M. & K.*, 443; *Cookson* v. *Cookson*, 8 *Simons*, 529; *Townsend* v. *Devaynes*, 11 *Simons*, 498, note; *Dyer* v. *Clark*, 5 *Metcalf*, 562; *Howard* v. *Priest*, 5 *Metcalf*, 582; *Story on Part.*, *sec.* 92, 93; 3 *Kent's Com.*, 64, 5*th ed.*)

PEW HOLDER.

The right of a pew holder to a pew in a meeting-house is subordinate to the rights of the owners of the house. He has an exclusive right to occupy his pew, when the house is used for the purposes for which it was erected; but he cannot convert his pew to other uses, not contemplated. If the house is taken down, as a matter of convenience or taste by the owners thereof, the owner of the pew is entitled to compensation; but if the house is taken down as a matter of necessity, and because it has become ruinous, and wholly unfit for the purposes for which it was erected, the owners of the house are not liable to make any compensation to the separate pew holders, but may take the avails of the materials, of which the house is built, for the purpose of erecting another house in its place.

The owner of a pew in a meeting-house may sustain an action of trespass on the case against one, who unlawfully disturbs him in the possession of his pew. But he holds his pew subject to the right of the owners of the house to take down and rebuild the house, in case of necessity, without making him compensation.

The correctness of the doctrine laid down in *Daniel* v. *Wood, et al.*, 1 *Pick.*, 102, in reference to the right of pew owners, recognized.

Where land was leased to a town in 1797, by durable lease, for the purpose of erecting and continuing thereon a meeting-house, and a meeting-house was accordingly erected there by the town, under the statute then in force, and the pews in the house were then sold by the town in town meeting, and, in 1814, a Religious Society was organized in the town under the provisions of the statute of 1814, and the Society continued to occupy the house for the same purpose for which it had been previously occupied, and the town subsequently conveyed to the Society all the interest of the town in the land and house; it was held, that the Society succeeded to all the rights of the town, and became the owners of the house and land; and might, in case of necessity, take down and rebuild the house, without making compensation to the pew owners.—*Kellogg* v. *Dickinson*, 18 *Vermont R.*, *p.* 266. (1847.)

PHYSICIAN—EVIDENCE.

One who is not engaged in the practice of physic, may nevertheless be competent to testify, if he shows that he had studied the science of medicine, and felt competent to express a medical opinion upon a particular disease. The fact that he was not a practising physician would go to his credit.—*Tullis* v. *Kidd*, 12 *Alabama R.*, *p.* 648. (1848.)

(Ormond, J., cited *Washington* v. *Cole*, 6 *Ala.*, 212; *Commonwealth* v. *Mendum*, 6 *Rand.*, 709.)

POLICY OF INSURANCE.

A policy of Insurance must be in writing. A *verbal* waiver of the forfeiture of a policy of insurance, is not binding.

A *verbal* agreement that a policy which has been forfeited by a transfer of the interest of the assured by judicial sale, that on repurchase by the assured of the property originally insured, the policy shall re-attach and continue in force during the unexpired term, must, whether regarded as a waiver of a forfeiture, or a verbal policy, or an agreement to continue the old policy, to have any binding force, be in writing.—*Cockerille* v. *Cincinnati Mutual Ins. Co.*, 16 *Ohio R.*, *p.* 148. (1848.)

(*Taft, Key & Mallon*, cited 1 *Phil. Ins.*, 2; 1 *Duer Ins.*, 60, 61; *Giddon* v. *Man. Ins. Co.*, 1 *Sumner*, 232; *Crowningshield* v. *N. Y. Ins. Co.*, 3 *Johns. Cas.*, 142; 1 *Phil. Ins.*, 372; *Head & Amory* v. *Prov. Ins. Co.*, 6 *Cranch*, 166–169; *Beatty* v. *The Marine Ins. Co.*, 2 *Johns.*, 109; *Angell & Ames on Corporations*, 236; 1 *Con. U. S. Sup. Court R.*, 371; *Ducany* v. *Gill*, 4 *Car. & P.*, 121; 1 *Duer*, 64 *sec.* 9.)

POSSESSION.

Where the owner of a dwelling house, having a right of entry therein, but in which the plaintiff had recently been dwelling, and which he and his family had then left, finds the doors open and no one in the house, he may lawfully enter into the possession thereof, remove what furniture there was therein belonging to the plaintiff, in a careful manner, and store it safely near by for his use; and the owner may afterwards lawfully retain the possession thereof, thus acquired.—*Rollins* v. *Mooers*, 25 *Maine R.*, *p.* 192. (1847.)

POWER OF ATTORNEY.

Where a power of attorney authorizes the person appointed to appoint an attorney *under him*, and to revoke such appointment at his pleasure, the death of the principal attorney necessarily revokes the power of the substitute.—*Watt* v. *Watt*, 2 *Barbour's Ch. R.*, *p.* 371. *N. Y.* (1848.)

PRE-EMPTION.

A mere right of pre-emption is not a title, it is only a proffer to a certain class of persons that they may become purchasers, if they will; without payment, or an offer to pay, it confers no equity; and only confers one where the party has consented to accept the offer by payment, or by claiming the benefit of the law in the proper manner, within the required time—*Grand Gulf Railroad and Banking Co. et al.* v. *Bryan*, 8 *Smedes & Marshall's R.*, *p.* 234. *Miss.* (1847.)

Action for damages for a trespass committed by defendants on lands possessed by plaintiffs as owners, and defence that the lands belong to the United States, and that defendants entered thereon for the purpose of acquiring a pre-emption right thereto: *Held*, that the title of one possessing as owner cannot be subjected to investigation at the instance of a mere trespasser; and that a party cannot be permitted, under pretext of an intention to purchase from the United States, to assume that land, in the possession of another, is public, and liable to be entered on at pleasure.—*Bonis et als. v. James et als.*, 7 *Robinson's La. R.*, *p.* 149. (1847.)

APPEAL by Hornsby and Printey, two of the defendants, from a judgment of the District Court of Pointe Coupée, in favor of the plaintiffs.—DEBLIEUX, J.

Johnson and *Janin*, for the plaintiffs.
Ratliff, *Boyle* and *Paterson*, for the appellants.

GARLAND, J.—This is a possessory action, in which the plaintiffs allege, that they are possessors as owners for more than a year, of a tract of land, at a place called the Racourci Bend, on which the defendants have entered and are committing waste by cutting timber, cordwood, &c. Writs of sequestration and injunction were issued, to arrest the commission of further trespasses and waste. In their petition, the plaintiffs, for the purpose of showing the extent of their possession, set forth the titles under which they hold, commencing with that derived from the Spanish Governor, Carondelet, in 1796.

The defendants, after a general denial, and a special denial of an amicable demand to quit the premises, aver that the land on which they are, and on which the alleged trespasses are said to have been committed, is public, and belongs to the United States; that they have taken possession of it, and expect, in due course of time, by complying with the requirements of the pre-emption laws passed by Congress, to secure a right and title to said land; and that, therefore, they have a right to possess it. The taking possession by the defendants was in the months of December, 1841, and January, 1842, a few months after the passage by Congress of the pre-emption law of 4th of September, 1841. *See Acts of 1st Session, 27th Congress, Laws United States, vol. 10, p. 155.* This suit was instituted in March, 1842, and the answers of the defendants filed in the month of May following, at which time they had not made any application at the Land Office of the District to purchase the land; nor does it appear to have been legally surveyed.

By documents given in evidence it appears, that on the 10th January, 1796, Ursin, and Dominique Bouligny, each applied to Gov. Carondelet for a tract of land of forty *arpents* front, by the ordinary depth, within the limits of the post of Pointe Coupée, at a place called *La Laguana del Racourcy*, upon which the usual orders were issued, directing the surveyor of the province to put each in possession; and on the tract now occupied by the plaintiffs, a settlement was made shortly after. In the year 1808 the Boulignys presented their claims, in the same notice, to the land officers in New Orleans. Their lands are described as being situated "in the County of Pointe Coupée, containing eighty *arpents* in front, on the right bank of the Mississippi, by forty *arpents* in depth." With this notice and the title papers, a plat of survey made by Charles Morgan, a surveyor, was presented, on which the upper boundary of the eighty *arpents* is represented as being on or near the bank of the river, which it follows down for a considerable distance, until it reaches a hackberry tree, growing on what is represented and called a *willow-point;* thence the line changes its course, and seems to run along or near to the edge of the willow-point for upwards of forty *arpents*, to the lower boundary. With the exception of a very small portion of the lower end of the lagoon, (laguna,) it is all represented as within the front line; and it is evident, that the surveyor did not intend to make the tract front on it. On the outside of the line a trace or road is represented, as is also the Mississippi river, and a large point or batture covered with willows. But along, or near this line, the parol evidence shows, that there was some high ground on which other trees grew, such as gum, cotton-wood, ash, &c. Upon the title papers, plat, and evidence of settlement, the title for forty *arpents* front was confirmed, so as to include the improvements. *See vol.* 2, *State Papers, Public Lands, p.* 332. At a subsequent period, a claim for the remaining forty *arpents* front was presented, and recommended for confirmation. *See vol.* 3, *State Papers, Public Lands, p.* 257. It is there stated as being on the right bank of the river, at the place commonly called Racourci. In the year 1818, Dominique Bouligny sold to one Martin Tournoir five *arpents* front of the same tract, which the plaintiff claims, with a reservation to himself of the alluvion or batture in front of it. In January, 1830, Bouligny and Jean Mercier, sold to Martin Bourgeat thirty-five *arpents* front of the same tract. They describe it as being at a place called the *Baie du Racourci*, upon the right bank of the river Mississippi. They then proceed to describe the front, side and rear lines, giving courses and distances, as the whole will appear by a plat said to be annexed to the sale, but which is not produced. They say nothing about a batture or alluvion, but sell the tract as described, with all its appurtenances. On the 7th February, 1833, the heirs of Bourgeat sell something over twenty-one *arpents* front of the land to Bonis and wife. They describe the land by lines, courses and distances, and say it has its *face sur la baie*, with such depth as may be found, &c., situated at the place commonly called Racourci. To the land so described they give a warranty. They then proceed to say, that they sell without warranty, all the rights they have or may have to the portion of the alluvion or batture in front of said tract of land. About the same time the aforesaid heirs sold the remainder of the tract of land to one John C. Turner. It is described as having eight *arpents* front, by a certain depth. They also sell, "a riparious right to the batture, but without warranty." The plaintiffs Turnbull and wife, hold under Turner, with a transfer of all his rights. About the time these sales were made to Turner and Bonis and wife, H. T. Williams, a United States Surveyor, being engaged in making surveys in that section of the country, undertook to locate the Bouligny claims. He seems not to have been very accurately informed as to their titles, nor was he requested by any one interested, so far as the record informs us, to locate the claims, nor were any of the claimants present. He placed the front line of the claim under which the plaintiffs hold, a considerable distance from the river, following very near the lines of Morgan, which were run in 1808; and he represented the land between that line and the *river*, as public. This survey has never been approved, and the surveyor, becoming himself Surveyor General, declined approving his own work, in consequence of representations being made to show its want of accuracy. The present Surveyor General of the United States also declines approving it. Since the institution of this suit, in consequence of representations made by one or more of the defendants, a survey was ordered by the Surveyor General now in office; but as soon as he was more fully informed he arrested the execution of his order, and has never approved the work of his deputy. Upon a sketch or plat made by the deputy surveyor last mentioned, the defendants, Hornsby and Printey, presented themselves at the Land Office, more than one year after the commencement of this suit, and claimed a pre-emption right on proof of settlement, but could not complete the purchase, as there was no approved township map in the office.

The parol testimony is voluminous, and shows what has been the condition of the land for more than forty years. The witnesses who have known the point or batture longest, say that, in front of the lagoon or *baie*, there was at their earliest recollection a ridge of high land, on which cane and trees of a large size grew, which was not overflowed except at the very highest stage of the river; and on this the road ran. There were other ridges and sloughs across the point, in early times. They all seem to have been annually covered with water. The point or batture has increased in dimensions, and become higher every year. There are now large trees in many places, and land susceptible of cultivation, showing that the formation was ancient. What the situation of the batture was at the time the land was granted in 1796, is not shown; but it is difficult to believe that the Spanish Governor intended that there should be a narrow slip of high ground in front of the land he granted, thus preventing the grantees from getting to the river. It is apparent, from the plat of Morgan's survey, made in 1808, that he did not intend that the lagoon should be the front; and it would also seem, that he ran the line as near to the willow bank as it could well be done. We know it is not the practice of surveyors in measuring a base or front line, to follow the bends of the stream to get the distance or quantity wanted; but to run their lines straight, changing their direction only when necessary to enable them to reach the point of destination. It is, therefore, not at all surprising that some spots of high land should be found outside of the front line, as run by the surveyor.

The main question in the cause is, was it intended that the claim of Bouligny should front on the river? When we take into consideration the usages and laws under the Spanish Government, they raise a strong presumption that such was the intention. When we look at the confirmation of the titles by the United States, we see the lands described as on the right bank of the river. These terms are not generally used to describe land lying at a distance from the bank. In 1818, the grantee, Bouligny, certainly conceived that he had some right to the batture, as he reserved it in his sale to Tournoir. The vendors of the plaintiffs, in 1833, supposed that they had some claim to it also, as they sold all their rights to the plaintiffs, who possessed under this claim of right, until disturbed by the defendants. But, say their counsel, Bourgeat did not acquire any right to the batture by his purchase from Bouligny and Mercier, and, therefore, could not transfer it, even admitting that the last were entitled to it. This is perhaps true; yet his heirs sold all their rights to the plaintiffs, whatever they were; and they had possessed as owners for more than eight years under these sales, previous to the defendants going on the land. In this action we cannot inquire into the validity of the plaintiffs' titles to the property. The question is simply one of possession. For several years before the defendants went on the premises, the plaintiffs occupied them, under notarial acts of sale. Two or more small houses had been erected, some fences had been put up, and wood had been cut at different places. Open and public acts of ownership were exercised. Shortly after the defendants took possession, they were notified of the claim of the plaintiffs, notwithstanding which they persisted in remaining on the land; and, more than a year after the institution of this suit, endeavored to get a title of it, by the presentation of an unapproved and unauthorized plat of survey to the Register of the Land Office, and by attempting to prove a settlement on land to which, at the time, they knew that others set up a claim.

When persons wish to obtain a right of pre-emption from the United States, they must take care to settle on land belonging to the government, and not on those notoriously possessed by others as owners, under an apparent title. It cannot be permitted to any one, under the pretext of an intention to acquire a title by purchase from the United States, to assume that the land he fancies, though in the possession of another, is public, and therefore liable to be entered on at pleasure, and the possessor's title subjected to investigation at the instance of a trespasser.—3 *Rob.*, 318. *Code of Pract., art.* 47.

Judgment affirmed.

PRESENTMENT—RESIDENCE.

The holder of a note not payable at any particular place, must present the same for payment, at maturity, at the known place of residence of the maker, though it be in a foreign country; if he means to hold the endorser.—*Gilmore et als.* v. *Spies*, 1 *Barbour's R., p.* 158. *N. Y.* (1848.)

PRINCIPAL AND AGENT.

The principal is not a competent witness for the agent, in a suit brought by him against an attorney, for the recovery of a debt due the principal, which the agent had placed in the attorney's hands for collection; as the record would be evidence for the principal, of the amount recovered, in a suit by him against the agent.—*Wallace et al.* v. *Peck et al.*, 12 *Alabama R., p.* 768. (1848.)

PRINCIPAL AND SURETY.

As between the principal debtor and his surety, the property of the former is primarily liable, and should be first resorted to, for the payment of the debt. And where the sheriff, with a full knowledge of the fact, wilfully violates the principles of equity in this respect, the Court of Chancery, upon a bill filed for that purpose, will relieve the surety.

if the surety cannot obtain satisfaction for the injury by an action upon the case against the sheriff—*Boaghton* v. *The Bank of Orleans*, 2 *Barbour's Ch. R.*, *p.* 458. *N. Y.* (1848.)

Where the judgment has been rendered against principal and surety, and the principal is insolvent, a Court of Chancery will entertain jurisdiction of a suit brought by the surety for the purpose of reaching credits of the principal, and appropriating them in payment of the judgment, although the surety has not paid the money.—*McConnell* v. *Scott et als.*, 15 *Ohio R.*, *p.* 401. (1847.)

This is a case in Chancery, reserved in the county of Morgan.

The bill is filed by the complainant as surety for the principal debtor, against him and others, in whose hands the principal debtor has credits. The bill states, that judgment at law has been rendered against both principal and surety; that the principal debtor is insolvent, and seeks the appropriation of the credits of the principal, in the hands of the debtors, to the satisfaction of the judgment against both him and the complainant, who is his surety.

The bill makes the judgment creditor a party merely, that he may receive the money on his judgment.

Some of the defendants have answered, but the judgment creditor and the principal debtor do not defend.

Welch, for the complainant. In support of the position, that Chancery had jurisdiction in a case like this, the following authorities were quoted: *Stump* v. *Rogers*, 1 *Ohio*, 533; *King* v. *Baldwin*, 2 *Johns. Ch.*, 561; *Rees* v. *Bersington*, 2 *Ves. Ch.*, 540; *Hayes* v. *Ward*, 4 *Johns. Ch.*, 132; *Wright* v. *Simpson*, 6 *Ves.*, 734; *Mit. Eq. Pl.*, 148; *Lord Ranebaugh* v. *Hayes*, 1 *Vern.*, 190; *Ward* v. *Henry*, 5 *Cowen*, 596; *Nesbit* v. *Smith*, 2 *Brown's Ch.*, 451; *Williams* v. *Helme*, 1 *Dev.*, 162; *Tankersley* v. *Anderson et al.*, 4 *Des.*, 47; *Taylor* v. *Heriot*, 4 *Des.*, 227; *Bank of Lake Erie* v. *Western Reserve Bank*, 11 *Ohio*, 449; *Hampton* v. *Levy*, 1 *McCord*, 116; *Gilmore* v. *Miami Ex. Co.*, 2 *Ohio*, 294; *Piatt* v. *St. Clair's Heirs*, 6 *Ohio*, 227.

It was further contended, that the defendants, by answering, admitted the jurisdiction of the Court over the subject matter, and that it was now too late to object that the Court had not, according to the usages of a Court of Chancery, the power to grant the relief sought; in support of which the following authorities were adduced: *Rees* v. *Smith*, 1 *Ohio*, 127; *Gilmore's History and Practice of Chancery*, 219.

Goddard, for the defendants.

Wood, C. J.—The question raised by the counsel is, whether a Court of Equity will entertain jurisdiction in a case like this? It is insisted, in argument, that the complainant is without remedy in any form, until the actual advance of the money due from his principal. At-law, the position is doubtless correct. An action to recover for money paid for another, does not lie, unless payment is made and proved on the trial, nor can the principal debtor be made liable at law for subjecting his surety to the peril of paying this debt, until the injury actually accrues by payment. This is all very true; but there is, nevertheless, a great variety of circumstances, where equity steps in, for he reason that the law affords no adequate redress, and prevents impending or threatened injury.

The surety, however, occupies ground peculiar to his own relation, and is favored in both legal and equitable tribunals. Numerous cases are cited by counsel, where principles analogous to those sought to be applied here, have been recognized in equity; and we think the complainant is within the authority of such adjudications. Indeed, in 1 *Ohio*, 533, the precise question now raised received the sanction of this Court, and in our view, the authority of that case should not be shaken.

What are the obligations of the principal debtor to his surety? Certainly to save him harmless from every injury which may result from such relation; and a promise is implied to this effect, as valid as if made in express terms, between the parties. 5 *Cowen*, 596. There is no adequate remedy at law, when the principal debtor is insolvent, by which his effects and credits in the hands of others can be made to be applied for the benefit of the surety. Certainly not, as we have already said, without the surety first pays the debt. And such payment may be attended with great inconvenience and severe sacrifices of property; burdens which surely ought not to be imposed, if they can, with propriety and justice, be avoided. In 6 *Vesey*, 734, it is said, "that equity will compel the principal to pay the debt, after due, at the instance of the surety." In 4 *Def.*, 47, "that it would be hard on sureties, if they were compelled to wait until judgment against them, or they had paid the debt, before they could have recourse to their principal, who might waste his effects before their eyes." Other cases might be cited to the same import.

If, then, the principal debtor may be forced to pay the debt at the instance of the surety, it would seem to follow, that the property, credits or effects of such principal may be followed into the hands of others. It must not be understood that the judgment creditor can be delayed in his remedy against the surety. He has his judgment, and may take out his execution at pleasure; but if he has not collected his money of the surety, and the surety has made it out of the property or credits of the principal, equity will decree its application in discharge of the creditor's judgment against the surety.

Decree for complainant.

PRIOR JUDGMENT.

Although a party has a right, as a general rule, to bring a suit upon a prior judgment, still the Supreme Court has such a control over its own process that it ought not to permit it to be perverted or used for any improper purposes.

Where a person who has recovered a judgment, brings successive suits thereon, in different courts, without issuing any execution, and he admits that such suits were brought for the purpose of coercing payment of his debt by accumulating costs, the Court in which the last suit is brought will grant a perpetual stay of proceedings in all the suits in that Court except the first.

A plaintiff will not be allowed to make use of the costs in the suit by way of penalty, in order to compel the defendant to pay his debt.—*Keeler* v. *King*, 1 *Barbour's R.*, *p.* 390. *N. Y.* (1848.)

PRISONER—CONFESSION OF.

When, after due warning of all the consequences, and sufficient time allowed for mature reflection, a prisoner makes a confession of his guilt to a private person, having no control over the prisoner or the prosecution, although he may have influence and ability to aid him, such confession is properly allowed as evidence for the jury.—*The State* v. *Kirby*, 1 *Strobhart's R.*, *p.* 155. *S. C.* (1847.)

PROCHEIN AMI.

A trial of right of property may be prosecuted in the name of an infant, by a *prochein ami*, who may execute the bond, and if necessary make the affidavit required by the statute.—*Strode et als.* v. *Clarke*, 12 *Alabama R.*, *p.* 621. (1848.)

PROMISE.

A promise to pay a sum of money for the delivery of a valuable paper, to which the person in possession has no claim, but which belongs to another, cannot be enforced. Nor will it vary the case, that the note which was given for the production of the paper, was made payable to a third person.—*McCaleb* v. *Price*, 12 *Alabama R.*, *p.* 753. (1848.)

PROMISSORY NOTE.

In an action upon a promissory note, made payable at a place certain and on demand after a specified time, no averment or proof of a demand on the part of the plaintiff is necessary to entitle him to maintain his suit.—*Gammon* v. *Everett*, 25 *Maine R.*, *p.* 66. (1847.)

(Whitman, C. J., cited *McKinley* v. *Whipple*, 21 *Maine*, 98; *Car-*

ley v. *Vance*, 17 *Mass.*, 389; *Bacon* v. *Dyer*, 3 *Fairf.*, 19; *Walcot* v. *Van Santvoord*, 17 *Johns.*, 248; *Huxton* v. *Bishop*, 3 *Wend.*, 13.)

A promissory note cannot be given in evidence without proo of its execution, unless specially declared upon.—*Somers* v. *Harris*, 16 *Ohio R.*, *p.* 262. (1848.)

(Hitchcock, J., cited *Putnam's Ex'r* v. *Clark*, *Wright*, 695; *Hamilton* v. *Phelps*, *Wright*, 689; *Harris* v. *Clarke et al.*, 10 *Ohio*, 5.)

When the maker of a promissory note dies before it becomes payable, the endorsee should make inquiry for his personal representative, if there be one, and present the note, on its maturity, to him for payment.

If it should be made to appear, that the endorser knew that the note would not be paid on presentment, and that the maker had deceased and his estate was insolvent, such knowledge would not relieve the holder from his obligation to make presentment and give due notice of its dishonor.—*Gower* v. *Moore*, 25 *Maine R.*, *p.* 16. (1847.)

(Shepley, J., cited *Nicholson* v. *Gouthit*, 2 *H. Bl.*, 609; *Clegg* v. *Cotton*, 2 *B. & P.*, 239; *Prideaux* v. *Collier*, 2 *Starkie*, 57.)

PROTEST—NOTICE OF.

Where the holder of a protested note and the party entitled to notice reside in the same town or city, notice should be given to the party entitled to it, either verbally or in writing, or a written notice must be left at his dwelling-house or place of business.

The term "holder," includes the bank at which the note is payable, and the notary who may hold the note as the agent of the owner for the purpose of making demand and protest.—*Bowling* v. *Harrison*, 6 *Howard's U. S. R.*, *p.* 248. (1848.)

The holder of a promissory note on which there are several endorsers, is only bound to give notice of protest to the one whom he intends to hold liable. If the endorser so notified wishes to secure his recourse against the others, he must give notice himself, where it has not been done by the holder.

Where in an action against the endorser of a note the holder relies on a promise to pay, made after the endorser had been discharged by the *laches* of the holder, it is incumbent on him to show that the promise was made by the endorser with full knowledge that he had been so discharged. But an actual payment furnishes a presumption of indebtedness; and where an endorser seeks to recover back the amount of a note on the ground that it was paid by him in ignorance of the fact that he had been discharged, he must show that he was so discharged.

One who alleges error as the basis of his action must show it, or show, at least, that the evidence of it is exclusively in the power of his adversary.

As a general rule, he who affirms must prove; but as there are many negative proposition which it would be impossible to prove directly, the burden of proof, in such cases, is thrown on the opposite party.—*The Union Bank of La.* v. *Hyde, et als.*, *7 Robinson's La. R.*, *p.* 418. (1847.)

PUBLIC WORSHIP.

A disturbance of a single member of a congregation engaged in religious worship, is an indictable offence within the statute of 1801, *Ch.* 35.

The Act of 1801, provides that "if any person shall interrupt a congregation assembled for the purpose of worshipping the Deity, such person shall be dealt with as a rioter at common law."—*Cockreham* v. *The State*, *7 Humphrey's R.*, *p.* 11. *Tenn.* (1847.)

PURCHASER.

A purchaser of real estate, *pendente lite*, will be bound by the decree. —*Green et als.* v. *White*, *7 Blackford's R.*, *p.* 242. *Ind.* (1847.)

RAILWAY COMPANY.

The plaintiff, who was a shareholder in a projected railway company, but who had refused to pay £100, a sum fixed by the executive committee as his share of the expenses incurred, filed his bill to restrain a creditor of the company from prosecuting an action at law against him to recover a debt, in the bill stated to have been assigned to the committee, in order that they might use it as a means of compelling payment of the £100, and also to restrain the executive committee of the company from commencing any action against him or parting with the deposits in their hands, except in payment of the liabilities of the company; and praying that accounts might be taken of the assets and liabilities, plaintiff offering to pay what might properly be found due by him.

The managing committee (all of whom, together with the creditor, were defendants) demurred for want of equity, and for want of parties: *Held*, that although a plaintiff may have a good defence to an action at law, he is not on that account precluded from proceeding in equity to restrain the action.

That the defendants must distribute the assets in their hands in discharge of the liabilities of the company, and were not justified in attempting to extort by means of an action an arbitrary sum, which the directors had fixed as plaintiff's share of the expenses. Demurrer overruled.—*Fernihough* v. *Leader et als.*, 4 *Railway Cases R.*, p. 373. *Eng.* (1848.)

RECEIVER.

A receiver, upon the passing of his accounts, is not entitled to an allowance out of a fund in his hands as receiver, for counsel fees which he has paid on an unsuccessful defence to a suit brought against him by the owner of such fund; nor for the expenses of an unsuccessful appeal brought by him from the decree in such suit.—*The Utica Insurance Company* v. *Lynch*, 2 *Barbour's Ch. R.*, p. 573. *N. Y.* (1848.)

RECOGNIZANCE.

It is essential to a recognizance for the appearance of the conusor to answer to charges against him, that it show the cause of taking it.

A recognizance must stand or fall by itself; and if not good on its face by failing to specify the offence for which the accused is arrested and bound to appear and answer, parol evidence is inadmissible to supply the defect.—*Nicholson* v. *The State of Georgia*, 2 *Kelly's R.*, p. 363. *Ga.* (1847.)

RECORD.

The caption of a record must show the Court was held at the place required by law.—*Bob, a slave* v. *The State*, 7 *Humphreys' R.*, p. 129 *Tenn.* (1847.)

RENT.

A note given for *rent of a store-house* is described in the plaintiff's writ as given for rent, omitting the words *of store-house*. *Held*, not to be a fatal variance under our statute.

In cases of express contracts to pay rent, the destruction of the premises by fire, or violence, or any casualty whatever, is not a good defence to an action to recover the rent, unless there is also an express stipulation to that effect. Nor will a Court of Equity relieve against such contracts under such circumstances.—*White et al.* v. *Molyneux*, 2 *Kelly's R.*, p. 124. *Ga.* (1847.)

REPLEVIN.

In replevin a plea that the goods and chattels in the declaration mentioned were not the property of the plaintiff, without showing whose they were, is bad. It should have averred that they were the property of the defendants or of some third person, naming him, *and* not the property of the plaintiff.—*Anstice* v. *Holmes*, 3 *Denio's R.*, *p.* 244. *N. Y.* (1848.)

(BRONSON, C. J., cited *Wildman* v. *Norton*, 1 *Vent.*, 249; *Wildman* v. *North*, 2 *Lev.*, 92; *Butcher* v. *Porter*, *Carth.*, 243; 1 *Show.*, 490; 1 *Salk.*, 94, *S. C.*,; *Harrison* v. *McIntosh*, 1 *Johns.*, 380; *Rogers* v. *Arnold*, 12 *Wend.*, 30; 8 *Went. Pl.*, 16, 17; 2 *Lill. Ent.*, 358; 3 *Chit. Pl.*, 1044, *Ed. of* '37; *Bull. N. P.*, 54; *Presgrave* v. *Saunders*, 1 *Salk.*, 5, *S. C.*; 6 *Mod.*, 81; 2 *Ld. Raym.*, 984, *S. C.*)

RESCISSION OF CONTRACT.

It is no ground for the rescission of a contract for the sale of land, that one who sold the land as agent, had no authority to act, if the principal ratifies his act, and is able and willing to make title.—*Alderson* v. *Harris et al.*, 12 *Alabama R.*, *p.* 580. (1848.)

RIPRARIAN RIGHTS.

Where the streets of a town bordering on navigable water, are dedicated to the use of the town and public, if there is no limitation, the dedication will extend across the shore to low water mark, as the shore may be reclaimed, or filled up by accretion, and become part of the town.—*Doe ex dem. Kennedy's Ex'rs* v. *Jones*, 11 *Alabama R.*, *p.* 63. (1847.)

ROBBERY.

To constitute robbery, it is not necessary that the person robbed must have been first in fear of his person or property; if the goods be taken either by violence or by putting the owner in fear, it is sufficient to render the felonious taking a robbery.—*McDaniel* v. *The State*, 8 *Smedes & Marshall's R.*, *p.* 401. *Miss.* (1847.)

ROBBERY AND REWARD.

The defendant, who had been robbed of jewelry, published an advertisement, headed "£30 Reward," describing the articles stolen, and concluding thus:—"The above sum will be paid by the adjutant of the 41st Regiment, *on recovery of the property, and conviction of the offender*, or in proportion to the amount recovered."

A., a soldier, on the 10th of *June*, informed his sergeant that B. had admitted to him that he was the party who had committed the robbery, and the sergeant gave information at the police-station. On the 14th the plaintiff, a police-constable, learning from one C. that B. was to be met with at a certain place, went there and apprehended him. The plaintiff, by his activity and perseverance, afterwards succeeded in tracing and recovering nearly the whole of the property, and in procuring evidence to convict B.:—*Held*, that the plaintiff was not, but that A. was, the party entitled to the reward.—*Thatcher* v. *England*, 3 *Common Bench R.*, *p.* 254. *Eng.* (1848.)

SALE.

A party who upon the sale of goods receives from the purchaser a promissory note made by a third person in payment, and afterwards sues the purchaser for goods sold, on account of fraudulent representations made by him as to the solvency of the maker, by which he was induced to receive the note, must, in order to recover, show that he returned or tendered the note to the defendant before suit brought. If he have recovered judgment against the maker he must tender an assignment of it.—*Baker* v. *Robbins*, 2 *Denio's R.*, *p.* 136. *N. Y.* (1847.)

(Beardsley, J., cited *Masson* v. *Bovet*, 1 *Denio*, 69; *Pierce* v. *Drake*, 15 *Johns.*, 475.)

An absolute sale of personal property, where the possession remains with the vendor, is void as to creditors and purchasers, though authorized by the terms of the bill of sale.—*Rhines* v. *Phelps et al.*, 3 *Gilman's R.*, *p.* 455. *Ills.* (1847.)

(Purple, J., cited *Thornton* v. *Davenport*, 1 *Scam.*, 296.)

A sale is not divested of the characteristics of a "Sheriff's sale," because the plaintiff and defendant, in execution, direct the Sheriff to sell on a credit; and a purchaser, at such sale, with a knowledge of the fact, must abide the rule of *caveat emptor.*—*Kilgore* v. *Peden et al.*, 1 *Strobhart's R.*, *p.* 18. *S. C.* (1847.)

Where the State sells a privilege, it cannot complain of the necessary consequences of its exercise.—*Tymannus* v. *Williams*, 7 *Humphreys' R.*, *p.* 80. *Tenn.* (1847.)

SALE—FRAUDULENT.

If a creditor purchase property of his debtor in satisfaction of his own debt, and the debts of other favored creditors, and buy a large surplus over, to the exclusion of a particular creditor, whose suit is pending, it is a badge of fraud.

The possession of property, real or personal, remaining with the vendor after an absolute deed of conveyance, is an evidence of fraud.

A creditor, or third person, may pay a full and fair price to an insolvent debtor for property; still, if the purchase is made to delay or defraud creditors of their rights, it is void as to them.

The declaration and other original papers of file in the clerk's office, may be used in evidence, in the same Court to which they belong.

An application for a new trial will not be granted on the ground that the verdict is contrary to evidence, provided there was testimony enough to warrant the finding, and the Court was satisfied, that justice had been done. Neither will the motion be sustained for the reason, that the verdict was contrary to the charge of the presiding judge if the charge itself was erroneous.—*Peck* v. *Land*, 2 *Kelly's R.*, *p.* 1. *Ga.* (1847.)

SALE—RESERVATION.

Where the owner of ground, in dividing into lots for sale, reserves a part for a public alley, and subsequently sells the lots with reference to a plan on which the alley is described, and as fronting on the alley, the ground set apart for the alley must be considered as dedicated to public use; and the purchasers of the lots have a right to insist upon its being kept open for the purposes for which it was thus dedicated.—*McDonough* v. *Calloway et als.*, 8 *Robinson's La. R.*, *p.* 92., (1847.)

SCIRE FACIAS.

A *scire facias* was served two days after the return day. *Held*, that it amounted to nothing, the writ having lost its validity.—*Hitchcock* v. *Haight*, 2 *Gilman's R.*, *p.* 603. *Ills.* (1847.)

SEAL.

Many obligors may adopt one seal or one scroll; and the question as to whether the instrument is a sealed or unsealed instrument, is one of intention, and the *onus* lies on the plaintiff to prove that the party adopted the seal or scroll.—*Hollis et als.* v. *Pond*, 7 *Humphrey's R.*, *p.* 222. *Tenn.* (1847.)

SET-OFF.

Upon a suit by husband and wife, on a note given to them jointly, for a debt created *with* the defendants, by the dealing of the wife with the consent of the husband, the defendants may set off an account, not included in the note, created in the same course of dealing.—*Case et al.* v. *Byrne*, 12 *Alabama R., p.* 115. (1848.)

The maker of a promissory note, in an action by the endorsee who received it after due, cannot set off a demand against the payee, unless such demand is connected with, or grew out of, the original transaction for which the note was given, or attaches to the note itself; he cannot set off a demand arising out of collateral matters.

To authorize a defendant to set off a demand under the 24th section of the Judiciary Act of 1799, such demand must be against the plaintiff in the action.—*Tinsley* v. *Beall*, 2 *Kelly's R., p.* 134. *Ga.* (1847.)

It is impossible, at law, to set off unliquidated damages against a fixed money demand; therefore, to an action on a note for a fixed sum, an offset cannot be made of the value of a slave of the defendant, alleged to have been converted by the payee of the note to his use.—*Whittaker et al.* v. *Robinson*, 8 *Smedes & Marshall's R., p.* 349. *Miss.* (1847.)

In error from the Circuit Court of Monroe county; *Hon. Francis M.* Rogers, *Judge.*

James H. Robinson sued William L. Whittaker and George Hardy, as makers, and John Smith, as payee and endorser of a note; Whittaker and Hardy plead payment, and filed with the plea this account of offset: "John Smith to Abner Prewett, for the use of William L. Whittaker, Dr., for one negro man, Jerry, aged about twenty-eight years, converted to your use."

It is not deemed necessary to notice the testimony on the part of the defendant; the jury found for the plaintiff the full amount of the note sued for, and interest, and the defendant sued out this writ of error.

Davis, for plaintiffs in error.

1. Can an open account be transferred by delivery, or endorsement, so as to make it the subject of set-off? The case of *Glass* v. *Moss*, 1 *How.*, 519, is believed to be conclusive upon this point.

2. It was assumed below, and may again be repeated, that, admitting Smith took the boy Jerry, it was a trespass for which case was the remedy, and that assumpsit would not lie. The doctrine that you may waive the tort, and rely upon the implied assumpsit, is too well understood to admit of discussion at this day.—*Chit. on Cont.*, 18, *and notes* 1 *and* 20.

Lindsay and *Copp*, for defendant in error.

1. In *Ellzey et al.* v. *Stone*, 5 *S. & M.*, 21, the Court say, "where

the facts of the case are fairly left to the consideration of the jury, the verdict will not be disturbed, unless a great preponderance of testimony appears against it."

Whether it was right or not to leave the facts of this case to the jury, we shall presently inquire; but that they were left fully, and, in the sense of the Court, fairly, to the jury, the record discloses.

2. The Court, in *Glass* v. *Moss*, 1 *How.*, 519, say, that it is not necessary that an assignment should appear on a promissory note, to enable the holder to tender it in offset. The Court use this language: "The possession of a promissory note, is *prima facie* evidence of ownership, and I take the rule to be equally applicable, whether it has been transferred by endorsement or delivery. The instrument introduced as an offset, is clearly a promissory note, and being transferred by delivery, Lemuel C. Glass acquired the beneficial interest in it, and had a right of action. That an action on the instrument must have been brought in the name of Joel Glass, for his use, cannot alter the case."

The Court here put it expressly, as we think, upon the ground that the property in the note was legally vested in the holder.

Does the same principle apply to an open account? We have never seen such an authority in any reported case, and do not think it can be drawn from this case of *Glass* v. *Moss*, or any statute of the state.

3. The set-off is not allowable for another reason. This account is for unliquidated damages, and it is a settled principle that unliquidated damages cannot be set off either in law or equity, against a legal demand.—*Webster* v. *Couch*, 6 *Rand.*, 519; *Murray* v. *Toland*, 3 *Johns. Ch.*, 575; *Howlit* v. *Strickland*, *Cowp.*, 57; *Bank* v. *Howard*, 13 *Mass.*, 235; *Goodwin* v. *Cunningham*, 12 *Mass.*, 193; *Braynard* v. *Fisher*, 6 *Pick.*, 355. And demand must be ascertained, and not a trespass or tort.—*Gibbs* v. *Mitchell*, 2 *Bay's S. C. R.*, 120; *Adams* v. *Manning*, 17 *Mass.*, 178; *Edwards* v. *Davis*, 1 *Halst.*, 394; *Weigall* v. *Waters*, 6 *T. R.*, 488. And it must be a legal and not an equitable demand.—*Wake* v. *Tinkler*, 16 *East*, 36.

4. One of two defendants cannot set off a debt due to him alone from the plaintiffs.—*Walker* v. *Leighton*, 11 *Mass.*, 140; *Porter* v. *Neckervise*, 4 *Rand.*, 359; *Kinnerly* v. *Hossack*, 2 *Taunt.*, 170.

This account is assigned to Hardy alone.

Mr. Justice Thacher delivered the opinion of the Court.

This was an action of assumpsit upon a promissory note, on which Whittaker and Hardy were makers, and Smith endorser. Whittaker and Hardy, the plaintiffs in error, pleaded payment, and filed as a set-off, a claim assigned by one Prewitt to Whittaker against Smith for damages, in consequence of Smith's alleged conversion of a slave belonging to Prewitt. The jury found in full for the plaintiff below, upon which defendants there claimed a new trial, and upon its refusal bring the cause here.

Without referring to other reasons, it is enough to say that this was an attempt to set off unliquidated damages against a fixed money demand, which is well settled to be impossible at law.

Judgment affirmed.

SHERIFF.

A person deputed to serve a writ has all the powers which may be exercised by a sheriff in executing any process, except that he is not to be recognized or obeyed as a sheriff, or known officer, but must show his authority, and make known his business, if required by the party who is to obey the same.

If the goods of the debtor are secreted in the store or warehouse of a third person, the sheriff will be justified in breaking open the outer door for the purpose of taking them by due process of law, if admittance is refused to him, after he has demanded it from the proper person; and he may do this in the night, as well as day.

And if admittance is demanded by the sheriff of the person having the key of the warehouse, it is sufficient; and the sheriff is not bound to make inquiry as to the manner, in which such person came in possession of the key.

If a warehouseman receive goods, and the bailor has no title to the goods, and they are taken from the custody of the warehouseman by authority of the law, as the property of a third person, the warehouseman may show this in defence of an action brought against him by the bailor for the goods.

This was an action of trespass, for breaking and entering the plaintiff's warehouse and taking from thence certain goods. The defendants pleaded that they took the goods, by virtue of legal process, as the property of a third person, and that they broke into the warehouse for the reason that they were refused admittance upon demand. The plaintiffs replied that the goods were the property of A., and not of the debtor, as whose they were taken, and that they had received the goods to keep for A. The defendants rejoined in estoppel, that A. had brought an action of trespass against them for taking and carrying away the same goods, and that issue had been joined in that action upon the question of A.'s title to the goods, and that judgment had been rendered thereon in favor of the defendants. And it was *held*, on demurrer to this rejoinder, that the matter was well pleaded as an estoppel, and that the defendants were entitled to judgment.—*Burton et al.* v. *Wilkinson et al.*, 18 *Vermont R.*, p. 186. (1847.)

Trespass *quare clausum fregit*. It was alleged, in the declaration, that the defendants, on the 17th day of October, 1842, broke open the door of the plaintiff's warehouse, and took and carried away from thence a quantity of butter, belonging to the plaintiffs. The defendants pleaded that one Curtis had sued out a writ of attachment against one Royal Cutter, and that the defendant Wilkinson was specially authorized to make service of the writ, and that the butter in question was the property of Cutter, and was stored in the plaintiffs' warehouse, and that Wilkinson demanded the key of the warehouse of Hubbard B. Bogue and J. H. Walker, in whose possession the key was, or that they should permit Wilkinson to enter the warehouse and attach the butter, and that, upon their refusing to do so, Wilkinson, as authorized officer, and the defendant Nutting, as his servant, broke open the door of the warehouse and took the butter; and the defendants alleged, that this was the supposed trespass complained of in the declaration. The plaintiffs replied, that previous to the attachment by Wilkinson the butter had been sold by Cutter to Joel Houghton, and that notice of the sale had been duly given to them by Houghton, and that they had undertaken and promised to keep the butter for Houghton, and to deliver it to him on demand, and that the defendant, in the night time, broke and entered the plaintiffs' warehouse and carried away the butter. The defendants rejoined, as an estoppel to the plaintiffs' relying upon the facts set forth in the replication, that Houghton, subsequent to the attachment, had brought an action of trespass against the defendants for taking and carrying away the butter, and that issue had been joined to the Court, in that suit, upon the question as to the title of Houghton to the butter, and that the Court rendered judgment, upon that issue, in favor of the defendants. To this rejoinder the plaintiffs demurred.

The County Court—ROYCE, J., presiding—adjudged the rejoinder sufficient; to which decision the plaintiffs excepted.

Beardsley, for plaintiffs.

1. The plaintiffs are not estopped by the judgment set up in the rejoinder. In order to make that judgment conclusive upon them, they must have occupied such a position, as would have rendered the judgment conclusive in their favor in a suit brought against them by Houghton for not safely keeping the property. The plaintiffs, by their undertaking to keep the property for Houghton, admitted his title, and are estopped from denying it in a suit brought against them by Houghton. If so, the judgment specified in the rejoinder could not be made available for them to defeat such action.—*Gosling* v. *Birnie*, 20 *Eng. Com. Law*, 153; 3 *Stephens' N. P.*, 777; 2 *Camp.*, 243, 344; 25 *Eng. Com. Law* 118; 9 *Eng. Com. Law*, 170.

2. The plaintiffs, as warehousemen, had a lien upon the property for storage, and were entitled to retain possession of it, until that lien was satisfied.—*Donnelly* v. *Crowther*, 22 *Eng. Com. Law*, 416.

3. An officer is not justified in breaking the door of a warehouse, except at a reasonable hour, and not in the night season.

Smalley, Adams & Hoyt and *Hunt & Nutting*, for defendants.

1. The plea in bar discloses a perfect justification of the trespass alleged in the declaration. Although a man's dwelling house is his castle, for defence and repose, yet it is not clear that he can therein defend the person or goods of another.—*Wats. on Sheriff*, 43–58, 59; 4 *Bac.*

Ab. Sheriff, N. 3; 4 *Com. Dig. Execution,* 65; 2 *Aik.*, 416. It is a personal privilege, annexed to the house for the protection of a man and his family, and has always been construed strictly. *Lee* v. *Gansel, Cowp.*, 1; *Lloyd* v. *Sandilands,* 4 *Eng. Com. Law,* 92. It has never been extended to any other building, detached from a dwelling house. 3 *B. & P.*, 226. On the contrary, it has always been held, that an officer, to serve process, might break open a store, warehouse, or barn, as well as the inner door of a dwelling house, trunks, &c., even without request to the owner to open.—*Wats. on Sheriffs,* 43, 59; *Haggerty et al.* v. *Wilber et al.*, 16 *Johns.*, 287; 4 *Bac. Ab. Sheriff, N.* 3; *Petersd.*, 397, 596 *in notes.* The defendant Wilkinson, being duly authorized, had all the powers of a sheriff.—*Rev. St.*, 172, *sec.* 23.

2. The judgment in the suit in favor of Houghton against the defendants is conclusive against Houghton as to the right of property in the butter in question. 1 *Phil. Ev.*, 321; *Outram* v. *Morewood,* 3 *East,* 354; *Church* v. *Leavenworth,* 4 *Day,* 274; *Canaan* v. *Greenwoods Turnp. Co.*, 1 *Conn.*, 1; *Howard* v. *Mitchell,* 14 *Mass.*, 241; *Jackson* v. *Stone,* 13 *Johns.*, 447; *Dewey* v. *Osborne,* 4 *Cow.*, 329; *Young* v. *Black,* 2 *U. S. Cond. R.*, 23; *Crandall* v. *Gallup,* 12 *Conn.*, 365; 1 *Stark. Ev.*, 193; *Wright* v. *Butler,* 6 *Wend.*, 284; *Viles et al.* v. *Moulton,* 13 *Vt.*, 510. The plaintiffs in their replication, set up no independent right or title, to the property in question, but identify themselves with Houghton's title, and make claim under him as his agents and bailees. Whatever, therefore, is evidence against the one, is evidence against the other. The recovery, being conclusive on Houghton's title, is equally binding and conclusive on the plaintiffs' claim, resting on that title.—1 *Phil. Ev.*, 324; *Adams* v. *Barnes,* 17 *Mass.*, 365; *Hutton* v. *Barber,* 2 *Wash. C. C. R.*, 64; *Wood* v. *Jackson,* 8 *Wend.*, 9; *Betts* v. *Starr,* 5 *Conn.*, 550; *Dennison* v. *Hyde et al.*, 6 *Conn.*, 508; *Lady Dartmouth* v. *Roberts,* 16 *East,* 334; *Noy's Maxims,* 4, 13; *Greenl. Ev.*, 220–222, 562, 563, 573, 574; *Kinnersby* v. *Orpe, Dougl.*, 56.

3. The recovery in the suit in favor of Houghton against the defendants, being conclusive as to the title to the property, is properly pleaded by the defendants by way of estoppel to the title attempted to be set up by the plaintiffs in Houghton.—*Noy's Maxims,* 4, 13; 4 *Com. Dig. Estoppel B.*

The opinion of the Court was delivered by

WILLIAMS, C. J.—But two questions have presented themselves to the consideration of the Court in this case. 1. As to the power of a person, specially deputized to serve a writ, in relation to the breaking of doors. 2. As to the claim set up by the plaintiffs under the title of Houghton.

A person deputed to serve a writ, as was the defendant Wilkinson, has all the powers, which may be exercised by a sheriff in serving or executing any process, except that he is not to be recognized or obeyed as a sheriff, or known officer, but must show his authority, and make known his business, if required by the party who is to obey the same,

In this particular he represents a special bailiff, rather than a known officer. To make an attachment, or to levy an execution on goods, the sheriff cannot break open the outer door of the debtor's dwelling house. It is otherwise, if the goods of a stranger are secreted in the dwelling house. A barn, or out-house, adjoining to and parcel of the house, or within the curtilage, may be broken open to make such levy; but a request must first be made for admittance. A barn in the field may be opened without request. *Penton* v. *Brown*, 1 *Keb.* 698; 19 *Vin.*, 432; *Haggerty* v. *Wilber*, 16 *Johns.*, 287. There is nothing to prevent a sheriff from serving an execution in the night, as well as in the day-time. Wilkinson was therefore justified in breaking into the warehouse in question, to serve an attachment on the goods of any person therein;—but he must first demand admittance.

In this case it is stated, that he did demand admittance of the persons who had the key; but it is objected, that the plea does not state but that the persons who had the key were wrongfully in possession. We think this was not necessary. If he demanded admittance of those who had the custody and care of the key, and who could have let him in without compelling him to resort to force, it was all that was necessary; and he was not bound to inquire how, or in what way, they became possessed of the same. A demand of the plaintiffs for admittance could have been of no use, as they could not have unlocked the door, while Bogue and Walker had the key. If there has been any collusion between the defendants and Bogue and Walker, which would have made the defendants liable, it should have appeared in the replication. A sheriff would have been justified in breaking open the warehouse of the plaintiffs to do execution on the goods of Cutter, having first demanded admittance of the persons who had the key.

The next inquiry is, whether the plaintiffs, having undertaken to keep the butter for Houghton, are bound to keep it for him at all events, and are estopped from setting up against him the proceedings had in the suit in favor of Houghton against the defendants, in which the decision was against Houghton's claim. It is undoubtedly true, that, when a wharfinger receives goods, or acknowledges the title of another, and agrees to receive or keep goods for such persons, he cannot dispute the title, in an action brought by such person against him. The cases of *Goslin* v. *Birnie*, 7 *Bing.*, 339; 20 *Eng. Com. Law*, 153; *Holl* v. *Griffin*, 10 *Bing.*, 246; 25 *Eng. Com. Law*, 118; *Harmon* v. *Anderson*, 2 *Camp.*, 243; and *Stonard* v. *Dunkin et al.*, 2 *Camp.*, 344; establish this point. The wharfinger is the agent of the person, of whom he receives the goods, and cannot dispute the title of his principal, in an action brought by the principal against him. But this cannot protect the goods thus received, from an execution against the person thus depositing them; and if they are taken from the wharfinger, or warehouseman, by lawful process, the wharfinger, or warehouseman, can protect himself, in a suit brought against him by the owner. If the person, from whom the wharfinger, or warehouseman, receives the goods, claims the same by a title illegal, so that he cannot lawfully hold them, and they are taken by authority of the law out of the custody and care of the wharfinger, the latter may show this in excuse for not delivering them.

The plaintiffs in this case, set up a title in the property in Houghton; but if Houghton himself has set up the same title against these defendants, and it has been decided against him, he would be estopped thereafter from claiming the same goods under the same title. We cannot therefore doubt, that if a suit were now instituted by Houghton against the plaintiffs, founded on their recognition of his title, it would be competent for them to defend against such suit, by showing that the butter was taken from their possession by process of law against Cutter, and that Houghton has instituted a suit against the officer serving the process, and that his *title* has been found defective and the officer serving such process justified in taking the property. The liability of the plaintiffs to Houghton for the butter, did not protect it against the creditors of Cutter, if Houghton's title has been found and adjudged to be invalid, as against such creditors. The rejoinder, therefore, fully answered the replication.

The judgment of the County Court is therefore affirmed.

Where the old Sheriff fails to deliver to his successor an execution placed in his hands during his term of office, and receives money thereon fourteen days after the appointment and qualification of the new Sheriff, his securities are not liable in an action on the bond, to account to the defendant for said money, notwithstanding he has been compelled to pay it a second time to the plaintiff.—*McDonald* v. *Bradshaw*, 2 *Kelly's R.*, *p.* 248. *Ga.* (1847.)

A person specially deputed under the hand and seal of the sheriff of the county, is an officer *de facto*.

The validity of the act of an officer *de facto* can only be inquired into in a suit to which he is a party.

A writ will not be abated because the officer who served it has not taken the oath of office.—*Merrill* v. *Palmer*, 13 *New Hampshire R.*, *p.* 184. (1847.)

Assumpsit. The action was commenced by a writ of attachment. After enrolling the writ, declaration, and officer's return, the defendant pleaded in abatement of the writ that the officer who served and returned the writ, was not, before the service and return, sworn to the faithful discharge of the duties of his office.

Upon examination of the writ and officer's return thus enrolled, it appeared that the officer in the service of the writ, acted by virtue of a special deputation under the hand and seal of the sheriff of the county endorsed upon the back of the writ.

The plaintiffs demurred generally.

Thompson for the plaintiffs.
Quincy, for the defendant.

Woods, J.—The matter of the plea in this case is insufficient to abate the writ. Hadley, who served the writ, was specially authorized for that purpose by virtue of a deputation under the hand and seal of the sheriff of the county in which the service was made.

The exception taken to the sufficiency of the service is based upon the alleged want of legal authority for that purpose in the deputy, for the reason that he had not taken the usual official oath for the faithful discharge of the duties of his office.

But being commissioned by the Sheriff, he acted under color of office. He was an officer *de facto*, and that was sufficient. Whether he was an officer *de jure*, was a question which could not be inquired into between these parties. The fact that he was an officer *de facto* was conclusive evidence of the legality of the authority under which he assumed to act, as between third persons. The question of its legality would be open, and could only be made upon an issue to which the officer was a party.

The authorities upon the question under consideration are uniform and conclusive.—*Moore* v. *Graves*, 3 *N. H.*, 408; *Morse* v. *Calley*, 5 *N. H.*, 222; *Tucker* v. *Aikin*, 7 *N. H.*, 118; *Lisbon* v. *Bow*, 10 *N. H.*, 167; 9 *Mass.*, 231; 15 *Mass.*, 180.

The judgment of the Court, therefore, is that the plea is insufficient to abate the writ, and that the defendant must answer farther.

SHERIFF—DEATH OF.

A sheriff, having collected money on an execution, died without having paid over the money, and the judgment was afterwards reversed. *Held*, that a suit on the sheriff's bond, on the relation of the execution-defendant, against the sureties of the sheriff for the money so collected, would not lie.—*The State* v. *Vananda*, 7 *Blackford's R.*, *p.* 214. *Ind.* (1847.)

SHERIFF—RESIDENCE.

A writ against a town cannot be served upon the town by a sheriff, who has ratable estate in the town, for which he is rated and taxed, though he be not at the time of making the service, a resident inhabitant of the town.

Form of a sufficient plea in abatement in such case.—*Evarts* v. *Town of Georgia*, 18 *Vermont R.*, *p.* 15. (1847.)

In this case the original writ was made returnable to the County Court, and at the term at which the action was entered in Court, the defendants appeared and pleaded as follows:

"And now the defendants here in Court defend the wrong and injury when, &c., and pray judgment of the plaintiff's writ, and that the same may be abated, quashed and held for nought, because they say that Decius B. Bogue, by whom the said writ was served, executed and returned, was, at the time said writ was served, the legal owner of a large real and personal estate, of the value, to wit, of three thousand dollars, situate and being in said town of Georgia, which said estate then was ratable and liable to taxation by and for said town of Georgia, and on which taxes were then raised, and that said Bogue was then liable to be taxed for the same, and that there is no other service of said writ, than the service so made and returned by said Bogue, as appears by the said writ and said Bogue's return thereon. Wherefore, for want of a legal service of said writ, the defendants pray judgment of the said plaintiff's writ, and that the same may be abated and quashed, and for their costs."

To this plea the plaintiff demurred, and assigned, as special causes for demurrer,—1. That it does not appear by said plea that said estate is, or was, set in the list of said Bogue in said town, or of any tenant of said Bogue in said town;—2. That it does not appear, but that said estate may have been in the possession of some tenant, or tenants, of said Bogue, and said tenant, or tenants, resident out of said town;—3. That it does not appear that said Bogue is a resident of said town;—4. That it does not appear, that taxes were then raised on said property by said town, or that said Bogue was liable to be rated and taxed for said property by said town, or that said Bogue was rated and taxed for the same by said town, unless argumentatively;—5. That the averment, that the said estate was ratable and liable to taxation by and for said town, is too general.

The County Court adjudged the plea sufficient; to which decision the plaintiff excepted.

Stevens & Seymour, for plaintiff.

1. The sheriff, though interested, may serve the writ.—*Rev. St. c.*, 11 *secs.* 4, 40; *c.* 13, *sec.* 60; *Slade's St.*, *p.* 200, *sec.* 2; *p.* 64, *sec.* 24.

2. A town is a public corporation.—7 *Vt.*, 19.

3. The officer must be rated, 6 *Vt.*, 51, that is, have taxable property and a *list*.—7 *Vt.*, 20, 48.

4. The argument *ab inconvenienti* applies.—9 *Vt.*, 170; 7 *Vt.*, 166.

Beardsley, for defendants.

1. The plea is substantially sufficient. *Rev. St.*, 77, *sec.* 40. It is difficult to discover any distinction between the case at bar and the cases of *Holmes* v. *Essex*, 6 *Vt.*, 47; and *Fairfield* v. *Hall*, 8 *Vt*, 68. It is true that the officer did not, at the time of service, reside in the town of Georgia; nor is this material. The interest is not created by the fact of residence, but by the fact that he is ratable by reason of having property in the town, on which he pays and is liable to pay taxes.

2. The objection that it is not alleged in the plea, that the estate was

set in the list of Bogue, in the town, is frivolous. The interest does not arise from this, but from the fact that it is ratable, or liable to be taxed.

3. It cannot be important, whether the estate was in possession of a tenant, nor whether he resided in or out of the town, if the officer was liable to pay taxes on the estate, and was taxed for the same, which facts the plea directly alleges.

4. It is sufficient to allege the fact, that the estate was ratable, and liable to taxation, without pointing out how, or to what extent, or in what form, the estate was ratable.

The opinion of the Court was delivered by

ROYCE, J.—In the case of *Holmes* v. *Essex*, 6 *Vt.*, 47, the sheriff of the county was a rated inhabitant of Essex, but the writ was served by his deputy, who was not alleged to have been an inhabitant of that town, or personally interested in the suit. Here the sheriff himself served the writ, having ratable estate in the town of Georgia, for which he was rated and taxed, though he does not appear to have been, at the time of serving the writ, a resident inhabitant of that town. This latter fact makes the only difference between the two cases, which can possibly tend to aid the service in the present instance. But the place of the officer's residence is not made a test of qualification by the statute, nor was it at all relied upon in the case cited. That decision proceeded solely on the ground of interest, and must therefore govern the present case.

Judgment of the County Court affirmed.

SHERIFF'S SALE.

If a bidder at sheriff's sale of real estate prevent others from bidding, by representations respecting the object of his bid, and then buy the property at the sale at a price much below its value, the sale is void as against public policy, and as a fraud upon the judgment-debtor and his creditors.—*Bunts* v. *Cole et al.*, 7 *Blackford's R.*, p. 265. *Ind.* (1847.)

A purchaser at sheriff's sale under an order for the sale of mortgaged premises, is invested with the interests of the mortgagee in the land, and so far as the land is concerned, is subrogated to all the rights of the mortgagee.

As between mortgagor and mortgagee, and those claiming under them, after condition broken the estate becomes absolute in the mortgagee, subject, however, to be redeemed at any time before foreclosure.

A purchaser from the mortgagor, whose purchase was made subsequent to the date of the mortgage, cannot maintain ejectment against the purchaser at sheriff's sale; although such subsequent purchaser was not made a party to the proceedings in Chancery. But he may have a bill to redeem.—*Frische* v. *Kramer's Lessee*, 16 *Ohio R.*, p. 125. (1848.)

A purchaser of land at sheriff's sale, under a judgment against a person who had conveyed the land to defraud his creditors, stands in the place of a creditor of the fraudulent grantor, and has the same rights.—*Scott* v. *Purcell et als.*, 7 *Blackford's R.*, *p.* 66. *Ind.* (1847.)

(DEWEY, J., cited *Hildreth* v. *Sands*, 2 *Johns. Ch.*, 35; *Sands* v. *Hildreth*, 14 *Johns.*, 493; *Ridgeway* v. *Underwood*, 1 *Wash. C. C. R.*, 129.)

SIGNATURE.

The signature of the name of a person not a party to the suit written under the attestation of the clerk of the Court from which process issued, and not opposite to the seal where the name of the security for costs was intended to be placed, is not such a bond for costs as the statute requires; and it is not competent to show by extrinsic proof, for the purpose of sustaining a *sci. fa.* on the bail bond, that the person so signing intended to make himself a surety for the costs.—*Keeland* v. *Harper*, 10 *Alabama R.*, *p.* 178. (1847.)

A written instrument, not attested by a subscribing witness, is sufficiently proved to authorize its introduction, by competent proof that the signature of the person whose name is undersigned, is genuine. The party producing it is not required to proceed further, upon a mere suggestion of false date when there are no indications of falsity upon the paper, and prove that it was actually made on the day of its date.—*Pullen* v. *Hutchinson*, 25 *Maine R.*, *p.* 249. (1847.)

SIGNATURE—ALTERATION OF.

If a note signed by several, be written, "I promise," a change of the word "I" into "we," will be a material alteration, which will render the note void, if made without the assent of the signers.

But a subsequent ratification of the alteration will be equivalent to an original authority to make it.—*Humphreys* v. *Guillou*, 13 *New Hampshire R.*, *p.* 385. (1847.)

(GILCHRIST, J., cited *March* v. *Ward*, *Peake*, 130; *Clark* v. *Blackstock*, *Holt*, 474; *Hemmenway* v. *Stone*, 7 *Mass.*, 58; *Master* v. *Miller*, 3 *T. R.*, 329; *O'Neale* v. *Long*, 4 *Cranch*, 60.)

SLANDER.

To maintain an action for words spoken, on the ground that they were injurious to the plaintiff in his business or occupation, the words must relate to his business character, and must impute to him misconduct in that character.

If the words are imputations on his morality, temper or conduct generally; which would be injurious to him, whatever were his pursuit, they are not actionable, *per se*.

Accordingly, a charge against the proprietor of a public house and garden, that he was a dangerous man; that he was a desperate man; that the declarant was afraid to go to such public house alone; and that the declarant was afraid of his own life; was held not to be actionable. —*Ireland* v. *McGarvish*, 1 *Sandford's R.*, *p.* 155. *N. Y.* (1849.)

(VANDERPOEL, J., cited *Van Tassel* v. *Capron*, 1 *Denio*, 250.)

The words "you hooked my geese" are not actionable in themselves.

Words not actionable in themselves may express a criminal charge, by reason of their allusion to some extrinsic fact, or of their being used and understood in a different sense from their natural meaning, and thus become actionable.

An *innuendo* cannot change the ordinary meaning of language.—*Hays et ux.* v. *Mitchell et ux.*, 7 *Blackford's R.*, *p.* 117. *Ind.* (1847.)

ERROR to the Bartholomew Circuit Court.

DEWEY, J.—Slander by Mitchell and wife against Hays and wife. Among the words laid in the declaration are the following: "You hooked my geese," *innuendo*, that the wife of Mitchell had stolen defendant's geese. Plea, general issue; Verdict and judgment for the plaintiffs.

The Court charged the jury, in substance, that the above words were actionable in themselves, and, if proved, would sustain the action, unless it appeared from all the circumstances of the case they were spoken in an innocent sense.

We think this instruction was erroneous. The common and ordinary meaning of the word "hook" is not *steal;* nor does its connection with the rest of the sentence naturally give it that signification or any other criminal meaning. Words not actionable in themselves may express a criminal charge by reason of their allusion to some extrinsic fact, or in consequence of being used and understood in a particular sense different from their natural meaning, and thus become actionable. And when such is the case, it is as necessary to prove the extrinsic fact, or the particular and offensive sense in which the words were used, as it is to establish the words themselves. The charge of the Court was a violation of this principle.

The declaration in this cause is not so framed as to make the words stated a good cause of action. Something more than an *innuendo* was necessary for that purpose. An *innuendo* cannot aver a fact, or change the natural meaning of language. There should have been a prefatory allegation of some extrinsic matter, or an explanation of the particular and criminal meaning of the words. This introductory matter having been stated, the *colloquium* should have connected with it the speaking of the words complained of, leaving to the *innuendo* its proper office of giving to those words that construction which they bore in reference to the extrinsic fact, or explanation of their particular meaning. In slander for words not actionable in themselves, the inducement in the declaration showing their actionable character should, of course, conform to the truth of the facts. If a crime has really been committed, and the words sued for were spoken in reference to it, that matter should be averred. *Linville* v. *Earlywine*, 5 *Blackf.*, 469. Or if the defendant has been in the practice of using the words to express the commission of a crime, that fact should be alleged. *Goldstein* v. *Foss et al.*, 4 *Bing.*, 489; *Angle* v. *Alexander*, 7 *Bing.*, 119. Or if a word or phrase has a particular and criminal meaning, different from its ordinary import, and was used in its opprobrious sense by the defendant, those facts should appear. *Forbes* v. *King*, 1 *Dowl. P. C.*, 672; 2 *Chitt. Pr.*, 549, *n. y.*; *Day* v. *Robinson*, 1 *Adol. & Ell.*, 554; 4 *N. & M.*, 884. It is usual to state such and similar matters in a distinct allegation; but they may be incorporated into the *colloquium*.—*Ricket et ux.* v. *Stanley*, 6 *Blackford*, 169.

PER CURIAM.—*The judgment is reversed with costs. Cause remanded, &c.*

SLAVE.

In an action instituted by one held as a slave to establish his right to freedom, the only issue which can be presented is *liber vel non*. Plaintiff cannot contest the title of the defendant but by establishing his own right to freedom. A slave is incapable of appearing in Court for any other purpose than that of claiming his freedom.—*Lewis* v. *Cartwright*, 7 *Robinson's La. R.*, *p.* 186. (1847.)

APPEAL from the District Court of the first District, BUCHANAN, J.

Van Matre and *Schmidt*, for the appellant.
Larue and *Preston*, for the defendant.

BULLARD, J.—The plaintiff claims his freedom, on the ground that he was carried by his master from the United States into Texas, at that time one of the States of the Mexican confederation, where slavery, as he alleges, was not tolerated by the constitution and laws at that time in force. He is appellant from a judgment against him, rejecting his pretensions. The only part of the "constitution and laws" which have been furnished us, is the constitution of the State of Coahuila y Tejas, which appears to have been adopted on the 11th of March, 1827. The 13th article contains the following disposition: "*En el estado nadie nace esclavo desde que se publique esta constitucion en la cabecera de cada partido, y despues de seis meses tampoco se permite su introduccion bajo ningun pretesto.*"

This article of the constitution by no means declares that slavery shall no longer exist, but provides, on the contrary, for its gradual

ual extinguishment, by declaring the children born of slave mothers, after the publication of the constitution, to be absolutely free, and prohibiting the further introduction of slaves from abroad six months thereafter. It is clear, that such slaves as existed in that State previous to the establishment of the Constitution, did not thereby become free.

But even admitting that such persons as were introduced afterwards in violation of that prohibitory clause in the constitution became *ipso facto* free, the evidence in this case, is quite vague, as to the time at which the plaintiff was carried to Texas. The only witness who testifies upon that point says, that he (the witness) resided in Texas from 1822 to 1828, during the whole of which time that State formed an integral portion of the Mexican Republic; that he knows the plaintiff, and recollects having hired him of Prior to aid him in clearing some land, in the neighborhood of St. Philip de Austin, *about the year* 1826; that he was in his employ for two or three weeks; and that he saw him frequently during the ten or twelve months afterwards. Prior called himself his master.

Thus it appears that the plaintiff was in Texas, with his master, before the adoption of the constitution, and could not consequently have acquired his freedom by being introduced afterwards. Indeed, there is no evidence of his having been carried to Texas, after the spring of 1827.

The counsel for the appellant contends, that the Court erred in giving judgment for the defendant, without proof that he had any title to the plaintiff as his slave, but with evidence on the contrary, that if a slave at all, which is denied, he belongs to one Roberts.

The plaintiff has no capacity to contest the title of the defendant. The only question properly presented by the pleadings, or which could be presented, was *liber vel non*. Slaves are incapable of appearing for any other purpose.—4 *Mart.*, 577; 8 *Mart.*, 158; 9 *La.* 158.

Judgment affirmed.

SPECIFIC PERFORMANCE.

No rule is better settled, than that a party cannot compel the specific performance of a contract in a Court of Equity, unless he shows that he himself has specifically performed, or can justly account for the reason of his non-performance.

If a party seeking to enforce a specific performance wishes to set off against the amount to be paid by him an indebtedness to him from the other party, he should lay the proper foundation for it in his bill, or he cannot be relieved.—*Scott* v. *Shepherd et ux.*, 3 *Gilman's R.*, p. 483. *Ills.* (1847.)

(*Peters* cited *Doyle* v. *Teas*, 4 *Scam.*, 204; 2 *Story's Eq. Jur.*, 79, *sec.* 789; 1 *Sug. Vend.*, 91.)

To entitle one party to the specific performance of a contract, it is not necessary that he should have performed or be able to perform his part of the contract to the letter; it is sufficient if he shows that he has not been in fault, and that he has taken all proper steps towards the performance.

Where one party to a contract has so far performed his part, that he cannot be placed in *statu quo*, a Court of Equity will decree specific performance by the other.

A party may by parol waive his right to call for a specific performance of his contract, but such waiver must be clearly and distinctly proved. Slight circumstances will not prevail to establish it; they must tend absolutely and unequivocally to show an intention to waive the right. —*McConkle* v. *Brown et al.*, 9 *Smedes & Marshall's R.*, *p.* 167. *Miss.* (1848.)

(SHARKEY, C. J., cited 1 *Story Eq.*, *sec.* 772; *Price* v. *Dyer*, 17 *Vesey*, 356.)

STAGE PROPRIETORS—LIABILITY OF.

The principle of necessity, which enables a party under certain circumstances, to prove the contents of a lost box or trunk, applies with as much, if not greater force, to the wife as to the husband.

Either husband or wife may be admitted to prove the quantity and value of the wearing apparel belonging to each, including in the catalogue the wife's jewelry, and every other article pertaining to her wardrobe that may be necessary or convenient to either in travelling.

In a suit against stage owners for loss of baggage, payment of the fare need not be expressly proved. It may be inferred without violent implication, as it is seldom if ever neglected. Even if not paid, the passenger is liable for it; and this obliges the owners of a stage coach to the exercise of ordinary diligence.—*McGill et al.* v. *Rowand*, 3 *Barr's R.*, *p.* 451. *Pa.* (1847.)

ERROR to the District Court of Allegheny County.

This was an action on the case brought by John Rowand, plaintiff below, and defendant in error, against Arthur McGill, Edward W. Hays, James Stewart, Griffith Bennett, and Prescot Metcalf, defendants below, and plaintiffs in error, to recover the value of two trunks and their contents.

It was testified on the trial, in substance, that the defendants were owners of the line of stages from Pittsburgh to Meadville; that the plaintiff and wife were passengers in the stage from Pittsburgh to Meadville, in July, 1843; that two large trunks of the plaintiff were replaced in the stage-coach at Butler; that after travelling eight or nine miles from there, the stage was met in a hollow about ten or eleven o'clock at night, by two men and a woman with a lantern. These persons stopped and talked with the driver for some time. When the driver parted from them he drove very fast up the hill. About an hour after this occurred, the two trunks of the plaintiff were missed, since which time nothing had been heard of them. There was some further evidence of singular behavior, on the part of the driver at the time, and afterwards, when searching for the trunks; and also of his singular account of the circumstances of the loss, leading to inferences of great carelessness, if not of collusion.

Plaintiff's counsel offered, and the Court admitted in evidence, under objection, the deposition of the plaintiff, containing a list of the articles in his trunk, with the values annexed; also the deposition of plaintiff's wife, containing a list of the articles in her own, and her husband's trunk. In the catalogue testified to, and valued by the wife, were a valuable diamond breast-pin, a gold breast-pin, and a miniature set in gold, with chain. To the admission of these depositions, defendants excepted, and the Court sealed bills of exceptions. Some additional evidence of the value of the diamond pin, miniature, and the more costly clothing, was given in the depositions of other witnesses.

Defendants requested the Court to charge the jury:

1. That the plaintiffs, having failed to prove the payment of stage fare from Pittsburgh to Meadville, the defendants are naked bailees, and not responsible, except for gross negligence of themselves or servants.

2. No proof of the value of the articles in the trunk having been made by the plaintiff, the jury cannot presume their value.

3. The defendants having no notice that the trunks in question contained jewelry, or other articles of greater value than ordinary wearing apparel, they are not liable for such articles as jewelry.

The Court refused to charge as requested, and the jury found for the plaintiff. Whereupon the defendants sued out this writ of error, and made the following assignments for error:

1. The Court erred in admitting the deposition of Mary Ann Rowand, the wife of the plaintiff below.

2. The Court erred in admitting the testimony of plaintiff and his wife, as to the value of the articles in the trunks.

3. The Court erred in their answers to the three several points submitted by the counsel of the defendants below.

McClure and *McCandless*, for plaintiffs in error.
Selden and *Dunlop*, contra.

Rogers, J.—The principle of necessity, which alone enables a party, under certain circumstances, to prove the contents of a box or trunk, applies, with as much, if not greater force, to the wife as to the husband. The wife *usually* packs her husband's trunk, and always her own, and therefore to say that she cannot in a proper case be a witness, will amount almost to a repeal of the rule, and in most cases to a denial of justice. We therefore see no reasonable objection to the admission of the husband or wife, or both, to testify to the amount of their wearing apparel, and to its value, belonging to each, including in the catalogue the wife's jewelry, and every other article pertaining to her wardrobe, that may be necessary or convenient to either in travelling. Nor is it very obvious in what manner the Court can restrict the quantity or value of the articles that may be deemed either proper or useful for their ordinary purposes. In the nature of things, it is susceptible of no precise definite rule, and when there is an attempt to abuse the privilege, we must rely upon the integrity and intelligence of the jury to apply the proper corrective ; and that there is but little danger to be apprehended on this score, the present case presents abundant proof.

There is no weight in the objection, that the plaintiff failed to prove payment of the stage-hire. Express proof, which in many cases would be difficult, in some impossible, is not required. That it is paid, may be inferred without any violent implication; as we all know, this is seldom, if ever, neglected. But, if not paid, the passenger is liable for it, and this, of itself, will oblige the owner of a stage-coach to exercise ordinary diligence. In order to charge a person as a common carrier, it is not necessary that a specific sum should be agreed on for the hire, much less paid for, if agreed on ; although not paid, he is entitled to a reasonable compensation. *Hay on Bail*, 327 ; *Seiter*, 505. That there was gross carelessness on the part of the driver, if not something worse, seems to be admitted. The cause of complaint by the owners of the coach is, therefore, not against the Court and jury, but against their own servant.

Judgment affirmed.

STATE COURT—CONSUL.

The privilege conferred upon the Consuls of foreign governments by the Constitution and Laws of the United States, of being sued in the Federal Courts only, does not extend so far as to enable a party, after a suit has been commenced against him in a State Court of competent jurisdiction, to divest that Court of jurisdiction by voluntarily accepting the office of Consul of a foreign power.

Where, subsequent to the commencement of a suit against a party, in a State Court, he accepted the appointment of Consul of a foreign power, by virtue of which he became exempted from liability to be prosecuted in the State Courts, but he proceeded to trial in the suit, upon the merits without suggesting his privilege to the Court, and afterwards brought a writ of error to the Supreme Court, to reverse the judgment of the Court below ; *Held*, that he was estopped from setting up his privilege, in bar of the jurisdiction of the State Courts.—*Koppel* v. *Heinrichs*, 3 *Denio's R.*, *p.* 449. *N. Y.* (1848.)

STATUTE LAW.

Where property is taken under a statute authority, without the consent of the owner, the power must be strictly followed ; and if any material link is wanting, the whole proceeding will be void.—*Doughty* v. *Hope*, 3 *Denio's R.*, p. 594. *N. Y.* (1848.)

(BRONSON, C. J., cited *Sharp* v. *Spier*, and *Sharp* v. *Johnson*, 4 *Hill*, 86, 92; *Striker* v. *Kelly*, 7 *Hill*, 9; 2 *Denio*, 323.)

STATUTE OF LIMITATIONS—BANK.

Money deposited with a banker by his customer in the ordinary way, is *money lent* to the banker, with a superadded obligation that it is to be paid when called for by check; and consequently, if it remain in the banker's hands for six years, without any payment by him of the principal or allowance of interest, the statute of limitations is a bar to its recovery.

An admission by a bankrupt in his balance-sheet will not take a debt out of the statute of limitations as against his assignees.

An admission in an unsigned letter, written and sent by the assignees of a bankrupt, by an accountant employed by them to wind up the affairs of the bankrupt estate, will not take a debt of the bankrupt out of the statute of limitations.—*Pott et als.* v. *Clegg*, 16 *Meeson & Welsby's R.*, p. 321. *Eng.* (1848.)

DEBT by the plaintiffs, as assignees of John Ryle, a bankrupt, against the defendant, as executor of William Turner, deceased, for money lent by the bankrupt before his bankruptcy to the defendant's testator, and on an account stated with him. The defendant pleaded, first, that the testator was never indebted; secondly, as to £918 13*s*. 8*d*, parcel of the monies demanded, a set-off for money lent by the testator to the bankrupt before the fiat, and without notice of any prior act of bankruptcy; thirdly, as to £1015, other parcel, payment by the defendant before action brought; and fourthly, as to the £918 13*s*. 8*d*, a set-off upon an account stated between the testator and the plaintiffs as assignees. The plaintiffs traversed the payment alleged in the third plea, and to the pleas of set-off replied the statute of limitations, on which issue was joined.

At the trial, before the late *Mr. Justice* WILLIAMS, at the last Spring Assizes at Chester, it appeared that the action was brought by the assignees of Mr. Ryle, who before his bankruptcy was a banker at Macclesfield, to recover the balance due upon a banking account of Mr. Turner, the defendant's testator. Mr. Ryle became bankrupt in 1841, at which time Mr. Turner had overdrawn his account to the amount of £1870. The defendant proved payment of £1015 to the plaintiffs, before the commencement of this action, whereby the balance was reduced to £855, which he sought to cover by the set-off alleged in the second plea. In order to establish that plea, he proved that, in the year 1826, an account had been opened with the bank in the joint names of the defendant's testator and one Mawdesley (as trustee), on which interest appeared to have been allowed to them at the rate of 3 per cent. per annum down to the year 1832, when the balance due to them was stated at £918 13*s*. 8*d*; but the books did not show any further transaction or entry relating to this account after that date, the balance remaining the same down to the period of the bankrupty. Mawdesley in January, 1839. The testator's separate account, on which this action was brought, was opened with the bank at a later period than the account with Turner and Mawdesley; both were entered in the same ledger, the latter being headed "Messrs. Turner and Mawdesley." And there were separate pass-books for each. On the separate account of Mr. Turner, interest at 5 per cent. per annum was charged against him from time to time in the bank books, down to the period of the bankruptcy.

It was contended by the defendant's counsel, that, under these circumstances, the statute of limitations was no answer to the set-off; for that, first, there was a duty implied by law on the part of the banker regularly to enter up the interest due upon the account of a customer, and so prevent the statute of limitations from attaching to the debt; and secondly, that the two accounts were for this purpose to be taken as one, and the part payments in respect of the account entered to Turner's debit kept alive both. But they relied also upon the following facts, as amounting to acknowledgments in writing sufficient to prevent the operation of the statute. In the first place, the bankrupt, on his final examination, in June, 1841, had entered in his balance sheet, which was signed by him, the sum of £918 13*s*. 8*d*, as due from his estate to the account of Turner and Mawdesley. Secondly, in the same year, an accountant employed by the assignees to wind up the affairs of the bank, had, by their direction, sent a letter to the defendant's testator, containing an unsigned copy of the entry in the ledger of the account between the bank and Turner and Mawdesley, in the following terms:—"Messrs. Turner and Mawdesley, Cr. £918 13*s*. 8*d*."—The learned Judge expressed his opinion that the set-off was barred by the statute of limitations, and under his direction the plaintiff had a verdict on all the issues except the third, damages £1030, leave being reserved to the defendants to move to enter a verdict for them on the plea of set-off; the Court to be at liberty to draw any inference which a jury might properly have drawn from the facts proved.

In the last Easter term, *Chilton* obtained a rule *nisi* accordingly, against which cause was shown in Michaelmas term, Nov. 13th and 14th, by

The *Attorney General* and *Welsby*.—The statute of limitations was a bar to the defendant's set-off. The relation between a banker and a customer who deposits money in his bank, is the ordinary relation of debtor and creditor, with the superadded obligation on the part of the banker, arising out of the custom of the trade, to honor the drafts of his customer; the breach of which duty is the subject of an action on the case, *Marzetti* v. *Williams*, 1 *B. & Adol.*, 415; or of an action of assumpsit, the tort being waived. But the deposit is no more than an ordinary loan. It was so expressly held by *Sir William* GRANT in *Carr* v. *Carr*, 1 *Meriv.*,

541, *n.*, and *Devaynes* v. *Noble*, 1 *Meriv.*, 568; by the Court of Queen's Bench in *Sims* v. *Bond*, 5 *B. & Adol.*, 38; and by *Lord* CHANCELLOR *Lyndhurst* in *Foley* v. *Hill*, 1 *Phillips*, 399, reversing the decision of VICE CHANCELLOR *Knight Bruce* in the same case, 13 *Law J. N. S. Chanc.*, 182. It has been held also, that money in a banker's hands will pass under a bequest of "ready money" in a will. *Parker* v. *Marchant*, 12 *Law J. N. S. Chanc.*, 385. The debt, therefore, which was due from the bankrupt to Turner and Mawdesley, was an ordinary debt, capable of being barred by the statute of limitations. Nor can it be said that the two debts—that due from Turner on the one hand, and that due to Turner and Mawdesley on the other—were so blended together as to form one account, and so to prevent the operation of the statute of limitations. The debt on the joint account of Turner and Mawdesley was kept altogether distinct from the other, and was barred by the statute of limitations before the death of Mawdesley in 1839, no interest having been paid in respect of it since 1832; whereas, on the debt of Turner to the bank, interest was charged at 5 per cent. down to the time of the bankruptcy. At all events, upon these pleadings the balance due to Turner and Mawdesley is treated as an ordinary debt, for money lent, to which therefore, prima facie, the statute of limitations is applicable.

Secondly, as to the facts relied upon to take the case out of the statute. The account sent to the testator by the accountant was unsigned; and besides, the acknowledgment signed by an agent is not sufficient. *Hyde* v. *Johnson*, 2 *Bing. N. C.*, 776. And the statement made by the bankrupt in his balance sheet cannot affect his assignees, whose title cannot be defeated by any act done by the bankrupt after his bankruptcy. *Eiche* v. *Nokes*, 1 *M. & Rob.*, 359, which may be cited as to this point, was an action against the bankrupt himself.

Chilton, *Townsend* and *Egerton*, in support of the rule.—If the argument on the other side be well founded, it follows that a banker, who neglects to balance the account of his customer for six years, may keep for his own use the money deposited with him by the customer, who may have been abroad the whole time, and may have had no occasion to draw a check. Surely that would be contrary to the policy of the law. On the other hand, if a banker is in the situation of an ordinary debtor, any person who deposits money with him might (before the recent alteration in the law of arrest) immediately afterwards have made an affidavit of debt against him, and arrested him. But the true relation between the parties, is this, that the banker holds the money under a special contract to honor the checks of the customer; who on his part cannot, so long as the banker is solvent, support an action for it without a previous demand of it in writing. This view of the case appears to be supported by the decision in *Marzetti* v. *Williams*. In *Pothier on Contracts*, by *Evans*, Vol. II. p. 126, it is said—"Where a man deposits money in the hands of another, to be kept for his use, the possession of the custodee ought to be deemed the possession of the owner, until an application and refusal, or other denial of the right; for until then there is nothing adverse; and I conceive that, upon principle, no action should be allowed in these cases, without a previous demand; consequently that no limitation should be computed further back than such demand." In *Norton* v. *Ellam*, 2 *M. & W.*, 461, PARKE, B., says: "Where money is lent simply, it is not denied that the statute begins to run from the time of the lending. Then is there any difference where it is payable with interest? It is quite clear that a promissory note payable on demand is a present debt, and is payable without any demand, and the statute runs from the date of it. Then the stipulation for compensation in the shape of interest makes no difference, except that thereby the duty is continually increasing *de di in diem*. It is quite different from a note payable at sight, because there, by the terms of the contract, it must be shown before the action is brought." This is analogous to the case of a note payable at sight, and therefore the statute did not begin to run until the bankruptcy, in 1841, rendered any formal demand of the deposit unnecessary. [ROLFE, B. The passage cited from *Evans's Pothier* certainly goes to show that the money owing by a banker to his customer is not an ordinary debt, but one of a special nature, for which no action can be brought without a previous demand. But supposing that to be so, should you not have raised the question by your pleadings? Whereas here the plea treats it as an ordinary debt for money lent. PARKE, B.—It has been held, *Gale* v. *Capern*, 1 *Ad. & E.*, 102, that a plea of the statute of limitations admits the original debt, and only denies its having been due within the six years. It is therefore admitted by these pleadings, that the bankrupt was originally indebted to Turner and Mawdesley in the sum of £918 13*s*. 8*d*, for money lent; whereas you are now arguing that he never was.] Then the facts proved in evidence take the case out of the statute; for supposing the remedy to have been barred by the lapse of time in 1838, it has been revived by the payments made on Turner's account within the six years, and after the death of Mawdesley. [PARKE, B.—The fact of the bank charging interest on the money advanced by them to Turner, after the death of Mawdesley, is very strong evidence that the money was advanced by way of independent loan to Turner, and not by way of part payment of an antecedent debt.] But further, the admission of the bankrupt in his balance-sheet was a sufficient acknowledgment to take the debt out of the operation of the statute. *Eiche* v. *Nokes; Ex parte Seaber*, 1 *Deacon*, 543. And although the account sent in by the accountant, by the authority of the assignees, might not be sufficient for this purpose, it constitutes a fresh cause of action on an account stated, within the fourth plea. *Smith* v. *Forty*, 4 *C. & P.*, 126; *Ashby* v. *James*, 11 *M. & W.*, 542. [POLLOCK, C. B.—In *Ashby* v. *James*, the parties met and stated accounts, and struck a balance; that was equivalent to a payment by one, and a repayment by the other.]

Cur. adv. vult.

The Judgment of the Court was now delivered by

POLLOCK, C. B.—The question in this case is, how far the defendant is entitled to avail himself of an old banking account, on which a large balance has been standing for many years, and to which the statute of limitations would apply under ordinary circumstances. And a question arose whether this could be considered in any other light than an ordinary debt; there being, undoubtedly, several authorities in which it is distinctly laid down that money deposited in a banker's hands is equivalent to money lent; and the majority of the Court are of that opinion. I entirely concur in the judgment of the rest of the Court, that the set-off, in the present case, cannot be made available; for even assuming that this account ought not to be treated as money lent, but that there are peculiar circumstances in a banking account which distinguish it from any other, yet none of those circumstances appear on these pleadings, so as to justify us in considering this case differently from what we should if it were an ordinary case of money lent; and I therefore concur with the rest of the Court, that the present rule must be discharged. At the same time, I must certainly, with considerable doubt and diffidence, confess the hesitation of my own opinion, whether there is not a special contract between the banker and his customer as to the money deposited, which distinguishes it from the ordinary case of a loan for money. It seems to me that is a question for the jury, who ought to decide what is the liability of the banker, and whether the money deposited with him is money lent or not. I could not concur in the judgment of the rest of the Court without expressing this doubt, in which, however, they do not partake, as they are of opinion that money in the hands of a banker is merely money lent, with the superadded obligation that it is to be paid when called for by the draft of the customer.

Rule discharged.

An account, in which a part of the items are within six years, and part of them are beyond six years, is not saved by the former from the operation of the statute of limitations against the latter, where there are no items of account on the other side.

There must be items of account on both sides, to make a *mutual account;* and it is only in mutual accounts, that an item within six years saves those beyond from being barred by the statute.—*Hallock* v. *Losee*, 1 *Sandford's R.*, *p.* 220. *N. Y.* (1849.)

(*Buckham & Nelson* cited *Kimball* v. *Brown*, 7 *Wend.*, 322; 2 *Rev. St.*, *p.* 3, *Ch.* 4, *art.* 2; *Rodman* v. *Hadden*, 10 *Wend.*, 498; 2 *Cowen's Treatise*, 760; *Graham's Prac.*, 109.

OAKLEY C., J., cited *Kimball* v. *Brown*, 7 *Wend.*, 322; *Edmonstone* v. *Thomson*, 15 *Wend.*, 554.)

A cause of action against an officer, for not paying money collected by him on execution does not accrue until demand is made on him for payment; and the statute of limitations begins to run from the time of the demand.—*Weston* v. *Ames*, 10 *Metcalf's R.*, p. 244. *Mass.* (1847.)

SUNDAY.

A person who travels on the Lord's day, neither from necessity nor charity, cannot maintain an action against a town for an injury received by him, while so travelling, by reason of a defect in the highway which the town is by law obliged to repair.—*Bosworth* v. *The Inhabitants of Swansey*, 10 *Metcalf's R.*, p. 363. *Mass.* (1847.)

(*Battelle & Williams* cited *Story on Con.*, *secs.* 162, 219, *and cases there cited*; *Lyon* v. *Strong*, 6 *Vermont*, 219; *Story on Con.*, *sec.* 221; 23 *American Jurist*, 10, 11.

Shaw, C. J., cited *Smith* v. *Smith*, 2 *Pick.*, 621; *Howard* v. *North Bridgewater*, 16 *Pick.*, 189; *Adams* v. *Carlisle*, 21 *Pick.*, 146; *Lane* v. *Crombie*, 12 *Pick.*, 177.)

Where a horse is sold on Sunday, and a note taken for the purchase money on the same day, both the contract and the note are void, and though the purchaser retain the horse in his possession, without objection or demand by the seller, the law will not *imply a promise* to pay the stipulated price or what the horse is reasonably worth. Such a contract being void, no property passed to the vendee, and he would be chargeable in *trover* upon proof of demand and refusal, or in *assumpsit* upon an express promise to pay, subsequently made, in consideration of the retention of the horse.—*Dodson* v. *Harris*, 10 *Alabama R.*, p. 566. (1847.)

(Collier, C. J., cited *O'Donnell* v. *Sweeney*, 5 *Ala.*, 467; *Pierce* v. *Hill*, 9 *Porter*, 151; *Shippey* v. *Easterwood*, 9 *Ala.*, 198.)

During the progress of a trial for murder, one of the jurors, while one of the counsel for the prisoner was addressing the jury, had a chill, and was, by order of the Court, placed upon a pallet, and for a time did not fully comprehend the whole of the argument, being in a drowse, though he had understood all of the evidence, and all that had been said by counsel previously. The fact that he was asleep was known to the prisoner, but the attention of no one was called to it: *Held*, under the circumstances, to be no ground for setting aside the verdict.

Courts cannot pronounce a judgment, or do any other act strictly judicial on Sunday, unless expressly authorized by statute so to do. A verdict of a jury, however, may be received on that day.

A jury, in a trial for murder, returned a verdict of guilty into Court, against the accused, and the Court pronounced a judgment thereon on

Sunday: *Held*, that the verdict was properly received, but that the judgment of the Court was absolutely null and void.—*Baxter* v. *The People*, 3 *Gilman's R.*, *p.* 368. *Ills.* (1847.)

(*Skinner* cited 3 *Thomas' Coke*, 354; 4 *Black. Com.*, 278; 2 *Tomlin's Law Dic.*, *title* "*Sunday*," 538; 7 *Comyn's Dig.*, 399, *B.* 3; *Mackeldey's Case*, 5 *Coke*, 66; *Dakin's Case*, 3 *Saund.*, 290; *Swan* v. *Broome*, 3 *Burrow*, 1595; *Story* v. *Elliott*, 8 *Cowen*, 27; *Pearce* v. *Atwood*, 13 *Mass.*, 347; *Bayley* v. *Smith*, 12 *Wend.*, 59; *Frost* v. *Hall*, 4 *N. H.*, 158; *King* v. *Strain*, 6 *Blackf.*, 447; *Arthur* v. *Mosby*, 2 *Bibb*, 589; *Shaw* v. *McCombs*, 2 *Bay*, 232; *Nabors* v. *The State*, 6 *Ala.*, 200.)

SURETIES.

If sureties neglect, when judgment is rendered, to cause the entry to be made, that they are sureties, as required by the statute, Chancery will not compel the judgment creditor to exhaust, first, the property of the principal.

Two executions of the same kind may be issued on the same judgment, and Courts of law, having the authority to restrain any abuse of process, on the part of the judgment creditor, Equity will not interfere. —*Elliot et al.* v. *Armstrong et als.*, 16 *Ohio R.*, *p.* 27. (1848.)

Where one surety on a note pays it, and files a bill against a co-surety for contribution, the defendant may prove by parol evidence the engagement actually undertaken by him when he signed the note.

In a controversy between two sureties on a note for contribution, the principal being equally liable to both, stands indifferently between, and is a competent witness.—*Hunt* v. *Chambliss*, 7 *Smedes & Marshall's R.*, *p.* 532. *Miss.* 1847.)

TAX SALE.

A defective description of land, listed for taxation, cannot be cured by the description and recitals in the tax deed, nor by other proof.

A tax deed, under the statute, is only *prima facie* evidence of title, and its validity may be destroyed by showing that the requisitions of the statute, authorizing the sale, have not been complied with.

To list land, as a specific number of acres, in an original survey, without specifying in what part of such survey, is too vague; and a sale for taxes, by such description, will pass no title to the purchaser.—*Turney* v. *Yeoman et als.*, 16 *Ohio R.*, *p.* 24. (1848.)

A tax title is utterly void, if the land be sold in a wrong name, under a wrong assessment.—*Stansbury* v. *Taggart*, 3 *McLean's U. S. R.*, *p.* 457. (1847.)

TENANT IN COMMON.

Where one tenant in common lays out money in improvements on the estate held in common, although the money so expended does not in strictness constitute a lien on the estate, yet a Court of Equity will not grant a partition without first directing an account, and a suitable compensation; or else in the partition, it will assign to such tenant in common that part of the premises on which the improvements have been made.

To entitle a tenant in common to an allowance, on a partition in equity, for improvements made by him on the premises, it is not necessary for him to show the assent of his co-tenants to such improvements, or a promise on their part to contribute their share of the expenses; nor a previous request to join in the improvements, and a refusal.—*Green* v. *Putnam*, 1 *Barbour's R.*, *p.* 500. *N. Y.* (1848.)

(PAIGE, J., cited 1 *Story Eq. Jur.*, *sec.* 655, 656, *b.*; *Swan* v. *Swan*, 8 *Price*, 518; *Town* v. *Needham*, 3 *Paige*, 546, 553; 3 *Paige*, 470.)

TENANT—BANKRUPTCY.

A discharge under the late bankrupt act, is not a bar to the recovery of rent which accrued after presenting the petition in bankruptcy, upon a lease executed by the bankrupt, as lessee before that time.

Therefore, where the plaintiff, prior to May, 1, 1842, demised a house to the defendant for one year from that day, for a certain rent payable quarterly, and the defendant occupied during the term, but on the 12th day of December, 1842, petitioned to be declared a bankrupt, and obtained his certificate in August, 1843; *held*, that the discharge was not a bar to an action on the lease for the last quarter's rent falling due May 1, 1843.—*Stinemets* v. *Ainslie*, 4 *Denio's R.*, *p.* 573. *N. Y.* (1849.)

(*Noyes* cited *Owen on Bank*, 59; *Copeland* v. *Stevens*, 1 *Barn. & Ald.*, 593; *Doe* v. *Andrews*, 4 *Bing.*, 348; 12 *Moore*, 601; 2 *Car. & Payne*, 598; *Dark* v. *Sharp*, 3 *Moore & P.*, 390; 5 *Adolph. & Ellis*, 366; *Henley's Bankrupt Law*, 237, 9; *Id. Appendix*, 78; *Mills* v. *Auriol*, 1 *H. Bl.*, 433; *S. C.*, 4 *T. R.*, 94; *Com. Land. and Ten.*, 247; *Archb. Bank Law*, 193; 1 *Cooke's Bank Law*, 5; *Parslow* v. *Dearlove*, 4 *East*, 438; *Brix* v. *Braham*, 1 *Bing.*, 281; 2 *Caine's Cas. in Err.*, 311; *S. C.*, 1 *Johns. Cas.*, 73; *Lansing* v. *Prendergrast*, 9 *Johns.*, 127; *Stebbins* v. *Wilson*, 14 *Johns.*, 403; *M. & F. Bank* v. *Capron*, 15 *Johns.*, 467; *Hodges* v. *Chase*, 2 *Wend.*, 248; *Brown* v. *Fleetwood*, 5 *Mees. & Wels.*, 19; *Wells* v. *Mace*, 2 *Wash. Vt.*, 503; 2 *Barr*, 343; *Crouch* v. *Gridley*, 6 *Hill*, 250; *Thompson* v. *Hewitt*, 6 *Hill*, 254.)

TENANT—BOND.

The defendant entered into a bond to the plaintiffs, in the penal sum of £250, which recited, that whereas R. J. had agreed to become tenant to the plaintiffs of a public-house, and it was stipulated, on the letting, that R. J. should take from the plaintiffs all the ale, spirits, &c., which should be consumed on the premises, and that he should become bound with a surety to pay for all the ale, &c., which he should receive from the plaintiffs, to the amount of £50, before he should have a fresh supply from them of the same, and so should continue to do from time to time, so long as he should continue tenant of the plaintiffs; and that when he should cease to be such tenant, the surety should be liable to the plaintiffs for such sum not exceeding £50, which the said R. J. should or might then owe to the said plaintiffs for ale, &c., supplied by them to him. The condition then was, that, if R. J. should from time to time pay to the plaintiffs for all the ale, &c., which he should from time to time have had from them to an amount not exceeding £50, before he should have had a fresh supply of the same, and when he should become indebted to them in that sum; and if the said R. J. should pay the plaintiffs all sum and sums of money which he should owe them for ale, &c., not exceeding £50, when he should cease to be their tenant, the bond to be void: *Held*, that under this bond the surety was not liable for any sum, not exceeding £50, which R. J. might owe the plaintiffs at the end of the tenancy, although he might have had from them a further supply of ale, &c., at a time when he owed them £50 and upwards.—*Seller et al.* v. *Jones*, 16 *Meeson & Welsby's R.*, p. 112. *Eng.* (1848.)

(*Bovill* and *Wise* cited *Bonsor* v. *Cox*, 6 *Beav.*, 110; *Whitcher* v. *Hall*, 5 *B. & C.*, 269; *Holl* v. *Hadley*, 4 *Bing.*, 54; *Dimmock* v. *Surla*, 14 *M. & W.*, 758; *University of Cambridge* v. *Baldwin*, 5 *M. & W.*, 580; *Evans* v. *White*, 5 *Bing.*, 485.)

TRESPASS.

In an action of trespass for goods taken and carried away, which the plaintiff, before action brought, demanded to be returned to him, and which the defendant promised to return, but which were attached on a writ against the plaintiff while the defendant was preparing to return them, the measure of damages is the same that it would have been if the defendant had returned the goods.—*Kaley* v. *Shed*, 10 *Metcalf's R.*, p. 317. *Mass.* (1847.)

The owner of improved land may use all lawful means within his power, to enforce his right to exclusive possession of his land, although the land may not be surrounded by a legal fence.

If cattle trespass upon improved land, which is not surrounded by such a fence, as required by statute, the owner of the land may drive them off, and may, for this purpose, set a dog upon them, provided he is not in any way wanting in ordinary care and prudence, arising from the size and character of the dog, or in the manner of setting him upon the cattle and afterwards pursuing them.—*Clark* v. *Adams, et al.*, 18 *Vermont R., p.* 425. (1847.)

Possession of personal property in the plaintiff is sufficient evidence of title, to enable him to maintain trespass therefor, unless the defendant exhibits a superior title.

If the owner of land has been disseized thereof, he cannot after that time maintain an action founded upon possession, until he has regained it; but by such disseizin, merely, the disseizor would not acquire a legal interest in the rents and profits, or in timber trees severed from the freehold. And should the disseizor cut the trees and appropriate them to his own use, he would be accountable to the owner for their value, after he had regained the possession, but would not be accountable for trees cut by a third person without his consent or connivance.

Where the owner of land has been disseized thereof for the term of six years, and has brought a writ of entry to obtain the possession, and the disseizor has put in his claim for improvements made by him during his possession, and the amount thereof has been found by the jury, and the owner of the land has elected to retain it and pay for the improvements, the disseizor should not be made accountable for timber trees cut upon the land, during the disseizen, by another without his consent or connivance; and if the timber, thus cut, has come into the actual possession of the owner of the land, and it is afterwards taken from him by the disseizor, he may maintain trespass therefor against the disseizer for such taking during the pendency of the writ of entry.—*Brown* v. *Ware*, 25 *Maine R., p.* 411. (1847.)

At the trial before Tenney, J., after the evidence was before the jury, on both sides, the substance of which is given in the opinion of this Court, the presiding judge intimated an opinion, that the action could not be maintained; and thereupon the plaintiff consented, that a nonsuit might be entered, to be taken off, and the action to stand for trial, if in the opinion of the Court it could be maintained; and a nonsuit, on these terms, was then ordered.

McCrillis and *Paine*, argued for the plaintiff, citing *Stat.*, 1821, *c.* 47, *sec.* 1; 1 *Greenl. Ev.*, 19 *and* 22; 1 *Chitty on Pl.*, 521, 522; *Stat.* 1821, *c.* 62, *sec.* 5; 10 *Mass.*, 146; 5 *Pick.*, 131; 1 *Kinne's Law Compendium*, 338, *and authorities there cited;* 6 *Metc.*, 407; 4 *Mass.*, 416; 3 *Hill*, 348.

Kent & Cutting, argued for the defendant, and cited 10 *Pick.*, 161; 17 *Mass.*, 299; 14 *Mass.*, 96; 1 *Metc.*, 528; 8 *Mass.*, 415; 15 *Pick.*, 33; 22 *Maine*, 451.

The opinion of the Court was drawn up by

Shepley, J.—This is an action of trespass brought to recover the value of certain mill logs cut during the former part of the year 1841, on lots numbered six and seven, in the town of Argyle, under a permit from Luther Lewis. The plaintiff had purchased them of the persons, who had cut them, and was in possession of them, when they were taken by the defendant. That was sufficient evidence of title to enable him to maintain the action, unless the defendant exhibited a superior title. His title was derived from Joseph Kinsman. He purchased of the Commonwealth of Massachusetts its title to a tract of land, including those lots, in February, 26, 1833, and conveyed a part of it, including them, on March 20, 1833, to Hollis Bowman, who on the same day reconveyed the premises to Kinsman in mortgage, who assigned the mortgage to the defendant on Dec. 22, 1838.

To defeat this apparently good title, the plaintiff exhibited proof of a conveyance from the Commonwealth to John Bennock, on December 1, 1815, of a tract of land including those lots, and of conveyances of them from Bennock through several persons to Isaac Williams and Joseph Cotton, by whom they were conveyed to Luther Lewis on February 6, 1838. If these conveyances were all operative, he became the legal owner of the lots. It appears, however, that Kinsman had disseized Williams and Cotton, before they conveyed to Lewis. And the owners would not after that time be able to maintain an action founded upon possession, until they had regained it. But Kinsman by such disseizen, merely, would not acquire a legal interest in the rents and profits, or in timber trees severed from the freehold. For the owners, after they had regained the possession, might recover the value of them in an action for the mesne profits. The disseizor would be considered, by cutting the trees and appropriating them to his own use, as obtaining their property and not his own.

Did the proceedings in the action of entry, prosecuted by Lewis in the names of his grantors to recover the lots, change the aspect of the case, and transfer the mill logs from the owners of the land to their disseizor? The tenant alleged, that the premises were holden by virtue of a possession and improvement for more than six years before the commencement of the action; and filed a claim to have the jury find the increased value of them by reason of any buildings and improvements. And the demandants filed a claim to have them find what would have been their value without such improvement. A verdict was found for the demandants by the jury, who also found the value of the land and the value of the improvements. The demandants made their election and paid the tenant for the improvements. The mill logs were cut, while the premises were held by virtue of that possession and improvement. But they were not cut by the tenant or by his consent or connivance. The tenant would become the owner of wood or timber cut on the premises during that time, by him or by his agency. For all his proceedings in the management of the estate, must be taken into consideration, to estimate the value of the improvements, or benefits to the estate. All questions respecting them would be adjusted by the finding of the jury; and no action for mesne profits could be maintained against him for his acts during that time. But he could not, in that estimate, be made responsible for the illegal acts of others, committed without his knowledge or connivance, on the premises; although their value might thereby be materially diminished. The jury are not by the statute required to consider or find, what damage has been occasioned by the acts of others without the fault of the tenant. The loss occasioned by such acts must in any event fall upon the owner of the land. Should he elect to pay for the improvements he would receive his land, diminished in value by them. Should he abandon it to the tenant, the price obtained for it would have been fixed at a less sum by reason of them.

In this case there is no proof, that the tenant was, or could have been made responsible for the acts of those persons, who cut the logs under Lewis; or that he could have obtained any title to them by the estimate made of the value of his improvements. The defendant can have no better title.

Nonsuit taken off, and action to stand for trial.

Under a declaration in trespass, which alleges that the defendants on a certain day, and on divers other days and times between that day and another day specified, broke and entered the plaintiff's barn and took and carried away his hay, the plaintiff may recover for as many distinct acts of trespass, as he can prove were committed by the defendants between the days mentioned in his declaration.

But if several persons are made defendants, and the plaintiff proves several distinct acts of trespass, in some of which a part, only, of the defendants were concerned, he can only recover against all the defendants for those acts in which all participated.—*Myrick* v. *Downer et al.*, 18 *Vermont R.*, *p.* 360. (1847.)

TREES.

Growing trees or grass may be severed in law, from the land, and become personal property, without an actual severance; as where the owner in fee of the land, by a valid conveyance in writing, sells the trees or grass to a third person; or where he sells the land, reserving the trees or grass.—*Bank of Lansingburgh* v. *Crary*, 1 *Barbour's R.*, *p.* 542. *N. Y.* (1848.)

(PAIGE, J., cited *Toll. Law of Ex'ors*, 194, 3 *Bac. Abr.*, 64.)

TRUST AND TRUSTEE—AGENT.

Trustees under an assignment for benefit of creditors employ an agent to proceed to America to recover part of the assigned property. Afterwards the debtors become bankrupt, and three of the trustees are appointed assignees:—*Held*, that under the circumstances of the case the assignees ought to be allowed in their accounts the expense of employing the agent.

For the purpose of bringing expenses within the description of just allowances, it is not necessary to show that they have actually benefited the estate, if there was a fair probability of their doing so.—*Ex parte Shaw*, 1 *De Gex's R.*, p. 242. *Eng.* (1849.)

(THE CHIEF JUDGE cited *Ex parte Christy*, 3 *M. & A.*, 90.)

TRUSTEE.

A trustee who accepts the trust, must do all acts which are necessary and proper for the due execution of the trust; he must act with reasonable diligence, and be vigilant in the discharge of his duties. To entitle him to the protection of the Court, he must act as a prudent man would act in relation to his own property, in those matters where he has a discretion. A trustee who permitted the debtor to retain the possession of the trust estate, waste it, and use it as his own, was held responsible for the injury to the trust fund, out of his own estate.—*Harrison et al.* v. *Mock et al.*, 10 *Alabama R.*, p. 185. (1847.)

TRUSTEE—PUBLIC CHARITY.

Though a trustee for a public charity is not called on for twenty years by the body to whom he is accountable to account, yet it is his duty to tender his accounts to such body without requisition; and if he do not, he is liable to the costs of an information filed to compel an account; even although in the result the charity prove to be indebted to such trustee.—*Attorney-General* v. *Gibbs*, 1 *De Gex & Smale's Ch. R.*, p. 156. *Eng.* (1849.)

TROVER.

Trover will lie against an officer, who takes property upon an execution, which is by law exempt from attachment.

In such action, brought against the officer by the execution debtor, who is the owner of the property attached, the property being exempt from attachment, the writ need not be served upon the officer eighteen days before the return day.

If a debtor being possessed of several cows, sell all but one, and that one, being attached, and sold on execution, bring trover against the attaching officer, the question may be submitted to the jury, whether the sale of the other cows was intended to operate as an actual transfer of the property, or was merely colorable, not intended to change the ownership. It is not sufficient, to entitle the defendant to recover, to prove merely that the sale of the other cows was fraudulent in fact; for, if so, those cows might be taken by the creditors of the plaintiff.—*Sanborn* v. *Hamilton*, 18 *Vermont R.*, p. 590. (1847.)

UNAUTHORIZED BANKING.

The sixth section of the title of the Revised Statutes relative to unauthorized banking, applies to foreign as well as domestic corporations. And foreign corporations are still prohibited from keeping any office in this State, for the purpose of receiving deposits, or for discounting notes or bills.

Where such a corporation authorizes one of its officers, or an agent, to attend from time to time at certain known places in this State, for the purpose of receiving deposits, or for the purpose of discounting notes or bills, with the funds of the corporation, and for its benefit, such known places of attendance are to be considered as offices of discount and deposit, of the corporation, illegally kept for the purposes prohibited by the statute.

And the officer or agent of a foreign corporation who thus carries on the business of discounting notes and bills in this State, with the funds of such corporation, and for its benefit, renders himself personally liable to the penalties prescribed by the seventh section of the act relative to unauthorized banking.

He cannot, therefore, be compelled to make a discovery of such violation of the statute, to aid the defence in a suit at law, brought in his own name, upon a note thus discounted by him as the officer or agent of a foreign corporation.

A defendant is not bound to answer or disclose any facts showing that he has been guilty of any act for which he is liable to an indictment, or which can subject him to a penalty, or forfeiture.—*Taylor* v. *Bruen*, 2 *Barbour's Ch. R.*, p. 301. *N. Y.* (1848.)

(The Chancellor cited *Matter of Kipp*, 1 *Paige*, 601; *City Bank of Baltimore* v. *Bateman*, 1 *Har. & John.*, 104.)

UNCURRENT MONEY.

Loaning uncurrent money, upon an agreement that the amount loaned shall be repaid in current funds, does not amount to usury where the discount upon the money loaned is very trifling, and the same will pass current in the market, in the way of trade.

Such a loan is not a violation of the statute, unless there is something in the transaction from which it is to be inferred, as a matter of fact, that it was a mere contrivance to obtain more than the legal rate of interest by loaning bills which were not intrinsically worth their nominal amount; and where it does not appear that the money loaned was not worth, to both parties, the amount at which it was received by the borrower.—*Slosson* v. *Duff*, 1 *Barbour's R.*, *p.* 432. *N. Y.* (1848.)

UNLAWFUL CONTRACT.

No principle is better settled, than that where two or more persons embark in an unlawful transaction, and one gets the advantage of the other, and appropriates more than his proportion of the spoils to himself, the Court will not interfere to make him divide with the others.—*Miller et al.* v. *Davidson*, 3 *Gilman's R.*, *p.* 518. *Ills.* (1847.)

VENDOR AND PURCHASER.

Persons having distinct claims against another, arising upon separate and independent contracts, cannot join in a bill to enforce such claims; where there is no proof of a common interest in the subject matter.

A purchaser of land has a right to buy up a prior contract between his vendor and another person for the sale of the land, with a view of extinguishing an outstanding incumbrance, and charging the vendor with the consideration money. But he has no right to procure such contract for the purpose of defeating the title under which he claims, and under which he is in possession of the land. That the law will not, and ought not to tolerate.—*Wood* v. *Perry*, 1 *Barbour's R.*, *p.* 114. *N. Y.* (1848.)

Where there has been a public sale of personal property, the purchaser may leave it with the former owner, upon a contract, or from motives of benevolence, and if the act is *bona fide*, it will not be liable to the debts of the former owner.—*Simerson* v. *The Branch Bank at Decatur*, 12 *Alabama R.*, *p.* 205. (1848.)

(*Campbell* cited *Watkins* v. *Birch*, 4 *Taunt.*, 283; *Joseph* v. *Ingraham*, 8 *Taunt.*, 338; *Latimer* v. *Batson*, 4 *B. & C.*, 652; *Leonard* v.

Baker, 1 *M. & S.*, 251; *Laughlin* v. *Ferguson*, 6 *Dana*, 118, *and cases cited;* 4 *Porter*, 252.

Ormond, J., cited *Kidd* v. *Rawlinson*, 2 *B. & P.*, 59; *Watkins* v. *Birch*, 4 *Taunt.*, 823; *Joseph* v. *Ingraham*, 8 *Taunt.*, 338; *Leonard* v. *Baker*, 1 *M. & S.*, 251; *Latimer* v. *Batson*, 4 *B. & C.*, 652; *Bank of Ala.* v. *McDade*, 4 *Porter*, 266; *Abney* v. *Kingsland*, 10 *Ala.*, 363.)

VENDOR AND VENDEE.

When goods are sold, to be paid for by a promissory note payable at a future day, with surety, and the vendee neglects or refuses to deliver the note, the vendor cannot sustain an action on book account for the goods, until after the time at which the note would have become due. The proper remedy is by a special action upon the contract.—*Eddy* v. *Stafford*, 18 *Vermont R.*, *p.* 235. (1847.)

Where the vendee went into the possession of a settlement of land purchased of the vendor upon the faith of his representations as to the title thereto, which representations were false and fraudulent, and known to have been so by the vendor at the time of making them, it was *held*, a Court of Equity would retain a bill at the instance of the vendee to rescind the contract, notwithstanding the vendee had not been evicted from the possession of the premises, nor abandoned the possession thereof, nor had offered to do so.—*Coffee et als.* v. *Newson*, 2 *Kelly's R.*, *p.* 442, *Ga.* (1847.)

(*Whitfield* and *Cole* cited *Neville* v. *Wilkinson*, 1 *Brown's Ch.* (*Percins' ed.*) 475; *Boyce's Ex'ors* v. *Grundy*, 3 *Peters*, 210; *Smith* v. *Richards*, 13 *Peters*, 26; 1 *Sugden on Vendors*, 5, 7; *Edwards* v. *McLeay*, *Coop.*, 308; 1 *Sugden on Vendors*, 284; 1 *Story Eq. Jur.*, 201, 202, 207; 2 *Johns. Ch.*, 519; 1 *Brown's Ch.*, 546; 1 *Bailey*, 250, 259; 2 *Keen*, 222; 2 *Kent's Com.*, 471; *Cooper Eq. R.*, 308; 14 *Ves.*, 144; 2 *Scho. & Lef.*, 486; 2 *Swanst.*, 388; 2 *Bay*, 76, 588; 1 *Nott & McCord*, 78; 2 *N. & McC.*, 184, 189; 1 *McCord*, 470; 1 *Serg. & R.*, 438; 5 *Serg. & R.*, 204.

Warner, J., cited 1 *Story Eq.*, 200, 201, 202, 419; 420; *Smith* v. *Richards*, 13 *Peters*, 26; *Camp* v. *Camp*, 2 *Ala.* (*N. S.*), 632; *Bacon* v. *Bronson*, 7 *Johns. Ch.*, 201.)

One who receives property upon condition that it is to belong to him, provided he pays for it a certain sum by a time specified, acquires no attachable interest in the property by paying a portion, only, of the purchase money.

And, if a third person purchase the interest of such conditional vendor and vendee in the property, paying each for his proportion, according to the amount paid under the contract, and then leave the property in the possession of such conditional vendee, the property is not subject to attachment by the creditors of the person thus in possession, unless fraud in fact is proved.—*Smith* v. *Foster*, 18 *Vermont R.*, p. 182. (1847.)

VENDOR—MISTAKE.

Where, by the mutual mistake of vendor and purchaser, as to the duration of a leasehold interest, it had been sold at a price considerably below its value, and the conveyance had been executed, and the purchaser let into possession;—*Held*, upon a bill filed some years afterwards by the vendor against the representatives of the purchaser, that the vendor was not entitled to be relieved against the mistake.—*Okill* v. *Whittaker*, 1 *De Gex & Smale's Ch. R.*, p. 83. *Eng.* (1849.)

(*Russell* and *Chandless* cited *Dowel* v. *Dew*, 1 *Y. & C.* (*C. C.*), 345; *Muskerry* v. *Chinnery*, *Lloyd & G. t. Sugd.*, 185; *Bree* v. *Holbeck*, 2 *Doug.*, 632; *Cripps* v. *Reade*, 6 *T. R.*, 606.)

VERDICT.

If a general verdict for the plaintiff be taken upon several counts in a declaration, and one of the counts is fatally defective, judgment will be arrested, on motion, though other counts, not liable to objection, were covered by the verdict.—*Sylvester* v. *Downer*, 18 *Vermont R.*, p. 32. (1847.)

(ROYCE, J., cited *Hazeltine* v. *Weare*, 8 *Vt.*, 480; *Harding* v. *Cragie*, 8 *Vt.*, 501; *Walker* v. *Sargent*, 11 *Vt.*, 327; *Needham* v. *McAuley*, 13 *Vt.*, 68.)

VESSEL.

When the owners of a vessel have let her on shares, for a certain time, to the master, who is to victual and man her, they cannot maintain an action for freight earned by the vessel during that time: such action can be maintained by the master only.—*Manter et als.* v. *Holmes et al.*, 10 *Metcalf's R.*, p. 402. *Mass.* (1847.)

(SHAW, C. J., cited *Reynolds* v. *Toppan*, 15 *Mass.*, 370; *Taggard* v *Loring*, 16 *Mass.*, 363; *Thompson* v. *Hamilton*, 12 *Pick.*, 425.)

WARRANTY.

A warranty of soundness covers all diseases which affect the value of the thing sold, whether temporary or permanent.—*Kornegay* v. *White*, 10 *Alabama R.*, p. 255. (1847.)

(*Edwards*, cited 18 *Johns.*, 141; 3 *Stark. Ev.*, 1666.)

WIDOW.

The right of a widow to the personal estate of her deceased husband, until a division thereof has been made, is a mere *chose in action*; and if she marries again, and her husband does not reduce the same into his possession, the right will survive to her on his death.

The right of a husband to his wife's interest, in the personal property of which a former husband of his wife died seized is inchoate, and his title is complete only when a division thereof has been made and he has reduced the same into his possession.—*Harper* v. *Archer et al.*, 8 *Smedes & Marshall's R.*, p. 229. *Miss.* (1847.)

(Clayton, J., cited *Wade* v. *Grimes*, 7 *How.*, 433; *Henderson* v. *Guyot*, 6 *Smedes & Marshall*, 211.)

WIFE—MORTGAGE.

Where a wife mortgaged her property, and then sought relief in Chancery upon the ground that the contract was void in consequence of her disability to contract, and it was shown that the lender acted in good faith; proceeded cautiously under legal advice, under assurances that the loan was for the exclusive use of the wife, to whom the money was actually paid; the interest upon the loan paid for several years; the mortgaged property insured by her, and the policy assigned to the mortgagee;—a bill to relieve her from the contract cannot receive the sanction of a Court of Equity.—*Beine et ux.* v. *Heath*, 6 *Howard's U. S. R.*, p. 228. (1848.)

WIFE—SEPARATE PROPERTY.

When property is conveyed absolutely, to a married woman, by a stranger, the statute of frauds has no application, in a contest between the wife and the creditors of the husband; it is therefore unimportant, whether the instrument is, or is not recorded.—*Newman* v. *James et al.*, 12 *Alabama R.*, *p.* 29. (1848.)

(*Leslie* cited *Swift* v. *Fitzhugh*, 9 *Porter*, 58; *Thomas & Howard* v. *Davis*, 6 *Ala.*, 113; *Catterlin* v. *Hardy et al.*, 10 *Ala.*, 511.

ORMOND, J., cited *Hartley* v. *Hurle*, 5 *Ves.*, 541; *Clancey on Rights*, 267; *Ex parte Ray*, 1 *Madd. C.*, 199, *Am. ed.*, 115; *Myers* v. *Peek*, 2 *Ala.*, 655; *Oden* v. *Stubblefield*, 4 *Ala.*, 40; *Swift* v. *Fitzhugh*, 9 *Porter*, 39; *O'Neil et als.* v. *Teague*, 8 *Ala.*, 349.)

WIFE—TESTIMONY.

The testimony of the wife can never be received against her husband, except in proceedings instituted against him on her behalf.

This rule holds not only during the coverture, but also continues to apply after a dissolution of the marriage contract, as regards transactions which took place previous to such dissolution.—*Barnes* v. *Camack*, 1 *Barbour's R.*, *p.* 392. *N. Y.* (1848.)

(BARCULO, J., cited 1 *Phil. Ev.*, 83; *Cowan & Hill's Notes*, 1554; *State* v. *Phelps*, 2 *Tyler*, 374; *Ratcliff* v. *Wales*, 1 *Hill*, 63.)

WILL.

Mere imbecility of mind in a testator, however great, will not avoid his will, provided he be not an idiot or a lunatic.

The term *unsound mind* in the statute concerning wills, is of the same signification as *non compos mentis;* and any one otherwise competent, to whom these terms do not apply, may make a valid will.—*Blanchard et als.* v. *Nestle*, 3 *Denio's R.*, *p.* 37. *N. Y.* (1848.)

A father bequeathed his business and stock in trade to his sons, with a declaration that a grandson, then an infant, should be admitted into the firm on attaining twenty-one, or in default thereof that the sons, or the survivor of them, should pay the grandson £1000 on his attaining twenty-one. On the bankruptcy of the surviving son before the grandson attained the age of twenty-one:—*Held*, that there was a right of proof for £1000 as a contingent debt.—*Ex parte Megary et als.*, 1 *De Gex's R.*, *p.* 167. *Eng.* (1849.)

It is a well established rule of construction of wills, that no form of words will constitute a condition precedent, when the intentions of the testator, to be collected from every part of the will, clearly indicate a different purpose.—*Stark et al.* v. *Smiley*, 25 *Maine R.*, *p.* 201. (1847.)

(*Bradbury* cited 4 *Kent*, 125; 2 *Black. Com.*, 154; *Co. Litt.*, 218; 1 *Salk.*, 170; 1 *Hill Abr.*, 247, 248; *Howard* v. *Turner*, 6 *Greenl.*, 106; *Currier* v. *Earl*, 1 *Shepley*, 216; *Morton* v. *Barrett*, 9 *Shepley*, 257; *Sayward* v. *Sayward*, 7 *Greenl.*, 210; 5 *Pick.*, 524; 3 *Peters*, 374; 1 *Bac. Abr.*, 642; 7 *Mass.*, 229; *Stearns on Real Actions*, 22, 23, 73; 6 *Maine*, 42.)

If a testator, after making his will, sell previously to his death, so great a part of the real estate devised, as to render it impossible to give effect to the dispositions of his will, it amounts to a revocation of the will. —*In re Cooper's Estate*, 4 *Barr's R.*, *p.* 88. *Pa.* (1847.)

A testator directed that it should be lawful for his wife to retain in her hands and employ in his business any part of his assets not exceeding £6000, so long as she should think fit if she should continue his widow, and appointed her and his son executor and executrix. The widow took the son into partnership with her in the trade, and they both became bankrupts:—*Held*, that the use of the £6000 in this trade was not an employment of it in the testator's business according to the direction of the will, but was a breach of trust on which proof might be made against the joint estate.—*Ex parte Butterfield*, 1 *De Gex's R.*, *p.* 319. *Eng.* (1849.)

Testatrix, by will, bequeathed £3000 in trust for C. for life, for her separate use, and after her death, for her children; and in case there should be no such children, in trust for P. By a codicil, stating that C. had been largely provided for from other sources, the testatrix deducted the sum of £2900 from the legacy of £3000, and revoked so much of the legacy accordingly, leaving only £100 as a remembrance of her affection:—*Held*, that the legacy of £3000 was revoked *in toto*, and that in lieu of it the legacy of £100 was given for the absolute benefit of C.; and that P. took no interest either in the £100 or any part of the £3000.—*Sanford* v. *Sanford*, 1 *De Gex & Smale's Ch. R.*, *p.* 67. *Eng.* (1849.)

Where a will contains different trusts, some of which are valid, and others void, or unauthorized by law; or where there are distinct and independent provisions as to different portions of the testator's property, or different estates or interests in the same portions of the property are created—some of which provisions, estates or interests, are valid, and others are invalid—the valid trusts, provisions, estates or interests, created by the will of the testator, will be preserved; unless those which are valid and those which are invalid are so dependent upon each other that they cannot be separated without defeating the general intent of the testator. *Haxtun* v. *Corse*, 2 *Barbour's Ch. R.*, *p.* 506. *N. Y.* (1848.)

(The Chancellor cited *Darling* v. *Rogers & Sagory*, 22 *Wend.*, 483; *Parks* v. *Parks*, 9 *Paige*, 117.)

WILL—ATTESTATION OF.

A will to be attested in the presence of the testator, must be witnessed within his view. It is not necessary to prove that he actually saw the witnesses attest the will; it is sufficient if, from their relative position, he could see them.—*Hill* v. *Barge*, 12 *Alabama R.*, *p.* 687. (1848.)

(ORMOND, J. cited 7 *Bac. Ab.*, 10; *Casson* v. *Dade*, 1 *Bro. C. C.*, 99; *Davey* v. *Smith*, 3 *Salkeld*, 395; *Doe* v. *Manifold*, 1 *M. & S.*, 294; *Todd* v. *Winchelsea*, 9 *Mood. & M.*, 12; 2 *C. & P.*, 488.)

WITNESS.

One joint maker of a note, not sued, is not a competent witness for his co-maker without a release.—*Kornegay* v. *Salle*, 12 *Alabama R.*, *p.* 534. (1848.)

(COLLIER, C. J., cited *Thompson* v. *Armstrong*, 4 *Ala.*, 383; *Lovell* v. *Adams*, 3 *Wend.*, 380; *Hall et al.* v. *Cecil et al.*, 6 *Bing.*, 181; *Pike* v. *Blake*, 8 *Vt.*, 400; *Pinney* v. *Bugbee*, 13 *Vt.*, 623; *Jewett* v. *Davis*, 6 *N. H.*, 518; *Spaulding* v. *Smith*, 1 *Fairf.*, 363; 3 *Phil. Ev.*, *C. & H.'s Notes*, 1520–1522.)

Where a deposition of a witness comes through the mail sealed, directed to the clerk of the proper Court, with the usual post marks, it may be published, although the name of the commissioner is not written across the seal.—*Park* v. *Bancroft*, 12 *Alabama R.*, *p.* 468. (1848.)

(GOLDTHWAITE, J., cited *Glover* v. *Millings*, 2 *S. & P.*, 28.)

A witness who has no interest in the subject of the suit, but who is liable for *costs* only, is disqualified from testifying, the law looking only to the *nature*, and not the *quantum* of interest.—*Vason* v. *The Merchants' Bank of Macon*, 2 *Kelly's R.*, *p.* 140. *Ga.* (1847.)

(LUMPKIN, J., cited 1 *Greenl. Ev.*, *secs.* 347, 401, 402; *Townsend* v. *Downing*, 14 *East*, 565; *Hubly* v. *Brown*, 16 *Johns.*, 70; *Scott* v. *McLellan*, 2 *Greenl. R.*, 199; *Bottomley* v. *Wilson*, 3 *Starkie*, 148; *Harman* v. *Lasbrey*, 1 *Holt Cases*, 390; *Edmonds* v. *Lowe*, 8 *B. & C.*, 407.)

Where money has been received by a witness upon a judgment for costs from the hands of the sheriff, and such judgment is set aside on a motion to correct the taxation, an action lies to recover the money back from the plaintiff in the execution, and not from the witness.

Where a witness is examined, he is entitled to his fees, though he be incompetent. His incompetency may be waived, or his interest released; and it does not follow that he was not examined, because he appears of record to have been incompetent.—*Gray* v. *Alexander*, 7 *Humphrey's R.*, *p.* 16. *Tenn* (1847.)

A promise to pay a witness $150 for his attendance as a witness, which was to be reduced one half if the party promising did not succeed in the cause, is against sound policy, and cannot be enforced.—*Dawkins* v. *Gill*, 10 *Alabama R.*, *p.* 206. (1847.)

(ORMOND, J., cited *Loomis* v. *Newhall*, 15 *Pick.*, 159; *Roby* v. *West*, 4 *New Hamp.*, 285.)

After the testimony of a witness has been taken upon a commission, and the commission returned, the party cannot have a new commission, to re-examine the witness, merely on the expectation that he may now swear more definitely than before; in the absence of any suggestion that the witness has made a mistake, or that new evidence has been discovered.—*Raney* v. *Weed*, 1 *Barbour's R.*, *p.* 220. *N. Y.* (1848.)

Where upon the trial of an issue, the evidence of a material witness, being uncorroborated, and being in other respects unsatisfactory, has been discredited by the judge, and the jury have given a verdict against the party producing that witness, this Court, upon being satisfied, by affidavits filed since the trial, that the evidence of the witness may be substantially corroborated, will grant a new trial.—*Shields* v. *Boucher*, 1 *De Gex & Smale's Ch. R.*, *p.* 40. *Eng.* (1849.)

A witness in narrating a conversation held between himself and another, cannot be permitted to testify what he meant by the questions asked by himself; but his meaning must be gathered from the import of the language, without the aid of a subsequent explanation of his own meaning.—*Haywood* v. *Foster*, 16 *Ohio R.*, *p.* 88. (1848.)

When a note is attested by a subscribing witness, and such witness resides in another of the United States, and beyond the reach of the process of the Court at the time of the trial, evidence of the handwriting of the witness, and of the maker of the note, may be produced, and is competent proof of its execution.—*Dunbar* v. *Marden*, 13 *New Hampshire R.*, *p.* 311. (1847.)

(WOODS, J., cited 1 *Phil. Ev.* 473, *2d ed. by Cowen & Hill*; *Sluby* v. *Champlin*, 4 *Johns.*, 401; *Holmes* v. *Pontin*, *Peake's Cas.*, 99; *Cooper* v. *Marden*, 1 *Esp.*, 1; *Burt* v. *Walker*, 4 *B. & A.*, 697; *Dudley* v. *Sumner*, 5 *Mass.*, 462; *Cook* v. *Woodrow*, 5 *Cranch*, 13; *Livingston* v. *Burton*, 11 *Johns.*, 64; *Wallis* v. *Delancey*, 7 *T. R.*, 266, *n.*; *Whittemore* v. *Brooks*, 1 *Greenl.*, 57, *and note.*)

WITNESS—DEATH OF.

A count on an instrument of writing by which the defendant acknowledged he had received, by the hand of J. S., $200 in favor of the plaintiffs, is sufficient.

It is necessary to the admission of evidence of what a deceased witness swore to on a former trial, that it be proved by the record of that trial that the suit was between the same parties and for the same cause of action.

And the precise words of the deceased witness, and not merely the substance of them, must be proved.—*Ephraims et al.* v. *Murdoch*, 7 *Blackford's R.*, *p.* 10. *Ind.* (1847.)

WRIT OF ERROR.

A plaintiff in error, in a cause where the people are defendants in error, who succeeds in reversing the judgment against him, is only responsible for the costs made by him in the prosecution of the writ of error.—*Sans* v. *The People*, 3 *Gilman's R.*, *p.* 338. *Ills.* (1847.)

INDEX.

ABATEMENT.

ACCEPTANCE.

ACCEPTOR.

ACCIDENT.

ACCOMMODATION.

ACKNOWLEDGMENT.

ADMINISTRATION.

ADMINISTRATOR.

ADVANCES.

AFFIDAVIT.

AGENT.

AGREEMENT.

ALIEN.

ALTERATION.

AMENDMENT.

ANCIENT LIGHTS.

ANNUITY.

APPEAL.

ARBITRATORS.

ASSAULT AND BATTERY.

ASSETS.

ASSIGNEE.

ASSIGNMENT

ASSIGNOR.

ASSUMPSIT.

ATTACHMENT.

ATTORNEY.

AUCTION.

AWARD.

BAGGAGE.

BANK.

BANKERS.

BANKRUPT.

BANKRUPTCY.

BAR.

BETTING.

BILL OF DISCOVERY.

BILL OF EXCEPTIONS.

BILL OF EXCHANGE.

BILL OF REVIEW.

BILL OF SALE.

BOND.

BOOKS.

BREACH OF TRUST.

BURGLARY.

CARGO.

CAVEAT EMPTOR.

CERTIFICATE.

CESTUI QUE TRUST.

CHALLENGE.

CHANCERY.

CHARTER.

CHATTELS.

CHECK.

CHOSE IN ACTION.

COLLATERAL.

COMMON CARRIER

COMMON LAW

COMPENSATION.

COMPLAINANT

CONSIDERATION

CONSIGNEE.

CONSTABLE.

CONSTRUCTION OF STATUTE.

CONSUL.

CONTRACT.

CONTRIBUTION.

CONVERSION.

CONVEYANCE.

CONVICTION.

CORPORATION.

COSTS.

COURTS.

COURTS OF CHANCERY.

COVENANT.

CREDITOR.

CREDITOR'S BILL.

CRIMINAL.

CROSS NOTES.

DAMAGES.

DEATH.

DEBT.

DEBTOR.

DECLARATION.

DECREE.

DEED.

DEFAULT.

DEFENCE.

DEFENDANT.

DELIVERY.

DEMAND.

DEMURRER.

DEPOSIT.

DEPOSITION.

DEPUTY SHERIFF.

DESCENT.

DETINUE.

DEVASTAVIT.

DEVISE.

DILIGENCE.

DISCHARGE.

DISTRIBUTEES.

DIVORCE.

DOMICIL.

DOWER.

EASEMENT.

EJECTMENT.

ENDORSEE.

ENDORSEMENT.

ENDORSER.

EQUITY.

ERASURE.

ERROR.

ESTATE.

EVIDENCE.

EXECUTION.

EXECUTOR.

EXEMPTION

FACTOR.

FALSE IMPRISONMENT.

FALSE PRETENCES.

FELONY.

FEME COVERT.

FIERI FACIAS.

FORECLOSURE.

FORGERY.

FRAUD.

FRAUDULENT.

GARNISHMENT.

GOODS.

GRAND JURY.

GRANTEE.

GRANTOR.

GUARDIAN.

HANDWRITING.

HEIRS.

HIGHWAY.

HOLDER.

HUSBAND.

HUSBAND AND WIFE.

INDICTMENT.

INFANT.

INJUNCTION.

INSANITY.

INSOLVENT DEBTOR.

INSTRUCTIONS OF COURT.

INSTRUMENTS.

INSURANCE.

INSURERS.

INTEREST.

INTESTATE.

JUDGMENT.

JUDGMENT CREDITOR.

JUDGMENT DEBTOR.

JURISDICTION.

JUROR.

JURY.

LACHES.

LAND.

LANDLORD.

LARCENY.

LEASE.

LEGACY.

LEGATEE.

LEVY.

LIABILITY.

LIBEL.

LIEN.

LIFE INSURANCE

LOSS.

LUNACY.

MAINTENANCE.

MANDAMUS.

MANSLAUGHTER.

MARRIAGE.

MASTER OF VESSEL.

MEMORANDUM.

MISDEMEANOR.

MISREPRESENTATION.

MISTAKE.

MORTGAGE.

MORTGAGEE.

MORTGAGOR.

MURDER.

NEGLIGENCE.

NEGOTIABLE.

NEW TRIAL.

NEXT OF KIN.

NON-PAYMENT.

NON-RESIDENT.

NON-SUIT.

NOTARY.

NOTE.

NOTICE.

OBLIGEE.

OBLIGOR.

OFFICER.

OMISSION.

ORDER.

OWNER.

PARENT AND CHILD.

PAROL.

PARTIES.

PARTNERS.

PARTNERSHIP.

PAWNEE.

PAYEE.

PAYMENT.

PERFORMANCE.

PETITION.

PEW HOLDER.

PLAINTIFF.

PLEA.

POLICY.

POSSESSION.

POWERS.

PRE-EMPTION.

PRESENTMENT.

PRESUMPTION.

PRIMA FACIA.

PRINCIPAL.

PRISONER.

PROBATE.

PROFITS.

PROMISE.

PROMISSORY NOTE.

PROOF.

PROPERTY.

PROPRIETORS.

PROTEST.

PURCHASE.

PURCHASER.

REAL ESTATE.

RECEIPT.

RECEIVER.

RECOGNIZANCE.

RECORD.

RECOVERY

RELEASE.

RENT.

REPLEVIN.

REPLICATION.

REPRESENTATIONS.

REPRESENTATIVE.

RESCISSION.

RESIDENCE.

RETURN DAY.

ROBBERY.

SALE.

SCIRE FACIAS.

SEAL.

SECURITY.

SET OFF.

SETTLEMENT

SHERIFF.

SIGNATURE.

SLANDER.

SLAVE

SPECIFIC PERFORMANCE.

STAKEHOLDER.

STATUTE.

STATUTE OF LIMITATIONS.

SUBPŒNA.

SUICIDE.

SUIT.

SUNDAY.

SUPPLEMENTAL BILL.

SURETIES.

TENANT.

TENANT IN COMMON.

TESTATOR.

TESTIMONY.

TITLE.

TRANSFER.

TRESPASS.

TRIAL.

TROVER.

TRUST.

TRUSTEE.

UNDERWRITERS.

USURIOUS.

VARIANCE.

VENDEE.

VENDOR.

VERDICT.

VESSEL.

VOID.

WAIVER.

WAREHOUSEMAN.

WARRANTY.

WIDOW.

WIFE.

WILL.

WITNESS.

WRIT.

WRITTEN CONTRACT.

WRIT OF ERROR.

Lightning Source UK Ltd.
Milton Keynes UK
UKHW010803101218
333747UK00015B/1096/P